Adapting to Change: Occupational Pension Schemes, Women and Migrant Workers

ELAINE A. WHITEFORD

Adapting to Change: Occupational Pension Schemes, Women and Migrant Workers

An examination of the extent to which occupational pension
schemes in the UK, the Netherlands and Germany enable
women and migrant workers to accrue adequate pensions

| KLUWER SOVAC
SERIES ON SOCIAL
SECURITY |

Kluwer Law International
The Hague • London • Boston

Library of Congress Cataloguing-in-Publication Data is available

Published by Kluwer Law International
P.O. Box 85889
2508 CN The Hague, The Netherlands
Tel.: + 31 70 308 1560
Fax: + 31 70 308 1515

Sold and distributed in the USA and Canada by
Kluwer Law International
675 Massachusetts Avenue
Cambridge, MA 02139, USA
Tel.: + 1 617 354 0140
Fax: + 1 617 354 8595

Sold and distributed in all other Countries by
Kluwer Law International
P.O. Box 85889
2508 CN The Hague, The Netherlands
Tel.: + 31 70 308 1560
Fax: + 31 70 308 1515

Cover design: Robert Vulkers bNO

Printed on acid-free paper

ISBN 9041103511

© 1996 Kluwer Law International, The Hague, The Netherlands

Kluwer Law International incorporaties the publishing programmes of Graham & Trotman Ltd.
Kluwer Law and Taxation Publishers and Martinus Nijhoff Publishers.

TABLE OF CONTENTS

PART I: INTRODUCTION

CHAPTER 1
INTRODUCTION AND DELIMITATION
OF THE RESEARCH   3

1.1   Changes in the Labour Market   3
1.2   The Demographic Challenge   7
       1.2.1   A FAVOURED ALTERNATIVE   16
1.3   The Delimitation   19
       1.3.1   WHICH ISSUES?   19
       1.3.2   WHICH SCHEMES?   21
       1.3.3   WHICH BENEFITS?   22
       1.3.4   WHICH MEMBER STATES?   24
1.4   The Structure   28

CHAPTER 2
PENSION PROVISION IN THE UK, THE NETHERLANDS
AND GERMANY   30

2.1   The UK   31
       2.1.1   STATUTORY PROVISION   31
       2.1.2   SERPS   34
       2.1.3   CONTRACTING-OUT   35
                COSR - Pre-April 1997   37
                COSR - Post-April 1997   40
                COMP   43
       2.1.4   TAX RULES   45
2.2   The Netherlands   49
       2.2.1   STATUTORY PROVISION   49
       2.2.2   OCCUPATIONAL SCHEMES   50
       2.2.3   TAX RULES   56

2.3	**Germany**	59
	2.3.1 STATUTORY PROVISION	59
	2.3.2 OCCUPATIONAL PENSIONS	62
	2.3.3 TAX RULES	71
2.4	**A Brief Comparison**	75

PART II: PENSIONS AND EQUALITY

CHAPTER 3
STATUTORY PENSION SCHEMES AND EQUALITY 81

3.1	**Introduction**	81
3.2	**The Discriminatory Features of Statutory Pension Provision**	82
3.3	**EC Law - The Background**	87
	3.3.1 THE PAUCITY OF TREATY SOCIAL PROVISIONS	87
	3.3.2 SEX EQUALITY LAW IN THE TREATY AND BEYOND	91
3.4	**Directive 79/7 - Personal Scope**	95
3.5	**Directive 79/7 - Material Scope**	97
3.6	**Directive 79/7 - Discrimination and Justifications**	99
3.7	**Directive 79/7 - Exceptions and Exclusions**	104
3.8	**Evaluation**	106

CHAPTER 4
OCCUPATIONAL PENSIONS AND EQUALITY 113

4.1	**Discriminatory Features of Occupational Pension Schemes**	114
4.2	**Directive 86/378**	115
4.3	**Article 119 - Some General Observations**	117
4.4	**Pensions as Pay**	122

	4.4.1	THE UK	130
	4.4.2	THE NETHERLANDS	131
	4.4.3	GERMANY	132
4.5	**Access**		133
	4.5.1	THE UK	140
	4.5.2	THE NETHERLANDS	144
	4.5.3	GERMANY	147
	4.5.4	CONCLUSIONS ON ACCESS	150
4.6	**Pensionable Age**		151
	4.6.1	THE TEMPORAL LIMITATION	156
	4.6.2	INTRODUCING EQUAL PENSIONABLE AGES	164
		The UK	168
		The Netherlands	170
		Germany	171
		Conclusions relating to pensionable age	171
4.7	**Contributions**		176
4.8	**Benefits**		183
	4.8.1	SURVIVORS' PENSIONS	184
		The UK	188
		The Netherlands	189
		Germany	191
		Conclusions concerning survivor's pensions	192
	4.8.2	ADDITIONAL VOLUNTARY CONTRIBUTIONS	194
	4.8.3	LUMP SUMS	196
4.9	**Links with Statutory Schemes**		196
	4.9.1	THE UK	205
	4.9.2	THE NETHERLANDS	206
	4.9.3	GERMANY	208
4.10	**Directive 86/378: A Recapitulation**		209
4.11	**Evaluation**		211

PART III: PENSIONS AND MOBILITY

CHAPTER 5
STATUTORY PENSIONS AND MOBILITY 221

5.1 **Introduction** 221

5.2 **Problematic Features of Statutory Pension Schemes** 222

5.3 **EC Law - The Background** 224

    5.3.1 FREE MOVEMENT OF WORKERS 225

5.4 **Social Security** 232

    5.4.1 INTRODUCTION 232

        The Options 233

    5.4.2 THE MAIN FEATURES OF THE COMMUNITY SYSTEM OF CO-ORDINATION 238

        Personal Scope 238

        Material Scope 241

        Applicable Legislation 242

        Non-discrimination 243

        Exportability 244

        Aggregation and Apportionment 244

        Rules against Overlapping 246

5.5 **Exceptions and Exclusions** 248

5.6 **Conclusion** 252

CHAPTER 6
OCCUPATIONAL PENSIONS AND MOBILITY 253

6.1 **Waiting Periods and Vesting** 255

    6.1.1 THE UK 256

    6.1.2 THE NETHERLANDS 258

    6.1.3 GERMANY 259

    6.1.4 COMPARISON AND COMMENT 263

6.2   Early Leavers - Short Service Benefits 265

      6.2.1   THE UK 266

      6.2.2   THE NETHERLANDS 268

      6.2.3   GERMANY 270

      6.2.4   COMPARISON AND COMMENT 273

6.3   Early Leavers - Transfers 274

      6.3.1   THE UK 275

      6.3.2   THE NETHERLANDS 278

      6.3.3   GERMANY 284

      6.3.4   COMPARISON AND COMMENT 287

6.4   Taxation 290

      6.4.1   TAXATION OF PENSIONS 292

      6.4.2   TAXATION OF TRANSFERS 295

6.5   Evaluation 296

6.6   Conclusion 298

PART IV: CONCLUSIONS

CHAPTER 7
SUMMARY AND CONCLUSIONS 311

7.1   Introduction 311

7.2   Pensions and Women 314

      7.2.1   STATUTORY SCHEMES 314

      7.2.2   OCCUPATIONAL SCHEMES 316

7.3   Pensions and International Migrants 322

      7.3.1   STATUTORY   PENSIONS   AND

              MIGRANTS 322

      7.3.2   OCCUPATIONAL   PENSIONS   AND

              MIGRANTS 324

7.4   Which is Better? 329

      7.4.1   WOMEN 329

      7.4.2   MIGRANTS 333

7.4   Conclusion 335

BIBLIOGRAPHY 341

TABLE OF CASES 363

INDEX 371

SUMMARY IN DUTCH 377

ABP	Algemeen Burgerlijk Pensioenfonds
ANW	Algemene Nabestaandenwet
AOW	Algemeen Ouderdomswet
AWW	Algemeen Wedeuw- en Wezenwet
BAG	Bundesarbeitsgericht
BB	Der Betriebs-Berater
BetrAVG	Betriebliche Altersversorgung
BPL	British Pension Lawyer
CML Rev.	Common Market Law Review
COMP	Contracted-out Money Purchase
COSR	Contracted-out Salary Related
DB	Der Betrieb
EL Rev.	European Law Review
ELJ	European Law Journal
EuZW	Europäische Zeitschrift für Wirtschaftsrecht
ICLQ	International and Comparative Law Quarterly
IJCLLIR	International Journal of Comparative Labour Law and Industrial Relations
ILJ	Industrial Law Journal
IRJ	Industrial Relations Jounal
JCMS	Journal of Common Market Studies
JSWFL	Journal of Social Welfare and Family Law
LIEI	Legal Issues in European Integration
MLR	Modern Law Review
NILQ	Northern Ireland Law Quarterly
NJB	Nederlands Juristenblad
NJCM Bulletin	Nederlands Tijdschrift voor de Mensenrechten
NJW	Neue Juristische Wochenschrift
NLJ	New Law Journal
NZA	Neue Zeitschrift für Arbeitsrecht
PA	Pensions Act
PSA	Pension Schemes Act
PSW	Pensioen- en Spaarfondsenwet
RdA	Recht der Arbeid
S.E.W.	Sociaal Economische Wetgeving

SSB	Short Service Benefit
SR	Tijdschrift voor Sociaal Recht
TvA	Tijdschrift voor Arbeidsvraagstukken
TvP	Tijdschrift voor Pensioenvraagstukken
WFR	Weekblad voor Fiscaalrecht
YEL	Yearbook of European Law
ZIAS	Zeitschrift für Internationales Arbeids- en Soziaalrecht

PART I

INTRODUCTION

INTRODUCTION AND DELIMITATION
OF THE RESEARCH

In the period which followed the second world war, the countries of Europe embarked on a programme of reconstruction. This programme was not merely concerned with rebuilding the shattered infrastructure and economies of the states, it also involved redesigning the systems of social security, particularly pensions, which had been developing in the decades before the war, but which had been decimated by its effects. In redesigning these schemes, the now Member States of the European Union put in place regimes which differed widely in their detail and even in their principles. Some states opted for systems covering the entire population of their territory, while others preferred to use social security only to cover those who were in paid employment. Differences could also be seen in the level of benefits paid, from subsistence level benefits, to those providing a reasonably high degree of income replacement.

As the end of the century approaches, the Member States of the EU are grappling again with the shape and form of their pension systems. The factors prompting the Member States to act in this manner will be outlined in the next sections.

1.1   Changes in the Labour Market

The pensions schemes which were put in place in the countries of the EU in the post-war period were designed to protect people in defined situations, which varied between the Member States. Basically, either all residents, or all employees, were insured and individuals who were insured either had to pay contributions to the scheme or they were credited with them. Individuals who were not insured for the entire period required by the legislation in question received a reduced level of

entire period required by the legislation in question received a reduced level of pension.

The schemes also operated on the basis of a number of assumptions. In this respect, the most important of these was that married women were either explicitly or implicitly assumed to be financially dependent upon their spouses, and consequently, they often accrued no independent right to a pension. Alternatively, particularly in schemes in which employment was the basis for insurance, the different employment patterns followed by women and men resulted in lower levels of pensions being paid to women.[1]

It can therefore be stated that the schemes created in the post-war period either gave no thought to the specific pension needs of women, or where they were considered, they were assumed to (wish to) be financially dependent upon a spouse. The appalling pension position of many women has however been found to be unacceptable for a number of reasons. The first is that, however disputed by some,[2] women as a group live longer than men.[3] Consequently, they are more concerned with retirement income than men, because they can expect to be in receipt of it for longer. Second, since the early 1970s, women have begun to

---

[1]   M. Landenberger, "Familiepolitische Maßnahmen und ihre Wirkungen auf Arbeitsmarktchancen und soziale Sicherung von Frauen", in C. Gather, U. Gerhard, K. Prinz and M. Veil (eds.), *Frauenalterssicherung. Lebensläufe von Frauen und ihre Benachteiligung im Alter*, Berlin 1991 at pp. 83-105 at pp. 85-86 indicates that women's pensions in Germany are typically 60% of those paid to men. M.M.H. Kraamwinkel, (*Pensioen, emancipatie en gelijke behandeling*, Deventer, 1995) cites figures at p. 9 which demonstrate that on average a married Dutchman receives ƒ24,500 p.a. from his occupational pension scheme, whereas a married woman generaly receives ƒ8200.

[2]   See the discussion in Chapter 4 below.

[3]   For example, Dutch figures indicate that by 1993, women could expect to live to the age of 80 as compared to men's life expectancy of 74; E. Lutjens and F.W.A. van Poppel, *Levensverwachting en pensioen. Geslacht afhankelijke of sekse-neutrale actuariële factoren?*, Deventer, 1995 at p. 47. The European average life expectancy figures for 1990 were 72.7 for men and 79.3 for women; see D. Taverne, *The Pension Time Bomb in Europe*, Federal Trust Report, London, 1995, appendix 1. 2/3rds of people over the age of 75 are women; J.B. Kuné, "Een ouder wordende wereldbevolking in een studie van de Wereld Bank. Pensioenvoorzieningen in mondiaal perspectief; met bijzonder aandacht voor de Nederlandse situatie", TvP (1995), 95-98 and 114-116 at 95.

participate in economic activity in ever-greater numbers,[4] increasing their economic power and rendering outmoded an assumption that they are financially dependent upon their spouse. Additionally, the rise in the divorce rate has made the assumption that a married woman can be provided for by her spouse increasingly unreliable.[5] The first challenge facing pension schemes has therefore been how to adapt their rules to the changed role of women in society, to enable women to accrue pensions adequate to their needs.

Pension schemes have already begun to adapt to this challenge. A singnficant role has been played in this regard by the law of the EU, one of the fundamental principles of which is that there is to be no discrimination on grounds of sex.[6]

A second challenge has emerged for pension schemes in ensuring that individuals accrue maximum benefit entitlement. In the post-war period, the market has internationalised, perhaps most obviously in Europe, where an increasing number of states have decided to participate in creating a single market - the EC - within which the factors of production are free to move in an area of undistorted competition. One of the factors of production the movement of which is to be encouraged and facilitated is that of workers. This poses a challenge for pension schemes as a consequence of their territorially limited scope. Insurance is generally only provided in relation to those resident and/or employed within the territory in question. If by moving from one Member State to another an individual lost accrued social security benefits and/or was excluded from the scope of schemes operating in his host Member State, a significant barrier would be erected to the practical exercise of one of the Treaty freedoms, and the pension to which this individual accrued entitlement would be correspondingly diminished.

Pension schemes have adapted to this challenge also. Article 3 of the EC

---

[4]   According to the Commission, female participation in paid employment had increased from 34% in 1960 to 67% in 1992. Commission of the EC, *Werkgelegenheid in Europa*, Brussels 1994 at p. 10 and 49-50.

[5]   G.M. Backes, "Was bedeuten sich verändernde Lebens- und Arbeitsbedingungen von Frauen für ihre künftige Situation im Alter?" in Gather et al, loc. cit. pp. 266-276 at p. 268 cites statistics which indicate that 20% of 1970 marriages ended in divorce.

[6]   See the discussion in Chapters 3 and 4 below.

Treaty declares that the common market which it was one of the main objectives of the EU to create, is to be characterised by the abolition between the Member States of barriers to the free movement of, inter alia, workers, a provision which has been worked out in more detail in Title III Chapter 1 of the Treaty.[7] Article 51 in turn provides the Council with the competence to adopt those measures in the field of social security which are necessary to ensure the free movement of workers. However, Article 51 also makes it clear that what is to be brought about is not harmonisation but coordination of social security schemes,[8] since it merely provides that the Council's measures should serve to bring about the exportation of benefits and the aggregation for the purposes of acquisition, maintenance and calculation of benefits on the basis of periods of employment carried out in different Member States. In other words, the Treaty required that national social security schemes be made to fit together to prevent the migrant worker from suffering in terms of social security coverage, while the substantive content of the individual national schemes remained within the exclusive competence of the Member States themselves.

There is also a third development which is seen as posing a fundamental challenge to the pension schemes of the Member States. The final challenge facing the pension schemes put in place in the post-war period is that posed by predictions as to the demographic composition of the population of the EU in the years to come. As shall be outlined in the next sections, these predictions have persuaded some that the only secure future for pension provision is one in which the state plays only a residual role, with primary responsibility lying with individuals and their employers. They are persuaded that fundamental reform is vital, shifting the main burden of retirement income provision from statutory to employer-based, occupational schemes.

This final challenge is thus seen by some as requiring that the structures and principles of the existing regimes be altered. However, whatever solution is found for this perceived challenge to the status quo, it will also have to be able to

---

[7]   This will be discussed at greater length in Chapter 3.

[8]   For a discussion of harmonisation techniques, and of coordination, see H.G. Sevenster, *Milieubeleid en Gemeenschapsrecht. Het interne juridische kader en de praktijk*, Deventer, 1992 at pp. 13-22 and 65-75 and the literature cited therein.

meet the challenges posed by the increased levels of economic activity of women, and the internationalisation of the market. Consequently, it would seem appropriate to consider whether the purported solution to the third challenge to existing pension provision is able to provide adequate pensions to women and international migrants, and indeed, whether it represents an improvement in terms of the possibilities it offers these specific individuals.

In the next section, the stimulus towards shifting the burden of retirement income provision from the state to the private sector - demographic predictions - and its perceived consequences for current pension provision will be outlined, before moving on to describe why it is that it is considered that occupational provision offers a better alternative. The main body of this research will be composed of assessing the adequacy of this alternative form of pension provision in dealing with the two challenges which have already come to face statutory pensions - the increased economic activity levels of women and the increased internationalisation of the market, and the greater employee mobility which, in the EU context at least, it seeks to encourage. Thereafter, the precise parameters of this research project will be outlined.

1.2   The Demographic Challenge

The major challenge facing statutory pension schemes in the EU at this time is not in fact that the market is internationalising, nor that more women than before are undertaking economic activities, but rather that the population of the EU is ageing. In absolute terms, the population is ageing because average life expectancy at birth for the population of the EU has increased from 67 in 1950 to 74.4 in 1980.[9] In other words, people are living longer. The population can also be described as ageing if population age is expressed in relative terms, in that the ratio of retired persons to members of the age group assumed to be economically active[10] is also

---

[9]   P.J. Besseling and R.F. Zeeuw, *The financing of pensions in Europe: Challenges and Opportunities*, CEPS Research Report No. 14, November 1993, Brussels at p. 25. It should however be noted that these figures do not include Sweden, Finland and Austria.

[10]   If unemployment is higher than estimated, this will distort the ratio produced.

changing, from an EU average of 21.2 in 1990 to an estimated 42.8 in 2040.[11] This relative ageing can partly be explained by the reduction in the fertility rate which has dropped from approximately 2.6 children per female to 1.5,[12] a rate which is clearly inadequate to maintain current population levels.[13]

Irrespective of the level of pension which a state pays to its retired population, these developments raise issues with which these schemes must grapple.[14] The ageing of the population means that not only will pensions have to be paid to a larger group of individuals than in the past (because there are more people over pensionable age), but also generally for a longer period of time

---

[11]   Besseling and Zeeuw, op. cit. at p. 20. See also "When George Soros meets Granny Smith", *The Economist*, 22 April 1995 at pp. 81-82 and 87, where a table indicates that the population aged 65 and over is estimated to reach 50% in Holland, and only in Ireland is it expected to remain below 30%. Similar figures are to be found in Taverne, loc. cit. appendix 2. The European Commission predicts that by 2020, the EU average ratio of persons over the age of 65 to those in the working population will reach 45%. COM (95) 466 final at p. 6.

[12]   CEPS, Working Party Report No. 9, November 1993, *Financing Retirement in Europe*, Brussels at p. 11. See also, for example, K. Achenbach and E. Haneberg, "Rentenversicherung: Ermutigende Zukunftsperspektiven", *Bundesarbeitsblatt* 11/1995, 5-11 at p. 6 which indicates that since the mid-1970s the German "net reproduction rate" has virtually halved, from 1.2 to 0.66.

[13]   Indeed, the Commission of the EC (hereafter, Commission) admits that studies which indicate that the total EU population will remain constant may be over-optimistic, since fertility rates are in fact lower than thought when the calculations were made. See COM (95) 466 final at p. 6.

[14]   This phenomenon has consequences for other areas of state social spending. In particular, because the number of (extremely) elderly people in the population is increasing, it can be expected that an ever larger number of individuals will make use of health care services, meaning that society will have to spend more money on health care. It is apparently the case that 90% of the cost of health care for the average individual is incurred in the last 6 months of life. See J. Plender, "Retirement isn't Working", *Financial Times Weekend*, 17 June/18 June 1995 at I. See also World Bank, *Averting the Old Age Crisis. Policies to Protect the Old and Protect Growth*, Oxford, 1994 at pp. 2, 31 and 43; J.B. Kuné, "Bevolkingsveroudering en de financiering van de AOW-voorziening. Is het creëren van een schommelfonds zinvol?", TPV (1996), 31-34 at 33.

(because they are living longer).[15] Consequently, it appears that if state pension schemes remain unchanged, more money will have to be spent on them. However, this increased spending will be required at precisely the point in time when statistics tell us that there will be fewer people in the working population.

Indeed, if this challenge is to be met, there does seem to be unanimity between studies that spending on pensions will have to rise to meet this challenge. By contrast, there is no uniformity as to whether the increases in expenditure caused by the increase in the numbers of elderly people in the population will be offset by savings incurred by virtue of the fact that the active population is smaller. Although the drop in fertility will mean that there are fewer children, and therefore that spending on the young *ought*[16] to drop, off-setting somewhat the increase in social spending caused by the health care and pension costs of the elderly,[17] it has been suggested that there will nevertheless be a net increase in social spending because, in OECD countries at least, social services spending per elderly person is generally two to three times that spent per child.[18] On the other hand, figures calculated for Germany suggest that social expenditure will in fact fall in the future![19] Equally, it might be suggested that the smaller working population will mean that savings will be made on unemployment benefits. Again, although some degree of saving would seem to be probable, it would be naive to assume that this will balance out the increased costs of the elderly population, since unemployment is caused in part by a shortage in appropriately skilled employees in the

---

[15] In part because of (expensive) medical advances. "Richer countries have more expensive health facilities that keep people alive longer increasing the demands on their pension systems." World Bank, op. cit. at 43.

[16] Note that the World Bank study (op. cit. at 31-32) indicates that where there are fewer children, it is even likely that more will be spent per child than is spent when there are many children, casting doubt on even this assertion.

[17] Note that a study for the Institute of Public Policy Research by the Health Economics Research Unit at Aberdeen University found that the projected increase in costs to the NHS from ageing had been exaggerated; *The Independent*, 4 September 1996 at p. 2.

[18] World Bank, op. cit. at 31.

[19] R. Hageman and G. Nicoletti, *Ageing Populations: economic effects and implications for public finance*, OECD 1989, table 11 at p. 45.

marketplace.[20] Consequently, it would appear that unless the schemes are reformed, the proportion of state spending which is devoted to pensions will increase and that it is unlikely adequately to be offset by savings made elsewhere.

However, at the same time, other factors have conspired to create an incentive for members of the EU to cut social security spending, especially in relation to pensions. In the context of Economic and Monetary Union, Article 104c EC provides that the governments of the Member States will avoid excessive government deficits. Failure to maintain government deficits below thresholds set by the Protocol on the excessive deficit procedure, can lead to measures being taken against the Member State in question, including reassessment of European Investment Bank lending policy towards that state, fines, and requiring the Member State to make a non-interest bearing deposit with the Community until the deficit has been corrected.[21] For Member States wishing to qualify for EMU, this may form an incentive to cut spending, on top of the demographic considerations already outlined which suggest that the system will become more expensive.[22] According to one set of calculations, if the real future cost of state pension provision appeared in government budgets, public debt in Europe would double

---

[20]   Kuné 1995, op. cit. at 95.

[21]   Article 104c(11) EC.

[22]   It appears that governments tackling public spending are already citing the need to conform with the EMU convergence criteria as a justification for their actions (EIRR 264 (1996) at 1). M. Green, "Social Security in Europe: The Only Certainty is Change", 25 *Benefits and Compensation International* no. 10 (1996), 2-7 at 2-3. For example, in Italy, reform of the state pension scheme is seen as essential if its public debt - 125% of GDP - is to be reduced. See R. Graham, "Italy on brink of pension reform deal", *Financial Times*, 8 May 1995, p. 2; "Pensions reform in force", EIRR nr 264, (1996), 31-34; P. Conci, "Pensions Reform in Italy", 7 *International Insurance Law Review* (1996), 229-231; A. Salafia, "Italy. The draft legislation for reform of Italy's statutory and complementary pension schemes", 48 *International Social Security Review* (1995), 143-150. See also the statements of the Dutch government in *Regeerakkord "Keuzen voor de toekomst"*, Stcrt. 156, 1994, 6-11 at 6. Additionally, much of the disruption which recently took place in France was in reaction to Juppé's proposals to reform the French social security system. See "France racked by massive crisis over social security reforms" EIRR 264 (1996) 6; "Social summit defuses crisis while reform continues", EIRR 265 (1996), 15-17. M. Voirin, "Private and public pension schemes: Elements of a comparative approach", 48 *International Social Security Review* (1996), 91-141 at 101.

as a percentage of GDP.[23]

In short, the demographic predictions which can now be made indicate that the bill for pensions will rise at a time when governments are under pressure to reduce state spending.

Despite the fact that when considering pensions, one tends to focus upon the amount of money paid periodically to the beneficiaries of the scheme, it is not in fact the *levels* of benefit per se which are causing the current crisis in statutory pension provision.[24] Rather it is the method by which statutory pension schemes are funded which has allowed the projected demographic developments, and EMU constraints to be interpreted as posing such a threat to their continuation.

The Member States of the EU currently finance their statutory schemes on what has come to be known in English as a "Pay-As-You-Go" basis.[25] Pay-As-You-Go means that current contributors, usually but not necessarily including the State,[26] are responsible for paying the benefits of those currently in receipt of

---

[23]   See J. Plender, op. cit. at I. In 1993, social protection expenditure per head amounted to 27.5% EU12 GDP, ranging from 34% for the Netherlands, to 16% for Greece. See COM (95) 466 final at p. 13. See also World Bank, loc. cit. at pp. 90-92 where what is termed "the implicit public pension debt" is discussed. S. Hutton, S. Kennedy and P. Whiteford, (*Equalisation of State Pension Ages: The Gender Impact*, EOC Research Discussion Series No. 10, Manchester, 1995 at p. 14) indicate that between 1960 and 1987 public pension expenditure as a % of GDP has increased from 9.6%-15.2% for Austria; 8.4% (1971)-11.9% (1979) for Belgium; 4.6%-8.5% for Denmark; 3.8%-7.1% (1984) for Finland; 6.0%-13.9% for France; 9.7%-11.5% for Germany; 4.3% (1965)-10.7% (1985) for Greece; 2.5%-5.4% (1985) for Ireland; 5.5%-15.6% (1985) for Italy; 4.0%-10.5% for the Netherlands; 1.4% (1965)-7.2% (1985) for Portugal; 3.2% (1970)-8.6% (1984); 4.4%-11.3% for Sweden; 4.0%-6.8% for the UK. However, as R. Beattie and W. McGillivray ("A risky strategy: Reflections on the World bank Report *Averting the old age crisis*", 48 *International Social Security Review* (1995), 5-22 at 8) point out, this need only be a problem if the debt had suddenly to be paid off.

[24]   Plender, op. cit. at I; "A Mountain of Money", *The Economist* 22 April 1995, p. 14. SEC(91) 1332 final at pp. 9-11; Kuné 1995, op. cit.; The Retirement Income Inquiry, *Pensions: 2000 and Beyond*, London 1996 (hereafter *Pensions 2000*).

[25]   In Dutch, *omslagstelsel*; in German, *Umlageverfahren*; in French, *répartition*.

[26]   The Dutch scheme, for example, only introduced a state contribution to the AOW in 1965. See M. Westerveld, *Keuzes van gisteren...een blauwdruk voor morgen? Honderd jaar sociale-verzekeringspensioenen in de Bondsrepubliek Duitsland, Groot-Brittannië en Nederland*, 1994, Den Haag at pp. 124 and 261-2.

benefits under the scheme and it offers a number of clear advantages to scheme
designers which alternative methods of funding lack. For example, it allows
schemes to be introduced virtually instantaneously, with benefits being granted to
a generation of pensioners who have never contributed to the benefit which they
receive.[27] This contrasts with the situation for pre-funded schemes[28] in which an
individual's benefit funded by his (and his employer's) contributions may require
40 years to reach maturity. Another advantage of Pay-As-You-Go when viewed
from the perspective of the legislator is that by allowing current employees to fund
current benefits by paying contributions based on their salaries, the income of
pensioners can fairly painlessly rise in line with increases in earnings, fostering
social solidarity and generally allowing pensioners to share in any increase in the
prosperity of society. It also makes the scheme easily adjustable to changed
circumstances[29] and frees it of the risks associated with investments of funds on

---

[27]   In the UK, for example, Beveridge originally proposed that his scheme be introduced over
        20 years. However, the government in power at the time did not follow this part of his
        recommendations. See Westerveld, loc. cit. at pp. 70-1, 75-76. Also L. Hannah, *Inventing
        Retirement. The Development of Occupational Pensions in Britain*, Cambridge, 1986 at pp.
        53-54. In Germany, in introducing the 1957 *Rentenversicherung* (Pension insurance), the
        government opted for Pay-As-You-Go, but it was only fully introduced in 1969. See
        Westerveld, loc. cit. at pp. 35, 171-174. According to Plender, op. cit. at I, state schemes
        of this type in fact benefit early entrants at the expense of later entrants "who may suffer
        negative returns on their money." E. Philip Davis, *Pension Funds. Retirement-Income
        Security and Capital Markets. An International Perspective*, Oxford, 1995 at pp. 35-40
        discusses the pro's and con's of pay-as-you-go versus funded schemes. See also Beattie and
        McGillivray, op. cit.; E. Reynaud, "Financing retirement pensions: Pay-as-you-go and funded
        systems in the European Union", 48 *International Social Security Review* (1995), 41-57;
        L.H. Thompson, "The advantages and disadvantages of different social welfare strategies",
        48 *International Social Security Review* (1995), 59-73; Voirin, op. cit.

[28]   In Dutch, funded by *kapitaaldekking*; in German, *Kapitaldeckungsverfahren*; in French
        capitalisation.

[29]   For example, should the exclusion of a particular group from entitlement to benefit be found
        to be illegal, a small increase in premiums paid allows the scheme to adapt. See for
        example, Joined Cases C-87-89/90, *Verholen and others* v. *Sociale Verzekeringsbank*, [1991]
        ECR I-3757.

capital markets.[30]

However, Pay-As-You-Go depends upon a considerable degree of inter-generational solidarity as it requires that the current working generation foregoes some of its income by paying social contributions in the interests of the current generation of pensioners in return for no more concrete a guarantee of similar sacrifices by future generations than a political promise to continue to operate the scheme.[31] Contributors assume that they will receive levels of benefit from the state scheme roughly concommitant to the contributions which they have paid.[32] The demographic projections as to the future composition of Europe's population suggest that the existing balance between what current contributors pay in and the amount which they will receive in benefits in the future can only be maintained either by raising the levels of contributions to be paid by the smaller group of contributors,[33] or by increasing the contributions paid by the State.[34]

---

[30]   For an economic description of the differences between funding and Pay-As-You-Go, see Philip Davis, loc. cit. at pp. 35-40, who also discussed at pp. 127-229 the questions of the performance of pension funds as financial institutions, their effects on capital markets, pensions funds and corporate finance and international investment. See also SEC(91) 1332 final at pp. 8-9.

[31]   P. Alcock, "The advantages and disadvantages of the contribution base in targeting benefits: A social analysis of the insurance scheme in the United Kingdom", 49 *International Social Security Review* (1996), 31-49 at 42.

[32]   M. Westerveld, "Pensioenen in de 21e eeuw: gouden bergen, diepe dalen", NJB nr. 28 (1996), 1103-1109.

[33]   For example, according to figures calculated for the Netherlands, this could result in a situation that if the old age pension is not altered, premiums for the old age pension would have to rise from 14.25% in 1994, to 22.1% in 2030, 23.3% in 2035 and 20.9% in 2040. J.H.M. Nelissen and H.A.A. Verbon, "Ouderen voor jongeren", ESB 1993, 817-821, at 819. In Germany, it appears that the proportion of workers to retirees will shift from 2 contributors to each pensioner to one to one (Achenbach and Haneberg, op. cit. at 5) Although commentators hope that the reforms to the statutory scheme introduced in 1992 will safeguard the German state pension scheme, these predictions are based on the German economy continuing to grow and may require adjustment in the light of the already deteriorating economic situation. Indeed, calls have already been heard to cut the levels of social security contributions which Germans have to pay from 41.1% to 37%. See "German plan for growth and jobs", *Financial Times*, 16 January 1996 at p. 2) In the UK, the ratio of people of working age to pensioners is predicted to drop from 3:1 to 1.6:1 and restoring pensions to 1979 levels would cost an estimated £50 billion in by 2030. See "Call for action on pensions 'time bomb'", *The Independent*, 24 January 1996 at p. 2. Assuming price, as

Increasing the level of contributions required from workers in the future is not without its problems. First, levying a high rate of contributions suggests to the contributors that they will receive concommitant benefit levels.[35] Consequently, high contribution rates can be seen to burden the social security scheme in the future at a time when it is not clear what the size of the working population which would have to finance the pensions will be. Second, and probably more importantly, high levels of contributions may be seen as taxes, encouraging evasion and a retreat into the "black economy".[36] This in turn disadvantages more than merely contributions to the pension scheme. General state revenue obtained from taxes and social security contributions and used for a wide range of purposes suffers, reducing the funds available for other areas of expenditure.[37] Additionally, high payroll taxes (or contribution rates) may lead to increased wage demands, in turn fuelling inflation. Finally, relatively high perceived levels of taxes and contributions may encourage employers to transfer their operations to jurisdictions levying lower rates. For all these reasons, therefore, raising contribution rates is not

---

opposed to wage inflation, the most recent review carried out by the Government Actuary predicts that the contribution rate will have to increase from the current 16.6% (1991) to a peak of 17.9% in 2030 (Hutton et al, loc. cit. at p. 41).

[34]   An additional measure which can be taken is to raise pensionable age. This will be discussed in Chapters 3 and 4 below in the context of equality between women and men. For these purposes, however, raising pensionable age offers States a method of saving money on pension payments because the pensions will be payable for a shorter period of time. As will be discussed *infra* it is not a particularly easy policy to introduce. Additionally, it will result in the working population being larger than would otherwise have been the case, with favourable consequences for the numbers of contributors to the scheme. But it also suggests that the savings made in unemployment benefit payments will be less than would otherwise have been the case.

[35]   Kuné 1996, op. cit. at 32.

[36]   The "black economy" is a term used to describe employment carried outwith the framework of the law, in that it does not result in the employee or employer paying taxes or social security contributions in relation to it. Additionally, the employee does not enjoy the protection of labour laws designed to protect him.

[37]   For example, the current problems facing the Italian pension scheme are seen partly to have been caused by the fact that only 40% of the population are in regular paid employment, by which is meant, employment as a result of which taxes and social security contributions are paid; see "Pensions reform in force", op. cit. at 32.

seen as an attractive response to the challenges currently facing the statutory schemes.

The second main way of maintaining benefit levels in the future would be to increase the contributions paid by the state. However, this would mean a choice between cutting expenditure in other areas which may be neither possible nor desirable, or increasing state revenue through increased levels of taxation, which has the negative consequences already described. Although increasing the level of tax paid by pensioners would offer a means of increasing revenue, it will reduce pensioners' disposable incomes, reduce the spending power of that sector of the economy, and may push some into poverty by taking their benefit levels below that deemed the minimum acceptable. The most usual response to that situation is to provide a state financed means tested top up, which, of course, does not reduce the state's social spending.[38] However, perhaps more importantly, it should also be borne in mind that increasing the levels of tax paid by pensioners is itself a difficult political course to follow in a period in which the numbers of retired persons are set to increase, since they become a large interest group for the preservation of the status quo, and one with the time to campaign on the issue.[39]

Finally, it is possible to raise pensionable ages. This has the benefit that individuals will be able to contribute to the scheme for longer, and ought to be in receipt of their pension for a correspondingly reduced period and as such, this approach has the potential to offer schemes considerable savings. However, first there is a marked trend towards not later but earlier retirement.[40] Second, it is politically extremely difficult to raise pensionable ages other than by very gradual

---

[38]   See for example, Beattie and McGillivray, op. cit. at 18.

[39]   An example of the increasing political weight of pensioners can be seen to be provided by the formation of political parties in the Netherlands campaigning on specific pensioner issues.

[40]   For example, Taverne (loc. cit., appendix 5) indicates that male activity rates have dropped from an EC average for 50-54 year olds of 91.1% in 1983 to 88.9% in 1991; for the age group 55-59, the drop is from 75.5% to 72.7%; for those aged 60-64, the figures are 42.3% to 37.1%; for 65-69 year olds, the figures are 13.1% and 11.3%. Finally, those over 70 have dropped from 5.3% to 3.8%.

steps.[41] Consequently, it is not to be expected that raising pensionable age will do anything to address what are seen as the fundamental difficulties of statutory schemes at present.

These alternative methods of maintaining the balance in the current scheme have proved politically unattractive. Instead the Member States have begun to consider the fundamental reform of their systems of retirement income provision.[42]

1.2.1   A FAVOURED ALTERNATIVE

The perceived problem with Pay-As-You-Go is that it is considered to be unable satisfactorily to deal with a situation in which the retired population is larger than the working population. A variety of different solutions have been offered to address the problem, but a common feature of many such proposals is the recommendation that the degree to which pensions are funded in advance (pre-funded) ought to be increased.[43]

---

[41]   See the proposals of the UK and German governments discussed in Chapter 4. Details of similar cautious approaches taken in other jurisdictions are given in Voirin, op. cit. at 102-103.

[42]   See for example, "A Mountain of Money", *The Economist* 22 April 1995, p. 14; Philip Davis, loc. cit. at pp. 40-52; COM(95) 466 final; H. Verbon, "De financiering van de oudedagsvoorziening", 18 *Tijdschrift voor Politieke Ekonomie* (1995), 32-51; Kuné 1996, op. cit; P. Johnson, *The Pensions Dilemma*, IPPR, London, 1994; B. Davies, *Better Pensions for All*, IPPR, London, 1993; Commission on Social Justice, *Social Justice. Strategies for National Renewal*, London 1994, at pp. 221-305; Taverne, loc. cit.; *Pensions 2000*, op. cit.; B. Castle and P. Townsend, *We CAN Afford the Welfare State*, London, 1996. As the World Bank study (loc. cit.) shows, this discussion is taking place worldwide. N. Ploug and J. Kvist, (*Social Security in Europe. Development or Dismantlement?*, Deventer, 1996) demonstrate that the debate is not confined to pensions, but covers the entire social security system.

[43]   Note that it is not my intention here to discuss the relative merits of Pay-As-You-Go as opposed to funded schemes (on which see Philip Davis, loc. cit. at pp. 35-40; World Bank, loc. cit. at pp. 10-19, 73-100; Beattie and McGillivray, op. cit.; Reynaud, op. cit.; Thompson, op. cit.; Voirin, op. cit.; Taverne, loc. cit.) or the spectrum of options which have been proposed. The political decision that pre-funding is better will be taken as the basis for the discussion which follows. The only assessment which will be made is of whether the one or the other better serves the groups with which this research is concerned.

In a pre-funded scheme, the contributions paid by and on behalf of a particular individual are invested for him and the resulting capital is used to fund his benefits. Because money contributed by and on behalf of the individual funds his benefits, pre-funding is seen basically to be immune to the difficulties which the shift in the balance between the active and non-active population has been seen to create for Pay-As-You-Go schemes,[44] although opinions on this are far from united.[45]

However, it is not just in relation to the method of financing that reform is contemplated. It will be recalled that states searching for alternatives to Pay-As-You-Go have also been desirous to reduce their social expenditure. This in turn explains why the proposals of those whose solution to the difficulties facing Pay-As-You-Go schemes is to increase the role of pre-funded schemes and to place responsibility for making and financing such provision on the individual and his employer rather than the state, have proved so politically popular.[46] While reducing the role of the state in this field can be "sold" to the electorate on grounds

---

[44]   As Kuné 1996, op. cit. discusses, where the working population is smaller than the retired population, Pay-As-You-Go results in there being a relative scarcity of savings in the economy as the retired population ages. This may lead to capital shortage, and lack of investment. Pre-funding is said to offer a (widely disputed, see for example, Beattie and McGillivray, op. cit. at 14-15; Castle and Townsend, loc. cit.; Reynaud, op. cit. at 55-6; Thompson, op. cit. at 68-9) method of ensuring that there is a sufficient level of savings in the economy. This is because it involves the small working population also accruing funds, which are available to the economy at a time when the large group of pensioners are drawing their benefits, and the national savings are reducing accordingly. See also D. Miles, "No free lunches in providing for an ageing population", *The Independent*, 19 August 1996, 17; B. Reading, "Ease those pension worries", *Financial Times Weekend Money*, 7-8 September 1996.

[45]   See for example, Beattie and McGillivray, op. cit. at 14-15.

[46]   The World Bank study recommends that no more than 20% of total retirement income be provided by the state. These proposals for reform of pensions can be seen to dovetail nicely into the "deregulatory" "privatizing" initiatives being followed in a number of jurisdictions, as is observed by Voirin, op. cit. at 117 and 135-136; Beattie and McGillivray, op. cit. at 21 "it is unfortunate that the issue of pension reform has been mixed up with the wider debate about privatization and the role of government". However, it should be recalled that where the state seeks to use the private sector to provide pensions, it will be forced to regulate the institutions closely and so "deregulation" is hardly an appropriate term; Thompson, op. cit. at 70.

of "maximising individual choice and responsibility",[47] it offers governments an easy method of massaging social spending figures.[48] Reducing the levels or availability of state pensions[49] allows the social security budget to be cut.[50] It also influences the apparent social costs to employers of operating within a particular jurisdiction, because such figures rarely include obligations imposed on employers to fund occupational benefits.[51]

Consequently, a number of arguments have been mustered to argue that the best response to the perceived current crisis in statutory provision is to increase the role played by pre-funded employer-based "occupational" pension schemes,

---

[47]   The UK government heralded its 1985 Pension reforms (on which see Chapter 2) with the declaration "We want to give greater responsibility and greater independence to the individual" Green Paper, *Reform of Social Security*, Cmnd. 9517, Chapter 1 (also cited in Westerveld, loc. cit. at pp. 374-375). The government's rejection of the recommendation of the report *Pensions 2000* that occupational provision be made compulsory is also based on its ideological conviction as to the role of the state. See "Pension Reform would make the wealthier save more", *Financial Times*, 24 January 1996 at p. 9. For the Dutch government's view of the role of occupational pension schemes see *Nota Aanvullende Pensioenen*, TK, 1990-1991, 22 167, nr. 2. And *Regeerakkord "Keuzen voor de toekomst*, op. cit. at 6.

[48]   W. Streeck, "Neo-Voluntarism: A New European Social Policy Regime?", 1 ELJ (1995), 31-59.

[49]   It should be noted that it is virtually impossible to envisage scrapping statutory pension provision, because need will continue to exist in the poorest sectors of society for which private provision will be unable to provide (because of the low earnings of the individuals concerned, their interrupted employment patterns, and the lack of solidarity within occupational schemes). Where private provision is not compulsory, state provision will also remain necessary for those whom private provision has decided not to provide. For the variety of methods through which occupational schemes have denied particular classes of individuals pension rights see Chapters 4 and 6 below.

[50]   It should be noted that even in countries in which the state makes no direct contribution to occupational pension provision, this does not mean that it is cost-free for the state. Contributions made to occupational pension schemes generally enjoy some form of tax benefit. Consequently, the exchequer will forego some current income, receiving (lower amounts, because of the effects of marginal tax rates) income in the future as a consequence of taxing the benefit. It has been calculated that in the UK, for example, the tax advantages offered to occupational schemes cost the exchequer £7,700 million in 1993, C. Daykin, *Pension Provision in Britain*, London, 1994 at p. 46.

[51]   See for example, L. Barber, "Shaky truce on social battlefield", *Financial Times*, 5 August 1996, 13.

despite the fact that

> "at the end of the day, the question of how far resources should
> be extended to the welfare state is a political one, just as much
> as is the question of how these resources are to be
> distributed."[52]

If a brief overview is taken of developments in the Member States of the EU, it becomes clear that this is precisely the path which governments are following.[53] In the light of this trend away from statutory pension schemes, occupational retirement provision will form the main focus of this research, the precise delimitation of which will be provided in the final sections of this Chapter.

1.3   The Delimitation

1.3.1   WHICH ISSUES?

As should have become clear from the preceding sections, the future shape of European pension provision is currently a topic of heated discussion. A number of commentators consider that increasing the role played by pre-funded employer based occupational schemes is the most appropriate response to the demographic challenges facing statutory schemes. The appropriateness per se of this conclusion will not be the focus of this work.[54] Rather, the evaluation of occupational provision which will be made will concern its ability to provide women and international migrants[55] with adequate[56] levels of retirement income.

---

[52]   Ploug and Kvist, loc. cit. at pp. 38-39. This is echoed by Castle and Townsend, loc. cit. at p. 19.

[53]   See, for example, the overviews provided by Green, op. cit.; Reynaud, op. cit.; Voirin, op. cit.; Thompson, op. cit.

[54]   See for example, the opinions expressed by Beattie and McGillivray, op. cit. at 14-15; Castle and Townsend, op. cit.; Kuné, op. cit.; Reynaud, op. cit. at 55-6; Thompson, op. cit. at 68-9.

[55]   It is true that the international migrant is unlikely to face more significant difficulties than the job-changer within a Member State. However, for reasons of symmetry with the brief discussion of the statutory position, only the position of the international migrant will be considered. R. Cornelissen ("The Principle of Territoriality and the Community Regulations

As will be elaborated upon shortly, I intend to do so on the basis of detailed examination of the regulation of occupational schemes in the jurisdictions in which coverage is most widespread. This should enable some conclusions to be drawn as to the extent to which existing schemes will have to adapt their rules. However, equally, it should indicate the paths which states seeking to encourage occupational provision ought to avoid, if they wish women and migrant workers to be enabled to accrue maximum levels of occupational benefits, and to avoid occupational pension schemes being used to partition the labour market.

It has been stated that the statutory pension schemes operating in the Member States have already been forced to respond to the challenges of providing for women and international migrants. The EC legislator acted in relation to labour mobility and social security in 1958. 20 years later legislation was adopted to introduce equality into social security schemes. The law is well-known and developed. However, the situation in relation to occupational schemes is much less clear. First, it has only been relatively recently that the schemes have been forced to consider the position of women workers. They are currently struggling to eradicate discrimination from their rules. This would accordingly seem to be an appropriate time to carry out a detailed examination of whether this action goes far enough. Second, in relation to international migrants, occupational pension schemes are a particularly interesting subject for research, because there have been no detailed studies into the ways in which occupational schemes may hinder labour mobility. Research of this nature at this time can highlight the difficulties for the labour market which widespread transition to occupational provision could bring. This would allow these problems to be avoided.

---

on Social Security (Regulations 1408/71 and 574/72), 33 CML Rev. (1996), 439-471) indicates at fn. 16 at 444 that the number of EU migrant workers is only about 2 million.

[56]   For the purposes of this research, an adequate pension will be defined as follows: the maximum pension to which any particular scheme enables individuals to accrue entitlement. The reason for this definition is that every scheme provides benefits of a particular standard to individuals who satisfy all its requirements. In this regard, the frame of reference for the adequacy of the pension benefit is internal to the scheme in question, rather than some external standard.

1.3.2   WHICH SCHEMES?

It has been stated that the main focus of this project will be occupational schemes. These are the pension schemes offered to employees by their employers as part of their contracts of employment. No consideration will however be given to individual pension schemes. A number of factors informed this decision. First, the individual nature of the pension policy concluded means that the free movement problems which may arise with this type of contract are of a different nature to those arising in the group oriented occupational scheme. Equally, the individual nature of the insurance contract, separate from any employment contract, also means that any equality issues which arise in individual contracts are different from those in the occupational schemes. These differences would seem adequately to justify excluding individual pension arrangements from the scope of this research.

Another kind of pension scheme which will not be considered specifically here is the pension paid to the public servant. Despite the Court of Justice's holding in the *ABP* case[57] that pension schemes which pay benefits to civil servants fall within the scope of Article 119 EC,[58] and that a coordination regime has to be created for the social security rights of migrants covered by such schemes,[59] they will remain outwith the scope of the present study. The reason for this exclusion is that occupational pension provision for civil servants is often made within an entirely different legal framework than that operating for private sector employees. One crucial difference is that they are frequently funded on a Pay-As-You-Go basis. In this respect they resemble statutory schemes more than they do occupational ones and consequently, the exclusion of civil service schemes can be justified by reference to the fact that although fulfilling the function of an occupational scheme, the methods of statutory provision are adopted.

Although the resulting public sector schemes operate in a manner not

---

[57]   Case C-7/93, *ABP* v. *Beune*, [1994] ECR I-4471.

[58]   This will be elaborated upon in more detail in Chapter 4.

[59]   Case C-443/93, *Vougioukas* v. *Idryma Koinonikon Asfalisscon (IKA)*, [1995] ECR I-4033, discussed by Cornelissen, op. cit. at 444. This is discussed at greater length in Chapter 5.

entirely different from private sector schemes, to have included discussion of them would have increased the complexity of this work, without however adding any substantive points to the discussion. Consequently, consideration of the detailed regulatory frameworks governing civil service schemes has been ommitted, although the conclusions which are reached as to the discriminatory effects of occupational schemes, and their potential to form barriers to free movement of workers can be expected to be equally applicable to these public sector schemes.

This study will focus on the occupational pension schemes. This is not to say that no attention whatsoever will be paid to the statutory schemes. At least a brief description of the statutory basis will be required if occupational provision is to be understood in context.[60] This is because all occupational pension schemes build upon the basis provided by the statutory scheme. As has already been observed, statutory schemes have already been the focus of the European legislator's attention in relation both to free movement and sexual equality. These activities will be outlined and the reforms to which they have led discussed, before moving on to consider occupational provision in more detail. This will enable an evaluation to be made of whether the two groups of workers with which this research is concerned will find accruing an adequate pension easier within a statutory or occupational scheme.

1.3.3   WHICH BENEFITS?

In relation to the benefits covered, this volume is limited to retirement pensions paid by occupational pension schemes.[61] It does not therefore include supplementary health benefits provided by many employers to their employees and

---

[60]   Voirin, op. cit. at 93.

[61]   Indeed, it is limited to retirement benefits paid to individuals who reach pensionable age, and any benefits paid to their survivors. No specific consideration is given to the invalidity pensions. The provisions governing invalidity pensions typically enable an individual to be treated as if he had been in pensionable employment until reaching pensionable age. Inclusion of separate sections on these pensions would however seem only to complicate this research, without adding significant substantive points. As far as international migrants are concerned, it seems unlikely that the obstacles created by invalidity pensions will be significantly different from those created by "normal" retirement pensions. Similar observations would seem to apply to women's pensions.

their families.[62] This exclusion is prompted by one major consideration. The nature of health insurance differs from old age insurance. Rights to old age benefits accrue over time and are dependent upon the individual reaching a specified age and the level of benefit paid out by a fund increases over time, or more precisely, increases in line with the individual's period of membership of the scheme. It is therefore of the greatest importance to the level of benefits which the employee will eventually receive, that on changing employment he does not forfeit his accrued rights.[63] By contrast, for health insurance benefits to be paid out, all that is required is that the individual be insured at the moment that the risk materialises; the level of benefit does not depend on the length of the insurance history of the individual member. Maintaining previously accrued rights is not important in health insurance[64] while it is vital in pension insurance.

Another difference between the two forms of insurance is that health insurance policies cover different ranges of risk. Pension schemes provide for the same risk - loss of income on reaching a specified age. Additionally health insurers are permitted to carry out risk selection, refusing insurance (or making it more expensive) to those they consider most likely to require the protection covered by the policy. By contrast, no risk selection takes place in pension schemes, at least in relation to offering membership or setting conditions to be fulfilled - individuals belonging to families with a predisposition for extreme old age are not refused membership, nor do those whose family histories suggest that they will live only

---

[62]   Given the developments outlined at the beginning of this research, it seems likely that supplementary health insurance will become increasingly common in the future as the cost of health care hits home. For a detailed treatment of supplementary health insurance in the European Union see, P.K. Meyer, *Auswirkungen des EG-Dirkriminerungsverbots von Mann und Frau auf das private und betriebliche Krankheits- und Altersvorzorge in Europa*, Karlsruhe, 1994.

[63]   Although he may not realise it.

[64]   Except to the extent that an individual moves from a scheme covering a wide range of risks, to a scheme with narrower coverage, or stricter qualifying criteria.

a few years beyond pensionable age enjoy lower premiums.[65]

These considerations suggest that the issues raised by pension insurance and health insurance are sufficiently different to justify the exclusion of supplementary health insurance from the scope of this research. Consequently, only retirement and survivor's pensions will be considered.

1.3.4   WHICH MEMBER STATES?

Occupational pension schemes are already in existence to a greater or lesser extent in the countries of the EU.[66] Recent estimates indicate that assets held to cover occupational pension liabilities in the then 12 EU Member States amounted to some 1,051,261 million ECU,[67] although there are significant variations between the Member States. It seems probable that Member States seeking to increase the role played by pre-funded occupational schemes in their jurisdiction will look to states in which this form of provision is more established for lessons from which they can learn.[68]

A major limitation in the scope of the research carried out - at least in relation to the comparative part - is that it centres on only three of the current fifteen Member States of the Union. The nature of this research - detailed examination of the specific features of national law and practice relating to occupational pension schemes which may penalise the two groups of employees with which this research is concerned - is such as to preclude examination of all

---

[65]   See however, A. Bailey, "Want a better pension? Don't get fit, get fat", *Independent on Sunday*, 7 July 1996 at 14 who reports that one company is paying higher periodic pensions to individuals who are considerably overweight, on the basis that they are unlikely to live as long as their thinner counterparts.

[66]   *Supplementary Pensions in the European Union: Developments, Trends and Outstanding Issues*, Report by the European Commission's Network of Experts on Supplementary Pensions, Brussels, 1994 (hereafter *Supplementary Pensions*).

[67]   *Supplementary pensions*, loc. cit. at p. 94.

[68]   Indeed, a brief examination of the proposals which have been presented in France and Italy suggests that precisely such an approach is being followed. See Conci, op. cit.; Salafia, op. cit.; A. Jack and D. Owen, "France to launch pension scheme by end of year", *Financial Times* 16 September 1996, p. 2.

the individual Member States. Were such an approach to be followed, either the resulting report would be unmanageably large or so superficial as to be of doubtful utility. Consequently, a selection has been made from amongst the Member States. The selection of which Member States to study was relatively simple. As recent figures demonstrate,[69] it is only in three Member States that a significant volume of assets has been accumulated to cover occupational pension liabilities, and these states also have the most extensive coverage of employees.[70] By focusing on these three Member States the most important and developed markets for occupational provision are isolated. My research consequently focuses on the regulation of occupational pension schemes in the UK, the Netherlands and Germany. The largest volume of pension scheme assets of any EU Member State is to be found in the UK where in 1991 they amounted to some 490,719 million ECU,[71] despite the fact that only around 48% of UK employees are members of schemes.[72] In Germany, figures for 1992 suggest that assets had been accumulated to cover occupational pension liabilities amounting to some 214,322 million ECU[73] with coverage in the private sector reaching 46.7% of employees.[74] The Netherlands on the other hand has coverage of approximately

---

[69] *Supplementary Pensions*, loc. cit.

[70] Ellison (*Pensions: Europe and Equality*, Longman Pensions Report, London, 1994) at p. 8 cited figures which suggest that the accessions of Austria, Finland and Sweden have changed nothing in this respect.

[71] *Supplementary Pensions* loc. cit. at p. 94.

[72] Government Actuary, *Occupational Pension Schemes 1991 Ninth Survey by the Government Actuary* (hereafter Government Actuary), London, 1994 at p. 4. Note that the numbers of individuals with benefits additional to those provided by the state is greater than this figure might suggest. In fact, if those with a contracted-out personal pension are included in the figures, 68% of workers are contracted out of SERPS (this will be discussed in more detail in Chapter 2). The figure rises to 73% if those who are contracted-in members of SERPS with additional occupational pension entitlement are included. An additional 12% of employees are entitled to a SERPS pension (with no additional entitlement). Only 15% of employees in 1991 did not have some form of second tier provision. *Pensions: 2000 and Beyond*, loc. cit. at p. 7.

[73] *Supplementary Pensions* loc. cit. at p. 94.

[74] Ibid at p. 60.

82%,[75] resulting in the accumulation of pension fund assets of some 187,953 million ECU. By contrast, the Member State with the fourth largest accumulation of pensions capital was Belgium where the assets amounted to a mere 44,873 million ECU.[76]

It has been stated that many states are searching for a replacement for their statutory pension schemes, or at least to shift the focus away from it. This is certainly true of the UK and the Netherlands, where government policy would seem clearly to be to stimulate occupational provision to allow the role played by the state to diminish in future. By contrast, in Germany developments demonstrate a political fidelity to the State as primary provider, despite reducing the generosity of the scheme in recent years.[77] The legislatures in these jurisdictions have selected different tools to encourage occupational provision, and a description of these methods should prove interesting to policy-makers seeking to engineer a similar growth in occupational provision. The fact that the backgrounds formed by the statutory schemes in these 3 States differ,[78] as do the roles played by

---

[75]   Figures cited by D. Harrison, *Pension Provision in the EC. Opportunities for the private sector in the Single Market*, London, 1992 at p. 11. Kraamwinkel, loc. cit. at p. 23. It is to be expected that the reason why coverage is so high in the Netherlands is because of the practice of making occupational schemes compulsory for entire branches of industry. This will be discussed in Chapter 2 below.

[76]   *Supplementary Pensions* loc. cit. at p. 94.

[77]   See the discussion in Achenbach and Haneberg, op. cit.; W. Niemeyer, "Die gesetzliche Rentenversicherung drei Jahre nach der Wiedervereinigung und Perspektiven für ihre Weiterentwicklung", in *Bewährungsprobe der Alterssicherungssysteme in Zeiten wirtschaftlicher Rezession*, Wiesbaden, 1993 at pp. 11-22; H. Rische, "Finanzierungsperspektiven der gesetzlichen Rentenversicherung im geeinten Deutschland", in W. Förster and N. Rössler (eds.), *Betriebliche Altersversorgung in der Diskussion zwischen Praxis und Wissenschaft. Festschrift für Peter Ahrend*, Köln, 1992, at pp. 58-68; W. Schmähl, "Unbau der sozialen Sicherung im Alter? - Zur Diskussion über die weitere Entwicklung der Alterssicherung in Deutschland", Staatswissenschaften und Staatspraxis (1995), 331-365; F. Schösser, "Muß die gesetzliche Rentenversicherung umgebaut werden?", 4 Neue Zeitschrift für Sozialrecht (1995), 193-197). For recent political confirmation of this, see N. Blüm, "Vertrauen in die Rentenversicherung", *Bundesarbeitsblatt* 3/1996 at 5-10.

[78]   The UK post-war pension scheme chose unambiguously to pay flat-rate benefits to all residents on retirement, a choice which was also made in the Netherlands. The German legislator took a different approach. The statutory scheme put in place in Germany was, from its very inception, earnings-related and over the years, it has gradually been extended to

occupational schemes - in the UK and the Netherlands occupational schemes build for a large number of employees upon flat rate statutory schemes;[79] in Germany they supplement for a relatively limited group of (more) highly paid employees the (more) generous earnings-related benefits provided by the State - means that the three states offer contrasting pictures of occupational provision.

By selecting Member States in which occupational pension schemes play an important role, it should be possible to isolate the main features of occupational pension provision which are likely to be problematic from the perspective of the two groups of employees with which this research is concerned. Additionally, it may be that the national legislatures have already begun to address any problems, offering some possible and contrasting solutions to problems which may arise.

Finally, the legal regimes within which occupational pension provision is made in both the UK and the Netherlands bear a number of striking similarities. Accordingly, the inclusion of Germany, a Member State in which a significant amount of capital is tied up in occupational pension schemes, but in which a different approach to the regulation of occupational pensions adds to the range of comparisons which can be made in the context of this research. Additionally, in terms of one strand of the research - equal treatment of women and men in occupational pension schemes - most of the references to the ECJ in this area originate from these three Member States, suggesting a keenly developed awareness of at least some of the problems which occupational pension schemes can raise in this respect. Consequently, it is hoped that the selection of Member States is such as to reveal the major features of occupational pension provision in the Union, and therefore also the majority of the problems which occupational pension schemes may cause for the two groups of workers with which this research is concerned.

---

cover previously excluded groups of the economically active population. More detailed treatment of the statutory schemes operating in these three states will be given in Chapters 2 and 3 below.

[79] Although in the UK, some individuals may be members of the State Earnings Related Pension Scheme (SERPS) on which see the discussion in Chapter 2.

1.4   The Structure

First the regulatory regimes within which occupational pension provision is made in the UK, the Netherlands and Germany will be described. This is necessary if a clear grasp is to be obtained of the dynamics of occupational provision. Additionally, it will demonstrate clearly the differences between the approaches taken by the various legislators. By providing detailed descriptions of the regulatory frameworks and the interaction between the occupational and statutory schemes in place in the jurisdictions in question, a full picture of occupational pension provision in the jurisdiction in question can be obtained. Second, it allows the features of occupational provision which form barriers to labour mobility, for example, to be discussed elsewhere in the book unencumbered by explanations of peculiarities of the national regulatory regime. This ought to make the resulting report considerably easier to read and understand. Finally, by providing detailed descriptions - complete with the full academic apparatus of footnotes and references - information is being made available in a comparative form which hitherto has only been available to those with working knowledges of German and Dutch. As such, it is hoped that this research will contribute to a broadening of the debate on future forms of retirement provision by providing detailed information on how provision is organised in other jurisdictions. It also provides an evaluation of the merits of pre-funded schemes but against a different set of criteria to those normally utilised.

The main body of this research is contained in Parts II and III of this book. In Part II, pensions are examined from the perspective of equality between women and men. In Chapter 3 a brief discussion is provided of the law in relation to statutory schemes, and the alterations to which it has led. In Chapter 4 a detailed description of given of the requirements of sex equality law in the field of occupational pensions and of the alterations to which it has led. At the end of the Chapter, some conclusions will be drawn as to the adequacy of the activity which has been undertaken to date, and an answer will be given to the first main question posed in this research: have occupational pension schemes already adequately adjusted to the equality principle, or will further action be necessary.

In Part III the focus of the discussion shifts to pensions and mobility. In Chapter 5, a brief introduction will be given to the requirements of EC law in relation to employee mobility and the regime which has been put in place to ensure that migrant workers do not suffer in terms of their statutory pension accrual because of their decision to migrate. The kinds of alterations to which this has led will also briefly be discussed. In Chapter 6 the rules of occupational pension schemes will come under the spotlight to see how (if at all) they could form obstacles to employee mobility. This will allow some conclusions to be drawn as to whether the rules of occupational pension schemes will require amendment to prevent them penalising migrant workers.

In Chapter 7, in Part IV, some conclusions will be drawn as to the extent to which it is true to say that pre-funded occupational pension schemes have already adapted to the challenges posed by the increased economic activity levels of women and the internationalisation of the market. Finally, some conclusions will be drawn as to whether shifting the emphasis of pension provision from the state to the individual/employer is likely to be a positive or negative development for the two groups of workers with which this research has been concerned.

PENSION PROVISION IN THE UK, THE NETHERLANDS
AND GERMANY

In the previous Chapter the demographic predictions and economic factors were discussed which have set in train a fundamental debate about the future form of pension provision in the Member States of the European Union. It was suggested that it was likely that the states seeking to reduce their future liability to make payments under the statutory scheme, might seek to shift the emphasis of provision to pre-funded occupational pension schemes. The three Member States with the most developed systems of occupational pension provision were selected for analysis in this research, because it seemed likely that states contemplating such reform would turn to these regimes for inspiration. The regulatory regimes which have been established to regulate occupational pension schemes in those jurisdictions will be described in this Chapter. These descriptions will form a vital framework for understanding the more detailed discussion of the problems which a shift from Pay-As-You-Go statutory schemes to pre-funded occupational schemes may cause workers defined by the scheme operated by their employer as "atypical" - migrant workers and women. In the descriptions of the individual regulatory regimes, it will become clear that occupational provision in these States is made in widely differing ways and in each description, emphasis will be placed not so much on the features which all jurisdictions share, but those which distinguish them from the others being considered.

Accordingly, in the Chapter which follows, the regulatory frameworks which have been established in these Member States to regulate occupational pension provision will be outlined. Prior to the description of the occupational framework, a brief outline will be given of the statutory scheme which underlies it. For as Philip Davies observes, "private-funded schemes cannot usefully be viewed in isolation ...(from) the state social-security scheme."[1]

---

[1]   Loc. cit. at p. 57.

2.1   The UK

2.1.1   STATUTORY PROVISION

The UK statutory pension scheme comprises a flat-rate component and and earnings-related supplement.[2] The flat-rate benefit was introduced in 1946[3] and at the time it was hoped that it would be sufficient to provide income adequate for subsistence to its recipients.[4] Although benefit levels were indexed to prices and often wages, the level provided was never adequate to enable pensioners to rely solely on state provision.[5] The formal link between benefit levels and average wages was finally severed as a consequence of the Social Security Act 1980 and by 1992 the level of benefit paid had dropped to approximately 18% of national average earnings.[6]

Currently, four different kinds of old age pension are paid, although only one - the Category A pension which is of significance to the greatest number of employees - will be considered here.[7] To qualify for a Category A pension, an

---

[2]   A detailed description of the UK statutory scheme is to be found in Ogus, Barendt and Wikeley, *The Law of Social Security*, 4th edition, London, 1995 at pp. 213-266.

[3]   Pursuant to the National Insurance Act 1946.

[4]   Ogus et al loc. cit. at p. 214; Westerveld, loc. cit. at pp. 70-71.

[5]   Ogus et al, loc. cit. at p. 214.

[6]   *Supplementary Pensions*, loc. cit. at 17. Note that on the basis that this policy continued and that earnings rise 1.5% p.a. faster than prices, the replacement rate of the statutory scheme would have fallen to 9% by 2030. See *Pensions: 2000 and Beyond*, loc. cit. at p. 4. It is reported that Michael Portillo MP has admitted that the value of the UK basic pension will have become nugatory by the beginning of the next century ("Tory Pension Policies Forecast to Fail", *UPS Intelligence*, vol 5 No. 1, 13 July 1996 at 2).

[7]   The Category B pension is payable to a dependent spouse on the basis of the contributions of the providing spouse. It will be discussed briefly in passing in Chapter 3. Category, C and D pensions will not be discussed. Both types of penson are non-contributory and were introduced to cover those who had been uninsured prior to 1948. For the details of Category, C and D pensions, see Ogus et al, loc. cit. at pp. 239-240.

individual must have paid contributions on the basis of earnings between the Lower Earnings Limit (LEL) and the Upper Earnings Limit (UEL) for 90% of his working life - 44 years for men, 39 years for women.[8] For each year during which insufficient credits have been paid, the pension will be reduced. If entitlement falls below 25%, no basic pension is payable.[9]

The low level of benefit provided by the state created considerable scope for a market to develop providing benefits to supplement those provided by the state. In fact, the first way of doing this is within the state scheme itself in the form of an earnings-related supplement to the flat rate basic pension. The first state initiative in the field of earnings-related pensions was the Graduated Pension Scheme (GPS) introduced in 1959.[10] However, it was widely perceived as inadequate and has been described as "a political gimmick, not a pension scheme."[11] It required those earning between the lower and upper earnings limits to pay contributions into the scheme which in turn was to provide benefits on retirement.[12] However, benefit levels were low and not protected against the effects of inflation. Additionally, employees were premitted to contract-out of the GPS where they belonged to a scheme offering them benefits roughly equivalent to those available under GPS, a facility which can be seen to demonstrate the absence of political conviction about the appropriateness of this scheme. As will emerge below, contracting-out has remained a feature characteristic of occupational pension provision in the UK.

In terms of the three Member States under examination, the introduction of the facility to contract-out of the state scheme is unique to the UK.

---

[8]   See on this difference in contributions Case C-9/91, *R.* v. *Secretary of State for Social Security, ex parte the EOC*, [1992] ECR I-4297.

[9]   Detailed treatment is given in Ogus et al, loc. cit. at pp. 222-233.

[10]   See the discussion in Westerveld, loc. cit. at pp. 76-80; Hannah, loc. cit. at pp.

[11]   T.E.J. Holland, of Norwich Union Insurance, quoted in *East Anglian Daily Times*, 1 March 1960, 5c, cited in Hannah, loc. cit. at p. 58.

[12]   It appears that the motives for its introduction included the perceived need to inject funds into the National Insurance Fund to pay the flat-rate benefits. See Ogus et al, loc. cit. at p. 218; Hannah, loc. cit. at p. 57 ; Westerveld, loc. cit. at pp. 78-9.

Nevertheless, its introduction can be seen to have been an entirely rational response to a specific situation. Although the first statutory pension scheme was introduced in the UK in 1908,[13] the first occupational pension scheme was reported to have existed as early as 1686[14] and as early as 1936, a survey covering the 6,544 private sector schemes known to exist revealed that 1.6 million employees were members of private sector schemes, which when added to the 1 million public sector employees belonging to schemes revealed that 13% of the working population was covered by an occupational scheme.[15] By 1956, prior to the introduction of the GPS, this figure had increased to 33%, with a total of 8 million employees (4.3 million private sector, 3.7 million public sector) being covered.[16] This in turn allowed the industry (pension funds and, more particularly, insurers) to lobby to retain their market when the government was contemplating introducing an earnings-related pension scheme.[17] Although the actual state of the market can be seen to have influenced the measures adopted by the politicians, it is worth noting that from the very first, the political ideology informing scheme design in the UK was that the state was to play a residual role and not stifle individual initiative.[18]

---

[13]   The Old Age Pensions Act.

[14]   This contributory scheme made a pension available to employees of Customs and Excise is the qualifying conditions were satisfied. For a detailed treatment of this subject, see Hannah, loc. cit.; briefer treatment is given to the subject in *Pension Law Reform. The Report of the Pension Law Review Committee, Chairman Professor Roy Goode* (hereafter the Goode Report), Cm 2342-1, London, 1993 at pp. 54-72; R. Nobles, *Pensions, Employment, and the Law*, Oxford, 1993 at pp. 1-8; for pension coverage since the war, see the surveys by the Government Actuary, most recently, Government Actuary, *Occupational Pension Schemes 1991 Ninth Survey by the Government Actuary*, London, 1994 at pp. 3-5.

[15]   Hannah, loc. cit. at p. 40.

[16]   Ibid.

[17]   A point made by Hannah, loc. cit. at p. 56; Westerveld, loc. cit. at p. 78.

[18]   This is demonstrated by the fact that the original legislation drew a distinction between the deserving and the undeserving poor in deciding who should qualify for state benefit. The terms of the 1908 Act provided that those who prior to reaching the relevant age had been dependent on poor relief, who had recently been released from prison or who had failed to maintain themselves did not qualify for the new benefit. See Westerveld, loc. cit. at pp. 57-

2.1.2   SERPS

The GPS was finally replaced by a more robust form of state earnings-related
pension scheme (SERPS) in 1975.[19] The flat rate pension was deemed to replace
earnings in full up to the level of 18% of national average earnings. On top of this,
SERPS would provide an earnings-related component of the pension replacing up
to 25% of individual earnings above that rate earned in the best 20 years of an
individual's career, subject to a ceiling.[20] An employer who wished could choose
to contract-out of SERPS where the occupational scheme provided by his
undertaking granted benefits at least as good as those to which the individual
would have become entitled under SERPS.[21]

    In recent years, however, the benefits to which SERPS grants entitlement
have been reduced. In the mid-1980s the Conservative government - prompted in
part by fears about its future costs - toyed with the idea of abolishing SERPS in
its entirety,[22] it eventually satisfied itself with reducing the value of the benefits
provided by replacing the best 20 years rule with a calculation based on the
individual's entire employment history.[23] The Pensions Act 1995 introduced
additional reforms which reduce further the value of SERPS to those accruing
rights under the scheme. SERPS were previously calculated by revaluing total
qualifying earnings for each year in line with the increase in average earnings, and
then the annual LEL was deducted from each year's revalued earnings. Under the

---

60.

[19]   Introduced by the Social Security Pensions Act 1975.

[20]   In practice this is for those earning 135% of national average earnings.

[21]   Because the provisions regulating contracting-out have exercised a strong influence on the
        shape taken by occupational pension schemes in the UK, the requirements of the contracting-
        out legislation will be considered below.

[22]   See the Green Paper on social security reform, Cmnd. (1985) 9517-9520, dicsussed at length
        by Westerveld, loc. cit. at pp. 374-387; Ogus et al, loc. cit. at p. 220.

[23]   For a discussion, see Westerveld, loc. cit. at pp. 386-388; B. Davies and S. Ward, *Women
        and Personal Pensions*, London, 1992 at pp. 17-19.

new regime, the annual LEL is deducted before revaluation, reeducing the value of SERPS by, it has been calculated, about 14% by the year 2020.[24]

2.1.3   CONTRACTING-OUT

It has already been stated that the facility to contract-out is an important feature of pension regulation in the UK. This observation is confirmed by statistics which show that of the 10.7 million individuals who belonged to occupational pension schemes in 1991, 9.7 million were in contracted-out schemes, with only 1 million in contracted-in schemes.[25]

Pension law in the UK has undergone a legislative revolution over the last few years. The undoubted catalyst for this was the misappropriation of some £400 million of pension fund assets belonging to the schemes assiciated with Mirror Group Newspapers by the late Robert Maxwell.[26] A Pension Law Review Committee[27] was established by the Secretary of State for Social Security on 8 June 1992

> "To review the framework of law and regulation within which occupational pension schemes operate, taking into account the rights and interests of scheme members, pensioners and employers; to consider in particular the status and ownership of occupational pension funds and the accountability and roles of trustees, fund managers, auditors and pension scheme advisers; and to make recommendations."

The Goode report observed that

---

[24]   M. Thomas and B. Dowrick, *Blackstone's Guide to the Pensions Act 1995*, London, 1995 at p. 147.

[25]   Government Actuary, loc. cit. at p. 7. It seems that once (unintended?) consequence of the reforms introduced by the Pensions Act 1995 may be that an increasing number of schemes will be contracted-in, offering benefits which supplement SERPS. This is already the course followed by, *inter alia*, GEC, Siemens and W.H. Smith. For a discussion of this see B. Davies, *The New Contracting-Out Requirements*, London, 1996.

[26]   See Social Security Select Committee, *2nd report, The Operation of Pension Funds*, House of Commons Papers Session 1991-1992, 61.

[27]   Under the chair of Professor Goode, it led to the 696 page Goode report which was published in September 1993 (Cm 2342-1, London).

"Pensions law is an amalgam of equity and trust law, contract
and labour law, heavily overlaid with complex legislation
governing the occupational pensions aspects of social security,
taxation and financial services. One can search in vain for a code
in which the essential rights and obligations flowing from the
establishment of pension schemes are clearly laid out. Much of
the law is to be found only in reports of court decisions about
the interpretation of scheme documents and the duties of trustees
and employers at common law. Legislation is at present spread
over more than thirty statutes and well over a hundred statutory
instruments."[28]

Partly as a result of its work, the situation is now marginally clearer. The majority
of the statutory provisions on contracting-out are now to be found in the Pension
Schemes Act 1993[29] (PSA), with amendments to this being introduced by the
Pensions Act 1995 (PA). The bones of this legislation are fleshed out by means of
a number of statutory instruments, to which reference will be made as necessary.

As has already been described, occupational pension schemes which
satisfy a number of legislative requirements are permitted to contract-out of
SERPS. The decision to contract-out and the decision to which classes of employee
the contracting-out decision will apply,[30] lie entirely in the hands of the
employer.[31] On a practical level, the consequence of a decision to contract-out is
that the National Insurance contributions which would have fallen due on earnings
between the lower earnings limit and the upper earnings limit are reimbursed and

---

[28]   The Goode Report, loc. cit. at p. 186.

[29]   SI 1994 No. 86 The Pension Schemes Act 1993 (Commencement No 1) Order 1994 laid
       down that the Act was to come into force on 7 February 1994 with the exception of
       prospective repeals of the equal access requirements and the re-enactment or amendment of
       provisions not yet in force. For a brief introduction into the Pension Schemes Act 1993, see
       A. Kam, "The Pension Schemes Act 1993", 55 BPL (1994), 12-13.

[30]   The only legitimate ground on which distinction may de drawn between employees is the
       nature of their employment. PSA 1993 s. 11(3).

[31]   PSA 1993, s. 11(1) and (2). See also SI 1984 No. 380, regs. 2-7; for post-5 April 1997
       service, these regulations are superceded by The Occupational Pension Schemes
       (Contracting-Out) Regulations 1996, SI 1996 No. 1172 (the 1996 Regulations). Note that s.
       160(1)(a) PSA 1993 renders void any provision which purports to make membership of a
       pension scheme compulsory. See also reg. 2(2)(a) of the 1996 Regulations.

no SERPS entitlement is accrued in relation to this period of employment.[32] It is possible to contract out of SERPS in a number of ways, which will be outlined briefly below, before moving on to consider the main determinant of the shape of pension schemes, the tax treatment of schemes. First, the position of contracted out salary related schemes (COSR) will be considered, and thereafter the position in relation to contracted out money purchase schemes (COMP) will be described.[33] The PA 1995 has introduced new rules for service falling after 5 April 1997 and so both the current and the future regimes will be described in turn.

COSR - Pre-April 1997

If he wishes to contract-out, an employer is required to apply to the Occupational Pensions Board for a contracting-out certificate[34] which provides conclusive evidence of the contracted-out status of the scheme[35] and which states whether the employer has contracted-out on a salary related or money purchase basis.[36] Having decided that he wishes to contract-out, the employer is obliged to issue

---

[32] PSA 1993 s. 41.

[33] S. 149 PA 1995 also creates the possibility for hybrid schemes to contract-out of SERPS after April 1997. These are schemes which provide both money purchase and salary related benefits. See the Occupational Pension Schemes (Mixed Benefit Contracted-Out Schemes) Regulations 1996, SI 1996 No. 1977. The basic effect of these Regulations is for such schemes to be treated, for the purposes of Part III of the PSA 1993, as if the separate parts of the scheme were separate schemes. In other words, they are to be treated as separate salary related and money purchase schemes. The position of these hybrid schemes will not be considered further here. Since in effect they are treated as two separate schemes, the descriptions of COSR and COMP which are provided would seem to suffice. Including a separate section on COMB (contracted-out mixed benefit) schemes would not seem to be necessary, but it is important that the existence of this possibility be noted.

[34] PSA 1993 s. 7(1)(a). For a personal pension scheme, this is referred to an appropriate scheme certificate, s. 7(1)(b).

[35] PSA 1993 s. 7(3).

[36] PSA 1993 s. 12(1); reg. 8 of the 1984 Regulations.

notice of his intention to the employees concerned and to trades unions where relevant.[37]

In relation to **salary-related** schemes,[38] all the provisions on contracting-out are designed to ensure that the individual does not suffer as a result of his decision to contract-out. To this end, the contracting-out scheme had to offer benefits at least equivalent to the Guaranteed Minimum Pension (GMP) under SERPS.[39] Additionally, the scheme must also provide a GMP for widows.[40] The scheme must also provide for the payment of a pension to an earner on reaching pensionable age[41] and, furthermore, that the pension must remain payable for the life of the earner.[42] To qualify for a contracting-out certificate, it is also necessary

---

[37]   Reg.s 3-7 of the 1984 Regulations govern this currently.

[38]   Until 1986 it was only possible to contract-out on the basis of a salary-related scheme.

[39]   PSA 1993 s. 9(2). The GMP is defined in s. 8(2) of the Act. An individual becomes entitled to a GMP if in any tax week during which he is contracted-out his weekly earnings exceed the current lower earnings limit. These translate into "earnings factors" of which "the appropriate percentage" (see s. 14(5) PSA 1993) will be paid as a weekly pension.

[40]   PSA 1993 s. 17. Note that the widower enjoys less favourable treatment than a widow. His right to a widower's GMP only relates to rights acquired from tax year 1988-1989. See Occupational Pension Scheme (Contracting-Out) Regulations 1984, SI No. 380 regs. 33B and 33C.

[41]   PSA 1993 s. 13(1)(a). Nevertheless, the payment of the pension may be deferred beyond pensionable age where the earner continues in employment. See s. 13(4) PSA 1993 and s. 15 which provides for the revaluation of the guaranteed minimum when the payment of the GMP is postponed. According to s. 13(5), the consent of the earner is required for any postponement based on employment to which that pension does not relate and for any postponement beyond 5 years beyond pensionable age.

[42]   PSA 1993 s. 13(3). A woman who has elected to pay lower levels of Class 1 contributions (by virtue of s. 19(4) of the SSCBA 1992) must be entitled to a pension at pensionable age even if she does not have a GMP under sections 14 and 16. This provision finds its basis in the old provisions according to which married women could elect to pay reduced rates of national insurance contributions and acquire derived rights through the contributions paid by their husbands. This facility is now only available to women who were and still are married or entitled to a state widow's pension and were paying reduced rate contributions in April 1978, or who had been doing so prior to 6 April 1977 and whose employment has not been interrupted for more than two years since 5 April 1978. Otherwise these women have to pay the standard National Insurance contributions.

that provision be made for the revaluation of the earnings factors of early leavers[43] which means that where an individual leaves the scheme prior to reaching pensionable age, the value of his accrued rights should be maintained. A final but important requirement if a contracting-out certificate is to be granted is that the employer is obliged to contribute to the scheme.[44]

All these provisions are intended to ensure that the employee does not lose any rights because of his employer's decision to contract-out of the SERPS scheme.[45] To try to ensure this end, section 23 requires that the OPB must be satisfied that the scheme complies with the requirements relating to the means of securing the GMP rights. These are set out in the Occupational Pension Schemes (Contracting-Out) Regulations.[46] The rights must be secured by irrevocable trust, policy of insurance or annuity contract which is a trust, policy or contract established, taken out or entered into by someone resident or with a place of business in the UK. Additionally, where the irrevocable trust is chosen, it must be one subject to the law of the UK. The insurance policy or annuity must be taken out with an insurer authorised under article 6 or article 27 of Directive 79/267.[47] Although these provisions do not apply to schemes administered outwith the UK, such schemes require the approval of the Board before they may contract-out, and it will require that similar safeguards are given in respect of GMP rights. The

---

[43]   Earnings factors are the "points" which he builds up on the basis of his remuneration between the lower and upper earnings limits. See PSA 1993 s. 16 and part IV of the Act.

[44]   S. 22 of the 1993 Act. Unless the scheme is enjoying a contributions holiday because it is in surplus (see s. 37 of the PA 1995). Note that s. 22 has been repealed by the PA 1995.

[45]   Technically, the decision could be said to be that of the employee since his employer can no longer compel his entire workforce to become members of his occupational pension scheme. However, in practice, since the employer is exclusively competent to decide to contract out, and, subject to the coutracting-out conditions outlined here, exclusively competent to determine the terms upon which contracting-out will take place, the decision must be deemed to be that of the employer. If this argumentation is rejected, the conditions for contracting-out suddenly represent a most uncharacteristic paternalistic attitude by the government for the individual in his relationship with his employer.

[46]   SI 1984 No. 380 reg. 30.

[47]   Directive on the coordination of laws, regulations and administrative provisions relating to the taking up and pursuit of the business of life insurance, O.J. 1979 L 63/1.

remaining requirements contained in section 23 relate to priority of GMP rights on the winding up of a scheme which, although undoubtedly of great practical importance, will not be considered further in this study.

The OPB must be satisfied that the scheme can meet its GMP liabilities and its other liabilities. This is done by requiring the Scheme Actuary to issue a solvency certificate and, for insured schemes, for the principle underwriter to submit annual returns.[48] It is also possible for the OPB to lay down requirements as to the proportion of the schemes investments which are invested in a particular class of investments. This has largely been used to limit self investment.[49]

COSR - Post-April 1997

Under the new rules, the decision to apply for a contracting-out certificate remains that of the employer and the same basic consultation requirements must be met.[50] However, the OPB is abolished[51] and once the regime takes effect, applications for contracting-out certificates will have to be made to the Secretary of State.[52] In fact, this function will be exercised on his behalf by the Contributions Agency.

The basis for the old contracting-out regime in relation to COSR was that the level of benefits provided by the scheme would not fall below a certain guaranteed minimum defined in the legislation. For service completed after 5 April 1997, this has been abolished[53] and replaced with an obligation to provide

---

[48]   The trustees of self-administered schemes must submit annual returns to satisfy this requirement. However, the subject of self-administered schemes falls outwith the scope of this research.

[49]   On the investment practice of pension funds, see Philip Davis, loc. cit. at pp. 203-229.

[50]   See regs. 2-7 of the 1996 Regulations.

[51]   S. 150 PA 1995.

[52]   Most of the OPB's functions are transferred to the newly-created Occupational Pensions Regulatory Authority (OPRA), established by ss. 1-15 and 96-108 and sch. 1 of the 1995 Act.

[53]   Note that transitional provisions cover the treatment of accrued GMP rights; see regs. 55-69 of the 1996 Regulations.

benefits which are broadly equivalent to or better than those of a defined reference scheme.[54] It is necessary that an actuary certify that the scheme is broadly equivalent to the reference scheme[55] which is determined in accordance with the guidance note issued jointly by the Institute and Faculty of Actuaries.[56] An actuary is precluded from issuing such a certificate if the pensions to be provided to more than 10% of earners and their widow(er)s collectively are not broadly equivalent to those to which they would be entitled under a reference scheme.[57]

The basic standard which must be satisfied is that the pension must be payable between the age of 65 and the member's death. It must have an accrual rate of 1/80th of average qualifying earnings in the last three tax years prior to the end of service for each year of service, up to a maximum of 40. Qualifying earnings are at least 90% of earnings upon which Band 1 National Insurance contributions are paid. Finally, spouse's pensions of 50% of the member's actual[58] or accrued[59] pension must be payable under the scheme.[60] Where a scheme offers different benefits to different categories of employees, the actuary must be satisfied that each part of the scheme complies with the statutory standard.[61]

---

[54]   S. 9(2B) PSA 1993, inserted by s. 136(3) PA 1995; ss. 12A and 12B PSA 1993, inserted by s. 136(5) PA 1995. See also reg.s 18-22 of the 1996 Regulations.

[55]   S. 12A(6) PSA 1993.

[56]   GN28, "Retirement Benefit Schemes - Adequacy of Benefits for Contracting-Out on or After 6 April 1997".

[57]   Reg. 23(b) of the 1996 Regulations.

[58]   If the death occurs after the member's pensionable age.

[59]   If the death occurs prior to the member's reaching pensionable age.

[60]   See s. 12B PSA 1993.

[61]   Reg. 22 of the 1996 Regulations.

Another very important change introduced by the PA 1995 is the Mimimum Funding Requirement (MFR).[62] It is intended to provide members with the security that irrespective of the fate of their employer, pensioner members can expect that their pensions will continue to be paid and that members not yet in retirement (active or sleeping[63]) can be assured of a fair representation of their accrued rights.

Section 56 requires that the assets of schemes be not less than the scheme's liabilities, but the detail on this is to be provided by means of regulations.[64] The White Paper suggested valuing assets and liabilities on a cash-equivalent basis, which for active and sleeping members means the cash-equivalent transfer value. In relation to pensioners, it means the cost of providing pensions in payment. One major difficulty is that since the assets are to be valued by reference to market values, this can fluctuate dramatically. Consequently, the White Paper allows for averaging over a reference period.[65]

As a consequence of section 57, trustees or managers are obliged to obtain periodic actuarial valuations of the scheme, and actuarial certification that the contributions being paid are adequate to ensure that the minimum funding requirements can be met. If he finds this to be inadequate, managers or trustees are obliged to obtain an actuarial valuation.

Additionally, it is now necessary that a schedule of contributions be prepared which the actuary must certify if he considers it adequate for the purposes of the MFR. This provides a method of monitoring the health of the scheme. Finally, section 60 provides for a means of restoring funding where it has dropped below 90% of the liabilities.

---

[62]   See ss. 56-61 PA 1995. See the discussions in the Goode Report, loc. cit. at pp. 232-251; Thomas and Dowrick, loc. cit. at pp. 84-92 describe the law as it has been adopted.

[63]   A sleeping member is someone who no longer contributes to a scheme (or on whose behalf no more contributions are being paid) but whose pension has not yet commenced. It typically occurs where someone changes employment and the protection given to early leavers will be discussed in Chapter 6 below.

[64]   See s. 56(3).

[65]   Thomas and Dowrick (loc. cit. at p. 88) suggest that this test is likely to produce undesirable changes in investment strategy.

One of the aims pursued by the 1995 reforms was to provide individual members with a greater degree of security that the pension promised would in fact be paid. The effectiveness of these reforms in realising this aim remains to be seen.

COMP

The provisions relating to contracting-out by **money purchase** scheme were introduced by the Social Security Act 1986, taking effect as of 1988 and are currently to be found at ss. 26-32 of the 1993 Act.[66] Where the basic objective of the COSR legislation is to ensure that the individual receive a pension of at least a particular specified value, the COMP provisions aim to safeguard an individual's "protected rights".[67] Subject to the rules of the scheme, the protected rights of a member are those deriving from minimum payments[68] together with any payments made by the Secretary of State under section 7 of the Social Security Act 1986.[69] These sums must be used to purchase money purchase benefits.[70]

---

[66] Note that parallel provisions allow contracting-out on a personal basis by taking out a personal pension. See PSA 1993 ss. 43-45 for the provisions on minimum contributions. Because personal pensions do not (necessarily) involve an employer (the 1991 survey by the Government Actuary reveals that it is not usual for an employer to contribute to a personal pension, op. cit. at p. 4), they fall outwith the scope of this study.

[67] S. 9(3) of the 1993 Act.

[68] "Minimum payments" are defined in section 8(2) of the 1993 Act as the rebate percentage (employee contributions rebate plus employer contributions rebate = 1.8% or earnings + 3% or earnings = 4.8% of earnings - section 41) of earnings factors between the lower and upper earnings thresholds. S. 137 of the PA 1995 inserts ss. 42A and B into the PSA which introduces age-related rebates for COMP, reflecting the greater expense in providing money purchase benefits for older individuals.

[69] This was an incentive payment made to schemes contracting-out for the first time between 1 January 1986 and 5 April 1993 and represented 2% of banded earnings for National Insurance purposes for each employee belonging to a COMP. After April 1993 the incentive payment fell to 1% of earnings for those aged 30 or more.

[70] Section 31(3)(a). Sums can be deducted for administrative expenses and or commission (s. 31(3)(i) and (ii)) but the amount of these can be limited by the OPB - s. 31(2)(i), (ii) and (iii).

Protected rights also include any rights to money purchase benefits which have been transferred from another occupational or personal pension scheme.[71]

The contracting-out requirements also lay down a number of requirements as to the treatment to be accorded to these protected rights. They must be identifiable and they must be treated no less favourably under the scheme rules than any other rights which the member enjoys under the scheme.[72] The rules of the scheme must provide for effect to be given to the protected rights of a member by the purchase of an annuity, the provision of a pension, the transfer of the protected rights or by the payment of a lump sum.[73] In this way, it is hoped that the individual will receive benefits roughly equivalent to those to which he would have been entitled under SERPS, although there is of course no guarantee that this will in fact happen.

Payment of a pension (or annuity) under a COMP scheme must commence when the beneficiary is between the ages of 60 and 65 unless the parties have agreed to later payment, and payment must continue until the member's death.[74] Where the member dies, his pension must be payable to the widow or widower (in prescribed circumstances for the prescribed period) at an annual rate which is at least[75] one half of that which would have ben payable to

---

[71]   Transfers will be considered in Chapter 6 below.

[72]   S. 27 of the 1993 Act. See now the Personal and Occupational Pension Schemes (Protected Rights) Regulations 1987 (SI 1987/1117) which will be replaced as of 6 April 1997 by the Personal and Occupational Pension Schemes (Protected Rights) Regulations 1996 (SI 1996/1537).

[73]   S. 28 of the 1993 Act. See the Personal and Occupational Pension Schemes (Protected Rights) Regulations 1987 (SI 1987/1117) which will be replaced as of 6 April 1997 by the Personal and Occupational Pension Schemes (Protected Rights) Regulations (SI 1996/1537). Note that s. 142 of the 1995 Act introduces interim arrangements for giving effect to protected rights.

[74]   S. 29 of the 1993 Act.

[75]   For the first five years - see s. 29(2).

the member had he been living at the time. In certain circumstances, this latter requirement may be satisfied by lump sum payments.[76]

The benefits must be paid by an insurance company which satisfies a number of prescribed conditions[77] and which has been chosen by the member.[78] The OPB (OPRA post-5 April 1997) can lay down a number of requirements in relation to investments, payments, investment gains, scheme expenses and commissions and the application of minimum contributions and minimum payments to the provision of money purchase benefits.[79]

2.1.4   TAX RULES

In the previous sections, the provisions have been described which schemes must satisfy if they are to be permitted to contract-out of SERPS. It is certainly the case that these provisions have played a considerable role in determining the shape of occupational provision in the UK. However, the contracting-out regulations are only part of the picture of the UK legislative framework for pensions. The major determinants of the shape of pension schemes are in fact the requirements of the Inland Revenue, and these will be touched upon briefly below.

The requirements laid down by the Inland Revenue for qualifying for the not inconsiderable tax advantages have played a formative role in the design of occupational pension schemes in the UK. These tax advantages have been designed to balance two objectives. On the one hand it is hoped that the tax advantages will

---

[76]   S. 29(2)(b)(ii) PSA 1993. See the the Personal and Occupational Pension Schemes (Protected Rights) Regulations 1987 (SI 1987/1117) which will be replaced as of 6 April 1997 by the Personal and Occupational Pension Schemes (Protected Rights) Regulations (SI 1996/1537).

[77]   See the Personal and Occupational Pension Schemes (Protected Rights) Regulations 1987, SI 1987/1117 which are to be replaced as of 6 April 1997 by the Personal and Occupational Pension Schemes (Protected Rights) Regulations 1996 (SI 1996/1537). Basically, the company must be authorised and must offer annuities in respect of protected rights without regard to the sex or marital status of the members.

[78]   The member is obliged to satisfy a number of requirements as to granting notice to trustees. See s. 29(4) of the 1993 Act and SI 1987/1117.

[79]   S. 31 of the 1993 Act.

stimulate the growth of occupational schemes, but on the other hand, the Inland Revenue wants to prevent unjustifiably large schemes being created merely to take advantage of the tax facilities. Thus, alongside the contracting-out certificate which a scheme must obtain from the OPB (or Secretary of State), the tax legislation requires that the Pension Schemes Office be satisfied that a number of conditions are met before the scheme is "approved" for the purposes of the Inland Revenue. As shall be demonstrated below, approval can be mandatory, discretionary or exempt.

For **mandatory** approval, the scheme must be bona fide established for the sole purpose of providing relevant benefits[80] in respect of service as an employee. The only benefits which may be paid out under an mandatory approved scheme are to the employee, his or her widow(er), or any children, dependants or personal representatives. The retirement benefit must be payable at a specified age between 60 and 75. The rate of accrual of the benefit may not exceed one-sixtieth of the employee's final remuneration[81] for each year of service, up to a maximum of forty. Additionally, the only form of assignation, surrender or commutation which will be countenanced is the payment, where foreseen in the scheme rules, of a lump sum. However, again this is subject to a statutory maximum and may not exceed three-eightieths of final remuneration for each year of service, again the maximum period of service being set at forty.[82] Similarly, the benefit payable to the widow(er) of the employee who has died in retirement may not exceed two-thirds of the benefits to which the employee had been entitled. These requirements,

---

[80] Relevant benefits are defined in s. 612 ICTA as: "any pension, lump sum, gratuity or other like benefit given or to be given on retirement or on death, or in anticipation of retirement, or, in connection with past service, after retirement or death, or to be given on or in anticipation of or in connection with any change in the nature of service of the employee in question, except that it does not include any benefit which is to be afforded solely by reason of the disablement by accident of a person occurring during his service or of his death by accident so occurring and for no other reason".

[81] Defined in s. 612 as "the average annual remuneration of the last three years' service". It should also be borne in mind that an earnings cap applies.

[82] The same figure may not be exceeded where there are two or more "relevant associated employments" or two or more "connected schemes". Relevant associated employments are defined in s. 590A ICTA.

particularly those relating to accrual, and the provisions on lump sums are fairly restrictive and therefore most schemes seek discretionary approval.

The PSO is able to grant **discretionary** approval to schemes which do not satisfy some of the requirements of mandatory approval. In particular, it is possible for a scheme to offer accelerated accrual of benefits where the reference period for service is less than 40 years.[83] However, in this regard it is necessary to bear in mind that the maximum pension accrual of two thirds of final salary is absolute. A scheme with discretionary approval can merely provide that this level is built up over a shorter period. Additionally, discretionary approval may be granted to a scheme which offers death in service benefits to widow(er)s, children and dependants. Where pursuant to this, the scheme chooses to offer a lump sum on death in service, this may not exceed four times the employee's final remuneration. Flexibility is also possible in respect of pensionable age under the discretionary approved scheme. Thus, a pension may be offered anywhere up to ten years prior to the age specified in the pension deed, or even earlier where the member has become an invalid. Similarly, discretionary approval may be granted to schemes which provide for a return of employee contributions in certain circumstances and the requirement that the employer contribute can be relaxed for schemes providing additional benefits to those provided by the scheme to which he does contribute. Finally, approval may be granted to a scheme relating to a trade or undertaking carried out partly in the UK and by a person not resident in the UK.

A scheme which satisfies the conditions for either kind of approval but which is also set up under irrevocable trust[84] qualifies the approved scheme as an **exempt** approved scheme.[85] Exempt approved status qualifies a scheme, the employer and employees for maximum tax advantages. This means that investment or deposit interest held for the purposes of the scheme will be exempt from income

---

[83]   See Schedule 23 to ICTA: Occupational Pension Schemes. Schemes approved before 23 July 1987.

[84]   See *inter alia*, Nobles, loc. cit. at pp. 10-13, 64-86, 97-111.

[85]   S. 592 ICTA.

tax.[86] Additionally, an employer can deduct any contributions he pays in respect of employees in an undertaking chargeable to UK income or corporation tax as an expense of management. These contributions are not taxable as income in the hands of the employee on whose behalf they are paid. Similarly, employee contributions can be deducted from their income liable to income tax under Schedule E to the extent that this sum does not exceed 15% of the remuneration paid in that year.[87]

By contrast, where a scheme does not enjoy exempt approved, but merely approved status, a less attractive tax picture emerges. There the employer's contribution is not taxable income in the hands of the employee by virtue of section 596(1)(a), but no exemption will be enjoyed in respect of income from investments or deposits, the employer's contributions or the employees' contributions. The pensions paid out under all approved schemes are taxable income in the hands of the employee.[88]

In short, the Inland Revenue makes it extremely attractive for an employer to structure his occupational pension scheme in such a manner as to qualify for exempt approved status. Although it is difficult to calculate the total value of these tax advantages, the Inland Revenue calculated that this system cost £7,700 million in 1993 alone.[89] Contrary to what might initially be expected, it is not the contracting-out regulations but the Inland Revenue requirements which shape most strongly the benefits provided by occupational pension schemes in the UK.

---

[86]   See. s. 592(2) ICTA.

[87]   The earnings cap applies here also.

[88]   S. 597 ICTA.

[89]   Figures cited in C. D. Daykin, *Pension Provision in Britain*, London, 1994 at p. 46.

2.2   The Netherlands

2.2.1   STATUTORY PROVISION

Like the statutory scheme in place in the UK, the Dutch statutory pension - the AOW[90] - provides a flat rate benefit.[91] Although it was originally envisaged that the AOW would provide only subsistence level benefits, by 1965 the political climate had changed and the scheme was altered so as to offer unmarried beneficiaries a benefit of 70% of the minimum wage.[92] Although the level of the AOW has traditionally been linked to the minimum wage, the recent government accord stated that benefit levels would not rise with wages during 1995, and only at 50% of such developments for the period 1996-1998.[93] In 1990, an individual earning twice the average wage in manufacturing with a full insurance record would receive an AOW payment amounting to 37% of his final salary on retirement.[94] Given the government's intention to freeze benefit levels, it is to be expected that this replacement rate will reduce.

The AOW is paid to all residents who satisfy the relevant criteria. To qualify for a full AOW, an individual must have been resident in the Netherlands, or working there and subject to its wages tax (*loonbelasting*) between the ages of

---

[90]   This is the abbreviation of the name of the legislation governing the benefit, the *Algemene Ouderdomswet*, Stb. 1956, 281, most recently consolidated in Stb. 1990, 129.

[91]   The approach of the Dutch Van Rhijn Commission which was set up by the government in exile in London during the second world war to study the future shape of the Dutch social security system, was greatly influenced by the Beveridge Report. For a detailed analysis of the developments in the Dutch system, see Westerveld, loc. cit. at pp. 99-125, 254-281 and 405-448.

[92]   Married individuals, and those treated as married (see the law of 11 November 1986, Stb. 563) are each entitled to benefits of 50% of the minimum wage. Where only one spouse is over pensionable age, a means tested supplement of up to 50% of the minimum wage is available. The various developments which preceded this arrangement will be discussed in Chapter 3 below.

[93]   See *Regeerakkord "Keuzen voor de toekomst"*, op. cit. at 6-11.

[94]   *Supplementary Pensions* loc. cit. at p. 12.

15 and 65. For any year in which an individual has not been insured, a pro rata reduction in benefit levels takes place.[95]

It is clear that like the UK scheme, the Dutch statutory scheme leaves considerable scope for occupational provision to develop, and coverage of Dutch employees is indeed high.[96] From the very birth of the statutory scheme, it has been government policy not to hinder the growth of occupational schemes[97] and although it accepts that it bears responsibility for providing residents with a basic level of retirement income, it encourages the social partners to make arrangements to supplement the statutory scheme.[98]

2.2.2   OCCUPATIONAL SCHEMES

Although successive Dutch governments have stressed the importance of occupational provision, an employer is, in principle, free to decide against offering his employees an occupational pension.[99] For many years, it was government

---

[95]   AOW, articles 2, 6(1), 7 and 13.

[96]   It is not easy to obtain an overview of the kind provided by the Government Actuary's surveys in the UK. However, it has been suggested that coverage in the Netherlands has reached 82%; Harrison, loc. cit. at p. 11; Kraamwinkel, loc. cit. at p. 23.

[97]   This was admitted in the parliamentary debates on the adoption of the AOW. See E. Lutjens, *Pensioenvoorzieningen voor werknemers. Juridische beschouwingen over ouderdomspensioenen*, Zwolle, 1989 (hereafter Lutjens 1989) at p. 18.

[98]   Even when increasing the AOW benefits to the social minimum, this perspective was maintained: "eventually, the AOW, together with company or undertakings pension schemes, should provide the employee with full protection, while at the same time providing the non-employee a basis upon which individual provision can be made." "*Op den duur tezamen met de bedrijfs- en ondernemingspensioenen, een volwaardige oudedagsvorziening voor werknemers zou bieden, terwijl voor de niet-werknemers zij een basis zou zijn, waarboven particuliere voorzieningen zouden kunnen worden getroffen.*" TK 1963-1964, 7762, p. 20. This was recently reaffirmed in the *Nota aanvullende pensioenen*, TK 1990-1991, 22 167, nr. 2.

[99]   In principle, because, for certain employer's in industry, a scheme will have been made compulsorily applicable, removing this element of choice. In the commercial sector, it can be doubted to what extent it is true to say that the employer is free in this respect, since, in a competitive market in which the main competitors make such provision available, the employer will in fact enjoy little freedom.

policy that an obligation would be introduced for employers to offer their employees an occupational pension.[100] However, by the time the relevant preparatory studies had been carried out, the relevant consensus had been lost and so the Dutch employer remains free to decide whether or not to offer a pension to his employees.

However, once such an undertaking has been made, a number of restraints are imposed on the employer's freedom, the majority of which are imposed in an attempt to ensure that the pension undertaking made is eventually paid. The Dutch Pension Schemes Act (*Pensioen- en Spaarfondsenwet* PSW)[101] aims to ensure that where an employer promises his employees a pension, this undertaking is indeed honoured.[102] This is to be brought about by by imposing a number of obligations on the employer.[103] An employer who makes a pension promise to his employees must utilise one of a limited number of vehicles for this promise:[104] an industrial pension fund,[105] a company pension fund[106] both of

---

[100]   See TK 1990-1991, 22 167, nr. 2 at pp. 24-28; Lutjens 1989, loc. cit. at pp. 36-38 and 770-771 who concludes that this would indeed be a good idea, at least is if were to be contained in three quarters binding law. For the government's rejection of such a scheme see the *Nota aanvullende pensioenen* TK 1990-1991, 22 167, nr. 2 at p. 27. C.C.H.J. Driessen, "Op weg naar een wettelijke aanvullende pensioenrecht voor werknemers", in M.M.H. Kraamwinkel, J.J. Schippers and Siegers, *De toekomst van de aanvullende pensioenen*, Zwolle, 1992 at pp. 35-42; P.J. van Eekeren, "De totstandkoming van aanvullende pensioenregelingen: verplichtingen van rechtswege", 1989 SR 165; in a different context, J. Dierx and M. Kraamwinkel, "Pensioenplicht", 1989 Nemesis 127.

[101]   Law of 15 May 1952, Stb. 275, reprinted at Stb. 1981, 18. Detailed examination of the PSW is to be found in Lutjens 1989, loc. cit. at pp. 28-36, 39-40, 98-119.

[102]   MvT PSW 1952, TK 1949-50 1730, nr. 3, p. 5. See Lutjens 1989, loc. cit. at p. 29.

[103]   Art. 2 PSW.

[104]   Art. 2 PSW.

[105]   *Bedrijfspensioenfonds.* This is defined in art. 1(1)(b) PSW as "a fund working in a particular branch of industry (*bedrijfstak*) in which, either only for persons employed in the industry or also for the benefit of those working in that branch in some other capacity, monies are gathered together with the objective of insuring for pensions." ("*Een in een bedrijfstak werkend fonds, waarin hetzij alleen ten bate van personen, die als werknemer, hetzij mede ten bate van personen, die in andere hoedanigheid in die bedrijfstak werkzaan zijn, gelden worden bijeengebracht, strekkende tot verzekering van pensioenen.*")

which must possess full legal personality,[107] group or individual life insurance policies.[108] Although the employer is in principle free to select between these possibilities, the PSW does require that where life insurance is chosen, the employee must be no better nor any worse off than would have been the case had the employer joined an industry pension scheme or attached a company fund to his undertaking.[109]

The essence of the obligation imposed pursuant to the PSW is to keep the pension money in a separate legal body, whether a pension fund or an insurer. By keeping the monies separate from the employer, maximum security for the employee is ensured, the objective behind the PSW. It should be stressed that responsibility for fulfilling the pension promise lies with the employer.[110]

Nevertheless, a slight gloss must be put upon this description of the freedom of the employer. An interesting feature of the Dutch occupational pensions system is that a representative of a substantial proportion of the organised participants in the sector[111] can request the Minister to make the scheme

---

[106]   *Ondernemingspensioenfonds.* Defined in Art. 1(1)(c) PSW as "a fund attached to an undertaking, in which for the benefit of persons attached to the undertaking, monies are brought together for the objective of pension insurance." ("*een aan een onderneming verbonden fonds, waarin ten bate van personen, die aan die onderneming verbonden zijn, gelden worden bijeengebracht, strekkende tot verzekering van pensioen.*")

[107]   Art. 4(1) PSW.

[108]   Art. 2(4)B and C PSW. The insurer must qualified under the Insurance Supervision Act (*Wet toezicht verzekeringsbedrijf* (WTV), Stb. 1994, 252. Such arrangements are subject to the provisions of the *Regelen verzekeringsovereenkomsten Pensioen- en spaarfondsenwet*, decision of 16 July 1987, Stcrt. 143, as most recently altered by decision of 15 July 1994, Stcrt. 136.

[109]   Art. 2(4), second sentence PSW.

[110]   Article 2(5) PSW.

[111]   There is no statutory definition of when a group will be deemed to be sufficiently representative. See the discussion in Lutjens 1989, loc. cit. at pp. 202-212.

compulsory[112] for all or part of the sector.[113] If the Minister is satisfied that a substantial proportion of the sector support the move, and he has consulted the relevant organs,[114] he will grant the request.[115]

A number of conditions must be satisfied before the Minister can decide that the scheme's scope should be extended.[116] The Minister can refuse to adopt

---

[112]   The ability to extend the scope of collective agreements beyond the instant parties to the agreement is an important feature of Dutch industrial relations. Fear of intersectoral "social dumping" appears to have prompted the introduction of this facility. Law of 27 May 1937, Stb. 1937, 801. See A.T.J.M. Jacobs, *Het recht op collectief onderhandelen in rechtsvergelijkend en Europees perspectief*, Alphen aan den Rijn/Brussels, 1986, at pp. 226-231. Nevertheless, the government seems to be having second thoughts about the desirability of this practice in the current economic climate, particularly in respect of the lower paid. In this regard, see *Algemeen verbindend verklaren van CAO-bepalingen*, TK 1993-1994, 23 532, nr. 1 and *Regeerakkord "Keuzen voor de toekomst"*, op. cit.

[113]   The Wet Bpf (Law of 17 March 1949, Stb. J 121) was adopted on 17 March 1949 to make the facility available in relation to pension funds which was available in relation to other aspects of labour agreements. The statute concerning collective agreements was unsuitable for this purpose because first, their duration is limited to a maximum of 5 years, a period much too short to be of significance in the pensions context, and decisions making collective agreements are limited to a two year period. For a detailed explanation of the working of the Wet Bpf, see Lutjens 1989 loc. cit. at pp. 200-230. As the parliamentary debates preceeding the adoption of this statute demonstrate, considerations relating to competitiveness played an important role. It was deemed unacceptable that an employer should be able to undercut his competitors by failing to offer his employees an occupational pension scheme. In this context, the question invariably arises of the compatibility of this practice with the provisions of articles 3(g), 5, 85, 86 and 90 of the EC Treaty. The ECJ was recently been asked about this in Joined Cases C-430 and 431/93 *Van Schindel* and *Van Veen* v. *Stichting Pensioenfonds voor Fysiotherappeuten*, [1995] ECR I-4705. However, it avoided answering the question. See, referring to a decision by a lower Dutch court, L.P. de Hon, "Verplichte bedrijfspensioenfondsen verenigbaar met Europees mededingingsrecht?", TvP 1992, 73-74.

[114]   The Head of the relevant department of general administration (*Departement van Algemeen Bestuur*), the Social and Economic Council (*Sociaal-Economische Raad*) and the Insurance Chamber.

[115]   Art. 3(1) Wet Bpf.

[116]   It is necessary that a pension scheme already be in existence the provisions of which do not conflict with the principle of equality between men and women. Additionally, article 5(2) I-V gives five grounds on which refusal is certain. First, if the Minister objects to the fund's financial basis, as emerges from the actuarial report. Similarly, if those matters listed under article 5(2)II are not to be found in the statutes and rules of the scheme, the Minister will also refuse to grant the decision. If the Minister considers that the scheme insufficiently

a decision if he considers that the scope of the scheme should be extended to embrace a larger group than that envisaged by the application. However, he does not have the power to extend the scope of a scheme in the absence of a specific request by the relevant representatives. Once granted, decisions may be revoked, for example where the statutes and rules of the scheme are altered without the approval of the Minister (article 3(5)).

It is possible for exemption to be granted from a decision extending the scope of a scheme.[117] Exemption must be granted where requested by an individual[118] who, for at least six months prior to the entry into force of the ministerial decision, was a member of a company pension scheme or contributed to a pension held by an insurance company. However, the existing scheme must offer at least the same standard of protection as the scheme from which exemption is sought.[119] At the end of 1988, there were approximately 1000 company pension schemes. In addition, there were 77 industrial pension schemes, of which 64 had been extended. Approximately 20 000 pension schemes were executed by insurers.[120] The significance of this power to declare schemes generally

---

safeguards the rights of members, no decision of general applicability will be taken. Where there is not equal representation of employers and employees on the board of the fund, again the request will be refused. Finally, if the fund does not have legal personality, permission must be refused.

[117]   Article 5(2)II(1) Wet Bpf. For details see Lutjens 1989, loc. cit. at pp. 231-262.

[118]   It may also be requested by the employer. In this situation, it must be clear that the majority of the workforce which will be affected by possible exemption support the employer's request. A number of government directives have been adopted outlining the policy to be followed. Decision of 29 December 1952, Stcrt. 1953, 1 most recently amended by decision of 15 August 1988, Stcrt. 158.

[119]   This does not necessarily apply where the scheme in question is being run down, or where the ministerial decision relates to one part of an industry, the major part of which belongs to another branch.

[120]   *Nota aanvullende pensioenen* TK 1990-1991, 22 167, nr. 2 at p. 20.

applicable to entire sectors of the economy should not be underestimated as a source of the high degree of coverage achieved by Dutch pension schemes.[121]

The PSW imposes a number of additional requirements on pension schemes, in the interests of protecting the interests of members of schemes. According to article 9 of the PSW, the capital contained in a pension fund destined for the provision of pensions must be used to transfer or re-insure the relevant risk. This should be accomplished by taking out an insurance policy with an insurer licenced under the WTV. Nevertheless, in certain circumstances defined to provide an equal level of member protection, exemption from this requirement will be granted. Thus, a scheme which operates on the basis of an actuarial[122] and financial management plan in which the plan's basis and financial structure are clearly explained, does not have to transfer or re-insure the risk covered by the pension scheme. It is however necessary that the plan itself have been approved by the Insurance Chamber, and every five years[123] the scheme's actuarial profit and loss accounts must be submitted to the Insurance Chamber for approval. Additionally, any proposed changes to accounts or plans which have already been approved by the Chamber, must be submitted for its approval before they are put into action.

As emerges from these provisions, in contrast to the AOW, occupational pension schemes must be pre-funded. This also follows from the requirement that the assets of the scheme, together with any anticipated income, must be sufficient to cover its anticipated liabilities.[124] In this way, it is hoped that the pension scheme will be more likely to be able to meet its committments, thereby ensuring that the member's expectations are met. Additionally. investments made by the

---

[121]   G.J.B. Dietvorst, *De drie pijlers van toekomstvoorzieningen en belastingen*, Deventer, 1994 at p. 57.

[122]   NB the Insurance Chamber must also approve of the actuary.

[123]   Or where it deems it necessary, at smaller intervals.

[124]   Article 13 PSW.

fund must be prudent, a concept which is not defined in the legislation,[125] and self-investment must not exceed 10% of the assets of the fund.[126]

Thus, it can be seen that the PSW and the Wet Bpf lay down a number of provisions whereby the freedom of the employer in making and designing his pension scheme is curtailed. In adopting these provisions, the legislator has been guided by what it considers to be the best manner of protecting the members expectation that a pension promise made will actually be paid out. As with the UK, the substantive limits on benefit levels are contained in the tax legislation which will be outlined below.

2.2.3   TAX RULES

The Wages Tax Law (*Wet op de Loonbelasting*)[127] contains a precise definition of what constitutes a pension from the fiscal point of view:

> "The term pension scheme covers a scheme which exclusively, or mainly,
> a. as its object has the care of employees and ex-employees in the event of invalidity or old age and the care of their spouses, children, step-children which have not yet reached the age of 21 and are neither married or divorced.

---

[125]   During the parliamentary debates preceeding the adoption of the legislation, some members inquired whether a more detailed definition of what is considered "prudent" would not be more useful. However, it was decided that since what will be considered is dependent on the existing financial basis of the fund, together with the characteristics of its members, that it woulld be impossible to give a definition which was useful enough without forming an impediment to other schemes with different needs.

[126]   Article 15. This can be derogated from in a situation where an employer wishes to increase the benefits offered by his scheme and where the Insurance Chamber has already approved his financing plan.

[127]   *Wet op de Loonbelasting*, Stb. 1964, 514, as most recently amended by the law of 23 December 1994, Stb. 927, 928, 932, 933 and 936.

b. provides a pension which does not go beyond that which by
social standards, in connection with length of employment and
remuneration received, can be deemed to be reasonable."[128]

The second leg of this definition imposes a substantive limitation on the levels of
benefit which may be provided by schemes, if fiscal advantages are to be
retained.[129] In practice, this requirement has been interpreted as indicating that
a scheme offering a benefit of no more than 70% of final salary over a 40 year
career will be considered to be reasonable by social standards.[130] If the criteria
contained in article 11(3) of the Wet LB are satisfied, a situation comes about
where the pension scheme in question is fiscally "pure" which means that the tax
advantages contained in the Wet LB are conferred on the situation. Briefly, if the
situation concerns a "pure" pension scheme, the premiums paid by an employee

---

[128]   *"Onder een pensioenregeling wordt verstaan een regeling die uitsluitend of nagenoeg
          uitsluitend:*
          *a. ten doel heeft de verzorging van werknemers en gewezen werknemers bij
          invaliditeit en ouderdom en de verzorging van hun echtgenoten en van hun
          kinderen en pleegkinderen die de leeftijd van 21 jaar nog niet hebben bereikt en
          niet gehuwd zijn of gehuwd geweest zijn, en*
          *b. een pensioen inhoudt dat niet uitgaat boven hetgeen naar maatschappelijke
          opvattingen, mede in verband met diensttijd en genoten beloning, redelijk moet
          worden geacht."* Article 11(3) of the Wet LB.

[129]   The rationale of such a requirement is, given the tax deductability of contributions to
          schemes which satisfy the tax provisions, to avoid huge accumulations of capital created
          merely for the purposes of avoiding paying high marginal tax rates.

[130]   The 70% norm was accepted by the STAR as the ideal to be aimed at by pension schemes.
          However, it appears that this norm has become a fiction for the majority of employees. This
          is a consequence of the (previous) difficulty of maintaining SSBs and the difficulty relating
          to taking a transfer. In addition to adopting legislation to cover these difficulties (see *infra*),
          the government also seems to be considering encouraging a change from final salary to
          average salary or money purchase schemes which do not cause the early leaver such
          problems. The advantage of these other pension forms is that they allow the older employee
          to move down salary scales prior to retirement without loss of pension rights. See TK 1990,
          22 167, nr. 2 where figures are cited demonstrating that 72.1% of employees who are
          members of occupational pension schemes are members of final salary schemes. This
          approach was confirmed in a letter from the Staatssecretaris van Financiën to the Second
          Chamber (1993-1994, 23 046, nr. 9). See on this subject, J. Th. L. Brouwer and H.M.
          Kappelle, "De maatschappelijke opvattingen omtrent pensioen bieden meer ruimte dan
          Financiën denkt", WFR 1994, 6116, 1243-1245.

can be deducted from his taxable salary,[131] the employer is permitted to deduct the premiums which he pays to the fund from his taxable profits[132] and the pension is taxed as income on payment.[133] Failure to satisfy the provisions of the Wet LB does not however mean that a payment can not be a pension within the meaning of the PSW. It merely means that the tax advantages granted to "pure" pensions are denied to "impure" schemes. Thus, by way of example, if the level of income replacement guaranteed by the scheme in question amounts to, say, 90% of the final salary received, this will be regarded as a fiscally "impure" scheme and some tax advantages will not be granted. However, the scheme in question is by no means void. The premiums paid by the employee will "merely" not be deductible from his taxable income.[134] Nevertheless, the employer will generally be allowed to deduct pension costs from his taxable profits[135] but the benefit will be taxable on receipt in so far as the benefits received exceed the payments made by the employee.[136] As this example makes clear, it is not possible to split the "pure" parts of a pension scheme from the "impure" parts.

---

[131]   Article 11(1)(i) of the Wet LB.

[132]   These will qualify as wage costs and can be deducted on the basis of article 7 of the Income Tax Act (*Wet Inkomstenbelastingen* - Wet IB) where the employer is a natural person, or on the basis of article 8(1) of the Corporation Tax Act (*Wet Vennootschapsbelasting* - Wet Vpb) if the employer is a legal person.

[133]   Article 10(1) of the Wet LB.

[134]   Because the possibility for deduction is only for a pension scheme within the definition contained in article 11(3) of the Wet LB.

[135]   Because articles 7 Wet IB and 8(1) of the Wet Vpb do not limit deductibility to situations where the pension is a pension within the meaning of the Wet LB.

[136]   Article 25(1)(g) Wet LB.

2.3   Germany

2.3.1   STATUTORY PROVISION

The statutory scheme operating in Germany offers a high level of earnings related benefits to beneficiaries, in contrast to the low-level flat-rate benefits paid in the UK and the Netherlands.[137] The objective served by the German statutory scheme is to provide the individual who has been insured for 45 years with a pension representing some 70% of the net average salary,[138] which reflects the belief that primary responsibility for providing retirement income lies with the State.[139] The earnings cap which is present in the system[140] is set at such a high level[141] that it seems reasonable to assume that the statutory scheme will provide for the major

---

[137]   On this subject, see generally W. Gitter, *Sozialrecht. Ein Studienbuch*, München, 1992; M. Kittner and O.E. Krasney, *Sozialgesetzbuch. Textausgabe mit Einleitungen*, 2nd ed., Bonn, 1991; for a detailed treatment of the history of statutory pensions, see Westerveld, loc. cit. at pp. 15-56, 165-199, 297-362.

[138]   W. Tegtmeier, "Supplementary Pension Schemes within the Overall System of Provision for Old-Age in the Federal Republic of Germany", in W. Schmähl (ed.), *The Future of Basic and Supplementary Pension Schemes in the European Community - 1992 and Beyond*, Baden-Baden, 1991 pp. 99-110, at p. 101. See Achenbach and Haneberg, op. cit. at 6. *Supplementary Pensions*, loc. cit. at 9.

[139]   See H.-D. Steinmeyer, "Nationaler Bericht Deutschland", in *Zusatzversorgungssysteme in der Bundesrepublik Deutschland, Frankreich und Großbritannien - Entwicklung, Tendenzen und offene Fragen*, Köln, 1994 (hereafter Steinmeyer 1994) at p. 18.

[140]   At the end of every year, the salary earned by the individual is translated into *Entgeltpunkten* (Salary Points). To calculate the number of Salary Points to which an individual is entitled, his salary is divided by the average salary earned in Germany that year. Thus, where the individual earns an average wage, he accrued 1 Salary Point for a year, whereas if he earns less than that, he earns a part of one Salary Point. These Salary Points are in turn multiplied by the *Rentenartfaktor* (a fixed percentage depending upon the type of benefit)(para. 67 SGB VI) and by the *aktuelle Rentenwert* (which is the means by which the level is translated into a DM value)(para. 68 SGB VI). In this way, subject to the operation of the ceiling, the earnings history of the individual is reflected in the level of statutory benefit which he receives. To ensure that the pensions retain their value, paragraph 65 provides for adjustment in the levels of pensions in payment annually on 1 July.

[141]   In 1993, 44,055 ECU when average earnings of non-manual workers in industry were 31,620 ECU. Both figures cited in *Supplementary Pensions*, loc. cit. at 10 and 11.

needs of most of the population. However, if a 20 year career is assumed, the replacement rate provided by the statutory scheme drops to 31% net.[142] Where the individual earns twice the average wage, 45 years' insurance provides a pension at 55% net of final salary, whereas an individual with an insurance history limited to 20 years enjoys a statutory pension of only 24% of his final earnings.[143] In 1990 the average number of years of insurance of retirees was 37.3 for men and 23.4 for women,[144] which suggests that the vast majority of individuals in Germany - at least the men - will receive statutory pensions providing them with a reasonable level of income on retirement.

In Germany, all those who are economically active are mandatorily insured for the old age pension scheme, with those not subject to mandatory insurance also being given the opportunity to purchase insurance under the scheme.[145] To qualify for a pension, an individual must have reached pensionable age and have satisfied the relevant waiting period.[146] The standard old age pension is payable from the age of 65, and the five year general waiting period must be satisfied.[147] Women can however retire from the age of 60 where they satisfy the waiting period of 15 years and where since reaching the age of 40 they have paid compulsory contributions for at least 10 years.[148]

In contrast to the situation pertaining in the UK and the Netherlands, there appears to be political confidence in Germany in the long-term viability of the

---

[142]   Cited in *Supplementary Pensions*, loc. cit. at 9.

[143]   Ibid. at 12.

[144]   These figures are for West Germany, the corresponding figures for East Germany were 47.1 years for men and 36.2 years for women, *Supplementary Pensions*, loc. cit. at 15.

[145]   Para. 7 SGB VI.

[146]   Para. 34 SGB VI.

[147]   The various waiting periods are laid down in para. 50 SGB VI.

[148]   Para. 39 SGB VI. The German government has announced that equal pensionable ages will be phased in. It should be noted that when equality has been introduced into the statutory scheme, different contributions from women and men are no longer allowed. See Case C-154/92, *Van Cant* v. *Rijksdienst voor Pensioenen*, [1993] ECR I-3811.

statutory scheme,[149] particularly after the recent reforms. In the light of the projected economic and demographic developments, the German legislator introduced amendments in 1989 (the *Rentenreformgesetz* RRG 1992) which were designed to safeguard the long-term viability of the scheme.[150] In designing the reforms, the legislator was influenced by five considerations.[151] First, the ratio of those contributing to the statutory scheme to those in receipt of benefits pursuant to it had increased and was forecast to double by 2030.[152] This alone could have been expected to impose significant financial pressures upon the German system of old age provision. However, these pressures were seen to be exacerbated by the fact that individuals are also living longer, with the result that pensions have to be paid for a longer period of time on average. At the same time, the periods of economic activity during which contributions were being paid dropped, partly as a consequence of lengthened periods of education. Additionally, the birth rate was dropping reducing the pool of economically active whose contributions finance current pensions. Finally, it was felt that the practice of taking early retirement was robbing industry of valuable resources, something which the legislator ought to discourage.[153]

---

[149]   See Blüm, op. cit.; Niemeyer, loc. cit. For academic support, see Steinmeyer (1994), loc. cit. at pp. 18-19; Schmähl 1995, op. cit.; Schösser, op. cit.

[150]   The *Rentenreformgesetz* (RRG) 1992 RRG of 18 December 1989, *Bundesgesetzblatt* (BGBl) I 2261.

[151]   For a discussion of the factors which prompted the RRG 1992, see Westerveld, loc. cit. at pp. 323-342; Kittner and Krasney, loc. cit. at pp. 401-406; W. Förster, S. Recktenwald and M. Trevisany, "Das Rentenreformgesetz 1992 und seine Auswirkung auf betriebliche Versorgungssysteme", BB (1990) Beilage 29.

[152]   For figures, see Kittner and Krasney, loc.. cit. at p. 404; equally bleak figures are cited by Förster et al op. cit. at 3; Achenbach and Haneberg, op. cit. at 6.

[153]   For example, male activity rates for those between 60 and 64 dropped by 50.8% between 1970 and 1990 and for those between 55 and 59. activity dropped by 10.5%. Figures cited in W. Trommel, *Eigentijds met pensioen. Een beschouwing over flexibele pensioenering en arbeidsdeelname in Nederland, aan de hand van Amerikaanse, Zweedse en Japanse voorbeelden*, Den Haag, 1993 at p. 15; see also the statistics cited by Achenbach and Haneberg, op. cit. at 6.

One of the reforms introduced pursuant to the RRG was to raise female pensionable age.[154] At the same time, the early retirement facility which was introduced by the 1972 reforms was tightened up slightly. As a consequence of this, all individuals with a full insurance record will be allowed to retire from the age of 62, but if they choose to do so, their pension will now be reduced proportionately. Similarly, those postponing retirement beyond the age of 65 will now receive increments to their pension. The final innovation of the 1992 RRG was to introduce the possibility for an individual to retire partially.[155] Paragraph 42 SGB VI enables an individual to opt for a full pension or a pension worth one or two thirds of the full pension. Taken together, it is hoped that these provisions will stimulate a delayed or phased move into retirement, reversing to some degree the trend towards increasingly early retirement, with positive spin-off effects for the financial viability of the statutory old age pension scheme. The final amendment has been to increase levels of pension benefits in line with net wage increases, rather than the previous gross wage figure.

2.3.2   OCCUPATIONAL PENSIONS

Despite the apparently healthy nature of the German statutory scheme, a not insignificant occupational pensions industry has grown up in Germany. A 1990 survey indicated that some 70% of employees (*Beschäftigten*) in Germany were members of an occupational pension scheme,[156] with 1992 figures suggesting that the capital collected to cover occupational retirement benefits amounted to some

---

[154]   From the year 2000, pensionable age will be raised in (monthly) steps until ages are equalised in 2012. Additionally, the provision according to which those with extremely long contributions records (35 year waiting period) (para. 36 SGB VI) could retire from the age of 63 was also abolished step by step (para. 41).

[155]   In its original form, the statutory scheme in the UK required that to gain entitlement to a pension, women between the ages of 60 and 65, and men between the ages of 65 and 70 had to have retired from regular employment. This was abolished in 1989, in the hope of encouraging people to continue working after reaching pensionable age. See Ogus et al, loc. cit. at pp. 227-230; Westerveld, loc. cit. at pp. 400-401.

[156]   Quoted in L.G. von Wartenberg, "Zur Bedeutung der betrieblichen Altersversorgung für die Finanzierung deutscher Unternehmen", in Förster and Rössler (eds.), loc. cit. pp. 141-159 at p. 143.

DM 433 thousand million, or 214,322 million ECUs. The equivalent ECU assets for the UK were 490,719 million and for the Netherlands 187,953 million. These figures themselves are impressive enough and demonstrate that there is a considerable pensions industry in Germany, even if its assets are lower than for the other Member States which are being considered in this research. However, a significant feature of the German situation is that the vast bulk of this capital (some DM 250,000 million or ECU 123,743 million) remains within the undertaking from which the pension promise emanates,[157] prompting the following observation:

"For many years now, occupational pensions have formed an invisible instrument for financing the German economy."[158]

Because the situation in Germany differs in a number of significant details from that pertaining in both the UK and the Netherlands, more attention will be paid to the development of occupational schemes there than for the others.

Occupational pensions began to spring up in Germany during the 19th century. However, as in the UK and the Netherlands, they were considered not to form part of the remuneration paid to the employee, but rather as an expression of the employer's paternalistic obligation to care for his employees (*Versorgung*).[159] Additionally, as their establishment became more widespread, a large body of opinion came to consider the pension paid to the employee, more often than not funded solely by the employer, as a reward for *Betriebstreue*, or company

---

[157] For the operation of this system, see below.

[158] "*Die betriebliche Altersversorgung is schon seit längerem zu einem unverzichtbaren "Finanzierungsinstrument" für die deutsche Wirtschaft geworden.*" von Wartenberg, loc. cit. at p. 142. See also "Corporate Germany's DM 30 billion hole", *The Economist* 22 April 1995 at p. 82.

[159] On the history of occupational pension schemes in Germany, see Commission of the European Communities, *De aanvullende regelingen van de sociale zekerheid in de landen van de EEG*, serie sociale politiek number 15, 1966, Luxembourg at p. 15 ; H.-D. Steinmeyer, *Betriebliche Altersversorgung und Arbeitsverhältnis - Das betriebliche Ruhegeld als Leistung im arbeitsvertraglichen Austauschverhältnis* (hereafter Steinmeyer 1991), München, 1991 at pp. 11-29; P. Ahrend, W. Förster and J. Rühmann, *Gesetz zur Verbesserung der betrieblichen Altersversorgung mit zivilrechtlichen, arbeidsrechtlichen, steuerrechtlichen Voorschriften und Erläuterungen* 5th ed., München, 1994 at pp. XV-XVI.

loyalty.[160] Entirely in character with this view, it became common for employers to include as a condition for entitlement to a pension, the requirement that the employee remain in the employer's employment until reaching pensionable age.[161] As a consequence of the freedom accorded to the employer in designing the shape of and conditions of the occupational pension scheme which he offered employees, the occupational pensions promise became known as the "goldene Fessel",[162] that is, the golden chain, which indicates the onerous nature of the conditions which employers chose to impose.

Although it has been recognised that pensions can be regarded as pay to the employee,[163] for the non-German commentator the situation in Germany continues to be characterised by an emphasis on the rights and freedoms of the employer to impose conditions on his promise of a pension to his employee which would not be considered acceptable in the UK or the Netherlands. As shall be described below, a German pension undertaking has to have been made to an employee for 10 years[164] before he obtains an enforceable right to a pension which stands in stark contrast to the much shorter period required in the Netherlands and the UK.[165] One explanation which could perhaps be found for this difference in approach is that, by contrast to the UK and the Netherlands, occupational pensions play a different role in Germany, topping up an already generous statutory system, as opposed to forming a necessary addition to a low

---

[160]   This is still the view defended by the employers. See Steinmeyer 1994, loc. cit. at p. 19.

[161]   See the example to be found at BB 1982, 1176.

[162]   Ahrend et al, loc. cit. at p. 3; Steinmeyer 1994, loc. cit. at p. 40.

[163]   See the discussion in Steinmeyer 1991, loc. cit. Even then, the BAG has traditionally taken the view that the pay is for loyalty rather than for services rendered. See the judgment of 10/3/72, BB 1972, 1005.

[164]   Or three years, where the employee has worked for the employer for 12 years. In both cases the individual must be over the age of 35 when he seeks to leave the employment, see infra.

[165]   Vesting periods will be discussed at greater length in Chapter 6 below.

level of statutory benefit. If the German occupational pension is viewed as a luxury, it may explain the general acceptance of harsher conditions.[166]

The major piece of legislation governing occupational pension schemes in Germany is the *Gesetz zur Verbesserung der betrieblichen Altersversorgung* (BetrAVG) which was adopted on 19 December 1974, entering into force on 22 December of that year,[167] in relation to all employment relationships existing at that date or coming into existence thereafter.[168] As its title suggests, the BetrAVG aimed to improve occupational pension provision but the government also hoped that the adoption of the legislation would broaden coverage, improve employee protection and encourage employee mobility.[169]

Although one of the objectives which was pursued by the BetrAVG was the improvement of employee protection, the first steps in this direction were taken prior to the adoption of the legislation. In a judgment of 10 March 1972,[170] the *Bundesarbeitsgericht* (BAG) held that an employee who had been affiliated to a company for more than 20 years and who was dismissed prior to reaching pensionable age retains the occupational pension rights which he has accrued to that date.[171] In other words, prior to the adoption of the legislation, the BAG tempered the freedom granted to employers to impose whichever conditions they saw fit for the acquisition of enforceable pension rights. In addition, the Court

---

[166]   It is interesting to note that, in contrast to the UK and the Netherlands, German unions have not been particularly concerned with occupational pensions. This reinforces the impression that occupational pensions are seen as a luxury in Germany. On the subject of unions and occupational schemes, see Steinmeyer, (1994), op. cit. at pp. 19 and 33.

[167]   BGBl I S. 3610, as most recently amended by the RRG 1992, BGBl. 1989 I S. 2261. See Ahrend et al, loc. cit.

[168]   Judgment of the BAG, BB 1982, 1176 at 1177.

[169]   Ahrend et al, loc. cit. at p. XV.

[170]   BB 1972, 1005; see Steinmeyer 1991, loc. cit. at pp. 23-25; Ahrend et al, loc. cit. at pp. 3-4.

[171]   However, a temporal limitation was imposed on the case, with the benefits of the judgment being restricted to those employees who left the employment after 1 January 1969.

recognised that pensions are a form of pay,[172] and deemed that company loyalty does not require to be demonstrated until pensionable age to earn a reward in the form of a pension.[173]

The period laid down in the judgment of the BAG was further reduced by the BetrAVG. Paragraph 1 provides that an individual obtains an enforceable pension right where the promise has been made to him for at least 10 years, or where he has been affiliated to the company for at least 12 years and the pension promise is at least 3 years old. In both cases, the individual in question must be over the age of 35 on leaving the employment, although the parties are free to agree terms which are more favourable to the employee.[174] Even without more favourable derogation, these provisions represent a significant improvement in the situation of the employee since he is now certain of retaining pension rights after this period and need not fear their loss if he decides to change employer. The employee's position is further improved by the provisions of paragraph 2 which lay down the methods by which the levels of the benefit to which the early leaver becomes entitled are to be calculated.[175]

As with the UK and Dutch provisions, the legislation in Germany requires that pension promises be administered by a particular form of institution.[176] Additionally, a distinction is drawn between direct promises (*Direktzusage* or

---

[172]   See the extensive discussion in Steinmeyer 1991, loc. cit.

[173]   This protection was extended in a 1975 judgment in which the BAG held that an individual who voluntarily leaves the service of an employer after a period of at least 20 years is also entitled to retain any pension rights which he has accrued. Judgment of 20 February 1975, 3 AZR 514/73 - DB 1975 S. 1274; Ahrend et al, loc. cit. at p. 3.

[174]   Steinmeyer 1994, op. cit. at p. 40 indicates that it is usual for the employers to operate at the highest threholds laid down in the law.

[175]   See the more detailed treatment of this subject in Chapter 6 below.

[176]   This is most clearly the case for the Netherlands and Germany. In UK the requirement of irrevocable trust must be satisfied if all the tax advantages are to be enjoyed by the scheme in question.

unmittelbare Verzorgungszusage)[177] and indirect promises (*mittelbare Versorgungszusage*). A unique feature of pension provision in Germany is that where the employer chooses to make a direct promise, he is not required to place the funds with a legally separate institution but is merely obliged to enter debit records in his company accounts representing his pensions liabilities. This is currently the most popular manner for the employer to make a pension promise to his employees with 53.2% of undertakings financing their pensions in this way, accruing assets of some DM 231.5 thousand million in 1991.[178] This popularity is easy to explain. The long vesting periods countenanced by the legislator for German schemes means that an employer need only actually seriously consider financing a pension for those of his employees who stay with him for at least 10 years while he may enjoy the tax benefits of making the promise immediately.

Where no separate pension fund is formed to protect the pension rights accruing to employees, the members of the pension scheme are in an extremely precarious position, since their pension "rights" are entirely at the mercy of the prosperity of the undertaking. This vulnerability is exacerbated if there is no requirement that the benefits be funded in advance. These considerations underly the decision of the UK and Dutch legislators to require that pension funds be pre-funded to a greater or lesser extent, and that the funds must be brought under the control of a financial institution separate from the employer. Recognising the potential vulnerability of the beneficiaries of direct promises, paragraphs 7-15 BetrAVG oblige the employer who has made such a promise to take out insolvency insurance.[179] Employers who have made direct pension promises are obliged to contribute to the *Pensions-Sicherungs-Verein Versicherungsverein auf Gegenseitigkeit* (PSVaG) by paying a levy which is calculated to plug the gap

---

[177] Also referred to as *Pensionszusage, Ruhegeldverpflichtungen, Pensionsverpflichtungen*, see Steinmeyer 1991, loc. cit. at p. 4.

[178] von Wartenberg, loc. cit. at p. 143; the same figures are also cited by C. Conrad, "Les Fonds de Pension Allemands", in Association Europe & Enterprises, *Fonds de Pension en Europe: Expreiences et Devenir*, Les Dorriers de l'AEE No. 5, Paris, 1994 pp. 39-42 at p. 32; Steinmeyer 1994, loc. cit. at p. 32.

[179] Para.s 7-15 BetrAVG; see Ahrend et al, loc. cit. at pp. 67-96; J. Paulsdorff, "Der Begriff der betrieblichen Altersversorgung als Gegenstand der Insolvenzsicherung" in Förster and Rössler (eds.), loc. cit. at pp. 195-207.

between the proceeds realised through bankruptcy proceedings and the cost of purchasing the annuity contracts in question.[180] In turn, the PSVaG takes out annuity contracts with insurers to buy out the benefits owed to the former employees of the bankrupt employer.[181] For an individual to benefit from the *Insolvenzsicherung* he must have an enforceable right to a pension, and although the period required for acquisition of this right is long, the insolvency insurance provisions undoubtedly represent an important safeguard for employees.

The employer making an indirect pension promise has a choice between three different financing vehicles. He can finance his pension promise by means of *Direktversicherung* (direct insurance), a *Pensionskasse* (a pension fund) or by an *Unterstützungskasse* (a support fund).[182] In *Direktversicherung* the employer concludes a life insurance contract with an insurance company on the life of the employee in question, although it is the employee and his survivors who gain entitlement to claim the resulting benefits.[183] 45.5% of undertakings making pension provision have chosen this form and some DM 30 thousand million in assets have been accrued.[184] The insurance company is subject to the supervision of the *Bundesaufsichtsamt für das Versicherungswesen* (BAV) to ensure its solvency and therefore the protection of the beneficiary. In contrast to the *Direktzusage* the only situation in which the employer using direct insurance has to take out insolvency insurance is where he has borrowed on the life insurance contract or transferred it. Additionally, if the rights can be revoked, insolvency insurance must be taken out as it must where bankruptcy proceedings have been commenced.

---

[180]   BetrAVG para.s 9(2) and 10; see *Supplementary Pensions*, loc. cit. at 78-9.

[181]   A ceiling of three times the social security contributions ceiling is set on the benefits protected by the *Insolvenzsicherung*. In 1993 this resulted in a ceiling of DM 259,200; see BetrAVG para. 7(3).

[182]   BetrAVG para 1; see Ahrend et al, loc. cit. at pp. 19-22.

[183]   Para. 1(2) BetrAVG. This is different from the Personal Pensions available in the UK, because there the contract is directly between the insurance company and the beneficiary. This is also the case for the C-policies available in the Netherlands.

[184]   See for example, Steinmeyer 1994, loc. cit. at p. 32.

Unlike the pension providers which have already been identified, the *Pensionskasse* grants rights directly to the employee and his survivors. It must be a legal person separate from the sponsoring employer and must be a competent care institution (*Versorgungseinrichtung*). It is the German pension provider which most closely resembles the pension funds operating in the UK and the Netherlands. Because it is separate from the employer and because it is obliged to operate on the basis of financial plans, the rights granted through *Pensionskassen* can be seen to be considerably more secure than those granted though, for example, direct promises.[185] This is reinforced by the fact that the *Pensionskasse* is also subject to the supervision of the BAV. Perhaps because of these protective measures, *Pensionskassen* are relatively rare in Germany, with only 8.6% of pension promises being funded in this way.[186]

14.8% of undertakings which have made pensions promises fund their scheme through the final method for making indirect pension promises - the *Unterstützungskasse* - and in so doing have ammassed assets of DM 30 thousand million. Here beneficiaries of the scheme are granted no legal rights to benefits. If BAV supervision is to be avoided, one of a number of legal forms must be selected. These are the registered society (*eingetragenen Vereins*), a private limited company (*GmbH*) or a foundation (*Stiftung*). The capital of which the *Unterstützungskasse* disposes is separate from that of the employer but it can be placed at the disposal of the sponsoring undertaking, subject to charging appropriate interest. As a consequence of the inability of the *Unterstützingskasse* to grant legal rights, in principle the promise can be revoked at all times, albeit subject to a requirement of good faith.[187] Employers who use *Unterstützungskassen* are obliged to take out insolvency insurance with the PSVaG,[188] thereby redressing in part the insecurity for the employee which is

---

[185]   Ahrend et al, loc. cit. at p. 71.

[186]   The assets accumulated with *Pensionskassen* were in 1991 estimated to amount to some DM 95 thousand million. *Supplementary Pensions*, loc. cit. at 94.

[187]   The sponsoring undertaking must suffer economic difficulties justifying the revocation.

[188]   Para. 9(2) BetrAVG.

engendered by the ability of the *Unterstützungskasse* to make its funds available to the employer and its inability to grant legal rights.

It is undoubtedly the case that employees are considerably more secure as a consequence of the provisions of the BetrAVG and that not insignificant restrictions have been placed on the previously unfettered freedom of the employer ins this field. However, in comparison with the UK and the Netherlands, the German situation is characterised by the relative strength of the employer. Additionally, the state intervenes much less in German schemes than it does in either of the other states. As has already been suggested, this is probably a result of the fact that occupational schemes play a different role in Germany than in the other countries studied, but regardless of the causes of these differences, it should be stressed that the extremely long vesting periods which German schemes are allowed to use, form a barrier to employee mobility.

To enjoy the protection provided for by the statute (or to be subject to its obligations, depending upon your perspective) it is necessary that the benefit offered by the scheme fall within the definition of occupational pension contained in the BetrAVG.[189] Paragraph 1 of the BetrAVG defines occupational pensions as

"benefits paid in relation to old age, invalidity or survivorship as

a consequence of the employment relationship".[190]

Three features can be distilled from this definition which give the core elements of the definition for Germany.[191] First, the objective served by the promise must concern caring for the individual in question. Second, the payment must be triggered by one of the listed eventualities and finally, the undertaking must find its roots in the employment relationship subsisting between the employer and the

---

[189]   H.-D. Steinmeyer, "Die Gehaltsumwandlungsversicherung als betriebliche Altersversorgung", BB (1992), 1553-1559 at 1553.

[190]   "*[D]em Leistungen der Alters-, Invaliditäts- oder Hinterbliebenenversorgung aus Anlass seines Arbeitsverhältnisses*". A considerable debate has taken place in Germany as to the precise characterisation which ought to be given to occupational pensions (pay, reward for loyalty, care payment?), on which subject, see generally, Steinmeyer 1991, loc. cit. for an extensive treatment, and the treatment of the same subject in Paulsdorff, loc. cit.

[191]   See F.H. Heither, "Aktuelle Rechtsprechung zu Fragen der betrieblichen Altersversorgung bei individualrechtlicher Ausgestaltung", DB (1991), 165-172 at 165.

beneficiary.[192] The pension undertaking can be contained in an individual contract of employment, or can form part of the collective employment conditions agreed with the union.[193]

In conclusion, it can be said that in comparison to the previous situation, the BetrAVG does offer the beneficiary of a pension promise a reasonable level of protection while leaving the employer with a considerable degree of freedom in deciding how to fund his benefit. This latter freedom is however, as with the UK and the Netherlands, in practice less than might appear on paper, because of the tax law provisions.[194]

2.3.3   TAX RULES

Originally, it was intended that the creation of inalienable rights in the BetrAVG would have been tax led. However, the judgment of the BAG of 1972 considered above led to the abandonment of this provision, with attention focussing instead on the provisions relating to labour law.[195] Nevertheless, tax law continues to play an important role in German occupational pensions law, influencing the employer in his choice of funding vehicle for the pension promise which he has made.

---

[192]   Note, it is not necessary that the promise be made during the life of the employment relationship. Promises made prior to the commencement of the employment relationship, and those made after the employment relationship has terminated are also covered.

[193]   It should be noted that where the pension promise is contained in a collective agreement, that will only bind the parties to the agreement. It is however possible to apply to the Minister of Labour and Social Order for a declaration that the collective agreement in question is of general applicability in the entire branch or undertaking concerned. This is different from the situation in the Netherlands where it is the pension scheme itself which can be made compulsory.

[194]   See generally, the comments in *Supplementary Pensions*, loc. cit. at 71-77.

[195]   See Steinmeyer 1991, loc. cit. at p. 6.

The *Einkommensteuergesetz* (EStG) 1990[196] provides that an employer
may deduct from his accounts sums set aside to cover pension promises
(*Direktzusage*) under certain circumstances. These are that the beneficiary must
have a right to a one-off or recurring benefit and the promise must not contain any
conditions that permit the employer to reduce or remove the right to benefit, unless
it would be considered reasonable in the circumstances.[197] It is also necessary
that the pension promise be contained in writing. It is worth stressing that the
individual need not yet have acquired an *unverfallbaren Anwartschaft* (vested right)
to benefit from the tax law provisions. The deduction can be made for the first
time in the financial year in which the pension promise was first made, but not for
any year in which the beneficiary was younger than 30.[198] The deduction can
only take place for a part of the value of the promise and tables are attached to the
legislation indicating the maximum allowable deductions. Where deductions have
been made for pension promises, they must be entered into the trade accounts of
the undertaking.[199] Any employer contributions to such schemes are not taxable
income in the hands of the employee.

As far as benefits are concerned, paragraph 19 EStG provides that
pensions paid as a consequence of a previous employment relationship fall subject
to tax in the hands of the recipient. Pursuant to paragraph 104 of the
Bewertungsgesetz (BewG)[200] where the pension promise satisfies the conditions
laid down in the EStG, the pension obligation can be deducted from the capital of
the undertaking. Any premiums which the employer is required to pay to the
PSVaG are deductible.

---

[196]   Para. 6a EStG 1990, BGBl. I 1898. The relevant provisions are reproduced in Ahrend et al,
        op. cit. at pp. 158-160. The provisions are elaborated upon in the *Einkommensteuer-
        Richtlinien* 1990, BStBl. I Special issue 2 (reproduced in Ahrend et al, at pp. 167-187).

[197]   One of the situations listed in the EStR as one in which it would be considered reasonable
        to revoke a pensions promise is where the tax law situation has changed significantly. See
        Ahrend et al, loc. cit. at p. 162.

[198]   For more detailed treatment, see Steinmeyer 1994, loc. cit. at p. 67.

[199]   Para. 249 *Handelsgesetzbuch*, BGBl.

[200]   BGBl. III 610-7.

As was mentioned above, the interesting feature of the *Unterstützungskasse* is the fact that the beneficiary does not obtain an enforceable right against the fund.[201] Thus, in terms of employee security, the *Unterstützungskasse* can be seen to be only marginally preferable to the *Directzusage*. The sponsoring undertaking pays contributions to the *Unterstützungskasse* which can be deducted when the statutory criteria are satisfied.[202] Ceilings are set for the maximum level of deductible contribution depending upon whether the institution pays life-long benefits or not.[203] Again, reference is made to a table included in the legislation which lays down the maximum levels of covering capital for benefits in payment, the basis for deductibility. Where the *Unterstützungskasse* receives its funding through an insurance contract, it is allowed to deduct the levels of the annual premiums which it pays to its insurer. However, these two different forms of deductibility do not apply cumulatively. Contributions paid to an *Unterstützungskasse* by an employer are treated as a business expense in the year in which they are paid. However, the contribution must be connected to the business if it is to be deductible. Like contributions to direct promises, contributions to *Unterstützungskassen* are not taxable income in the hands of the recipient, but the benefit is taxable.

An *Unterstützungskasse* is free from the obligation to pay corporation tax[204] where the fund is limited to employees of one or more economic units. Additionally, the fund must be run as a social institution[205] and its funds may not

---

[201]   An explanation is to be found at no. 27a. of the EStR 1990, quoted in Ahrend et al loc. cit. at pp. 154-159.

[202]   Para. 4d EStG 1990 covers contributions to *Unterstützungskassen*.

[203]   See the description at Steinmeyer 1994, loc. cit. at pp. 68-9.

[204]   See para. 5(3) *Körperschaftsteuergesetz* (KStG) 1991.

[205]   Defined in para. 1 of the *Körperschaftsteuer-Durchführungsverordnung* (KStDV) 1984. The recipients of the benefits may not be overwhelmingly entrepreneurs or companies, the monies collected in the fund may only be used to benefit the members and their dependents. Finally, for *Pensionskassen*, the conditions laid down in paragraph 2 KStDV 1984 must be satisfied, with *Unterstützungskassen* being obliged to satisfy the criteria of para. 3. Basically for *Pensionskassen*, particular benefit ceilings for different types of benefits are laid down. For *Unterstützungskassen*, the beneficiaries may not be obliged to contribute, beneficiary

exceed a given level.[206] To the extent that the funds collected within the *Unterstützungskasse* exceed the amounts laid down in the legislation, the excess falls subject to taxation, unless it is reduced in one of a number of ways within 18 months of the ceiling being exceeded.[207]

The *Pensionskasse* is the German pension institution which most closely resembles the pension funds operating in the UK and in the Netherlands.[208] However, according to the figures for 1991 cited above, only 8.6% of pension undertakings are funded in this way. Pursuant to paragraph 4c EStG 1990, contributions to *Pensionskassen* are deductible as a business expense of the employer to the extent that the contributions are required by the statutes of the fund or the financial plan (*Geschäftsplan*), or are for the purposes of making good a deficit. The contributions are however taxable in the hands of the employee,[209] and it is usual for the employer to pay 2/3 of the contributions.[210] Benefits are subject to reduced tax rates, with lump sums being tax free. The treatment of the profits made by the fund is identical to that meted out to the *Unterstütaungskasse* and outlined in the preceeding section. It should be noted that a *Pensionskasse* or *Unterstützungskasse* which uses the monies collected for objectives other than the payment of pensions instantly becomes liable to corporation tax. Again both these institutions can choose to pay capital sums so long as the ceilings laid down in the

---

involvement in contributions and the benefits must satisfy the same criteria as the *Pensionskassen.*

[206]   25% of the amount laid down in para. 4d EStG 1990; see para. 5(3)(e) KStG 1991.

[207]   Para. 6 KStG 1991. The ways of reducing the surplus are, with the agreement of the future beneficiaries, increasing the level of benefits, payment to the sponsoring undertaking, to set off against contributions paid by the sponsoring undertaking, to reduce future contributions.

[208]   An explanation of this type of institution is contained at no. 27 of the EStR 1990, quoted in Ahrend et al, op. cit. at pp. 153-154.

[209]   Para. 40b EStG 1990; see also no. 129 *Lohnsteuer-Richtlinien* 1990 (LStR), quoted in Ahrend et al, loc. cit. at pp. 173-178. They are taxable at a lower rate where they do not exceed a particular figure which was DM 3000 p.a. in 1993. See Steinmeyer 1994, loc. cit. at p. 66.

[210]   Steinmeyer 1994, loc. cit. at p. 38.

KStDV are not exceeded and the beneficiary does not as a consequence receive a higher payment than that to which he had been entitled.

The insurance claim financed through direct insurance[211] does not amount to a part of the company profits for the purposes of tax law.[212] Contributions paid to direct insurance constitute business expenses in their year of payment. It should be noted that pursuant to paragraph 40b EStG 1990, the employer is entitled to levy flat rate tax on contributions paid to direct insurance, subject to the condition that the insured event cannot materialise prior to the 60th birthday of the beneficiary. However, where the employer's contributions for the employee exceed a given amount, this provision does not apply. It would appear that investment income earned by the insurance company will be subject to corporation tax.[213]

2.4   A Brief Comparison

In the UK and the Netherlands, the statutory scheme has always provided a low level of benefit leaving plenty of scope for the private sector to supplement any perceived deficiencies in the level of state provision. By contrast, in Germany the generosity of the state scheme led to a situation in which occupational provision was only made for the better-paid members of the workforce. As was stressed repeatedly in the section on Germany, the overall impression which emerges from examination of the legislative framework for occupational provision there is that occupational schemes are a luxury offered only or mainly to the more highly-skilled and paid members of the workforce. This finds its most telling expression

---

[211]   See LStR 1990, quoted in Ahrend et al, loc. cit. at pp. 173-178.

[212]   Para. 4b EStG 1990. It should be recalled that the insurance contract is between the employer and the insurance company. Accordingly, without this provision, the employer (or the undertaking) would have the beneficial interest on the contract and would or could be subject to tax as a consequence. See the explanation contained at no. 26 of the EStR 1990, quoted in Ahrend et al, loc. cit. at pp. 152-153.

[213]   This can be deduced from the ommission of the *Directversicherung* from the list of bodies enjoying exemption from the KStG.

in the unwillingness to regard pensions as "pay" in the hands of the employee; something to which he or she has rights.[214] The situation is very different in the other two states examined, where occupational provision forms a vital supplement to the low level of benefits which the state provides and in which the remunerative character of the occupational pension is generally accepted. It is suggested that this fundamental difference in the role played by such schemes usefully explains many of the differences between the legislative frameworks in place in the UK and the Netherlands on the one hand, and Germany on the other.

In none of the states under discussion have occupational schemes been made compulsory in the sense that employers have been required by the legislator to make this form of provision. In the Netherlands although the government has remained faithful to its original view that occupational schemes are properly a matter for the social partners, the practice of declaring particular schemes compulsory for all or parts of particular branches of industry means in practice that employers in those sectors have little actual freedom of manoeuvre in this regard, although they do retain discretion as to which employees they offer membership to. In the UK, on the other hand, the employer is entirely free to decide whether or not to offer a pension to his employees. This freedom is however tempered by the market, in that a firm the major competitors of which offer significant occupational benefits to employees will often feel obliged to do the same. Additionally, pressure can also be expected to come from unions which have woken up to the importance of occupational pensions to their members.

By contrast, the German employer appears to enjoy the greatest degree of discretion in relation to the decision whether to offer employees the benefits of scheme membership, unfettered either by government pressure or substantial union demands. German employers have also managed to establish a powerful lobby[215] which they use with considerable success to campaign against the imposition of

---

[214]   This point lies at the heart of the differences between the protection given to those who leave employment prior to reaching pensionable age. The UK and Dutch legislative frameworks extend protection to individuals much more readily than is the case in Germany. Detailed treatment of these differences will be given in Chapter 6 of this book.

[215]   Which extends to its own press, which means that it is particularly vital when reading German pensions literature that the background of the writer be borne in mind.

more exacting legislative provisions.[216] They simply threaten to withdraw cover should requirements become too onerous, although it must be admitted that this is a common feature of all three jurisdictions examined.

As will emerge even more clearly in Chapter 6, in the UK and the Netherlands the legislator has imposed significant obligations upon employers operating occupational pension schemes, obligations which are more far-reaching than those imposed on German schemes. However, the UK and Dutch legislatures have sweetened the pill of obligations by offering significant tax advantages to employers who operate particular forms of scheme. Tax law is not used in Germany to encourage individuals to belong to pension schemes, and indeed the fact that in certain circumstances, contributions paid by employers to pension schemes are treated as current income in the hands of the employee can be seen to form a significant disincentive to membership of occupational schemes. Voices are increasingly being heard within Germany to improve the use of tax law to encourage employers to make occupational pension provision for their employees.[217]

In fact, the most significant difference between the regulatory systems can be traced to the fact that the most popular forms of pension provision in Germany are those to which employees are not permitted to contribute. This can be seen to encourage an environment in which pensions are not in fact perceived as "belonging" to the employee; as being something to which he or she enjoys rights. The fact that money collected for the purposes of funding occupational pensions in Germany mainly comes from the employer to the exclusion of the employee makes it easier for German employers to resist calls for greater rights to be granted to beneficiaries of such schemes.[218]

---

[216]   Legislation or judgments which are seen as too onerous are generally subjected to a barrage of criticism in the pensions press. See for example, C. Berenz, "Hat die betriebliche Altersversorgung zukünftig noch eine Chance?", 11 NZA (1994), 385-390, 433-438.

[217]   See for example, Festschrift Ahrend; A. Fischer, "German Bank urges fairer tax on pensions", *Financial Times*, 29 November 1995, at p. 3.

[218]   This will be discussed at greater length in Chapter 6 below where the specific rights of pension scheme members will be discussed.

By contrast, in the UK and the Netherlands, it is usual for employees also to contribute to the pension scheme to which they belong. This makes it easier to recognise that they have rights in relation to the scheme, rights deserving of particular standards of protection. It is suggested that the fact that members of schemes are perceived as having "rights" which also explains the UK and Dutch requirements that pension money be kept separate from the sponsoring employer as well as the fundamentally different approaches to when funding will be deemed adequate.[219]

The legal regulation of occupational pensions in the UK and the Netherlands involves the legislator imposing a large number of obligations on employers who wish to profit from all the tax advantages made available to employers offering qualifying schemes. The degree of legislative interference in occupational pension provision is much less in Germany. Ultimately, these differences must be traced back to the different roles played by occupational pension schemes in these Member States.

---

[219] Of course, as the Maxwell debacle demonstrates, this need not form a barrier to employers plundering pension funds.

PART II

PENSIONS AND EQUALITY

STATUTORY PENSION SCHEMES AND EQUALITY

3.1   Introduction

In Chapter 1 the three major challenges to statutory pension provision were outlined. One of these - the demographic predictions as to the future balance of the population - has been interpreted by some as signalling the end of the pension status quo, because these Pay-As-You-Go financed statutory pension schemes would become unaffordable. The boundaries of this research project were described as being to examine whether the proposed replacement for statutory provision - pre-funded, employer based occupational schemes - could deal adequately with the remaining two challenges to pension provision - the increased levels of participation in paid employment by (married) women, and the increased internationalisation of the market.

     The first of these two questions will be addressed in the next Chapter. In this Chapter, I would like briefly to examine the changes which women's participation in paid employment, and the changes in their role which has accompanied this, have required be introduced to statutory pension provision. A discussion of the changes brought about in statutory schemes will provide a context for considering the changes introduced into occupational schemes and will allow conclusions to be drawn in the final Chapter as to whether women are more likely to accrue adequate pensions within statutory or occupational schemes.

     In the next section, some background information will be provided about the ways in which statutory pension schemes in the jurisdictions being considered traditionally operated to the disadvantage of women, and why it was therefore that change was required. Thereafter, a description will be given of the main impetus behind change in this area - EC Directive 79/7.[1] First, its personal and material

---

[1]   Directive 79/7 concerning the progressive implementation of the principle of equal treatment for men and women in matters of social security. O.J. 1979 L 6/24.

scope will be outlined, before the exceptions which it contains are outlined. Thereafter, the impact of the Directive on the discriminatory features of the pension schemes of Member States selected will be outlined, before an evaluation is made of the extent to which the Directive has ensured that women are as able as men to accrue an adequate statutory pension.

3.2   The Discriminatory Features of Statutory Pension Provision

As the discussion in Chapter 2 reveals, the statutory pension schemes which operate in the jurisdictions under consideration, all reflect, to some degree or another, the contributory principle. This means that benefits received reflect somehow the levels of contributions paid in to the scheme. In statutory schemes, this usually occurs with contributions, or periods of insurance in the scheme resulting in credits, which are then revalued on retirement to produce the level of benefit to which the individual is entitled. In the UK and Germany, this has basically brought with it that the statutory pension scheme is concerned with those in paid employment; the fact that the basis for insurance in the Netherlands is residence within its jurisdiction, means that the Dutch system is exceptional in this regard.

However, there are also other assumptions underlying the pension schemes which were put in place in the post-war period.[2] For example, Beveridge, whose report was fundamentally important in shaping the statutory schemes in the UK and the Netherlands, assumed that most women would marry and upon doing so would and should leave the employment market to become part of a household, performing caring, household and other tasks in return for maintenance by a spouse. Indeed, his report stressed the important role to be played by married women in providing for the nation's future. Accordingly, to enable them to fulfill

---

[2]   For a detailed treatment of the development of the statutory pension schemes in place in these states see, Westerveld, loc. cit.; also M. Westerveld, "Yesterday's Choices ... Tomorrow's Blueprint? - One hundred years of Social Security Pensions in the Federal Republic of Germany, the United Kingdom and the Netherlands", in 10 IJCLLIR (1994), 16-35. J.A. Sohrab, *Sexing the Benefit: Women, Social Security and Financial Independence in EC Equality Law*, dissertation, Florence, 1994 at pp. 1-29 and 128-130. For descriptions of the systems currently in place, see the discussion in Chapter 2.

the role he saw for them, he proposed a system offering married women derived entitlement to benefits.[3]

The UK pension system[4] which emerged in response to his report reflected these assumptions, and indeed created incentives for couples to act in this way. Married women were offered the option of paying reduced contributions to the state scheme, in return for which they forfeited their right to a number of benefits. However, a married woman exercising this option "gained" entitlement to a dependent wife's pension on the basis of the contributions history of her spouse.[5] The idea of a wife's financial dependence on her spouse was also reflected in the provisions providing for payment of a widow's pension on the death of a husband, whereas no automatic provision was made in respect of widowers. As contemporary comentators observed, "in the case of the Beveridge Report, the recognition accorded to women's reproductive role had turned into prescription."[6]

A similar story can be told for the Netherlands where the Van Rhijn commission was strongly influenced by the Beveridge report.[7] The Dutch old age pension scheme, the AOW, was also premised on a wife's financial dependence on her spouse. Here, however, the married woman was given no "option". She simply obtained no right to an old age pension, but her husband was paid a

---

[3]   For some of the literature critical of Beveridge, see, for example, S. Baldwin and J. Falkingham, (eds.), *Social Security and Social Change. New Challenges to the Beveridge Model*, London, 1994; D. Groves, "Occupational Pension Provision and Women's Poverty in Old Age", in C. Glendinning and J. Millar (eds.), *Women and Poverty in Britain: the 1990s*, London, 1992 at pp. 193-206 (Groves 1992); J. Lewis (ed.) *Women's Welfare Women's Rights*, London, 1983.

[4]   See Ogus et al, loc. cit. at pp. 15-16, 61-62; Westerveld, loc. cit. at p. 95; J. Ginn and S. Arber, "Heading for Hardship: How the British pension system has failed women", in Baldwin and Falkingham (eds.), loc. cit. pp. 216-234 at p. 216.

[5]   See Ginn and Arber, loc. cit. at p. 217; Westerveld, loc. cit. at p. 151; S. Atkins and L. Luckhaus, "The Social Security Directive and UK Law" in C. McCrudden (ed.), *Women, Employment and European Equality Law*, London, 1987, pp. 103-122 at p. 106.

[6]   J. Lewis, "Dealing with Dependency: State Practices and Social Realities, 1870-1945", in Lewis (ed.), loc. cit. pp. 17-37 at pp. 19-20.

[7]   See Westerveld, loc. cit. at pp. 121-125, 254-262 and 415-442.

supplement in respect of her instead, to reflect the greater costs incurred by a two-person household. Like the British, the Dutch also made provision for payment of a widow's pension under the *Algemeen Weduwen- en Wezenwet* (AWW).[8]

The German system was less obviously premised on a wife's financial dependence her husband.[9] Pension rights were built up on the basis of an individual's employment history but this system too would often result in women becoming financially dependent upon their spouses.[10] Indeed, dependence was encouraged by the scheme in a manner similar to that in the UK in that married women could stop contributing.[11] The result of this system for a woman who gave up paid employment on marriage, or the birth of a child,[12] was that her pension accrual would cease, and even if she later returned to paid employment, the level of pension which she eventually received would be reduced as a result of time spent out of the employment market. So in fact, like her Dutch and British

---

[8]   Most recently consolidated at Stb. 1990, 127. See the discussion in L.G.M. Stevens (ed.), *Pensioen en andere toekomstvoorzieningen*, Deventer, looseleaf at III.C. Note that this has recently been replaced by the *Algemene Nabestaandenwet* (ANW), law of 21 December 1995, Stb. 1995, 690.

[9]   See Westerveld, loc. cit. at pp. 174-177, 308-323 and 352-354.

[10]   As a consequence of low pay and interrupted careers.

[11]   M. Veil, ""Es wächst zusammen, was nicht zusammen gehört" - Die Frau im Rentenrecht der ehemaligen Deutschen Demokratischen Republik und der Bundesrepublik Deutschland" in Gather et al (eds.), loc. cit. pp. 191-204 at p. 197.

[12]   It is apparently the case that women's disadvantageous position in relation to contributory social security schemes is caused not by marriage but by childbirth. G. Rolf, "Ideologiekritik am Rentenrecht und ein Reformvorschlag zur eigenständigen Alterssicherung von Frauen" in Gather et al, loc. cit., pp. 175-190 at pp. 177-185 produces tables which demonstrate how particular periods of time outside of employment, or in part-time employment, as a consequence of childcare affects pension accrual. A. Tölke, "Heirat und Geburt als Einschnitte in der weiblichen Erwerbsbiographie", in Gather et al, loc. cit., pp. 32-45 at pp. 37-41 discusses the effects of marriage and childbirth on women's participation rates in paid employment; see also K. Prinz, "Die Bedeutung der Kindererziehung für die Erwerbsverläufe und die Alterssicherung von Frauen in der Bundesrepublik Deutschland und der ehemaligen Deutschen Demokratischen Republik" in Gather et al, loc. cit. pp. 46-61 at pp. 56-59 discusses the effects of children and part-time work on wages, career and the fact that it increases the likelihood of unemployment. See in the Dutch context, *inter alia*, R. Holtmaat, *Met zorg een recht? Een analyse van het politiek-juridisch vertoog over bijstandsrecht*, Zwolle, 1992 at p. 52. For the UK, see Groves 1992, loc. cit. at p. 201.

counterpart on retirement she would receive a level of pension which resulted in her being financially dependent on her spouse. This conclusion is confirmed by the fact that the German statutory scheme also made provision for payment of a widow's pension.

Where provision was made for paying a woman a pension in her own right, the most obvious way in which the notion of dependence on men was reflected was in setting different pensionable ages for women and men. This was the practice in the UK[13] and Germany.[14] In the UK, the Widow's, Orphans and Old Age Contributory Pensions Act 1925 had provided pensions at the same age for women as for men. However, between 1925 and 1946, as a result of pressure from (ironically) the women's movement, women's pensionable age was lowered. It had been argued first, that single women above the age of 60 could not find employment and so should be paid their pension from this age. Second, it was argued that since women generally marry men a few years older than themselves, an equal pensionable age meant that in the first few years of retirement, the marital income dropped, which caused most married men to postpone retirement until their spouse also was 65.[15] By contrast, the justification for this practice in the German literature points to women's lower pensionable age as recognition of the fact that during their active lives, they are often burdened by both paid and unpaid responsibilities.[16]

---

[13]   Where women qualified for a full retirement pension aged 60, and in relation to which a full contributions history was 39 years. Men on the other hand, could claim their pensions from the age of 65, and a full contributions history was 44 years.

[14]   Currently, the standard old age pension is payable from the age of 65 for both women and men. However, women who satisfy the waiting period of 15 years and who have paid compulsory contributions for at least 10 years since reaching the age of 40 are entitled to retire at the age of 60 (para. 39 SGB VI).

[15]   See Westerveld, loc. cit. at pp. 60-62.

[16]   P. Ahrend and D. Beucher, "Die Gleichberechtigung der Geschlechter in der betrieblichen Altersversorgung seit dem Barber-Urteil des EuGH", BetrAVG 1993, 253-258; J. Rühmann, "Auswirkung der neueren EuGH-Rechtsprechung auf die Gestaltung betrieblicher Versorgungsregelungen", BetrAVG (1994), 107-114; J. Rühmann and E. Heissmann, "Sex Discrimination - The German View", International Pension Lawyer 1994, no. 16, 14.

Finally, schemes typically operated hours or earnings thresholds. These excluded from the scheme individuals earning below a particular amount and/or whose weekly or monthly working hourse fell below a nationally defined standard. The effect of these rules was generally to exclude women from scheme membership[17] and they represent the final main method through which it was made difficult for women to accrue independent social security entitlement.

As even this cursory glance at state provision in these jurisdictions reveals, pension provision was designed to reward men and those undertaking full-time uninterrupted employment.[18] Mechanisms were put in place to encourage men to organise their lives in such a way, with women being encouraged to adopt a subordinate, dependent role out of the labour market and to look to their spouse for their financial needs.

However, as was mentioned in Chapter 1, in the decades after the second world war, the position of women in society began incrementally to change. Increasing numbers of married women chose to continue in employment after their marriage.[19] They rejected the roles to which the pension schemes condemned them, as they began to enjoy the economic benefits of paid employment. Equally, the rise in the divorce rate convinced many women of the fact that it would be foolish to depend upon their marriage surviving until both parties reached pensionable age. In other words, a change took place in society, and it was necessary that the law adapt to reflect this. In the adaptations which took place in relation to statutory pension schemes, a key role was played by EC law.

---

[17]   For example, in the UK in 1990 some 2.25 million women were estimated to have been excluded from the compulsory contributory social security scheme because their earnings fell below the LEL. See C. McCrudden and J. Black, "Achieving Equality between Men and Women in Social Security: Some issues of costs and problems of implementation", in McCrudden (ed.) 1994, loc. cit. pp. 169-194 at p. 172. At para. 75 of his opinion in Joined Cases C-245/94 and C-312/94, *Hoever and Zachow* v. *Land Nordrhein-Westfalen*, opinion of 2 May 1996, Advocate General Jacobs cites statistics adduced by the German government to the effect that the overwhelming majority of those working part-time are women, and 75% of those working "insignificant" hours are women.

[18]   In the German context, Rolf, loc. cit. at pp. 175-176 discusses the patterns of employment which the statutory scheme is designed to reward. However, her observations are equally pertinent to the UK and the Netherlands.

[19]   See the figures cited by Tölke, loc. cit. at pp. 37-38.

3.3 EC Law - The Background

3.3.1 THE PAUCITY OF TREATY SOCIAL PROVISIONS

Any trawl through the TEU in search of a provision requiring that men and women be treated equally in relation to social security pensions will be in vain. In fact, a search for provisions concerning social policy will produce very little - Title VIII Chapter 1,[20] and, since the entry into force of the amendments agreed at Maastricht in December 1991, the Protocol and Agreement on Social Policy.[21]

---

[20] D. Collins, *The European Communities: The Social Policy of the First Phase*, Volume 2: *The European Economic Community 1958-1972*, London, 1975; L.H.J. Crijns, "Het Sociale Beleid van de Europese Gemeenschap", in F.A.J. van den Bosch and A.M. Dancot-Devriendt (eds.), *Sociaal en zeker*, Deventer, 1986, pp. 149-175; M. Shanks, *European Social Policy Today and Tomorrow*, Oxford, 1977; M. Shanks, "The Social Policy of the European Communities", 14 CML Rev. (1977), 375-383.

[21] On which see the various opinions expressed by, *inter alia*, C. Barnard, "A Social Policy for Europe: Politicians 1: 0 Lawyers", IJCLLIR (1992), 15-31; B. Bercusson, "Maastricht: A Fundamental Change in European Labour Law", 23 IRJ (1993), 177-190; B. Bercusson, "The dynamic of European Labour Law after Maastricht", 23 ILJ (1994), 1-31; B. Bercusson and J.J. van Dijk, "The Implementation of the Protocol and Agreement on Social Policy of the Treaty on European Union", 11 IJCLLIR (1995), 3-30; D. Curtin, "The constitutional structure of the union: A Europe of bits and pieces", 30 CML Rev. (1993), 17-69; B. Fitzpatrick, "Community social law after Maastricht", 21 ILJ (1992), 199-213; P. Lange, "Maastricht and the Social Protocol: Why did they do it?", 21 *Politics and Society* (1993), 5-36; P. Lange, "The Politics of the Social Dimension", in A.M. Sbragia (ed.), *Euro-Politics. Institutions and Policymaking in the "New" European Community*, Washington, 1992, at pp. 225-256; M. Rhodes, "The Future of the Social Dimension: Labour Market Regulation in Post-1992 Europe", JCMS (1993), 23-51; M. Rhodes, "The Social Dimension after Maastricht: Setting a new Agenda for the Labour Market", IJCLLIR (1993), 297-325; G. Schuster, "Rechtsfragen der Maastrichter Vereinbarungen zur Sozialpolitik", 1992 EuZW, 178-187; J.-C. Séché, "L'europe sociale après Maastricht", CDE (1993), 509-536; J. Shaw, "Twin-Track Social Europe - the Inside Track", in D. O'Keeffe and P.M. Twomey (eds.), *Legal Issues of the Maastricht Treaty*, London 1994, at pp. 295-311; E. Szyszczak, "Social Policy: a Happy Ending or a Reworking of the Fairy Tale?", in O'Keeffe and Twomey (eds.), loc. cit. at pp. 313-327; E. Szyszczak, "Future Directions in European Union Social Law", 24 ILJ (1995), 19-32; R. Vaubel, "Social Regulation and Market Integration: A Critique and Public-Choice Analysis of the Social Chapter", 50 *Aussenwirtschaft* (1995), 111-132; P. Watson, "Social Policy after Maastricht", 30 CML Rev. (1993), 481-513; M. Weiss, "The significance of Maastricht for European Community Social Policy", 1992, IJCLLIR 3-14; E.A. Whiteford, "De sociale dimensie van de EG na Maastricht: oude wijn in nieuwe zakken", 18 NJCM (1993), 110-132; E.A. Whiteford, "Social Policy after

The paucity of social provisions, despite the statement in the TEU that the objectives of the Union are

"to promote economic and social progress for their peoples, within the context of the accomplishment of the internal market ... and to implement policies ensuring that advances in economic progress are accompanied by parallel progress in other fields",[22]

is however easily explained.

The drafters of the Treaty of Rome sought to create a framework for the creation of a common market, in which all obstacles to intra-Community trade would be abolished to merge the national markets into a single market bringing conditions as close as possible to those in a genuine internal market.[23] The operation of this market was to be one of free and open competition[24] between economic operators. In designing the legal framework within which this market was to operate, one of the dilemmas which faced the drafters of the Treaty was whether it was necessary to harmonise social charges in the Member States in the interests of free and fair competition.[25]

Maastricht" 18 EL Rev. (1993), 202-222; E.A. Whiteford, "W(h)ither Social Policy?", in G. More and J. Shaw (eds.), *New Legal Dynamics of European Union*, Oxford, 1995 at pp. 111-128.

[22]   For the significance of the changes introduced into the list of objectives by the TEU, see the comments in Kapteyn, VerLoren van Themaat, *Inleiding tot het recht van de Europese Gemeenschappen - Na Maastricht*, Deventer, 5th ed. 1995 at pp. 69-87.

[23]   See for example Case 15/81, *Gaston Schul* v. *Inspecteur der Invoerrechten en Accijnzen*, [1982] ECR 1409, para. 33.

[24]   Art. 3(g) EC (formerly art. 3(f) EEC).

[25]   One of the clearest expositions of these arguments is to be found in ILO Studies and Reports (New Series) No. 46, *Social Aspects of European Economic Co-operation* (hereafter ILO Report), Geneva 1956. See also, R. Nielsen and E. Szyszczak, *The Social Dimension of the European Community*, Copenhagen, 1993 at pp. 16-18; P. Davies, "The Emergence of European Labour Law", in W. McCarthy (ed.), *Legal Intervention in Industrial Relations: Gains and Losses*, Oxford, 1992, at pp. 313-359; S. Deakin and F. Wilkinson, "Rights vs Efficiency? The Economic Case for Transnational Labour Standards", 23 ILJ (1994), 289-310; C. Barnard, *EC Employment Law*, Chichester, 1995 at pp. 81-87; S. Deakin and C. Barnard, "Social Policy in Search of a Role: Integration, Cohesion and Citizenship", in A. Caiger and D.A.M.-A. Floudas (eds.) *1996 Onwards: Lowering the Barriers Further*, Chichester, 1996 at pp. 177-195, esp at pp. 178-187.

For these purposes, social charges must be understood as covering matters with both direct and indirect pecuniary consequences for undertakings. An example of a rule with direct pecuniary consequences for an undertaking would be national legislation setting a minimum wage or requiring that a particular percentage of the pay roll be contributed to the state social security scheme. Rules with indirect pecuniary consequences for undertakings are, for example, those which provide employees with a high level of protection against dismissal or which prohibit them working above a particular weekly or daily hours threshold. These kinds of provision do not directly impose higher costs on employers but can, where an employer wishes to react swiftly to market conditions - a boom or sudden recession - impose obstacles to his ability to adjust his undertaking to the changed environment, and thereby force him to incur extra costs.

On one side of the argument as to the relevance of social costs to the Treaty were those who considered that differences in social costs could operate as a means of distorting competition. They took the view that firms in Member States in which workers enjoyed relatively high levels of protection would be seduced by the less expensive (but more exploitative) conditions existing in competing countries, to relocate their undertakings to these environments.[26] It was argued that without harmonisation, governments would either dismantle existing protective legislation or refuse to introduce improvements in the future for fear of the consequences of such actions for the competitiveness of undertakings established

---

[26] The decision of the Hoover company to relocate production from Dijon in France to Cambuslang in Scotland, allegedly because of less stringent employee protection in the latter, forms a recent example of the sort of conduct feared by proponents of this view. On the Hoover case see, "The Hoover Affair and Social Dumping", 1993 *European Industrial Relations Review* 230, at 14; Watson, op. cit. at 512-513; Editorial Comments, "Are European values being hoovered away?", 30 CML Rev. (1993), 445-448. Another more recent possible example was the decision of the German firm Siemens to open a major manufacturing plant in Tyneside in Northern England. On television interview, the representative of Siemens cited as an important factor infuencing their choice of location the "flexibility" of the workforce. He observed that it would be possible for the firm to operate 24 hours a day, 7 days a week with three shifts of workers. It was also a positive factor for the firm that there were plenty of individuals to be found who would be willing to work under such conditions. Placing these remarks in the context of European integration, it seems clear that the lower levels of legal protection enjoyed by British workers formed a major incentive to the firm to locate production there. (In addition to huge government subsidies, and unspecified levels of local investment aid.)

within their territory. Failure to harmonise social charges would, on this view, lead
to a reduction in social protection in the Union and potentially increase the
exploitation of the least protected.[27]

According to the opponents of this view, differences in social costs
generally reflect differences between the labour markets in the countries concerned,
such as higher productivity or skills.[28] Consequently, such differences rather than
distorting competitive conditions within the single market are in fact a necessary
component of the efficient operation of that market.

The drafters of the Treaty of Rome can be seen largely to have been
convinced by the arguments of the second group.[29] Although the Treaty seeks to
realise an improvement in the living and working conditions of Union citizens, the
primary vehicle through which this is to be achieved is the operation of the market.
In the eyes of the drafters, despite social policy's potential to impose different
costs on undertakings operating in different jurisdictions, it was not to be viewed
in primarily economic terms. Consequently, it was not seen to be central to the
European project as a result of which the Union was given scarcely any powers to

---

[27]   "The main economic argument for concerted international action in the field of social policy
        is that in the absence of international co-ordination the efforts of some countries to introduce
        improvements in social standards and conditions may be frustrated by the competition of
        other countries with a less developed social conscience." ILO Report, op. cit. at 85.

[28]   "Differences in the general level of labour costs do not give rise to special difficulties from
        the point of view of international competition, since countries with high labour costs per
        hour possess advantages which compensate for these high costs." ILO Report, op. cit. at 73.

[29]   As were the ILO Experts. They concluded that "[i]nternational differences in the general
        level of worker's remuneration, far from being an obstacle to freer international trade, are,
        so long as differences in productivity persist, indispensable, though not in themselves
        sufficient, to ensure the allocation of manpower and capital in each country to those
        industries in which it has the greatest advantages or the smallest disadvantages, so as to
        ensure maximum output and incomes in all participating countries." op. cit. at 111.
        Nevertheless, they did mitigate this conclusion somewhat, concluding that in some cases
        fixing minimum standards might eliminate abnormal competition and indeed contribute to
        freer international trade. Op. cit. at 71-2. Davies, loc. cit. observes that the crucial point
        about the ILO report is that the drafters' conception about how freer international trade was
        to be brought about and how its benefits would be diffused did not lead them to perceive
        many very substantial social problems needing Community solution.

adopt legislation in this field.[30] Nevertheless, as the discussion in the remainder of this Chapter and the next reveals, this has not prevented a significant body of law being adopted in the field of social policy, some of which has had far-reaching consequences for pension provision in the Member States.

3.3.2   SEX EQUALITY LAW IN THE TREATY AND BEYOND

The social provisions of the Treaty contained in Title VIII Chapter 1, have been described as "programmatic" in character, serving as an interpretative aid to other provisions of the Treaty rather than granting individuals specific substantive directly effective rights.[31] Consequently, it continues to be the case that competence in the social field remains squarely with the Member States.[32]

Article 119, which will be discussed at length in Chapter 4 below, is the exception to the largely programmatic character of most of the provisions in the social chapter of the Treaty. It requires that the Member States ensure that women and men receive equal pay for equal work and enjoys vertical and horizontal direct effects,[33] as a result of which it has had far-reaching consequences for the laws and practices of the Member States. Although the requirement that women and men receive equal pay for equal work can be seen to be an aspect of social policy, the inclusion of an equal pay norm in the Treaty was apparently prompted by

---

[30]   Social policy is often included in what has been termed "flanking policies". See R.C. Lane, "New Community Competences under the Maastricht Treaty", 30 CML Rev. (1993), 939-979; K. Mortelmans "De interne markt en het facettenbeleid na het Keck-arrest: nationaal beleid, vrij verkeer of harmonisatie", 42 S.E.W. (1994), 236-250 at 238-9; Kapteyn VerLoren van Themaat, loc. cit. at pp. 639-660.

[31]   Case 126/86, *Giminez Zaera* v. *Instituto Nacional de la Seguridad Social y Tesorería General de la Seguridad Social*, [1987] ECR 3697 at para.s 11 and 14. Article 117 does appear to have operated as an interpretative aid to Article 119 in Case 43/75, *Defrenne* v. *Sabena*, [1976] ECR 455 (*Defrenne II*) at para. 15. See also Joined Cases C-72/91 and C-73/91, *Sloman Neptun Schiffahrts AG* v. *Seebetriebsrat Bodo Ziesemer der Sloman Neptun Schiffahrts AG*, [1993] ECR I-887; see note by P.J. Slot, 31 CML Rev. (1994), 137-146.

[32]   Case 163/73, *Commission* v. *France*, [1974] ECR 359; Case C-113/89, *Rush Portuguesa* v. *Office National d'Immigration*, [1990] ECR I-1417.

[33]   Case 43/75, *Defrenne II*, cited *supra* at para. 39.

economic considerations.[34] More specifically, France, whose domestic sex equality legislation was more far-reaching than that of her future partners, feared that her industry would suffer competitive disadvantage if no such provision was included in the Treaty. She feared that firms established elsewhere would undercut French firms by using female labour which was less well paid than male labour.[35] Although economic considerations played a role in its inclusion in the Treaty, the Court has interpreted Article 119 as serving both economic and social ends,[36] and has even gone so far as to hold that sexual equality forms part of the foundations of the Community.[37]

However, in the first request for a preliminary ruling on this Article's scope, the Court took a cautious approach. It excluded from the ambit of the equal pay principle the pensions which were at issue in the case which were

> "directly governed by legislation without any element of agreement within the undertaking or the occupational branch

---

[34]   Barnard 1996, loc. cit. at pp. 321-334; Hoskyns, loc. cit. at pp. 43-59.

[35]   Prior to the signing of the Treaty of Rome, a committee of experts was convened under the auspices of the ILO to consider *Social Aspects of European Economic Cooperation* (ILO Studies and Reports (New Series) No. 46, Geneva 1956, discussed by Barnard, loc. cit. at pp. 81-87; Davies, loc. cit. at pp. 313-359; Deakin and Wilkinson, op. cit. at 289-310; Deakin and Barnard, loc. cit. at pp. 177-195; Nielsen and Szyszczak, loc. cit. at pp. 16-18. They basically concluded that there was no need to harmonise social costs among the Member States generally, but that "[w]age differentials according to sex constitute a particular case of low wages in industries in which a large proportion of female labour is employed. When such differentials are not the result of special circumstances affecting employment opportunities for female workers in certain areas but are due to such factors as tradition and the absence of effective organisation of female workers in trade unions, it will be desirable to create such conditions as will enable these differentials to be gradually abolished, taking into account the ILO Equality of Remuneration Convention." ILO Report, footnote at 112-113.

[36]   Case 43/75, *Defrenne II*, cited *supra* at paras. 8-10.

[37]   Case 149/77, *Defrenne* v. *SABENA*, [1978] ECR 1365, (*Defrenne III*) at paras. 26-27. See C. Docksey, "The Principle of Equality between Women and Men as a Fundamental Right under Community Law", 20 ILJ (1991), 258-280. For a more critical approach, see S. Fredman, "European Community Sex Discrimination Law: A critique", 21 ILJ (1992), 119-134; H. Fenwick and T.K. Hervey, "Sex Equality in the Single Market: New Directions for the European Court of Justice", 32 CML Rev. (1995), 443-470.

concerned ... obligatorily applicable to general categories of workers."[38]

It thus immediately excluded statutory pensions from the scope of Article 119. Consequently, if equality was to be introduced in this area as a result of Community law, further legislation would be required.

When equality between women and men is viewed through the optic of competition, it becomes logical to extend the principle through all aspects of the employment relationship. This was precisely the course of action followed by the Community.[39] Thus, the Council resolution concerning the Social Action Programme[40] expressed the political will to

> "undertake action for the purpose of achieving equality between women and men as regards access to employment and vocational training and advancement and as regards working conditions, including pay..."

This led first, to the adoption of the Equal Pay Directive[41] which the Court has held restates the principle of equal pay set out in Article 119, without altering its

---

[38]   Case 80/70, *Defrenne* v. *Belgian State*, [1971] ECR 445 (*Defrenne I*) at para. 7.

[39]   Streeck (op. cit.) suggests that the EC was able to make sex equality law its own because in none of the Member States had sex equality emerged as an important issue at the time. Consequently, the EC was not intruding upon well-developed areas of national law and policy.

[40]   Resolution on a Social Action Programme, O.J. 1974, C 13/1. The Social Action Programme was published at Bull. EC Supp. 2/74 at p. 8. In it, the Member States undertook to adopt between 30 and 40 measures over a three year period to realise the three main objectives of the programme: 1. full employment; 2. improvement in living and working conditions; 3. greater involvement of the social partners in European decision-making. Although many of the measures contained in the Action Programme were indeed undertaken, only a very small number required that legislation be adopted, perhaps reflecting the limitations of the Treaty. See the discussion in B. Bercusson, *European Labour Law*, London, 1996, at pp. 49-52; Crijns, loc. cit. at pp. 159-161. The most detailed treatment is to be found in Shanks, loc. cit.

[41]   Directive 75/117, O.J. 1975, L 45/19. E. Ellis, *European Community Sex Equality Law*, Oxford, 1991 at pp. 95-116; C. Hoskyns, *Integrating Gender. Women, Law and Politics in the European Union*, London, 1996 at pp. 78-96; S. Prechal and N. Burrows, *Gender Discrimination Law of the European Community*, Aldershot, 1990 at pp. 81-98.

content or scope.[42] However, the precise scope of the equal pay principle remained the subject of controversy. For example, while the Directive was being drafted, the subject of occupational pension schemes apparently arose.[43] Some delegations, prompted by the Commission, queried whether the equal pay principle covered, or ought to be interpreted as covering, occupational pension schemes. The Council decided that procrastination was best, and a reference to occupational schemes was ultimately ommitted from the Directive, on the ground that since occupational schemes supplement the benefits paid by statutory schemes, equality in the latter was a precondition for equality in the former. EC law did not require equality in statutory schemes, so equality could not be required from occupational schemes.[44]

However, the genie was by then well and truly out of the bottle. The next piece of legislation to emerge from the Social Action Programme was the Equal Treatment Directive.[45] This covered access to employment, vocational training and promotion, and working conditions. The original draft also sought to remove the "absurdity"[46] of discriminating against women in relation to pensions by requiring that men and women be treated equally in respect of social security. However, at the last minute the references to social security were dropped from the Directive,[47] and, at the insistence of the Commission, replaced with an

---

[42]   Case 96/80, *Jenkins* v. *Kingsgate (Clothing Productions) Ltd.*, [1981] ECR 911.

[43]   Prechal and Burrows, loc. cit. at pp. 165-166.

[44]   The Court's response to this argumentation will be discussed in the next Chapter.

[45]   Directive 76/207, O.J. 1976, L 39/40. See the discussions in Ellis, loc. cit. at pp. 117-178; T.K. Hervey, *Justifications for sex discrimination in employment*, London, 1993 at pp. 47-79; Hoskyns, loc. cit. at pp. 99-107; Prechal and Burrows, loc. cit. at pp. 104-164.

[46]   The EOC has observed, "There is in any case an absurdity, at least in terms of a consistent social policy, in securing for employees the right to equal pay throughout their careers, only in effect to abandon it at the point of retirement." EOC, *Unisex Pricing in Long Term Insurance: An Independent Report by Actuarial Consultants Tillinghast*, Manchester, 1989 at p. VI.

[47]   See for example, Hoskyns, loc. cit. at p. 105; C. Hoskyns and L. Luckhaus, "The European Community Directive on Equal Treatment in Social Security", 17 *Policy and Politics* (1989), 321-335 at 322; Sohrab, loc. cit. at pp. 61-62.

undertaking to adopt a separate Directive dealing with equality and social security schemes.[48]

The Directive obliging the Member States progressively to introduce equality into their social security systems was finally adopted in December 1978.[49] The original draft covered both occupational and statutory social security schemes but a last minute amendment was made to postpone mandating equality in occupational schemes until a later date.[50] In this respect, Directive 79/7 is merely a first step. It requires merely the *progressive* implementation of the principle of equal treatment for men and women in matters of social security, and is subject to a number of exceptions. The scope of the Directive will be discussed in the next sections.

3.4   Directive 79/7 - Personal Scope

The personal scope of the Directive is outlined in Article 2. It covers

"the working population - including self-employed persons, workers and self-employed persons whose activity is interrupted by illness, accident or involuntary unemployment and persons seeking employment - and to retired or invalided workers and self-employed persons."

Although the Directive does not explicitly state that it is concerned only with those members of the working population engaged in some form of earning activity, the Directive is in fact so limited as a consequence of the case law of the ECJ. In a number of cases, the Court has held that the Directive only applies to men and

---

[48]   Art. 1(2) of the Directive.

[49]   Directive 79/7, O.J. 1979, L 6/24. See, Ellis, loc. cit. at pp. 179-205; Hoskyns, loc. cit. at pp. 107-113; Hoskyns and Luckhaus, op. cit.; Prechal and Burrows, loc. cit. at pp. 165-203; Sohrab, loc. cit. at pp. 60-120; J.A. Sohrab, "Women and Social Security: the Limits of EEC Equality Law", *Journal of Social Welfare and Family Law*, (1994), 5-17. Actually, two Directives were adopted to deal with "social security". Directive 79/7 deals with statutory social security schemes, and shall be the subject of discussion in this chapter. In addition, Directive 86/378 (O.J. 1986, L 225/40) was adopted to deal with occupational schemes. The latter Directive will be discussed in Chapter 4 below.

[50]   This will be discussed in the next Chapter.

women in their capacity of workers,[51] by which it is clear that the Court means that the individual in question performs an "effective and genuine economic activity"[52] "for remuneration ... the nature of which [employment] is not determined by himself for and under the control of another, regardless of the legal nature of the employment relationship."[53] Although the case law on the concept of worker was developed in the context of the free movement of workers,[54] not sex equality, the Court has recently asserted that, as far as possible, the concept should have the same meaning irrespective of the area of Commuity law concerned.[55] As is clear from this outline, only those in paid activities are covered although persons who have never been employed will be covered by the Directive if they can demonstrate that they are seeking employment at the time the risk materialises.[56] The mere fact that national legislation concerning one of the risks covered by the Directive[57] covers a particular individual, is not sufficient to bring that person within the scope of the Directive.[58] They must also be able to demonstrate that they satisfy the requirements of the Directive.

The limitations in the personal scope of the Directive, reduce significantly its potential to eradicate discriminatory provisions and practices from statutory pension schemes. As a consequence of its preoccupation with paid employment,

---

[51]   See for example, Cases 48, 106, 107/88, *Achterberg te-Riele and others* v. *Social Verzekeringsraad*, [1989] ECR 1963. See the discussion in Sohrab, loc. cit. at pp. 63-67.

[52]   Case 53/81, *Levin* v. *Staatssecretaris van Justitie*, [1982] ECR 1035 at para. 19.

[53]   Case 66/85, *Lawrie-Blum* v. *Land Baden-Württemberg*, [1986] ECR 2121 at para. 17.

[54]   On which, see the discussion in Chapter 5 below.

[55]   Case C-317/93, *Nolte* v. *Landesversicherungsantalt Hannover*, [1995] ECR I-4625 at para. 21; Case C-444/93, *Megner and Scheffel* v. *Innungskrankenkasse Vorderpfalz*, [1995] ECR I-4741 at para. 20.

[56]   Case C-31/90, *Johnson* v. *Chief Adjudication Officer*, [1993] ECR I-3723.

[57]   For the material scope of the Directive, see the next section.

[58]   See Joined Cases C-87-89/90, *Verholen*, cited *supra*. Note the contrast between this and the position for Regulation 1408/71. On which see the discussion in Chapter 5 below.

it offers nothing to women who have carried out valuable unpaid activities at home. However, limiting the Directive to social security schemes providing protection to the economically active can be seen to be a logical consequence of the limitations of the competence which the Community enjoys in the social sphere.[59] Unfortunately, the limitations of the personal scope are exacerbated by limitations in the Directive's material scope, as we shall discover in the next section.

3.5 Directive 79/7 - Material Scope

The material scope of the Directive is to be found in Article 3 which provides:

> "This Directive shall apply to: (a) statutory schemes which provide protection against the following risks: sickness, invalidity, old age, accidents at work and occupational diseases, unemployment; (b) social assistance, in so far as it is intended to supplement or replace the schemes referred to in (a)."

In its early case law, the Court held that to fall within the scope of Directive 79/7, a benefit "must constitute the whole or part of a statutory scheme providing protection against one of the specified risks or a form of social assistance having the same objective."[60] In taking this approach, the Court appeared to be motivated by a desire to promote the uniform application of the Directive throughout the Community, irrespective of the idiosyncrasies of individual national regimes.[61]

However, recently the Court appears to have taken a more conservative turn. For a benefit to fall within the scope of the Directive it now appears that it must be "directly and effectively linked to the protection provided against one of

---

[59]   See the discussion in s.3.3 above.

[60]   Case 150/85, *Drake* v. *Chief Adjudication Officer*, [1986] ECR 1995 at para. 21.

[61]   See Case 150/85, *Drake*, cited *supra* at para. 23. See also the opinion of the Advocate General in Case C-243/90, *R.* v. *Secretary of State for Social Security, ex parte Smithson*, [1992] ECR I-467; Case C-228/94, *Atkins* v. *Wrekin District Council and Department of Transport*, judgment of 11 July 1996, nyr at para. 20.

the risks specified in Article 3(1)."[62] So the mere fact that one of the risks listed in Article 3(1) has materialised *vis-à-vis* an individual who is in receipt of a benefit is not sufficient to bring him or her within the scope of the Directive. For example, benefits paid to an individual who happens to be over pensionable age and not in paid employment do not fall within the scope of the Directive simply because the receiving individual can be defined as a pensioner. It is also required that the main aim of the benefit must be to provide income to pensioners if it is to fall within its scope.

This coupled with the restrictive personal scope of the Directive seems likely to exclude many women from its scope. For example, a woman who has ceased to work as a consequence of the birth of a child will fall outside the scope of the Directive.[63] Only once she is actively seeking employment does she again fall within its scope. Similarly, a benefit designed to provide financial support to individuals whose income falls below a particular level does not fall within the scope of the Directive, even if the individual in question is unemployed.[64] As such, it is clear that the Directive depends heavily upon the existing structures of benefits in place in the Member States

Finally, it is clear that social assistance in general falls outwith the scope of the Directive. It is only where it supplements or replaces[65] the social security protection (previously) provided in respect of one of the enumerated risks that it

---

[62]   See for example, Case C-243/90, *Smithson*, cited *supra* at para. 14; Joined Cases C-63/91 and C-64/91, *Jackson and Cresswell* v. *Chief Adjudication Officer*, [1992] ECR I-4737; Case C-228/94, *Atkins*, cited *supra*. See also L. Luckhaus, "Intentions and the Avoidance of Community Law", 21 ILJ (1992), 315-322; M. Cousins, "Equal Treatment and Social Security", 19 EL Rev. (1994), 123-145; Sohrab, loc. cit. at pp. 69-71.

[63]   Case C-31/90, *Johnson*, cited *supra*.

[64]   See for example, Joined Cases C-63/91 and C-64/91, *Jackson and Cresswell*, cited *supra*.

[65]   This formulation was presumably chosen to prevent the Member States from avoiding the obligations of the Directive simply by reclassifying benefits as social assistance. However, given the "direct and effective" test, it may be that such actions would now stand a greater chance of success than they would have done in the past. See also the observations below on justifications for discriminatory provisions.

falls within Directive 79/7.[66] This is another unfortunate limitation in the scope of the Directive when it is viewed from the perspective of improving the income provided to women. As Holtmaat has demonstrated,[67] women are more likely to be in receipt of social assistance benefits than social security benefits. Consequently, excluding this class of benefit from the Directive's scope limits significantly its potential to eradicate discrimination. The significance of this in this context is that given the difficulties which women have had in accruing adequate levels of pensions in the past, they are likely to be in need of social assistance benefits to supplement their own incomes but the benefits to which they are most likely to have recourse are precisely those in relation to which discrimination is still permitted.

3.6   Directive 79/7 - Discrimination and Justifications

According to Article 4, the implementation of the principle of equal treatment in statutory schemes requires the elimination of both direct and indirect discrimination on grounds of sex.[68] As the Court has repeatedly held, Article 4 enjoys direct effect,[69] requiring that as of 23 December 1984, the date from which the Directive had to be implemented, all discrimination must be removed from the statutory scheme, and that no discrimination which was practiced prior to this date

---

[66]   See the discussion on this point in Case C-228/94, *Atkins*, cited *supra* at para.s 22-31.

[67]   Holtmaat, loc. cit. This is corroborated by the findings of, *inter alia*, S. Field and H. Prior, *Women and Pensions*, DSS Research Report 50.

[68]   The Commission apparently doubted the necessity of introducing a reference to indirect discrimination, taking the view that indirect discrimination was inconceivable in social security schemes. As the following discussion will demonstrate, this view has proved ill-founded.

[69]   Initially in Case 71/85, *State of the Netherlands* v. *FNV*, [1986] ECR 3855.

be allowed to perpetuate.[70] As such, this would suggest that the Directive ought to have far-reaching consequences for the practices described at the beginning of this Chapter.

Direct discrimination occurs where the rule expressly differentiates on grounds of sex. So for example, it is directly discriminatory to offer a survivor's pension only to widows and not to widowers.[71] Indirect discrimination occurs where a rule which is prima facie neutral in formulation, can be demonstrated to affect one sex to a disproportionate extent.[72] A common example of indirect discrimination in social security legislation is the breadwinner requirement, offering a particular benefit only to someone with dependents. Although neutrally formulated, in fact more men than women will typically be able to qualify, because of the continuing prevalence of the traditional division of responsibilities within families. As such, a presumption of indirect discrimination will be raised, and the onus of proof will then shift to the state seeking to defend the provision to demonstrate that the rule is "objectively justified" by factors which have nothing

---

[70]   See Case 384/85, *Borrie-Clarke* v. *Chief Adjudication Officer*, [1987] ECR 2865; Case 80/87, *Dik* v. *College van Burgemeester en Wethouders der Gemeente Arnhem en Winterswijk*, [1988] ECR 1601; Case C-377/89, *Cotter and others* v. *Minister for Social Welfare and others*, [1991] ECR I-1155; joined Cases C-87-89/90, *Verholen*, cited *supra*; Case C-338/91, *Steenhorst-Neerings* v. *Bestuur van de Bedrijfsvereniging voor Detailhandel, Ambachten en Huisvrouwen*, [1993] ECR I-5475; Case C-410/92, *Johnson* v. *Chief Adjudication Officer*, [1994] ECR I-5483.

[71]   Note that although discriminatory, it is not contrary to EC law. On which see the discussion *infra*.

[72]   The classic formulation of indirect discrimination in sex discrimination cases is to be found in Case 170/84, *Bilka Kaufhaus* v. *Weber*, [1986] ECR 1607. Extensive treatment of indirect discrimination is to be found in, *inter alia*, Hervey, loc. cit. esp. at pp. 54-62, 68-78, 86-95, 100-106, 118-121, 126-136, 175-211; S. Prechal, "Combatting indirect discrimination in Community law context", (1993) LIEI 81-97; C. Blomeyer, *Das Verbot der mittelbaren Diskriminierung gemäß Art. 119 EWG. Seine Funktion im deutschen Arbeitsrecht*, Baden-Baden, 1994; S. Rating, *Mittelbare Diskriminierung der Frau im Erwerbsleben nach europäischem Gemeinschaftsrecht. Richterrecht des EuGH und die Voraussetzungen seiner Rezeption am Beispiel Spaniens und der Bundesrepublik*, Baden-Baden, 1994. Recent case law suggests that the Court may be changing its definition see Joined Cases C-399/92, C-409/92, C-425/92, C-34/93, C-50/93 and C-78/93, *Helmig* v. *Stadt Lengerig*, [1994] ECR I-5727 discussed extensively by R. Holtmaat, "Overtime Payments for Part-Time Workers" 24 ILJ (1995), 387-394; R. Holtmaat, "Deeltijdwerk, Gelijkheid en Gender", 12 *Nemesis* (1996), 4-17.

to do with discrimination on grounds of sex. The possibility of justification constitutes a recognition of the fact that a variety of different objectives may be pursued through social policy, which ought not to be precluded "merely" because they have a disparate impact on the sexes. However, the danger exists that if justifications are not subjected to a stringent examination they can hollow out the equal treatment norm of any capacity to bring about change in the existing rules of the social security system.

In fact, it would seem that the case law concerning objective justifications in social security cases has reduced significantly the potential of the Directive to bring about change. To be justifiable, the Court has held that the rule adduced must be necessary and appropriate to the pursuit of the objective in question. Although it has refused to accept "generalised statements concerning certain categories of workers",[73] it does consider that rules are acceptable where states can indicate that the measures "correspond to an objective necessary to its social policy" and are "appropriate and necessary to the attainment of that purpose."[74] Although this might sound like a reasonably strict test, in fact it is not.

This is because as we have already seen, social policy is an area in which the EC has only the most limited competence and in relation to which the Member States basically retain their full prerogatives. It is consequently very difficult for the Court to do other than approach with caution the justifications which the

---

[73]   Case 171/88, *Rinner-Kühn* v. *FWW Spezial-Gebädereinigung*, [1989] ECR 2743 at para. 14. This involved an allegation by the German government that their sick pay legislation, which required employers to pay six weeks' sick pay only to employees working more than 10 hours per week or 45 hours per month, was justified by the fact that part-time employees were less integrated into the workforce than their full-time counterparts.

[74]   For an example of a rule being found to fall foul of these requirements, see Case C-102/88, *Ruzius-Wilbrink* v. *Bestuur van de Bedrijfsvereniging voor Overheidsdiensten*, [1989] ECR I-4311. The justification alleged was found to fail on the facts. The Dutch rules on invalidity benefits sought to guarantee recipients a minimum subsistence income. Where the recipient was a part-time worker, the level of this assistance was linked to previous income. In response to a claim that this was indirectly discriminatory against part-time workers, the Dutch government argued that it would be unfair to full-time workers in receipt of the benefit to grant part-timers an allowance higher than the wages they had received in employment. Unfortunately, this is precisely what the rules did for low paid full-timers and students!

Member States plead in this context.[75] However, recent case law suggests that the Court has become too cautious and has found a rule compatible with Community law on the basis of only the most cursory consideration.

If we return now to the description at the beginning of the Chapter of the forms of discrimination against women which have been practiced by social security schemes, we will see that women have often been precluded from accruing social security entitlement as a consequence of the operation of hours or earnings thresholds. Such rules exclude large numbers of women participating in paid employment from being able to accrue pension rights.[76]

This aspect of the German pensions legislation was recently challenged in *Nolte*, *Menger* and *Scheffel*. The legislation excluded from the obligation to contribute - and the right to benefit from - the statutory pension scheme, all those working less than a certain number of hours per week, and earning less than a specified amount. Despite the rule's disproportionate impact on women, the Court held that legislation can legitimately exclude part-time employees working a substantial number of hours per week from the protection afforded by the statutory social security scheme.

Although couched in fairly unimpeachable Community law terms, the judgments are disappointing for a number of reasons. Rather than lay down stringent criteria for evaluating the kinds of justifications adduced by the intervening governments,[77] the Court merely accepted that the financial equilibrium of the scheme depended upon this rule[78] and that bringing such individuals within the scope of the scheme would encourage illegal work. There

---

[75]   Case C-226/91, *Molenbroek* v. *Bestuur van de Sociale Verzekeringsbank*, [1992] ECR I-5943.

[76]   For example, in the UK in 1990 some 2.25 million women were estimated to have been excluded from the compulsory contributory social security scheme because their earnings fell below the LEL. See McCrudden and Black, loc. cit. at p. 172.

[77]   Which the Court has not been shy to do in other areas of the law. See for example, the judgment in Case C-80/94, *Wielockx* v. *Inspecteur der Directe Belastingen*, [1995] ECR I-2493, discussed in greater detail in Chapter 5.

[78]   Which is difficult to accept on the facts, given that the rule excluded individuals from both the obligation to contribute and from the right to benefit.

was no real inquiry as to the appropriateness and necessity of the rule in question, as previous case law would have suggested The significance to individual women of being able to accrue independent pension entitlement is great and justifies a more critical consideration of the arguments put forward by intervening governments. However, the judgments amount to a rubber-stamping of a practice which excludes a significant number of individuals - usually women - from social security protection. Other justifications adduced by governments have received similar treatment. Although the Court has given short shrift to arguments that particular rules are necessitated by purely economic considerations,[79] it has been suggested that it may be more favourable inclined towards arguments that particular rules impose admininstrative burdens on undertakings.[80] Given the importance of the equality principle and its potential in this field to grant many women access to independent income, it is to be hoped that courts which are called upon to adjudicate on these matters will take a critical approach and consider seriously the appropriateness and necessity of the rules in question. Otherwise, the Member States will essentially remain free simply to replace their directly discriminatory rules with more neutrally formulated ones and the Directive will have been robbed of much of its potential to engender change.

In conclusion, although the Directive would appear to impose quite stringent requirements on the Member States, the justifications which the Court has been willing to accept have hollowed out to a considerable degree its potential of to bring about far-reaching alteration in the discriminatory social security schemes of the Member States. Directly discriminatory measures may not be included in social securiry schemes. However, it would seem that indirectly discriminatory measures can remain in place, largely unaffected by the existence of the Directive.

---

[79] Case C-343/92, *Roks and others* v. *Bestuur van de Bedrijfsvereniging voor Gezondheid, Geestelijke en Maatschappelijke Belangen and others*, [1994] ECR I-571 but see the discussion in relation to pensionable age below.

[80] See the observations of J. Steiner, "The Principle of Equal Treatment for Men and Women in Social Security", in T.K. Hervey and D. O'Keeffe (eds.), *Sex Equality Law in the European Union*, Chichester, 1996, at pp. 111-136 at pp. 125-126, citing the judgment of the Court in a different context in Case C-189/91, *Kirshammer-Hack* v. *Sidal*, [1993] ECR I-6185.

The areas excluded from the Directive reduce further its potential to require the Member States to eradicate discrimination from their social security schemes.

3.7   Directive 79/7 - Exceptions and Exclusions

In the introductory section of this Chapter, it was observed that this Directive only required the progressive implementation of the principle of equal treatment in social security. As this would suggest, the Directive contains a number of exclusions and exceptions. Thus, Article 3(2) excludes from the scope of the Directive survivors' benefits,[81] and family benefits, unless granted by way of increases to the benefits due in respect of one of the enumerated risks. If we return briefly to the outline of the main ways in which statutory schemes differentiated between women and men which is contained at the beginning of this Chapter, one of the main methods described there was providing for a widow's but not a widower's pension. Consequently, the exclusion of survivors' benefits from the scope of the Directive allows one of the most blatant forms of discrimination to continue unchecked.

Another method by which schemes differentiated between women and men was in relation to pensionable age. Member States may continue to differentiate in relation to

"the determination of pensionable age for the purposes of granting old-age and retirement pensions and the possible consequences thereof for other benefits."[82]

---

[81]   But see Case C-337/91, *Gemert-Derks* v. *Bestuur van de Nieuwe Industriële Bedrijfsvereniging*, [1993] ECR I-5435.

[82]   Article 7(1)(a). See also the discussion in Chapter 4 in relation to links between occupational and statutory schemes.

Thus the UK and German schemes are quite entitled to continue to pay women their pensions earlier than men, although both jurisdictions have recently announced the equalisation of pensionable age.[83]

However, the precise scope of this exception has been the subject of considerable controversy and the Court has been asked for its opinion on a number of occasions.[84] It takes the view that where different pensionable ages are maintained in the statutory scheme, the Member States may also require different contributions from members for the same benefits, where the financial equilibrium of the scheme depends on this.[85] Nevertheless, the phrase "possible consequences for other benefits" only covers other forms of discrimination which are

> "objectively necessary in order to avoid disrupting the complex financial equilibrium of the social security scheme or to ensure consistency between retirement pension schemes and other benefit schemes."[86]

Although differences in pensionable age may be mirrored in relation to contributory benefits,[87] this is not permissible in relation to non-contributory benefits.[88]

---

[83]   The UK has introduced equality in pensionable ages pursuant to s. 126 and Schedule 4 of the PA 1995. This will be achieved in steps by 2020. The German government, through the *Rentenreformgesetz* 1992 (RRG), has provided that from the year 2000, pensionable age will increase in monthly steps until it is equalised in 2012.

[84]   Note that although the ages from which statutory pensions are payable may differ, this can not justify compelling women to retire at an earlier age than men. See Case 152/84, *Marshall* v. *Southampton and South West Area Health Authority*, [1986] ECR 723. Also Case 151/84, *Roberts* v. *Tate and Lyle Industries Ltd.*, [1986] ECR 703; Case 262/84, *Beets-Proper* v. *van Landschot Bankiers NV*, [1986] ECR 773. Contrast the position for pensionable ages in occupational schemes Case C-262/88, *Barber* v. *Guardian Royal Exchange*, [1990] ECR I-1889 and the discussion in Chapter 4 below.

[85]   Case C-9/91, *EOC*, cited *supra*. Contrast the approach adopted in Case C-154/92, *Van Cant*, cited *supra*. For discussion, see Sohrab, loc. cit. at pp. 77-79.

[86]   Case C-328/91, *Secretary of State for Social Security* v. *Thomas and others*, [1993] ECR I-1247 at para. 12.

[87]   Case C-92/94, *Secretary of State for Social Security and the Chief Adjudication Officer* v. *Graham, Connell and Nicholas*, [1995] ECR I-2521.

[88]   Case C-328/91, *Thomas*, cited *supra*.

The other exceptions contained in Article 7(1) related to advantages granted in respect of old age pensions to persons who have brought up children, acquisition of entitlement following periods of interruption of employment due to bringing up children, granting old age or invalidity benefit entitlements by virtue of derived entitlements of a wife, granting increases to certain benefits, including old age pensions, for a dependent wife,[89] and for the exercise of options prior to the entry into force of the Directive.[90]

If these exceptions are reviewed, it becomes clear that their effect is to enable the Member States to keep in place the variety of measures through which they encouraged women to give up paid employment on marrying or having a child. While this might perhaps be entirely defensible in relation to women who have already acted in reliance upon these kinds of rules, allowing them to continue unaltered into the future perpetuates a legal situation in which women are encouraged to abandon their financial indpendence upon marrying or having a child.

3.8   Evaluation

In making an evaluation of the Directive, it is necessary to bear in mind that its aims were very limited: in essence it appears to have been designed with the objective of removing discrimination against married women from statutory social security schemes. However, as a consequence of a number of limitations to its scope, it appears that its success in achieving this objective - at least in the area of pensions will be limited.

First limiting the personal scope of the Directive to those engaging in paid employment, or who are seeking to do so excludes those in unpaid activities from its scope. Consequently, the Directive is unable to help those excluded from national social security schemes to accrue independent entitlement. The Directive

---

[89]   See the judgment of the Court in Case C-420/92, *Bramhill* v. *Chief Adjudication Officer*, [1994] ECR I-3191.

[90]   This refers to the "married woman's" option in the UK. See Sohrab, loc. cit, at p. 76.

is concerned with eradicating some discrimination from social security schemes, not with creating social security schemes which protect all, irrespective of the activities which they undertake during their working lives.

The conservatism of the drafters *vis-à-vis* the persons covered by the Directive is also reflected in the material scope of the Directive. It covers only the branches of social security concerned with protection against employment based risks. Significantly, social assistance, the branch of state support to which women are most likely to have recourse,[91] is not included and it can continue to be permeated by provisions assuming dependency in particular situations.

However, the impact of the Directive is limited even in relation to those women who are participating in paid employment, and who consequently fall within its scope. This is a result of the exclusions and exceptions from the Directive's scope. Thus for example, in the field of pensions, the exceptions which the Directive contains in relation to pensionable age and survivors' benefits effectively neuter the equality principle of its potential to force major change in this field. If we return for a moment to the description in section 3.2 of this Chapter of the major sources of discrimination against women in statutory pension schemes, then these excluded subjects feature strongly.

This is not to say that the treatment of women by statutory pension schemes is not improving, in part as a consequence of the Directive. Married women in the Netherlands owe their independent right to an AOW pension to the adoption of the Directive.[92] However, the decisions of the UK and German governments to equalise state pensionable age were not prompted by the Directive but largely by financial considerations: given that the costs of statutory pension provision are set to rise in the years to come, equalising pensionable ages offers governments a method of saving money.[93] In relation to survivors' pensions, the

---

[91]   See Holtmaat, loc. cit.

[92]   For an assessment of the impact of the Directive on the Netherlands, see A.F.M. Brenninkmeijer, "Vrouwenstudies kwam te laat voor de sociale zekerheid", in E.A. Alkema and A.Ph.C.M. Jaspers (eds.), *Lof der verscheidenheid. Rechtsgeleerden over vrouw en recht*, Zwolle, 1993 at pp. 17-28; Sohrab, loc. cit. at pp. 127-140; Westerveld, loc. cit. at pp. 415-435.

[93]   See *Options for Equality*, loc. cit.; Hutton et al, loc. cit.

UK continues to differentiate between women and men, although the Dutch[94] and German[95] legislatures have been provoked by their national judiciaries to introduce equality.

As has already been observed, the aim of the Directive was to remove discrimination against married women from the state social scheme.[96] It does not require the Member States to provide particular kinds of benefits, nor to structure their contributions systems in any specific manner, provided that the systems which are put in place are not directly discriminatory.[97] The Directive's limited scope can be seen to be the consequence of the Community's limited competence in the social field.[98] These limitations mean that the Court is virtually forced to accept as a ground of justification that a measure pursues a legitimate aim of social policy but without really being able to examine that aim.

As should have become clear from the discussion, the breadth of the exclusions from the Directive ensure that the Member States remain free to continue to apply rules which blatantly differentiate between women and men, and

---

94   See Rspr. SV 1989/67, CRvB 7-12-'88, AWW 1987/17 and AWW 1987/46. Westerveld, op. cit. at pp. 453-456; J. Borgesius, "Weduwenpensioen voor weduwnaars", TvP (1989), 6-10; T. Loenen, *Verschil in Gelijkheid. De conceptualisering van het juridische gelijkheidsbeginsel met betrekking tot vrouwen en mannen in Nederland en de Verenigde Staten*, Zwolle, 1992 at pp. 196-200.

95   In Germany, the *Gesetz über Hinterbliebenenrenten und Erziehungszeiten* BGBl. 185, 1450 has introduced equality in relation to survivors' pensions. This was prompted by a judgment of the BVerfG, BVerfGE 39, 169; see Westerverld, loc. cit. at pp. 188-190; J.W.P.M. van Rooij, J.L.M. Schell, S.M.E. Vansteenkiste and C.J.M.M. Verwijmeren, *Rechterlijke toetsing aan het gelijkheidsbeginsel in het sociale-zekerheidsrecht in rechtsvergelijkend perspectief*, Den Haag, 1994 at pp. 119-120.

96   That this need not always occur in a manner favourable to the recipients of benefits is demonstrated by the manner in which the Dutch government introduced equality into its social security scheme. See the discussion in Westerveld, loc. cit. at pp. 412-442; A.F.M. Brenninkmeijer, "Vrouwenstudies kwam te laat voor de sociale zekerheid", in E.A. Alkema and A.Ph.C.M. Jaspers (eds.), *Lof der verscheidenheid. Rechtsgeleerden over vrouw en recht*, Zwolle, 1993, pp. 17-28 at p. 18.

97   For a recent confirmation of this position, see Case C-343/92, *Roks and others v. Bestuur van de Bedrijfsvereniging voor Gezondheid, Geestelijke en Maatschappelijke Belangen and others*, [1994] ECR I-571.

98   See the discussion in section 3.3 above.

reward those who have followed "traditional" sex-specific patterns. In 1987, hard on the heels of the adoption of Directive 86/378,[99] the Commission presented a proposal for a Directive completing the implementation of the equality principle in social security.[100] In essence, this would have extended the equality principle to the areas excluded from the scope of Directive 79/7. Additionally, in its original form, the proposal encouraged the Member States to eradicate notions of dependence from their social security schemes and to work towards a system based upon individualised rights.[101] However, it has not been adopted, and indeed, it appears that it has not even been discussed since 1989.[102]

However, even had it been adopted, it seems unlikely that it would have been adequate to ensure that in the area of pensions, women accrued levels of benefits equal to those accrued by men. The source of the inadequacy of women's statutory pension entitlement in the UK and Germany is the systems' inability to deal adequately with what Holtmaat has characterised as women's risks,[103] more particularly in this context, care tasks. Both Member States relate the level of pension which an individual receives to the length of time for which that individual has been insured under the scheme. Where women stop work, even temporarily to have and care for a child, this reduces their working career and consequently their pension.

---

[99]   On which see the discussion in the next Chapter.

[100]   Proposal for a Directive completing the implementation of the principle of equal treatment for men and women in statutory and occupational social security schemes, O.J. 1987 C 309/10. COM(87) 494 final.

[101]   See the discussion of this principle in L. Luckhaus, "Individualisation of Social Security Benefits", in McCrudden (ed.), loc. cit. at pp. 147-162; Sohrab, loc. cit. at pp. 203-217.

[102]   See the observations of K. Banks, "Whither the Social Security Directives? Developments in Community Law Relating to Sex Equality", in McCrudden (ed.), loc. cit. pp. 55-68, at p. 64.

[103]   Holtmaat, loc. cit. at pp. 61-71. She identifies the risk of psychiatric and physical overburdening as a consequence of combining unpaid care and paid work; the risk of having children; the risk of becoming unfit for work (where she works at home, or where she works outwith the home); the loss of a breadwinner; unemployment; lack of schooling; discrimination.

Although the UK[104] and German[105] systems have made provision to take account of the fact that many women spend some time out of the employment

---

[104]   In the UK, for example, to obtain a full pension, an individual has to be insured for 9/10th of his working life, which is 44 years for a man and 39 for a woman. However, where someone has been insured for at least one half of that period, or at least 20 years if that is less, they will be treated as if they have been fully insured where they can prove that for all other years they were precluded from regular employment by responsibilities at home. Although this does protect some women, it should be noted that it only applies in respect of full years spent outside the employment market, and consequently, a woman who begins to work again in low paid employment may find that that year does not count at all. This is because a qualifying year for pension purposes is one in which the relevant amount of contributions have been paid. Individuals in low paid employment, and particularly those working part-time, or for part of a year, may find that they are unable to contribute the requisite amounts. See in general Davies and Ward, loc. cit. at pp. 14 and 15. Although provision for similar credit to be given are to be found in SERPS, they are a recent reform the recent reforms to which have devalued it in terms of providing women with adequate pensions. The replacement of the 20 best years rule with the lifetime earnings rule: ss. 18-19 of the Social Security Act 1986 (c. 50), amending s. 6 of the SSPA 1975. This reform aimed to reduce the cost of SERPS by around 50% from approx. £25.5 billion in 2033 to approx. £15 billion.

[105]   In Germany, a 1979 Committee of Experts recognised that the German scheme's reliance on earnings and employment history of an individual worked to the disadvantage of women. See Westerveld, loc. cit. at pp. 308-314. In recognition of the fact that women earn less than men,(Despite efforts to ensure equal pay, studies demonstrate that women are still receiving lower pay than men. See for example, Commission of the EC, *Wage Determination and Sex Segregation in Employment in the European Community*, Social Europe Supplement 4/94, Brussels, 1994) the *Rente nach Mindesteinkommen* (RnM) was introduced in 1972 to improve the pension position of women. This provides that those who were paid less than 75% of the average gross annual wage in any year, receive a pension of 75% of this average gross annual wage, where they have satisfied the waiting period. For detailed treatment, see Westerveld, loc. cit. at pp. 175, 177, 179, 183, 284-5, 315, 328-9, 336-338, 477. By paying a higher pension than would otherwise be the case, this ought to have improved the pension position of the (very) low paid. In addition, where someone has cared for a young child an extra three years can be added to their insurance history to cover this period spent away from paid employment. See Westerveld, loc. cit. at pp. 310-312, 320-323, 336-338, 341-2. In addition, longer periods spent caring for children can be counted for the purposes of satisfying waiting periods. The calculation which takes place in this situation is also on the basis of the same 75% figure as features in the RnM. Although in theory the benefit is open to both parents, it seems designed to encourage the least well paid in the unit to care for the child, which will generally be the woman. In the past, these provisions ensured that some part-time workers obtained a higher level of pension than that to which their own contributions would have entitled them. For example, where someone had worked a small number of hours for a long period of time. However, the 1992 pension reform put an end to this facility, with consequently negative effects for the levels of women's pensions. See Westerveld, loc. cit. at p. 338.

market, the provision which has been made is unable entirely to remedy its negative effects on their pension accrual.

Another consequence for women of having children is that many of those who continue to work do so on a part-time basis. If women are to be enabled to accrue adequate levels of retirement income, schemes will have to find a manner of dealing with this practice.[106] In this respect, the judgments of the Court in *Nolte* and *Megner and Scheffel* are disappointing since they allow the Member States to exclude individuals working quite substantial numbers of hours from their social security schemes.

In conclusion, it can be observed that the Directive has required that much direct discrimination be eradicated from the social security schemes operating in the Member States. In principle indirect discrimination must also be eradicated, but as we have seen, the justifications available to the Member States reduce the impact of this principle significantly. Those women following "male"[107] patterns of employment ought now to be able to accrue an adequate level of pension under the scheme, and provisions have been adopted to enable women taking career breaks for the purposes of childcare to continue pension accrual which ought to improve their pension position also. It can therefore be said that statutory pension schemes have come a considerable way towards adjusting to the challenges posed by the increase in women's participation in paid employment and offer women falling within their scope the opportunity of accruing an adequate level of retirement income.

---

[106] In 1992, 85% of part-time employees in the EC were women. See Commission of the EC, *Werkgelegenheid in Europa 1994*, Brussels, 1994 at p. 115.

[107] By which is meant, approximately 40 years, 48 weeks per year, 38 hours per week. See in this respect, Directive 93/104 on Working Time, O.J. 1993, L 307/18. Similar considerations played an important role in Joined Cases C-399/92, C-409/92, C-425/92, C-34/93, C-50/93 and C-78/93, *Helmig*, cited *supra*. Holtmaat, loc. cit. and Sohrab, loc. cit. See also J.D.N. Bates, "Gender, Social Security and Pensions: The Myth of the 'Everyday Housewife'?", in S. McLean and N. Burrows (eds.) *The Legal Relevance of Gender*, London, 1988, at pp. 119-145.

OCCUPATIONAL PENSIONS AND EQUALITY

In Chapter 1 the scope of this research project was delimited and a couple of questions were formulated which it was stated the objective of this research was to answer. One of these questions was whether if increasing reliance is placed on the kinds of pre-funded occupational pension schemes which are to be found in the UK, the Netherlands and Germany women would be able to accrue adequate levels of retirement income. In the preceding Chapter, the alterations which EC law has required statutory pension schemes to introduce to acknowledge this phenomenon were discussed. In this Chapter, the requirements of EC equality law in the field of occupational pension schemes will be outlined and the changes which they have required schemes to introduce will be discussed. Finally, an assessment will be made of whether the law as it currently stands goes far enough, or whether additional provision will have to be made to adapt occupational pension schemes to women's participation in the labour market.

In this Chapter, a slightly different approach will be followed to that of the previous Chapter. First, a brief introduction to discrimination in occupational schemes will be given. Thereafter, the EC law - which in this area also has been an extremely important cause of change - will be introduced. In the remaining sections, the specific requirements of the law will be outlined in relation to specific aspects of occupational provision - pensions as pay, access to schemes, pensionable age, contributions, benefits, survivor's pensions, additional voluntary contributions, lump sums, links with statutory schemes. After each individual section, the changes which schemes in the jurisdictions under consideration have been forced to introduce will be outlined. In keeping with the focus of this research on occupational provision, this approach provides detailed information about both the extent to which discrimination had been practised in the past, and the kinds of reforms which had to be introduced as a consequence of the equality principle. This should enable a clear picture to be obtained of the usefulness of these reforms in improving the levels of occupational pensions paid to women. Additionally, the

description will provide a good basis for moving on to the final evaluation of the
adequacy of the changes which have been introduced.

4.1   Discriminatory Features of Occupational Pension Schemes

As the discussion in Chapter 2 reveals, occupational schemes were originally
unilateral undertakings by employers to care for those employees whose illness or
infirmity made them unable to earn to support themselves, a situation which has
gradually altered. Of necessity, being employer initiated, they offer pensions only
to (some) ex-employees. In determining the groups of employees to whom the
benefits of membership were to be offered, schemes have gradually come to utilise
many of the assumptions and rules of statutory schemes, in particular, that the
majority of women would be provided for through a man. For example, it was not
uncommon for schemes to allow men to join some years earlier than women. The
higher age from which women were offered membership basically represented the
age by which it was assumed that an unmarried woman would be unable to find
a man to support her,[1] and consequently she would need the benefit of her own
pension. Another way in which the notion of female financial dependency on men
was reflected in occupational scheme practice was in the blanket exclusion from
pension schemes of married women.[2] Like the statutory schemes upon which they
built, those schemes which did admit (married) women to membership often
operated lower female retirement ages,[3] offered survivor's pensions only to female

---

[1]   For example, the scheme at issue in Case 69/80, *Worringham and Humphreys* v. *Lloyds
        Bank Ltd.*, [1981] ECR 767.

[2]   During the 1920s, a marriage bar was introduced into the professions in the UK, resulting
        in the dismissal of women from, for example, teaching and the civil service. See for
        example, Lewis, loc. cit, at p. 34.

[3]   This had a number of consequences. First, the woman would have a shorter career over
        which to accrue a pension, even if the scheme did not operate different entry ages.
        Consequently, unless women were offered accelerated accrual (extremely rare, if not unheard
        of), this would result in their accruing a smaller pension. It also exacerbates the difference
        in the cost of providing an occupational pension to a woman and that of providing a pension
        to a man.

survivors of male employees,[4] and offered them lower and different benefits than were offered to men. Finally, and more technically, where women were admitted to schemes, they often operated on the basis of mortality tables which differentiated between the sexes on the assumption that women outlive men. This in turn made it more expensive to provide the same level of benefit in respect of a woman than in respect of a man.[5]

In all these different ways, therefore, occupational pension schemes differentiated between women and men and it is to be expected that these rules have played an important role in ensuring that older women are generally poor. As shall become clear in the course of this Chapter, schemes have been required to eradicate many of these practices, which ought significantly to improve the levels of occupational pensions received by women in the future. The legal provisions which have led to these alterations will now be outlined.

4.2   Directive 86/378[6]

In the previous Chapter the requirements of Directive 79/7 were described and the alterations to which it had led assessed. It was noted that Directive 79/7 is limited to statutory social security schemes, Article 1(2) providing that the subject of equal treatment in occupational social security schemes would be dealt with in a later Directive. This later Directive was finally adopted in the form of Directive 86/378.

---

[4]   For example, this was the case in the scheme at issue in Case 192/85, *Newstead* v. *Department of Transport*, [1987] ECR 4753.

[5]   This will be discussed in greater detail in s. 4.7 on contributions below.

[6]   Directive 86/378 concerning the implementation of the principle of equal treatment for men and women in occupational social security schemes, O.J. 1986 L 225/40. See the opinions expressed in D. Curtin, "Occupational pension schemes and article 119: Beyond the fringe?", 24 CML Rev. (1987), 215-257; J. De Wildt, "Gelijke behandeling in aanvullende pensioenregelingen", TvP (1988), 73-77; A. Laurent, "The elimination of sex discrimination in occupational social security schemes in the EEC", 125 *International Labour Review* (1986), 675-683; Prechal and Burrows, loc. cit. at pp. 276-290; S. Prechal, "Ondeugdelijke communautaire wetgeving: de pensioenrichtlijn", NJB (1990), 1299-1303; A. Schermer, "Ontwerp vierde richtlijn", SMA (1985), 520-533.

This has as its objective to "implement, in occupational social security schemes, the principle of equal treatment for men and women."[7] It covers

> "schemes not governed by Directive 79/7/EEC whose purpose is to provide workers, whether employees or self-employed, in an undertaking or group of undertakings, area of economic activity or occupational sector or group of such sectors with benefits intended to supplement the benefits provided by statutory social security schemes or to replace them, whether membership of such schemes is compulsory or optional."[8]

However, like Directive 79/7, Directive 86/378 is limited in scope. Expressly excluded from its scope are individual contracts, schemes with only one member, insurance contracts to which the employer is not a party and the optional provisions of schemes offered to participants individually.[9]

The Directive applies to members of the working population, including the self-employed, and to individuals whose activity is interrupted by illness, maternity, accident or involuntary unemployment, persons seeking employment, and to retired and disabled workers.[10] It covers occupational schemes which provide cover against sickness, invalidity, old age, industrial accidents and occupational diseases and unemployment. It also covers benefits paid by the employer to employed persons or their families, by reason of the latter's employment.[11]

The principle of equal treatment which the Directive is designed to introduce in the field, is elaborated upon in Article 5 as meaning that there is to be no discrimination on the basis of sex as regards particularly the scope and conditions of access to schemes, nor may schemes discriminate as regards the obligation to contribute and the calculation of contributions. Finally, the non-discrimination principle is said to mean that benefits are to be calculated without discrimination on grounds of sex.

---

[7] Art. 1.

[8] Art. 2(1).

[9] Art. 2(2). See *infra*.

[10] Art. 3.

[11] Art. 4.

Like Article 7 of Directive 79/7, Article 9 of Directive 86/378 provides for a number of exceptions to the equality principle. According to Article 9(a), the Member States may defer the application of the equality principle in relation to pensionable age either until equality is required *vis-à-vis* the statutory scheme, or until required by another Directive. Similar provision is made in Article 9(b) in relation to survivors' pensions. Finally, Article 9(c) provides that different employee contributions can be levied where they reflect the use of actuarial tables which differentiate on grounds of sex,[12] until July 1999. According to Article 8(1) of the Directive, schemes had to be revised in the light of the Directive by 1 January 1993 at the latest. However, it is to leave unaffected any rights and obligations pertaining to periods of membership prior to its entry into force.

As even this sketch of Directive 86/378 suggests, this legislative initiative mirrors Directive 79/7. Consequently, it might be expected that this Chapter would bear a strong similarity to that preceding it. However, this is not the case. Directive 86/378 will in fact feature only in passing in this Chapter. It has largely been rendered otiose by the European Court of Justice's robust interpretation of the scope of the equal pay principle contained in Article 119 EC and it is to this provision that we will now turn. Given that this principle has had such dramatic consequences for occupational pension schemes, before its substantive provisions are outlined, its place in the Treaty and the basic mechanics of its operation will be described.

4.3   Article 119 - Some General Observations

As has already been touched upon in Chapter 3, although the requirement that women and men receive equal pay for equal work can be seen to be an aspect of social policy, the inclusion of an equal pay norm in the Treaty was apparently prompted by economic considerations.[13] More specifically, France, whose domestic sex equality legislation was more far-reaching than that of her future

---

[12]   This will be discussed in greater detail in s. 4.7 below.

[13]   Barnard 1996, loc. cit. at pp. 321-334; Hoskyns, loc. cit. at pp. 43-59.

partners, feared that her industry would suffer competitive disadvantage if no such
provision was included in the Treaty. She feared that firms established elsewhere
would undercut French firms by using female labour which was less well paid than
male labour.[14] Although economic considerations played a role in its inclusion in
the Treaty, the Court has interpreted Article 119 as serving both economic and
social ends,[15] and has even gone so far as to hold that sexual equality forms part
of the foundations of the Community.[16]

Article 119 requires that men and women receive equal pay for equal
work,[17]

---

[14]   Prior to the signing of the Treaty of Rome, a committee of experts was convened under the
        auspices of the ILO to consider *Social Aspects of European Economic Cooperation* (ILO
        Studies and Reports (New Series) No. 46, Geneva 1956, discussed by Barnard, loc. cit. at
        pp. 81-87; Davies, loc. cit. at pp. 313-359; Deakin and Wilkinson, op. cit. at 289-310;
        Deakin and Barnard, loc. cit. at pp. 177-195; Nielsen and Szyszczak, loc. cit. at pp. 16-18.
        They basically concluded that there was no need to harmonise social costs among the
        Member States generally, but that "[w]age differentials according to sex constitute a
        particular case of low wages in industries in which a large proportion of female labour is
        employed. When such differentials are not the result of special circumstances affecting
        employment opportunities for female workers in certain areas but are due to such factors as
        tradition and the absence of effective organisation of female workers in trade unions, it will
        be desirable to create such conditions as will enable these differentials to be gradually
        abolished, taking into account the ILO Equality of Remuneration Convention." ILO Report,
        footnote at 112-113.

[15]   Case 43/75, *Defrenne II*, cited *supra* at paras. 8-10.

[16]   Case 149/77, *Defrenne* v. *SABENA*, [1978] ECR 1365, (*Defrenne III*) at paras. 26-27. See
        C. Docksey, "The Principle of Equality between Women and Men as a Fundamental Right
        under Community Law", 20 ILJ (1991), 258-280. For a more critical approach, see S.
        Fredman, "European Community Sex Discrimination Law: A critique", 21 ILJ (1992), 119-
        134; H. Fenwick and T.K. Hervey, "Sex Equality in the Single Market: New Directions for
        the European Court of Justice", 32 CML Rev. (1995), 443-470.

[17]   And also for work to which equal value is attached by virtue of Article 1 of Directive
        75/117. The Court has held that the latter Directive is "principally designed to facilitate the
        practical application of the principle of equal pay outlined in Article 119 of the Treaty [and]
        in no way alters the content or scope of that principle as defined in the Treaty" (Case 96/80,
        Jenkins, cited *supra* at para. 22). See Case C-127/92, *Enderby* v. *Frenchay Health Authority
        and Secretary of State for Health*, [1993] ECR I-5535; Case C-342/93, *Gillespie and Others*
        v. *Northern Health and Social Services Board and others*, judgment of 13 February 1996,
        nyr; C. McGlynn, "Equality, Maternity and Questions of Pay", 21 EL Rev. (1996), 327-332;
        Barnard, loc. cit. at pp. 172-186; Ellis, loc. cit. at pp. 38-94; L. Boelens and A. Veldman,
        Gelijkwaardige arbeid, gelijk gewaardeerd, Utrecht, 1993; D. Curtin, "Simple Justice", 9

the central concept of "pay" having been defined by the Court as embracing

> "any other consideration, whether in cash or in kind, whether immediate or future, provided that the worker receives it, albeit indirectly, in respect of his employment from his employer."[18]

This has resulted in a wide variety of the fringe benefits offered by employers to their employees falling within its scope, regardless of whether they are contractual terms or *ex gratia*[19] advantages. Employer funded sick pay,[20] occupational pensions,[21] redundancy payments,[22] and travel concessions[23] form clear examples of the kind of fringe benefits offered by employers which the Court has found to fall within the concept of "pay."[24]

However, working conditions in general, even if they have pecuniary consequences, do not fall within the scope of Article 119.[25] It is only once women have begun to participate in economic activity that they may claim the equality required by Article 119. As a consequence of this interpretation the Court has left Article 119 with no role to play in projects of social engineering,

---

Nemesis (1993), 190-198; C. Kilpatrick, "Deciding when Jobs of Equal Value can be Paid Unequally: An Examination of s1(3) of the Equal Pay Act 1970", 23 ILJ (1994), 311-325; Prechal and Burrows, loc. cit. at pp. 48-80. Commission Memorandum on Equal Pay for Work of Equal Value, COM(94) 6 final.

[18]   See *inter alia* Case C-262/88, *Barber*, cited *supra* at para. 12.

[19]   See Case 12/81, *Garland* v. *British Rail Engineering Ltd.*, [1982] ECR 359.

[20]   Case 171/88, *Rinner-Kühn*, cited *supra*.

[21]   Case 170/84, *Bilka-Kaufhaus*, cited *supra*. This will be considered in more detail below.

[22]   Case C-262/88, *Barber*, cited *supra*.

[23]   Case 12/81, *Garland*, cited *supra*.

[24]   Barnard 1995, loc. cit. at pp. 173-175 provides a comprehensive list, to which can now be added maternity pay; see Case C-342/93, *Gillespie*, cited *supra* at para. 14, although Art. 119 does not require that women on maternity leave receive full pay. See the comments made by McGlynn, op. cit. at 330.

[25]   Case 149/77, *Defrenne III*, cited *supra*. This led to the adoption of Directive 76/207 on the implementation of the principle of equal treatment for men and women as regards access to employment, vocational training and promotion, and working conditions O.J. 1976 L 39/40.

dismantling traditional structures which have hindered women in the pursuit of economic independence.[26]

Although Article 119 obliged the original Member States to implement the principle of equal pay by the end of 1961, lip service, at best, was paid to it during the 1960s by both the Member States and the Commission.[27] The breakthrough came with the Court's recognition in *Defrenne II* that Article 119 enjoys both vertical and horizontal direct effect, as a result of which individuals can invoke Article 119 against both the state[28] (the vertical situation) and, significantly in this area, against their employer. As later case law has demonstrated, it is not merely the employee who can make such a claim but also the ex-employee[29] and his or her survivor.[30] Similarly, the circle of persons upon whom Article imposes obligations has been broadened to include not only the State and the employer but also those administering a pension scheme, in the UK context for example, the

---

[26]   See for example, in the context of Directive 76/207, Case 184/83, *Hofmann* v. *Barmer Ersatzkasse*, [1984] ECR 3047. For a discussion of this subject in an EC law context, see Fredman, op. cit.; Fenwick and Hervey, op. cit.; Bercusson, loc. cit. at pp. 174-180.

[27]   For details of the various means by which the Member States attempted to delay fulfilling their obligations under the Treaty, see the comments of the Court in Case 43/75, *Defrenne II*, cited *supra* at paras. 47-60. Also H. Warner, "EC Social Policy in Practice: Community action on behalf of women and its impact in the Member States", 23 JCMS (1984), 141-167; Crijns, loc. cit. at pp. 150-151.

[28]   In Case C-188/89, *Foster* v. *British Gas* [1990] ECR I-3313, the Court provided some general guidance as to what should be understood to be an "emanation of the state", the definition of which was held to be a matter of Community and not national law. The Court defined an emanation of the state as "a body, whatever its legal form, which has been made responsible pursuant to a measure adopted by the State, for providing a public service under the control of the State and has for that purpose special powers beyond those which result from the normal rules applicable in relations between individuals is included in any event among the bodies against which the provisions of a directive capable of having direct effect may be relied upon." See D. Curtin, "Delimiting the Direct Effect of Directives in the Common Law Context", 15 EL Rev. (1990), 195-223. But note the possibly more restrictive approach to the definition of the "state" contained in the judgment in Case C-91/92, *Paola Faccini Dori* v. *Recreb Srl*, [1994] ECR I-3325, noted by W. Robinson at 32 CML Rev. (1995), 629-639.

[29]   Case 12/81, *Garland*, cited *supra*.

[30]   Case C-109/91, *Ten Oever* v. *Stichting Bedrijfspensioenfonds voor het Glazenwassers- en Schoonmaakbedrijf*, [1993] ECR I-4879.

trustees of a pension scheme.[31] The norm of Article 119 prevails over legislation, contractual terms and the provisions of collective agreements,[32] and where discrimination has been found, requires that until the situation has been remedied, the individual who has been disadvantaged receive the same treatment as the previously favoured individual.[33]

Discrimination has been defined by the Court as being where different rules are applied to the individuals who are in the same situation, or the same rules are applied to individuals in different situations.[34] As has already been mentioned, a distinction is usually drawn between direct and indirect discrimination.[35] Direct discrimination on grounds of sex occurs where the difference is based directly on the sex of the individual,[36] for example, paying women a lower hourly rate for a particular activity than men.[37] Indirect discrimination covers the situation where

---

[31] Case C-262/88, *Barber*, cited *supra* at para. 29; Case C-200/91, *Coloroll Pension Trustees Ltd.* v. *Russell et al*, [1994] ECR I-4389 at paras. 20-24; Case C-128/93, *Fisscher* v. *Voorhuis Hengelo BV and Stichting Bedrijfspensioenfonds voor de Detailhandel*, [1994] ECR I-4583 at para. 31.

[32] Case C-109/88, *Handels-og-Kontorfunktionaerernes Forbund i Danmark* v. *Dansk Arbejdsgiverforening (acting for Danfoss)*, [1989] ECR 3199; Case C-33/89, *Kowalska* v. *Freie und Hansestadt Hamburg*, [1990] ECR I-2591; Case C-184/89, *Nimz* v. *Freie und Hansestadt Hamburg*, [1991] ECR I-297. Note that where two collective agreements have been concluded by the same employer with the same employee representatives for two groups of employees, comparison is possible (Case C-127/92, *Enderby*, cited *supra*.)

[33] *Inter alia*, Case C-184/89, *Nimz*, cited *supra*. For the limitations of this obligation, see Case C-408/92, *Smith and others* v. *Avdel Systems Ltd*, [1994] ECR I-4435 and Case C-28/93, *Van den Akker and others* v. *Stichting Shell Pensioenfonds*, [1994] ECR I-4527. This will be discussed in more detail in the section on pensionable age below.

[34] See for example, Case C-279/93, *Finanzamt Köln* v. *Schumacker*, [1995] ECR I-225 at para. 30; confirmed, in *inter alia*, Case C-342/93, *Gillespie*, cited *supra* at para. 16.

[35] This first appeared in a Community equality law context in Case 43/75, *Defrenne II*, cited *supra* at para.s 18 and 19.

[36] See for example, the definitions provided by Hervey, loc. cit. at p. 49; Prechal, op. cit. at 83.

[37] A recent example which received particular media attention in the UK was that the two leading actresses in the television programme *Men Behaving Badly* were paid 25% less per series than the two leading actors.

a provision which is neutrally formulated in fact affects a considerably larger proportion of persons of one sex, and there is no way of demonstrating that the provision is objectively justified.[38] Despite initial confusion,[39] it is now clear that Article 119 enjoys direct effect in relation to both direct and indirect discrimination,[40] allowing both blatant and more subtle forms of discrimination between women and men to be challenged by this route. By granting Article 119 direct effect and subjecting it to a broad interpretation the Court has equipped the individual employee who considers that he has suffered discrimination a valuable weapon which can be wielded before all national tribunals.

4.4   Pensions as Pay

One of the first Article 177 references on Article 119 raised the question of its applicability to pensions. In *Defrenne I*[41] the Court was asked whether a pension payable under the terms of social security financed by contributions from workers, employers and by State subsidy, constituted consideration which the worker received indirectly in respect of his employment from his employer. In answering this question in the negative the Court observed that

> "although consideration in the nature of social security benefits
> is not ... in principle alien to the concept of pay, there cannot be
> brought within this concept, as defined in Article 119, social
> security schemes or benefits, in particular retirement pensions,
> directly governed by legislation without any element of

---

[38]   See *inter alia* Case 96/80, *Jenkins*, cited *supra*; Case 170/84, *Bilka-Kaufhaus*, cited *supra*. See the formulations expressed by Hervey, loc. cit. at p. 54; Prechal, op. cit. at 84; indirect discrimination is discussed at length by Blomeyer, loc. cit.; Hervey, loc. cit. at pp. 54-62, 68-78, 86-95, 100-106, 118-121, 126-136, 175-211; Holtmaat (1995), op. cit.; Rating, loc. cit.

[39]   Caused by the Court in Case 43/75, *Defrenne II*, cited *supra* at para. 18 where it appeared to suggest that Article 119 enjoys direct effect only in relation to cases of direct discrimination.

[40]   Case 96/80, *Jenkins*, cited *supra* was the first case in which the Court recognised this.

[41]   Case 80/70, cited *supra*.

agreement within the undertaking or the occupational branch concerned, which are obligatorily applicable to general categories of workers."[42]

Additionally, it appeared to have attached significance to the fact that the benefit in question was partly financed by the State and that the entitlement to the benefit arose by virtue of fulfilling the legal criteria rather than because of the specific employment relationship existing between the individual and his employer.[43]

The *Defrenne I* judgment was drafted in "negative" terms in that it indicated what did not fall within the scope of the concept of "pay". The question was whether on a "positive" or *a contrario* reading of the judgment, it could be concluded that occupational schemes were caught by the equal pay principle. In *Defrenne I* the Advocate General had considered the question extensively, concluding that they did fall within its scope. This conclusion appears to have found its echo in other Community institutions and some of the Member States. While the equal pay, equal treatment and social security Directives were being negotiated, discussions took place on Article 119's applicability to occupational schemes. However, as has already been observed, the solution finally chosen was to evade the issue, first by excluding social security in its entirety from Directive 76/207 and then to exclude occupational schemes from the scope of Directive 79/7.[44] Nevertheless, this course of (in)action did not still the debate at national level and the Court was duly presented with its first reference on the point in 1980.

Worringham[45] concerned a British contracted-out occupational pension scheme.[46] All male employees were obliged to contribute to the scheme, but female employees had only to contribute after they had reached the age of 25. To cover the costs of the contributions paid by the men, Lloyds paid a supplement to

---

[42]   Case 80/70, *Defrenne I*, cited *supra* at para. 7.

[43]   Case 80/70, cited *supra* at para.s 8-10.

[44]   See the discussion in Hoskyns and Luckhaus, op. cit. at 321-335; Prechal and Burrows, loc. cit. at pp. 165-166.

[45]   Case 69/80, *Worringham*, cited *supra*.

[46]   See the explanation of "contracting-out" contained in Chapter 2.

their salary which was immediately deducted and paid to the pension trustees.[47]
The net salary received by both groups was the same, but the gross salary received
by the men was higher than that received by the women. Consequently, other
benefits (such as redundancy or unemployment benefits, family allowances and
mortgage and credit facilities) calculated on the basis of gross salary were higher
for the men than for the women. The national court asked the Court if employer's
contributions or the rights of a worker under such a scheme were pay within the
meaning of article 119.

In dealing with this case, the Court chose to re-formulate the questions
referred, thereby enabling it to avoid directly addressing the relationship between
Article 119 and occupational pension schemes. In reformulating its question, the
Court in fact chose to focus upon the differences in gross salaries paid to the men
and women in question. It then held:

> "...a contribution to a retirement benefits scheme which is paid
> by the employer in the name of the employees by means of an
> addition to the gross salary and which helps to determine the
> amount of that salary is "pay" within the meaning of article
> 119."[48]

This judgment seemed clearly to indicate that differences in gross salaries violate
Article 119, but appeared to reach no conclusion on the applicability of Article 119
to occupational schemes.[49]

It was 1986 when the Court finally addressed Article 119's applicability
to occupational pension schemes. The non-contributory occupational pension
scheme operated by the *Bilka-Kaufhaus* concern offered full-time employees the
right to a pension after 20 years full-time employment. By contrast, before a part-
time employee could obtain the right to a pension, he had to have been employed

---

[47]   On leaving the employment in question the individual could receive refunds of the
        contributions paid to the scheme.

[48]   Case 69/80, *Worringham*, cited *supra* at para. 17.

[49]   Interestingly, in Case C-152/91, *Neath* v. *Hugh Steeper Ltd.*, [1993] ECR I-6935 and Case
        C-200/91, *Coloroll*, cited *supra*, the Court cited *Worringham* as authority for its decision
        that employee contributions to occupational schemes are pay, which as this discussion
        indicates, is a somewhat "creative" interpretation of its judgment. See the discussion on this
        point *infra*.

full-time for at least 15 of a total of 20 years. Ms. Weber von Hartz considered that this amounted to a form of discrimination against women since they were more likely than men to work part-time and therefore more likely than men to suffer the disadvantage of the more onerous qualifying condition. In finding that benefits paid out under occupational pension schemes did constitute pay within the meaning of Article 119, the Court based its judgment on an *a contrario* application of its judgment in *Defrenne I*. It focused on the fact that the scheme was the result of negotiations between employer and employee representatives and constituted a contractual term of the individuals' employment contracts. Additionally, the Court appeared to attach significance to the supplementary nature of the benefits provided under the scheme *vis-à-vis* those provided by the State.

As a result of this judgment, it appeared that at least purely supplementary pensions, which form an element of the contractual relationship between employer and employee and which are funded entirely by the employer constitute pay within the meaning of Article 119, unlike statutory schemes. However, it was not clear whether Article 119 imposed similar obligations upon the other forms of occupational pension provision which are to be found in the European Union, a subject upon which the Court has gradually provided clarification.

It has already been observed that the Court was asked about Article 119 and contracted-out pension schemes in *Worringham*, a question which the Court decided to avoid addressing. It followed a similar path in the 1987 *Newstead* case.[50] Mr Newstead was a UK civil servant required to contribute to a contracted-out occupational pension scheme which made provision for widows' and orphans' pensions. All male civil servants were obliged to contribute to the scheme irrespective of their civil status. On the other hand, female civil servants were not allowed to contribute unless they could demonstrate that they were married and that their spouse was dependent upon them as a consequence of physical or mental disability. Male civil servants who remained unmarried while covered by the scheme were entitled to a refund of the relevant contributions plus interest when they left the scheme. Mr Newstead, a "confirmed bachelor" objected to the loss of current enjoyment of this part of his income and challenged the rules of scheme, a challenge which ultimately reached Luxembourg.

---

[50]   Case 192/85, *Newstead*, cited *supra*.

However, just as it had done in *Worringham,* in *Newstead* the Court managed to avoid making any finding as to whether or not contracted-out occupational pension schemes fall within Article 119. Instead, the Court focused on the fact that the disparity in net salaries was a consequence of men's obligation to contribute to a widow's pension. The Court continued that

> "[s]uch a contribution must therefore, like a contribution to a
> statutory social security scheme, be considered to fall within the
> scope of Article 118 of the Treaty, not of Article 119."[51]

However, later, in passing, the Court appeared to take the view that contracted-out occupational schemes were "social security schemes", and therefore like the scheme at issue in *Defrenne I*[52] fall outwith the scope of Article 119. This was confirmed by the reasoning of the Court in providing an answer to the third question asked by the national court. In determining whether the treatment at issue was prohibited by Directive 76/207 the Court focused on Directives 79/7 and 86/378 as demonstrating that Article 1(2) of the 1976 Directive was not relevant. At no time did the Court even hint that Article 119 might be relevant. Consequently, *Newstead* appeared to suggest that by virtue of the fact that contracted-out schemes replace the benefits provided by SERPS, they were not caught by Article 119.

However, in 1990, in *Barber,* the Court turned this conclusion on its head, concluding finally that contracted-out schemes do fall within the scope of Article 119. In so doing, the Court based its judgment on *Bilka.* Thus, the Court again focused on the agreement which had been reached between the employer and employees[53] and the absence of any contribution by the state. Additionally, it referred to the relatively limited personal scope of the scheme at issue: it was only available to employees employed by that employer rather than to more general categories of workers. Finally, and apparently most significantly, it noted that

---

[51]   Case 192/85, *Newstead,* cited *supra* at para. 15.

[52]   Case 80/70, cited *supra.*

[53]   And on the fact that entitlement to a pension could come about by the unilateral act of the employer.

contracted-out schemes play the same remunerative role *vis-à-vis* their beneficiaries as do the supplementary schemes operating in other Member States.[54]

This last consideration reveals that the Court has sought to ensure uniformity of application of Article 119 to occupational pension schemes throughout the Union, irrespective of the precise details of their operation and structure. Indeed, it has emphasised that,

> "the field of application of Article 119, ... is based on the close connection which exists between the nature of the services provided and the amount of remuneration"[55]

rather than the precise legal categorisation of form in which a particular arrangement is cast. This suggests that the Court would take a functional approach to defining the scope of Article 119, focusing on the substance of arrangements which are made, rather than upon their precise legal form. This motivation can clearly be witnessed in the *Ten Oever* judgment.[56] The Dutch scheme there had been extended to cover the entire branch of industry in question[57] and the question arose as to whether the state's involvement was such as to remove such schemes from the scope of Article 119. However, seeking to maximise the scope of Article 119 and to ensure its uniform application throughout the Union, the Court sought to analyze the arrangements in the light of its previous determinations. Hence it was able to conclude that since the rules of the scheme were in fact agreed by the social partners and that the state played no role whatsoever in the scheme's financing but merely responded to the sector's request that the scheme be made compulsory, Article 119 was applicable.[58]

---

[54]   Case C-262/88, cited *supra* at paras. 25-28.

[55]   Case 149/77, *Defrenne III*, cited *supra* at para. 21.

[56]   Case C-109/91, *Ten Oever*, cited *supra*.

[57]   See the description of this mechanism contained in Chapter 2.

[58]   Case C-109/91, *Ten Oever*, cited *supra* at paras. 10-11; O.W. Brouwer, "Bedrijfspensioenen: gelijke monniken, gelijke kappen", Staatscourant 3, 5 januari 1994, 5; B. Fitzpatrick, "Equality in Occupational Pension Schemes: Still Waiting for *Coloroll*", 23 ILJ (1994), 155-163 and 252; I. Piso, "Het Ten Oever-arrest van het Hof van Justitie", Sociaal Recht 1993 288-292; E.A. Whiteford, "Collectief Geheugenverlies? Het EG-recht en de aanvullende pensioenen", 18 NJCM (1993), 998-1004.

It therefore appeared finally to be clear: occupational pension schemes, whether purely supplementary to, or partly replacing the state scheme, contributory or non-contributory fell within the scope of Article 119 EC. Nevertheless, one question remained. By apparently requiring that the state play only a marginal role in schemes falling within Article 119, the Court raised the suspicion that national civil servants, employed by the State, did not enjoy the benefit of the guarantee of equality contained in Article 119. This issue was clarified in the *ABP* case.[59] The *Algemeen Burgerlijk Pensioenfonds* is the pension scheme to which Dutch civil servants are affiliated and its rules are contained in the Law relating to the ABP.[60] At the time in question, employer and employee representatives negotiated about the terms of the scheme, but the legislator was not bound to abide by decisions reached by these groups. The employer financed the scheme on a balance of cost basis, but the State as such was obliged to make up any financial shortfalls in given circumstances. The benefits which it provided supplemented those paid by virtue of the AOW. As this brief description of the scheme's features reveals, the linkage with the state was such as to place the ABP as it was at the time on the line in the case law dividing occupational and statutory schemes.

The Court examined its previous case law and concluded that when determining whether an occupational pension will be considered to be "other consideration ... which the worker receives, directly or indirectly, in respect of his employment from his employer"

> "the only possible decisive criterion is whether the pension is paid to the worker by reason of the employment relationship between him and his former employer, that is to say the criterion of employment based on the wording of Article 119 itself."[61]

---

[59]   Case C-7/93, *ABP*, cited *supra*. Although civil servants are not considered in this research, this case will nevertheless be discussed because of the clarification which it provides as to the scope of Art. 119.

[60]   Stb. 1986, 540 contains the most recent consolidated text. However, this has recently undergone change as a consequence of the legislator's decision to privatize the ABP. See *Wet Privatisering ABP*, Stb. 1995, 639.

[61]   Case C-7/93, *ABP* cited *supra* at para. 43.

The Court elaborated on this statement by observing that there will be the relevant nexus where the scheme relates only to a particular category of workers, the benefit is directly related to the period of service or its level is calculated by reference to the individual's final salary.[62] As might be expected given the diversity of methods by which pension provision can be made, the "form" in which a particular pension scheme is cast is not relevant.[63]

In essence, what the Court appeared to be stressing is that what is of relevance is the role which the scheme plays in overall retirement income provision. If the benefits provided supplement those paid by the state and are paid as a consequence of any employment relationship, Article 119 will be relevant, even if the state plays a role in the scheme. The broad interpretation accorded to Article 119 by the Court ensures that all employers within and across states are subject to the same obligations and that individuals are entitled to the protection of Article 119 irrespective of where and by whom they are employed.

After a stream of litigation stretching over more than 20 years it now appears to be the case that the benefits paid out under occupational pension schemes whether contributory or non-contributory, purely supplementary or partially replacing the statutory schemes in place, in a public or private law employment relationship fall within the scope of Article 119. The key factor influencing the Court in concluding that Article 119 is applicable to a given scheme has been the employment relationship. In the next three subsections, the

---

[62] Case C-7/93, *ABP* cited *supra* at para. 45. It is suggested that these conditions should not be read too literally. Note that the Court itself used "and" and not "or". However, there seems no reason to suppose that the Court would hold that a money purchase scheme - where the final benefit need bear no relation to the individual's final salary - does not fall within the scope of Article 119. Similarly, where the pension benefit offered is a lump sum, unconnected to salary levels prior to retirement, this would also seem to fall within the spirit of the judgments. This is confirmed by Case C-200/91, *Coloroll*, cited *supra* at para.s 57-60. See also the Court's observation in *Defrenne III* that the application of Article 119 depends upon the close connection which exists between the nature of the services provided and the amount of remuneration. Case 149/77, cited *supra* at para. 21.

[63] "The meaning and scope of [the principle of equal pay] cannot ... be determined by reference to a formal criterion, which is itself dependent on the rules of practices followed in the Member States. The need to ensure uniform application of the Treaty throughout the Community requires Article 119 to be interpreted independently of those rules or practices; Case C-7/93, *ABP* cited *supra* at para. 28.

equality legislation in place in the UK, the Netherlands and Germany will be outlined, and the place of occupational pensions in these frameworks discussed.

4.4.1   THE UK

Over the years, pensions have gradually come to be seen as a form of deferred pay received by employees by virtue of their employment contracts.[64] However, it has only been recently that the legislator has required that schemes offer equal benefits to women and men.

Both the 1970 Equal Pay Act[65] and the 1975 Sex Discrimination Act[66] excluded "terms related to death or retirement, or to any provision made in connection with death or retirement" from their scope because specific legislation was deemed necessary.[67] Although the Occupational Pension Schemes (Equal Access to Membership) Regulations 1976[68] required that men and women be offered access to occupational schemes on terms which were equal as to age and length of service and as to whether membership was compulsory or voluntary,[69] this was not interpreted as requiring that benefits be equal.[70] Consequently, as

---

[64]   See the observations of C. McCrudden, "Equal Treatment and Occupational Pensions: Implementing European Community Law in the United Kingdom following the Post-*Barber* judgments of the European Court of Justice", 46 NILQ (1995), 376-404; C. McCrudden, "Third Time Lucky? The Pensions Act 1995 and Equal Treatment in Occupational Pensions", 25 ILJ (1996), 28-42; Nobles, loc. cit. at pp. 1-8, 50-54.

[65]   1970 c. 41. The relevant s. was 6(1A)(b).

[66]   The latter was adopted to implement the obligations imposed by Directive 76/207. 1975 c. 65; the relevant s. was 6(4).

[67]   Nobles, loc. cit. at p. 199.

[68]   SI 1976 No. 142.

[69]   It will be recalled from the discussion in Chapter 2, that s. 15 of the Social Security Act 1986 (see now s. 160(1)(a) PSA 1993 and s. 2(2)(a) of the 1996 Regulations) rendered void any provision purporting to make scheme membership compulsory.

[70]   See the discussion on access *infra*.

shall emerge in the remainder of this Chapter, occupational pension schemes differentiated between women and men in a wide range of ways.

4.4.2   THE NETHERLANDS

A similar story can be told for the Netherlands. Although Article 1 of the 1983 Constitution contains a general equality clause, it has only limited horizontal effect[71] and Article 120 of the Constitution prohibits the national judge from evaluating legislation in the light of the Constitution.[72] The legislative response to Directive 75/117, the *Wet Gelijk Loon* (Equal Pay Law),[73] the *Wet Gelijke Behandeling* (Equal Treatment Law)[74] and the consolidating statute, the *Wet Gelijke Behandeling*,[75] all excluded rights and benefits from pension schemes from their scope,[76] as did article 1637ij of the *Burgerlijk Wetboek* (Civil Code - BW) which deals with private law relationships.[77] This suggests that, as was the case in the UK, European law will have formed the catalyst moving Dutch occupational schemes to introduce equality between their male and female members.

---

[71]   This is to be effected through the general equality law *Algemene Wet Gelijke Behandeling* (AWGB) which entered into force on 1 September 1994. On this subject, see I.P. Asscher-Vonk and K. Wentholt, *Wet Gelijke Behandeling van Mannen en Vrouwen*, Deventer, 1994; J.A.H. Blom, *De Effectiviteit van de Wet Gelijke Behandeling M/V*, The Hague, 1994. See also I.P. Asscher-Vonk, *European Community Equality Law: The Netherlands*, Deventer, 1994.

[72]   See L. Prakke and C.A.J.M. Kortmann (eds.), *Het Staatsrecht van de landen der Europese Gemeenschappen*, Deventer, 1993 at pp. 504-505; van Rooij et al, loc. cit.

[73]   Stb. 1975, 129. For a critical analysis of the application of the equal pay directive in the Netherlands see, Boelens and Veldman, loc. cit.

[74]   Stb. 1980, 86, the legislative response to Directive 76/207.

[75]   Stb. 1989, 168.

[76]   See in general Blom, loc. cit; Asscher-Vonk and Wentholt, loc. cit.

[77]   *Uitkeringen of aanspraken ingevolge pensioenregelingen.*

4.4.3   GERMANY

The situation in Germany contrasts with the situations in the UK and the
Netherlands. The *Grundgesetz* (the Basic Law, hereafter, GG) provides a general
equality clause,[78] an equal treatment clause[79] and a non-discrimination clause.[80]
Article 3 GG enjoys limited horizontal effect,[81] giving the employee whose
contract is subject to public law an enforceable right. A similar right was created
for employees in private law relationships by the *Arbeitsrechtliches EG-*
Anpassungsgesetz[82] which introduced paragraphs 611a - 612a into the *Bundes*
Gesetz Buch (BGB),[83] and the concept of indirect discrimination (*mittelbare*

---

[78]   Art. 3(1) GG. *Alle Menschen sind vor dem Gesetz gleich.* (All persons are equal before the
law). T. Würtenberger, "Equality", in U. Karpen (ed.), *The Constitution of the Federal*
Republic of Germany. Essays on the Basic Rights and Principles of the Basic Law with a
Translation of the Basic Law, Baden-Baden, 1988, at pp. 67-90.

[79]   Art. 3(2) GG, *Männer und Frauen sind gleichberechtigd.* (Men and Women have equal
rights). On 30 June 1994, the *Bundestag* agreed to an addition to Article 3(2) GG: *Der Staat*
fördert die tatsächliche Durchsetzung der Gleichberechtigung von Frauen und Männern und
wirkt auf die Beseitigung bestehender Nachteile hin. (The State will promote the actual
realisation of equal rights between women and men and towards the elimination/reduction
of existing disadvantage). See A. Mittmann, "Das Zweite Gleichberechtigungsgesetz - eine
Übersicht", NJW (1994), 3048-3054, at 3053-3054.

[80]   Art. 3(3) GG, *Niemand darf wegen seines Geschlechts,... benachteiligt oder bevorzugt*
werden (No-one may be disadvantaged or advantaged because of... sex) E. Bloch
(*Gleichbehandlung von Männern und Frauen im Verhältnis des Europäischen*
Gemeinschaftsrechts zum Deutschen Arbeitsrecht, Diss., Göttingen, 1988) observes at p. 82
that Article 3(3) GG adds little to Article 3(2).

[81]   See for example, Bloch, loc. cit. at pp. 83-4.

[82]   *Gesetz über die Gleichbehandlung von Mann und Frau am Arbeitsplatz und über die*
Erhaltung von Ansprüchen beim Betriebsübergang, law of 13 August 1980, BGBl. 1308.

[83]   This legislation was designed to implement Germany's EC law obligations. They were duly
found to be in breach in Cases 14/83, *von Colson and Kamann* v. *Land Nordhein-Westfalen*,
[1984] ECR 1891; Case 79/83, *Harz* v. *Deutsche Tradax GmbH*, [1984] ECR 1921. See
Bloch, loc. cit. at pp. 136-177; Hervey, loc. cit. at pp. 112-114. The final legislation fully
implementing the obligations is contained in the Second Equality law, *Gesetz zur*
Durchsetzung der Gleichberechtigung von Frauen und Männern, BGBl. I 1994, 1406; see
generally, Mittmann, op. cit.

Benachteiligungen) into German law.[84] As early as 1955, the BAG recognised that article 3(2) GG granted a right to equal pay for equal work[85] and in 1972 it recognised that occupational pension rights represent the employee's deferred pay.[86] As will emerge below, German law has been responsible for many of the changes which German pension schemes have been obliged to introduce. However, this is not to say that the role played by European law has been negligible.

4.5   Access

It is common for employers to offer occupational pensions only to some of their employees; before an individual can begin to accrue pension benefits, (s)he must be entitled to join the scheme. The most common conditions set for obtaining access to a pension scheme concern years of service with the employer, hours of work or seniority.

The Court first addressed the question of access to occupational pension schemes in *Bilka*.[87] It will be recalled that *Bilka* concerned the non-contributory occupational pension scheme offered to its employees by a German department store. To qualify for payment of the benefit, a part-time employee had to have been employed full-time for at least 15 years over a 20 year period. Ms. Weber argued that the imposition of a minimum requirement of full-time employment worked to the disadvantage of women and formed a discrimination prohibited by Article 119. The UK government had argued that the conditions placed by an employer on the admission of his employees to an occupational scheme did not fall

---

[84]   See H.J. Pauly, "Decisions by the Federal Labour Court and the Court of Justice of the European Communities on the Subject of Indirect Discrimination" in L. Mok (ed.), *International Handbook on Pensions Law and Similar Employee Benefits*, London/Dordrecht/Boston, 1989, pp. 601-610, at p. 602; Bloch, loc. cit. at p. 94; Blomeyer, loc. cit.; Rating, loc. cit.

[85]   BB 1955, 225; Bloch loc. cit. at p. 85.

[86]   BB 1972, 1005. confirmed and extended by the judgment of 20 February 1975, DB 1975 1274.

[87]   Case 170/84, *Bilka*, cited *supra*.

within the scope of Article 119. However, in finding that the scheme offered by *Bilka* discriminated between women and men, the Court not only confirmed[88] that the benefits paid out by occupational schemes are pay within the meaning of Article 119,[89] but that the conditions of access to such schemes also fall within its scope.[90]

In two recent cases, this approach has been confirmed. In *Vroege*[91] and *Fisscher*,[92] claims were raised by women who had been excluded from membership of their employer's pension scheme. They requested that they be granted membership of the scheme from the commencement of their employment or 8 April 1976,[93] whichever was later. The Court appeared to find no difficulty in holding that

> "the direct effect of Article 119 can be relied upon in order retroactively to claim equal treatment in relation to the right to

---

[88]   It can be considered to have confirmed what could be inferred from its judgment in Case 80/70, *Defrenne*, cited *supra*. This is certainly the view which the Court itself took. See Case 170/84, *Bilka*, cited *supra* at para.s 16-22.

[89]   Case 170/84, *Bilka*, cited *supra* at para. 22 ("Benefits paid to employees under the scheme therefore constitute consideration received by the worker from the employer in respect of his employment").

[90]   This emerges not only from the express terms of the judgment but also from the comparison which the Court made. In concluding that the scheme in *Bilka* discriminated against part-timers it compared the treatment of full-time and part-time workers (at para. 27 it considered that "Since ... a pension falls within the concept of pay for the purposes of ... Article 119 it follows that, hour for hour, the total remuneration paid by Bilka to full-time workers is higher than that paid to part-time workers"). Had the conditions of access to the scheme not fallen within the scope of Article 119, the appropriate comparison would have been between full-timers who were entitled to benefits under the scheme and part-timers who enjoyed similar entitlement.

[91]   Case C-57/93, *Vroege* v. *NCIV Instituut voor Volkshuisvesting BV and Stichting Pensioenfonds NCIV*, [1994] ECR I-4541.

[92]   Case C-128/93, *Fisscher*, cited *supra*.

[93]   The date from which the Court recognised that Article 119 has direct effect; Case 43/75, *Defrenne II* cited *supra*.

join an occupational pension scheme and this may be done as
from 8 April 1976"[94]

From this date, employers have been obliged to treat women and men equally in
relation to access to membership of occupational schemes. As the reasoning of the
Court in *Bilka* makes clear, employers are also obliged to ensure that the benefits
which accrue as a result of that membership are equal. To paraphrase the Court,
failure to grant a particular group of employees equal access to a pension scheme
results in these individuals receiving lower hourly pay. This observation can in turn
only be understood as requiring that equal benefits be provided. If this was not the
case, it would mean that the employer who offered scheme membership after, say,
two years employment, would merely be obliged to use the same period for male
and female employees. However, he would be allowed to offer men benefits of,
say, 70% of their final salary, and women a mere 50% - in effect, he would be
able to offer them equal access but to different things. This in turn would strip the
"equal" access provision of any real content.[95]

Holding that employers have been obliged to offer male and female
employees in equivalent employment equal access to occupational pension schemes
since 8 April 1976 seems deceptively simple. However, given that the judgments
were handed down on 28 September 1994, some 18 years from the date from
which this entitlement exists, difficult questions arise as to how, if an individual
has unlawfully excluded from a scheme, redress could be sought.

It has already been observed that in the UK and the Netherlands, the
legislator had exempted from the equality legislation provisions connected with
retirement. Consequently, differentiation between women and men will have been
widespread in the past. Merely holding that women are entitled to equal access
under equal terms to occupational pension schemes does not resolve all the
questions in this area. For example, most schemes in the UK are contributory, that

---

[94]   Case C-128/93, *Fisscher* cited *supra* at para. 27.

[95]   This conclusion is not affected by the temporal limitation which the Court imposed on the
effects in time of its judgment in *Barber*, on which see the discussion in s. 4.6.1.

is, they require that members pay contributions to the scheme.[96] If someone has been wrongfully excluded from scheme membership and wishes to claim this, must (s)he pay the contributions which would have been required had (s)he been offered membership at the time? Are they to be revalued in the line with wage/price inflation? For how far back can rights be claimed? Scheme funds earn investment income. If funds have not been invested, they will not be able to earn income. Who is responsible for making good this deficit? These are only some of the issues which arise in attempting to redress past discrimination.

In *Fisscher* the Court was asked what, if any, obligations Community law imposed on employers, schemes and employees in relation to redressing past discrimination. Most of the debate concerned the position of the employee. Should (s)he be obliged to make the contributions which (s)he had been precluded from making? The British government appears to have argued that Ms. Fisscher should be entitled to require payment of the pension to which she would have been entitled had membership been open to her, reduced by the value of the contributions which she did not make.[97] The Court rejected this argument,[98] holding that

> "...the fact that a worker can claim retroactively to join an occupational pension scheme does not allow the worker to avoid paying the contributions relating to the period of membership concerned."[99]

---

[96]   Government Actuary, loc. cit. at p. 40 from which it can be concluded that 90% of scheme members belong to a contributory scheme.

[97]   Cited at para. 29 of the opinion of the Advocate General.

[98]   Interestingly, the second largest pension fund in the Netherlands has already implemented these judgments by granting excluded part-timers back-dated membership to 8 April 1976. Apparently, the fund intends to treat the employer's contributions as having been paid and to deduct the missing employee contributions from the levels of benefit. See "PGGM repareert pensioen vrouwen", *NRC Handelsblad*, 20 January 1995 at p. 1; "PGGM 'repareert' pensioenen groot aantal deeltijdwerkers", *De Volkskrant*, 21 January 1995 at pp. 1 and 7. See also "Pensioen wordt een minder ver-van-uw-bed show" *OR Informatie*, 27 March 1996, 27-29 at 28. This appears to be precisely the approach argued (unsuccessfully) by the UK government.

[99]   Case C-128/93, cited *supra* at para. 37.

In this respect, the Court followed its Advocate General who considered that the course supported by the British Government would amount to unjust enrichment[100] and create a new discrimination, this time in favour of women (granting her the full benefits of membership, without having been obliged to pay contributions). As he emphasized at paragraph 30 of his opinion,

> "Occupational pension schemes are clearly based on a *quid pro quo* consisting of an indissoluble link between the (employee's and/or employer's) obligation periodically to pay contributions and the right to receive benefits upon attainment of a specific age."

If one right is to be claimed, the corresponding obligation must be respected, and consequently, women wishing to accrue pension rights in relation to periods of employment lying in the past will be required to pay contributions.

Although requiring that an individual must pay back-dated contributions to activate the right to equal access in the past can be seen to be reasonable,[101] there is nothing in the judgments to prevent the employer requiring that these contributions be paid in a lump sum. If this course of action were to be followed, it would create a significant barrier to individuals seeking redress of past discrimination. However, the Court's requirement that the exercise of a Community law right not be made impossible would seem to prevent employers following such a course of action.[102]

---

[100] Opinion of Advocate General Van Gerven in Cases C-57/93 and C-128/93, *Vroege* and *Fisscher* at para. 30. Unjust enrichment has featured in other EC law judgments, most notably in Case C-208/90, *Emmott* v. *Minister for Social Welfare and Attorney General*, [1991] ECR I-4269; see also Case C-132/92, *Birds Eye Walls* v. *Roberts*, [1993] ECR I-5579.

[101] As the Advocate General recognises, any other approach would grant a group of employees entitlement to benefits for which they have not fulfilled one of the conditions, payment of contributions.

[102] See Case 45/76, *Comet BV* v. *Produktschap voor de Siergewassen* [1976] ECR 2043; Case 177/78, *Pigs and Bacon Commission* v. *McCarren and Company Ltd.*, [1979] ECR 2161. Extensive discussion is to be found in D. Curtin, "Directives: The effectiveness of judicial protection of individual rights", 27 CML Rev. (1990), 709-739; D. Curtin, "Note on Case C-271/91, *Marshall* v. *Southampton and South West Hampshire Area Health Authority*", 31 CML Rev. (1994), 631-652. It is worth noting that all these cases are concerned with the obligations which Community law imposes on public bodies. It can be asked whether a different, less strict, approach would be taken *vis-à-vis* private individuals i.e. that an

Even should an individual be in a position to pay the sum required to redress, say, 18 years of discrimination, another aspect of the Court's judgments seems likely to prevent individuals claiming back-dated membership for significant periods of time.[103] The Court held that national time-limits for bringing actions are applicable to the rights flowing from Community law.[104] The only conditions which Community law imposes *vis-à-vis* such national rules is that they must not be less favourable than for similar types of action at national level and should not render the exercise of rights conferred by Community law impossible in practice. Since the Court held that claims to equal access can be lodged for periods of employment subsequent to 8 April 1976, apparently taking the view that the legal situation was clear for both employers and employees, it would seem to be the case that if national law requires that claims for equal pay be brought within, say, three years of the commencement of inequality, this period can, depending on the facts of the case, begin to run as of 8 April 1976. On this scenario, if claims had not been submitted by 7 April 1979, no redress for this period in the past could be obtained.[105]

---

employer would be entitled to take a course of action prohibited to a local authority. However, given the Court's attempts to make the distinction between public and private employers in this context as small as possible, it seems unlikely that such a course would be followed in this specific case. As the discussion above demonstrates, the Court has tried to ensure that the scope of Article 119 is unaffected by the precise legal character of the employer. Nevertheless, see the distinction which the Advocate General was willing to drawn in *Fisscher*, and the discussions in D. O'Keeffe, "Third Generation Remedies and Sex Equality Law" in Hervey and O'Keeffe loc. cit. at pp. 161-172; S. Moore, "Enforcement of Private Law Claims of Sex Discrimination in the Field of Employment", in Hervey and O'Keeffe, loc. cit. at pp. 139-159.

[103]   This is of particular relevance for those employers operating non-contributory schemes.

[104]   Case C-128/93, *Fisscher* cited *supra* at para. 39.

[105]   See on this point, Case 45/76, *Comet*, cited *supra*. Here in relation to national rules of procedure the Court held, in the context of a Treaty norm that national procedural rules govern the situation unless those rules in practice make the exercise of the right impossible. The Court therefore held that it was compatible with Community law for national legislation to lay down a reasonable period of time within which an action must be raised. In fact, the Court took the view that such national rules actually represent an application of the fundamental principle of legal certainty.

This part of the judgment will in fact ensure that few individuals - if any - are able to claim redress for the full period. However, national law will often also create other hurdles which an individual seeking to claim backdated membership of a scheme will have to clear. First, in employment law disputes, it is often the case that an action will have to be raised within a particular period, if not of the occurrence of the act complained of, but of the termination of the employment relationship.[106] If national law provides that all outstanding claims against an ex-employer must be raised within, say, 6 months of the end of the employment relationship, all individuals outwith that category will be unable to claim back-dated membership. In short, it seems that national law will be able to erect significant barriers to prevent individuals from claiming backdated membership.

However, the Court also made it clear that national rules must not make it impossible to rely on the Community law right in question. Thus the time bar may not prohibit a woman who has wrongly been excluded from membership of an occupational pension scheme from claiming her right to equal access for the future. Thus, a woman who is still in the same employment today would be entitled to raise a claim for equal access - she will merely be barred from back-dating her claim as far back as 8 April 1976. Indeed, it seems also to be the case that in raising her action, some degree of back-dating of the claim will be possible.[107] For example, national law may provide that where equal pay claims are brought, these may be back-dated no further than two years.[108] It is accordingly suggested that a woman who has wrongly been excluded from membership will be able to back-date her claim for membership for as long as such equal pay claims may be back-dated under national law.[109] Indeed, it would seem that where national law knows no such limits, the Court will allow the

---

[106] See in this regard, in the UK context s. 2(4) EPA.

[107] Case C-338/91, *Steenhorst-Neerings* cited *supra*.

[108] National pensions lawyers are already beginning to argue about which particular national provisions should apply to such claims. See for example in the Dutch context, van Veen, "Verjaring van pensioenopbouw", NJB 1995, 213-4; see also the answer to a parliamentary question at TK 1994-1995, *Aanhangsel*, 221-2.

[109] See the discussions *infra*.

national legislature to introduce such limits.[110] Thus not only can national law considerably limit the extent of redress which a woman obtains for discrimination, but the national legislature is even entitled to introduce specific legal provisions with that sole objective.

By expressly recognising that access and benefits fall within the scope of Article 119, the Court can be seen to have tried to maximize the effects of Article 119. Excluding access from the scope of Article 119 would have limited the group of employees protected by the norm to those who had already been granted membership. Holding that equal access must lead to equal benefits means that the access can be given a real content. Both these aspects of the Court's case law can be seen to offer women who were excluded from schemes in the past significant opportunities for redress and consequently to offer women with a method of significantly improving the level of pension which they receive. However, by requiring that contributions be paid if the access is to be back-dated, and by allowing national time limits to operate or even to be introduced, the Court has allowed national legislatures to ensure that only in exceptional cases will individuals obtain any significant level of redress.

4.5.1   THE UK

It has already been mentioned that although the Equal Access Regulations required that women and men be granted equal access to occupational schemes, this only extended to age and length of service conditions, and to whether membership was compulsory or voluntary. They did not require that the terms and conditions

---

[110]   This happened in Case 309/85, *Barra* v. *Kingdom of Belgium* [1988] ECR 355, where legislation was introduced to limit the financial consequences of the *Gravier* judgment (Case 293/83, *Gravier* v. *City of Liège*, [1985] ECR 593). In *Gravier* the Court had found a provision of Belgian law which required that foreign but not Belgian students pay a fee (the minerval) for a particular vocational course contrary to European law. However, after the judgment in *Gravier*, the Belgian legislature passed a law precluding reimbursement of minervals paid in error unless the action for repayment was brought before the courts before the date of the judgment in *Gravier*. Because it rendered "the exercise of the rights conferred by Article 7 of the EEC Treaty impossible" the Belgian legislation was impermissible. However, the judgment suggests strongly that had the legislation restricted, rather than made impossible, the right to reimbursement, a different outcome would have been reached.

offered to men and women once they belonged to the scheme be equal.[111] In other words, UK law allowed schemes to differentiate between women and men as regards the benefits offered. As might be expected, the judgments of *Vroege* and *Fisscher* have required that far-reaching alterations be introduced in this regard.

To comply with the requirements of European law, the Pensions Act 1995 introduces section 62(1) which implies into all schemes an equal treatment rule. This in turn is elaborated upon in s. 62(2) as covering the terms on which persons become members of a scheme **and** how they are treated.[112] As has been outlined above, men and women have been entitled to claim equal access to occupational pension schemes in relation to employment falling after 8 April 1976. The ECJ has held that those seeking to realise their rights will be under the same obligations as those who were favoured in the past by being offered membership. Thus, if male employees had to contribute to the scheme, women seeking redress for unlawful exclusion from the scheme will be required to pay the contributions which would have fallen due had they been offered membership originally. In the UK legislation, the government seems to have sought to bring about a situation more favourable to excluded individuals. Regulation 5 of the 1995 Equal Treatment Regulations inserts sections 7A and 7D into the EPA 1970. In essence, what these provisions do is to make the employer responsible for financing any back-dated membership. However, as has already been discussed, there are passages in the judgments of the ECJ which seem to preclude employers from waiving the contributions of previously excluded members and funding the retrospective membership themselves.[113] In the light of these passages, it would seem that the UK's new regulations are not in conformity with EC law, and the position is that

---

[111] See the comments of I.M. McCallum and I. Snaith, "EEC Law and United Kingdom Occupational Pensions Schemes", 2 EL Rev. (1977), 266-273.

[112] However, s. 63(6) provides that s. 62 is only operative in relation to periods of employment lying after 17 May 1990. See also in this respect, reg.s 6 and 11 of The Occupational Pension Schemes (Equal Treatment) Regulations 1995 SI 1995 No. 3138. This limitation is a consequence of the government's interpretation of the limitation of the effect in time of the judgment in *Barber* and the so-called *Barber* Protocol, on which see the discussion at s. 4.6.1. below.

[113] E.g. Case C-128/93, *Fisscher*, cited *supra* at para. 37.

if individuals wish to claim back-dated rights to scheme membership, they will have to pay their share of the contributions necessary to fund the benefits.

In relation to claiming back-dated rights, section 2(4) of the Equal Pay Act 1970 provides that applicants under the Act must have been employed by the employer in question within six months preceding the date on which the claim is brought. Section 2(5) provides that claims under the Act may not be back-dated by more than two years from the date on which proceedings are initiated. Regulations 5 and 10 of the 1995 Equal Treatment Regulations which insert sections 6A and 6D into the EPA, and section 63(4)(c) PA 1995 make express provision for these rules to be applied to occupational pension schemes. The Regulations came into force on 1 January 1996, replacing the provisions of The Occupational Pension Schemes (Equal Access to Membership) Amendment Regulations 1995,[114] which themselves amended the 1976 Occupational Pension Schemes (Equal Access to Membership) Regulations. The basic effect of these provisions is to allow individuals to claim equal access to pension schemes[115] from the later of 2 years prior to submitting the claim, or 31 May 1995.

However, anyone who raised a claim for back-dated membership prior to 31 May 1995 may find the provisions of sections 2(4) and (5) being applied by analogy to their case. This was the course of action taken by the Employment Appeals Tribunal in its judgment of 24 June 1996 in *Preston and Fletcher* v. *Wolverhampton Healthcare NHS Trust, Secretary of State for Health and others and Midland Bank Plc*. This course of action would seem clearly to be envisaged by the Court in its *Vroege* and *Fisscher* judgments, and consequently it seems unlikely that it will be found to violate EC law.[116]

Although the Government Actuary Surveys are very informative, they cast very little light on the extent to which male and female members accrued rights to

---

[114] SI 1995 1215.

[115] Without being obliged to pay contributions, but see the comments above.

[116] The EAT has asked for a preliminary ruling on the compatibility of the two year time limit contained in s. 2(5) with EC law; *Mrs B.S. Levez* v. *T.J. Jennings (Harlow Pools) Ltd*, Appeal No. EAT/812/94.

different levels of benefits.[117] However, they do reveal that it was common for employers to exclude their part-time employees from membership of schemes. The practice of excluding part-time employees from schemes has changed only slowly in the post-*Bilka* period.[118] In 1983, some 2 million employees were excluded from schemes because they carried out part-time work,[119] and by 1991 the figure had dropped by almost 50%. A mere 16% of part-timers were found by the 1991 survey to belong to occupational schemes, as compared to 57% of full-timers.[120] Furthermore, the 1991 survey reveals that 1,060,000 employees are still excluded from occupational pension schemes in the private sector because the scheme does not admit part-time employees. This would seem clearly to conflict with European law. A further 1,940,000 individuals belong to schemes in which between 9 and more than 26 hours per week must be worked to gain membership. 2,700,000 individuals belong to schemes in which only those working fewer than 8 hours per week are excluded.[121] Whether schemes which set hour thresholds for membership are acting in conformity with European law will depend upon whether the employer can produce an objective justification for his conduct. Given that a certain percentage of every contribution goes to defer administrative costs, it is conceivable that for those working very few hours per week, the resulting benefit will be so small as not to justify undertaking the administrative tasks involved in building up a pension under the scheme. However, the judgments in *Nolte*[122] and

---

[117]   They are however informative on the differentiation in relation to pensionable age and survivor's benefits. These subjects will be discussed in the relevant sections below.

[118]   See the comments of the EOC in the House of Lords Report, op. cit, at p. 27.

[119]   1983 Survey by the Government Actuary, quoted in EOC, *Response of the Equal Opportunities Commission to the DSS on the EC Draft Social Security Directive*, Manchester, 1988 at p. 7.

[120]   Government Actuary, op. cit at p. 10.

[121]   1991 survey, op. cit. at p. 37.

[122]   Case C-317/93, cited *supra*.

Megner and Scheffel[123] discussed in Chapter 3 suggest that relatively high hours thresholds could be considered justifiable.

As the figures cited above demonstrate, if the Court takes a similar approach to this issue in relation to occupational schemes as it has in relation to statutory schemes, it will allow significant numbers of individuals to be excluded from schemes. For this reason, it is to be hoped that a more critical approach will be taken to this issue when it finally reaches Luxembourg.

Irrespective of the conclusion which the Court finally reaches on this point, it seems clear that schemes are going to be forced to change their rules on access. As such, this should result in a significant increase in the numbers of women with some form of occupational pension entitlement. However, British schemes did not in 1976 commonly grant equal access to occupational schemes as required by EC law, nor does *Bilka* appear to have galvanised them into action on this point. Provisions of national law seem certain to ensure that only a few women receive any redress at all, and that the redress who they do obtain will be extremely limited. It can consequently be concluded that employers have been rewarded for inaction in the face of what the Court seems to think was clear law.[124]

4.5.2   THE NETHERLANDS

Since 30 June 1994 an employer has been precluded from excluding employees from his pension scheme solely on the basis that they work fewer than the normal working hours of the undertaking. The same legislative amendment requires that where membership is dependent on earning a particular wage, a pro rata calculation must be made for part-time employees.[125] This should ensure that pension schemes comply with the obligations imposed upon them in relation to part-time

---

[123]   Case C-444/93, cited *supra.*

[124]   The fact that the Court elected not to limit the effect of its judgment on access in time suggests that it considered that the law was clear.

[125]   Art. 2a PSW. See also *Wettelijk recht op deeltijdarbeid*, TK 1993-1994, 23 538, nr. 1.

workers by European law, although European law appears to have played no rôle whatsoever in persuading the government to introduce the amendment in question.

A 1990 research project[126] reveals that a mere 9.1% of the members of occupational pension schemes work part-time.[127] Of the schemes surveyed at that time, 15 excluded those working fewer than 50% of average hours from membership, while 28 schemes excluded those working less than 35% of average hours from membership. The report concluded that 45 schemes covering 73% of the trial group partially excluded part-timers. As with UK schemes, it seems likely that a certain proportion of those currently excluding part-time employees will be utilising a threshold which indirectly discriminates against women and consequently that as a consequence of *Vroege* and *Fisscher* they will be able to claim redress. Again, like the UK, it seems that not only was no action taken in 1976, but *Bilka* also failed to cause schemes to alter their existing practices.

In relation to *Vroege* and *Fisscher* claims, litigation is ongoing as to the precise period of backdating which individuals can claim. One argument is that rights have to be claimed within 5 years of the right arising,[128] in other words, within 5 years of 8 April 1976, or joining the employer's undertaking, whichever is later. On the other hand, Article 11 of the Equal Treatment Law provides that equal pay claims are barred after two years have elapsed from the date on which payment fell due. Finally, some consider that these claims ought to be treated as claims for compensation, in relation to which a 20 year prescription period applies.[129]

At the time of writing, conflicting approaches are being taken by the various lower courts. For example, the *Kantonrechter* at Utrecht has held that a 5

---

[126]   I. de Veer, R.A. de, Bruyn and M. van der Linden, *Gelijke behandeling naar geslacht in aanvullende pensioenregelingen. Juridisch, beleidsmatig en empirisch bekeken*, Den Haag, 1991. This is the most recent comprehensive research available.

[127]   De Veer et al, loc. cit. at p. 51.

[128]   See art.3:308 BW.

[129]   See art. 3:306 BW.

year period applies,[130] whereas the *Kantonrechter* at Rotterdam has held that a 20 year period applies.[131] However, it seems likely that these cases will be appealed to the level of the *Hoge Raad* and that certainty on this point is some way off.

It appears that Dutch pension schemes did not just practice indirect discrimination, but that direct discrimination also occurred. Of the 70 schemes examined in 1990, 3 still excluded women in general from membership, and another 4 excluded only married women.[132] This conduct is clearly in conflict with the requirements of European law and consequently the many women who appear to have suffered discrimination in the past will have to be offered redress.

In this respect, the Dutch legislator has recently taken an initiative to improve the position of these women.[133] As the discussion in Chapter 2 reveals, for a number of years, the Dutch toyed with the idea of making occupational pension provision compulsory. To that end, a fund, the *Fonds Voorheffing Pensioenverzekering* (FVP) was created,[134] *inter alia* to enable unemployed persons to continue to accrue pension rights.[135] However, pensions were never made compulsory, although monies were accrued as planned. The reforms of the PSW which were introduced on 30 June 1994 also altered the situation of the FVP. Its monies can now also be used to finance compensatory pensions (*inhaalpensioenen*)[136] for women who previously were the victims of direct

---

[130]   21 September 1995; *Pensioenjurisprudentie*, 1995/45.

[131]   15 September 1995, *Pensioenjurisprudentie* 1995/46.

[132]   Ibid. at pp. 60-61. Note that the position on pensionable age and survivor's benefits will be discussed below.

[133]   On which see M. Kraamwinkel, "Inhaalpensioen voor gediscrimineerde vrouwen" 50 SMA (1995), 644-650.

[134]   Initially created by the law of 13 December 1972, Stb. 702.

[135]   For a brief introduction see E. Lutjens and B. Wessels, *Aanvullend Pensioen. Civiel- en sociaalverzekeringsrechtelijke hoofdzaken van aanvullende pensioenen in het bedrijfsleven*, Deventer, 1991 at pp. 54-56.

[136]   The literal translation is "catch up" pensions.

discrimination by pension funds.[137] Another condition which has to be satisfied if a subsidy is to be obtained is that the woman must have been employed on 17 May 1990. Finally, to qualify for the 25% subsidy, it is necessary that the compensation must be a voluntary action by the employer or fund. If the woman has raised a legal claim, or if the law requires that compensation be offered, employers and funds do not qualify for the payment. This means that if the *Hoge Raad* finally decides the back-dating cases in line with the *Kantonrechter* in Rotterdam - the 20 year back-dating period - the FVP will only be available to subsidise voluntary back-dating to women who while still in the employment relationship on 17 May 1990, were excluded from membership before 1976 because they were (married) women. The group of such individuals seems likely to be small indeed.

At the time of writing it remains unclear what degree of redress women in the Netherlands will be able to obtain for discriminatory provisions concerning access to pension schemes. Women who suffered indirect discrimination may be able to claim up to 20 years of back-dated membership. Women who were victims of direct discrimination may be able in addition[138] to benefit from subsidisation by the FVP should their employer or pension fund decide to offer further redress.

4.5.3 GERMANY

It appears that in 1990, 31.5% of scheme members were women. Although this figure is low, it seems that women's under-representation in German occupational schemes can not be blamed on employers excluding part-time employees. In Germany,[139] legislative provisions have been designed to protect the part-time employee from discrimination in relation to his employment. The first avenue through which part-time employees can require equal treatment with their full-time

---

[137] For the rules, see *Staatscourant* 31 May 1991, nr. 103.

[138] But as the discussion reveals, this is unlikely to concern more than a handful of women, if that.

[139] On this subject, see M. Lubnow, "Die Rechtsprechung zur Gleichbehandlung von Teilzeitbeschäftigten in der betrieblichen Altersversorgung - Folgen und Fragen", in Förster and Rössler (eds.), loc. cit. at pp. 273-294.

colleagues is by means of the *Beschäftigungsforderungsgesetz* (BeschFG). Paragraph 2(1) of this statute defines part-time employees as those working fewer hours than are normally worked in the undertaking in question.[140] However, an employer need not treat his part-time employees in the same manner as his full-time staff where there are *sachliche Gründe* (factual grounds) for differentiation.

Despite the legislature's adoption of a specific statute to protect part-timers, it has played only a minor role in this field. This is because the BAG held that the norms contained in Article 3(2) GG and Article 119 EC are stricter than paragraph 2(1) which should basically be seen as a prohibition against arbitrariness.[141] As a consequence, elucidation as to the precise content of the exception for *sachliche Gründe* is to be found in the case law concerning equality between women and men rather than in that concerned with the BescFG.

The first case concerning the exclusion of part-time employees from occupational pension schemes reached the BAG in 1982.[142] Here it held that it was contrary to articles 3(2) and (3) GG for an employer to exclude part-time employees from his occupational pension scheme, with article 119 EC playing only a marginal role in the Court's reasoning. In deciding whether or not *sachliche Gründe* were present to justify the differentiation, it took the view that since the only difference between the work carried out by part-time employees and that carried out by their full-time counterparts was its quantity rather than its quality,[143] the occupational pensions offered to part-time employees need only

---

[140] This contrasts with the vaguely worded proposals submitted by the EC Commission in this field which refer to "shorter working hours than statutory, collectively agreed or usual working hours". Proposal for a Council Directive on certain employment relationships with regard to working conditions O.J. 1990 C 224/4.

[141] See judgment of 23 January 1990, BB 1990 1202.

[142] Judgment of 6 April 1982, BB 1176; for details, see Lubnow, loc. cit. at pp. 280-281; Bloch, loc. cit. at pp. 163-166.

[143] In this respect, Lubnow cites some interesting research from which it appears that part-time employees may actually be more productive than their full-time colleagues. Lubnow, loc. cit. at p. 293.

be proportionately smaller.[144] Thus, it did not justify excluding the part-timers in their entirety from occupational cover.

In 1989 and 1990, three further judgments of the BAG built on the foundations which it laid down in 1982. In the judgment of 14 March 1989,[145] the BAG made it clear that it considered the exclusion of part-time employees from an occupational pension scheme to be indirect discrimination against women. The protection offered to part-time employees was further extended by a judgment of 23 January 1990[146] where it was stated that an employer could not choose to exclude all employees working fewer than 30 hours per week from the scheme, although a window of opportunity was left open to permit the exclusion of those working extremely short hours.[147] Finally, in a judgment of 20 November 1990,[148] the BAG indicated that the employer could not introduce equality over a transitional period, basically because it considered that neither the legislation nor the case law handed down in Germany had given any indication that indirect discrimination could be reduced over time.[149] Accordingly, it would appear to be

---

[144]   It should be noted that the BAG made it abundantly clear that it was aware of the financial consequences of its judgment which it deemed could only be met by adjustments for the future, not be reducing accrued rights. An extensive debate has taken place in German legal literature as to the temporal effects of a number of judgments relating to occupational pension schemes. On this subject, see inter alia, G. Griebeling, "Gleichbehandlung in der betrieblichen Altersversorgung", RdA (1992), 373-378 who seems to indicate that the appeal by the undertaking that the case law offends against the *Rechtsstaatprinzip* is without any chance of success.

[145]   BB 2115.

[146]   BB 1991, 916.

[147]   Presumably at some stage, the extremely small number of hours worked will amount to a *sachliche Gründe*. This would seem to be in line with the judgment of the BAG in 1982 (supra) where it seemed to indicate that it would consider that *Betriebstreue* could be rewarded by means of a sliding scale of benefits, reflecting the reduced quantity of work performed. The logic of this position is that at some stage the level of benefit accrued will be so small that it will be disproportionate to require its payment.

[148]   BB 1991, 1570.

[149]   In this respect, the judgment can be seen to echo the BAG's judgment of 5 September 1989 concerning occupational survivors' pensions, on which subject, see the discussion in section 4.6.1.3, *supra*.

the case that a part-time employee who has been excluded from an occupational scheme can require this from 1972, the moment from which the BAG recognised pensions as forming part of the pay received by an employee from his employer.[150] This would seem to go further than European law, since Article 119 EC only became directly effective for periods of employment subsequent to 8 April 1976.[151]

However, once again, the provisions of national procedural law seem likely to ensure that women obtain only the most limited redress. As a matter of national law, rights relating to an employment relationship must be claimed within either 1, 3 or 6 months. Alternatively paragraph 611a BGB provides that the right to damages for a violation of the prohibition against discrimination prescribes after 2 years. Finally, paragraph 196 BGB provides that wage claims prescribe after 2 years of the end of the year in which the claim arose.

4.5.4   CONCLUSIONS ON ACCESS

The importance of granting equal access to membership of occupational pension schemes cannot be overemphasised. Obliging employers to admit men and women on equal terms to schemes will reduce significantly the differentiation which has so often taken place between women and men in this field. No longer may employers operate different age thresholds for admitting women to scheme membership,[152] nor may they use women's "atypical" employment patterns, when

---

[150]   This is again applying by analogy the BAG's case law relating to occupational survivors' pensions. This question gains relevance in the light of the judgment of the Court of Justice in *Vroege* and the practice, widespread in Germany of offering non-contributory schemes. See E.A. Whiteford, "Lost in the Mists of Time: The ECJ and Occupational Pensions", (hereafter Whiteford 1995b) 32 CML Rev. (1995), 801-840, at

[151]   See Case 43/75, *Defrenne II*, supra; confirmed in, *inter alia*, Case C-128/93, *Fisscher*, cited *supra*; Case C-57/93, *Vroege*, cited *supra*. Note the decision of the BAG of 7 March 1995 (3 AZR 282/94) holding that the Protocol does not affect the applicability of national provisions like Article 3(1) GG. Note that the Court has been asked to rule on whether the Protocol prevails over the GG which prohibits retroactivity; Case C-50/96, *Schröder* v. *Deutsche Bundespost Telekom*, O.J. 1996 C 133/12.

[152]   Limiting membership to those deemed to be spinsters without a male to care for them; see the discussion in Groves 1992, loc. cit.

compared to the "male" 38 hour, 40 year uninterrupted career, as a blanket excuse to exclude them from the substantial benefits of scheme membership.

The statistics quoted in the national subsections of this section demonstrate how widespread discriminatory conditions of access to schemes were, and the European Court's recognition that women have been entitled to claim equal access to schemes for service accruing after 8 April 1976 appeared at first glance to be courageous. However, on closer inspection it has left national law the power to limit significantly the redress which women will be able to require. This deferral to national law not only spares the European Court difficult decisions, but it also undermines the uniformity of European law.[153]

In all three jurisdictions considered it appears that national procedural rules will render the possibility of using the *Vroege* and *Fisscher* judgments to obtain significant periods of backdated membership illusory. For women currently in paid employment, the clear statement of their right to be admitted to an occupational scheme on equal terms with their male colleagues ought to ensure that in the future they will be more likely to have some entitlement to an occupational pension. However, for women employed and discriminated against between 1976 and 1994, the judgments have little meaning and consequently, for many years to come, significant numbers of women will continue to bear the consequences of their discriminatory treatment in relation to pension scheme access.

4.6 Pensionable Age

As has already been pointed out in Chapter 3, of the three Member States which form the subject of this research, only the Netherlands currently offers men and women statutory retirement pensions at the same age, although both the UK and Germany have plans for introducing equality in this respect over the coming

---

[153] See the discussion in Curtin 1994, op. cit.; W. van Gerven, "Bridging the gap between Community and national laws: Towards a principle of homogeneity in the field of legal remedies?", 32 CML Rev. (1995), 679-702; R. Canata, "Judicial protection against Member States: A new *jus commune* takes shape", 32 CML Rev. (1995), 703-726.

decades.[154] Because occupational pensions generally supplement those provided by the state, many occupational schemes simply copied the state pensionable age in laying down pensionable age under the scheme rules. Doing so has a number of consequences for the pensions accrued by members of such schemes. In final salary schemes, individuals commonly build up a certain percentage, say 1/60th, per year of service. The most common consequence of women's shorter working lives in this field is that women will accrue a greater proportion of their pension per year than men, to take account of their shorter working lives. Alternatively, where annual accrual is at the same rate, a woman's shorter working life will allow her the opportunity only of accruing a lower level of pension. On the other hand, where a man and a woman have both worked for the same number of years and built up the same level of pension rights, if the man wishes to retire at the same age as his female colleague, the level of his pension will generally suffer actuarial reduction[155] because of his decision to take this pension sooner than the rules had envisaged. As these examples demonstrate, setting different pensionable ages can be seen to disadvantage both men and women in different ways.

As a matter of EC law, the position relating to the use of different pensionable ages in occupational schemes is now clear. It is contrary to Article 119 to impose an age condition which differs according to sex in respect of occupational pensions,[156] even where this merely reflects differences in the

---

[154]   In the UK, all those born after 6 March 1955 will have equal retirement ages, i.e. 65. For those born prior to that, it will gradually be phased in, with equalisation being realised in 2020. In Germany, from the year 2000 pensionable age will increase in monthly steps until it is equalised in 2012. For details, see the discussion in Chapter 3 and the literature cited therein.

[155]   The use of actuarial tables which differentiate on grounds of sex will be discussed separately in s. 4.7.

[156]   Case C-262/88, *Barber*, cited *supra* at para. 32; Case C-110/91, *Moroni* v. *Collo GmbH*, [1993] ECR I-6591 at para. 20; Case C-408/92, *Smith*, cited *supra*; Case C-28/93, *van den Akker*, cited *supra*.

statutory scheme.[157] In other words, occupational pensions must become payable to men and women at the same age.

However, the position has not always been so clear. The question was first raised in *Defrenne III*.[158] In that case, it was a term of the contracts offered to female employees that they should retire at the age of 40, whereas no such condition was contained in the contracts offered to male employees. The Court found that this age condition was a condition of employment which, despite its pecuniary consequences, did not fall within the scope of Article 119.[159] In *Burton*,[160] the rules of a voluntary redundancy scheme allowed women to apply for redundancy 5 years earlier than men.[161] The Court defined the problem as concerning the conditions of access to a scheme, which formed a working condition falling within the scope of Directive 76/207. In this respect, the Court can be seen to have remained faithful to its approach in *Defrenne III*. Particularly interesting was the Court's view that the permissible differentiation relating to pensionable age in the statutory scheme could be reflected in the conditions of access to payments under the occupational scheme. In casu, this allowed the Court to find that the scheme provisions allowing women to apply for redundancy 5 years earlier than men did not violate EC law.[162] This aspect of the *Burton*

---

[157]   It will be recalled that article 7(1)(a) of Directive 79/7 permits Member States to defer the implementation of equality in relation to statutory pensionable age. The complex subject of to what extent links may be laid between statutory and occupational schemes will be discussed in more detail *infra*.

[158]   Case 149/77, cited *supra*.

[159]   Case 149/77, cited *supra* at para. 21. The Court's findings had to be limited to the context of Article 119 since the implementation period for Directive 76/207 had not expired at the time of the judgment.

[160]   Case 19/81, *Burton* v. *British Railways Board*, [1982] ECR 554; see K. St. C. Bradley, "Note on Case 12/81 and Case 19/81", 19 CML Rev. (1982), 625-634.

[161]   The difference in ages reflecting the different statutory pensionable ages for women and men in the UK.

[162]   In the UK the difference in statutory pensionable age was reflected in a number of different ways. For example, the Occupational Pension Schemes (Equal Access to Membership) Regulations 1976, SI 1976/142 reg. 4 permitted the maximum entry age for women to

judgment appeared to have been overruled by a series of judgments handed down four years later.[163] In *Roberts*[164] the subject of the litigation was a contractual provision laying down a single age for dismissal in a mass redundancy involving the grant of an early retirement pension. In *Marshall*[165] the contractual retirement age operated by the employer reflected the different pensionable ages operated in the statutory scheme. In *Beets-Proper*[166] a contractual term required women to cease employment at an earlier age than men.[167] In all three cases the Court followed the same reasoning as in *Burton* in relation to the age condition, defining it as concerning the termination of employment, that is, a condition of employment. However, the various examples of differentiation in the three later cases were all found to conflict with EC law. This was because by the time it handed down its judgments in the 1986 cases the Court had narrowed the scope of the exception contained in Article 7(1)(a) of Directive 79/7 to

> "the determination of pensionable age for the purposes of granting old-age and retirement pensions and the possible consequences thereof for other benefits *falling within the statutory social security schemes*". (emphasis added)[168]

This implied that the linkage which had been approved in *Burton* was no longer permissible. Setting different contractual retirement ages did not fall within this narrower exception and therefore, despite the clear link with differentiation in the

---

schemes to be set at up to 5 years lower than for men.

[163]   As was observed by A. Arnull, "Some More Equal than Others?", EL Rev. (1986), 229-232; Curtin 1987, op. cit; D. Curtin, "Scalping the Community legislator: Occupational pensions and "Barber", 27 CML Rev. (1990), 475-506; T. Millett, "European Community Law: Sex Equality and Retirement Age", 36 ICLQ (1987), 616-633.

[164]   Case 151/84, *Roberts*, cited *supra*.

[165]   Case 152/84, cited *supra*.

[166]   Case 262/84, *Beets-Proper*, cited *supra*.

[167]   Despite the equal pensionable ages contained in the Dutch statutory scheme.

[168]   Case 152/84, *Marshall*, cited *supra* at para. 246.

statutory scheme, was contrary to European law.[169] In all these cases from *Defrenne III* to *Beets-Proper* the Court appeared to take the view that age conditions formed conditions of employment which - despite their pecuniary implications - fell within the scope not of Article 119, but of Directive 76/207. Additionally, after the false start in *Burton*, these cases also seemed to state clearly that no differentiation in age conditions was permissible even where merely reflecting legitimate differences in the statutory scheme.

The latter proposition was confirmed in unequivocal terms in both *Barber*[170] and *Moroni*.[171] The schemes at issue in both cases offered particular benefits to men and women at different ages, the ages chosen corresponding with the normal (different) pensionable ages under the statutory scheme. In both cases the Court found that this practice was in conflict with European law.[172] However, unlike the previous cases, the schemes at issue in *Barber* and *Moroni* were found to violate Article 119 not Directive 76/207. In other words, as *Bilka* had already suggested,[173] the Court held that Article 119 not only embraced the level of benefit paid out under a scheme, but also extended to cover the conditions laid

---

[169]   To this extent it must be concluded that *Burton* has been overruled.

[170]   Case C-262/88, cited *supra* at para. 32.

[171]   Case C-110/91, cited *supra* at para. 20.

[172]   In his opinion in *Barber*, Advocate General Van Gerven had considered at length the compatibility of the *Burton* and *Bilka* case law. He concluded that the age condition ought to fall within the scope of Article 119, considering further that Article 119 covers working conditions which directly cover access to remuneration but not the conditions precedent thereto concerning the continuation of the employment relationship. This amounted to bringing some, but not all, conditions of employment within the scope of Article 119. This was the second of his three possible interpretations. Subsequent events would seem to indicate that the Court has taken the broad approach ultimately rejected by the Advocate General. See the observations of Curtin (1990), op. cit. at 482 footnote 32. See the discussion *supra* on access and *infra* on links between statutory and occupational schemes.

[173]   And as the Court would confirm unequivocally in Cases C-57/93, *Vroege*, cited *supra* and Case C-128/93, *Fisscher*, cited *supra*.

down for acquiring access to that benefit.[174] In another context, Nobles explains this perfectly:

> "Logically, accepting that pensions are deferred pay leads one to regard all the rules of the scheme as part of the pay arrangement"[175]

For the Court to set out on this road did however require it to reverse its earlier case law, which with *Barber* and the succeeding cases it can be seen clearly to have done.

4.6.1   THE TEMPORAL LIMITATION

It was not only the Court which laid false trails in this area. Recognising that occupational schemes often mimic statutory pensionable age, the Council included a provision excluding pensionable age from the scope of Directive 86/378 and suggesting that such differentiation would remain legitimate as a matter of Community law until an additional Directive had been adopted outlawing the practice.[176] The Court's unequivocal finding in *Barber* that different pensionable ages violate Article 119 suggested that Article 9(a) of the Directive was incompatible with the Treaty.[177] However, in so holding, the Court took account of the reliance which schemes might have placed on the Directive and limited the temporal effects of its judgment in the interests of legal certainty and the legitimate expectations of the parties. It observed that

> "... overriding considerations of legal certainty preclude legal situations which have exhausted all their effects in the past from being called in question where that might upset retroactively the financial balance of many contracted-out pension schemes.(....) Finally, it must be pointed out that no restriction on the effects of the aforesaid interpretation can be permitted as regards the

---

[174]   This will be discussed in the section on links between statutory and occupational benefits below.

[175]   Nobles, loc. cit. at p. 52.

[176]   Article 9(a).

[177]   See Curtin (1990), op. cit. at 488-491; Prechal, op. cit. at 1301.

acquisition of entitlement to a pension as from the date of this judgement.

It must therefore be held that the direct effect of Article 119 of the Treaty may not be relied upon in order to claim entitlement to a pension with effect from a date prior to that of this judgement...."[178]

Despite the wish that this would contribute to legal certainty, this part of the judgment in fact served to create a huge degree of uncertainty and sparked a heated debate[179] centring upon the meaning of "legal situations which have exhausted their effects in the past", and "acquisition" and "entitlement to a pension". A wide variety of possible interpretations were advanced in academic contributions, the main options being summarised as follows:

1. equality need only be ensured in relation to those becoming a member of a scheme after 17 May 1990;
2. equality need only be ensured in relation to periods of employment falling after 17 May 1990;
3. equality need only be ensured in relation to those retiring for the first time after 17 May 1990;
4. equality must be ensured in relation to all pension payments made after 17 May 1990.

The potential cost to pension funds of these various options differed greatly. Options 1 and 2 involved no retroactive costs whatsoever, with option 2 having the advantage that it introduced equality throughout the membership of schemes from an earlier date than option 1. However, even option 2 would have allowed the effects of pre-1990 discrimination to be felt some 40 years after that date, as members with pre-*Barber* service entered retirement. By contrast, options 3 and 4

---

[178]   Case C-262/88, *Barber* cited *supra* at paras. 44 and 45.

[179]   Compare Curtin 1990, op. cit. at 485-488; J.R. Dierx, "Barberisme", Nemesis nr. 4 (1991), 1-4; S. Honeyball and J. Shaw, "Sex, law and the retiring man", 16 EL Rev. (1991), 47-58; E. Hoving, "Gelijke behandeling mannen en vrouwen in pensioenregelingen. Commentaar op Hof van Justitie EG 17 mei 1990 (Zaak *Barber*), TvP (1990), 50-55; D. Hudson, "Some reflections on the implications of the *Barber* decision", 17 EL Rev. (1992), 163-171; K.J.M. Mortelmans, "Zaak C-262/88, Douglas Harvey Barber vs. Guardian Royal Exchange Assurance Group", 39 SEW (1991), 143-153; S. Prechal 1990, op. cit. at 1299-1303; C.M. Sjerps, "Van Doornroosje en haar hardnekkige prins, oftwel: hoe het EG-Hof de pensioenwereld probeert te wekken", Sociaal Recht (1990), 212-217; E. Steyger, "Hof van Justitie EG, 17 mei 1990", Actualiteiten nr. 116, Nemesis (1990), 210-215.

would, on the basis that men would have gained entitlement to unreduced pensions from the age of 60, require schemes to make payments for which they had not bargained. It would however mean that the "fundamental right to equality" would be respected from 17 May 1990, only the benefits paid prior to that date being left undisturbed.[180]

The other main controversy at that time was whether only the contracted-out schemes at issue in *Barber* were entitled to rely on the temporal limitation, or whether it extended to cover all kinds of occupational pension schemes.[181] A host of references from national courts quickly attested to the fact that the confusion was not confined to academics.[182]

In the meantime, the lobbyists for the pensions funds got down to work. They took advantage of the Intergovernmental Conferences preparing amendments to the Treaty to persuade the Dutch government that the uncertainty should be cleared up by means of a Treaty amendment. The Dutch government duly submitted the interpretation of the temporal limitation most favourable to the pension funds. The other governments with significant "*Barber*-problems" were

---

[180]   The cost to British industry was estimated to be between 5 billion and 40 billion. See House of Commons Foreign Affairs Committee, *Europe After Maastricht*, Session 1991-1992, 2nd report, 70, paras. 11-14. For the Netherlands it was calculated that the bill would amount to *f* 120 billion guilders; see *Rapport inzake de mogelijke consequenties van het Barber arrest*, Towers Perrin/Smit & Bunschoten, April 1991. These figures were not uncontroversial; see for example, J.R. Dierx, "De macht der gewoonte", Nemesis nr. 1 (1992), 1-2. A subsequent investigation produced a figure of 3 to 5 billion guilders; *Rapport inzake de mogelijke financiële consequenties van het Barber arrest voor pensioenregelingen in Nederland*, Pensioenadviesbureau Brueren en Van Dijk, 1993.

[181]   See for example, Curtin (1990), op. cit. at 485 who argued that the temporal limitation ought indeed to be limited to contracted-out schemes. Support for this point of view could be obtained from the passages in the judgment in which the Court referred its temporal limitation to the specific situations of contracted-out schemes: at para. 43 the Court stated "..., the Member States and the parties were reasonably entitled to consider that Article 119 did not apply to pensions paid under contracted-out schemes...").

[182]   The first references were Case C-109/91, *Ten Oever*, O.J. 1991 C 125/11; Case C-110/91 *Moroni* O.J. 1991 C 132/8; Case C-152/91 *Neath* O.J. 1991 C 203/8; Case C-200/91 *Coloroll* O.J. 1991 C 243/4.

happy to acquiesce in this initiative,[183] and the support of the remaining Member States was apparently obtained with little difficulty. Accordingly, Protocol number 2 appended to the Treaty on European Union[184] provides that

> "For the purposes of Article 119 of this Treaty, benefits under occupational social security schemes shall not be considered as remuneration if and in so far as they are attributable to periods of employment prior to 17 May 1990, except in the case of workers or those claiming under them who have before that date initiated legal proceedings or introduced an equivalent claim under the applicable national law."

Protocols form an integral part of the Treaty[185] and are therefore to be recognised as primary Community law. As such on its entry into force on 1 November 1993 the so-called *Barber*-Protocol would supersede any conflicting provisions.[186]

---

[183] As can be deduced from the written observations of the five governments which intervened in the "post-*Barber*" cases (the UK, the Netherlands, Germany, Ireland and Denmark). The deadlines for submissions in Cases C-109/91, C-110/91 and C-152/91 all lay prior to the conclusion of the IGCs. All governments supported interpretation 2. The Commission which had initially supported interpretation 3, miraculously underwent a conversion to the merits of interpretation 2 between its submissions in Case C-152/91 and C-200/91. In the period between these two sets of submissions, the TEU had been agreed.

[184] On the legal issues, see S. Prechal, "Bommen ruimen in Maastricht. Wijziging van Artikel 119 EEG", 67 NJB (1992), 349-354; T.K. Hervey, "Legal Issues concerning the *Barber* Protocol", in O'Keeffe and Twomey (eds.), loc. cit. at pp. 329-337; Curtin 1993, op. cit.

[185] Article 239 EC. Confirmed by the Court in Case C-57/93, *Vroege*, cited *supra* at para. 35.

[186] As was recognised by the Advocate General in his Opinion in Cases C-109/91, C-110/91, C-152/91, C-200/91, [1993] ECR I-4893 at para. 23. See also Prechal 1992, op. cit; Curtin (1993), op. cit. It is true that according to Articles B and C of the TEU the Union aims to maintain in full the *acquis communautaire* and build on it. Were the Court to have interpreted the temporal limitation in a manner different from the interpretation laid down in the Protocol, some interesting legal issues could have arisen (see Curtin 1993, op. cit.; Hervey 1994, loc. cit; Whiteford 1993b, op. cit.; S. Moore, ""Justice Doesn't Mean a Free Lunch": The Application of the Principle of Equal Pay to Occupational Pension Schemes", 20 EL Rev. (1995), 159-177). However, as will emerge, the Court chose to interpret its temporal limitation as being in conformity with the interpretation contained in the Protocol.

As it happened, the Court chose not to wait for the entry into force of the TEU to elucidate its temporal limitation in *Barber*. Instead, on 6 October 1993[187] it handed down its judgment in *Ten Oever*, holding that

> "the direct effect of Article 119 of the Treaty may be relied upon, for the purpose of claiming equal treatment in the matter of occupational pensions, only in relation to benefits payable in respect of periods of service subsequent to 17 May 1990..."[188]

It is clear that this formulation does not differ on any matter of significance from that laid down in the Protocol.

As has already been noted, the Court was prompted to impose its limitation on the effects in time of its judgment in *Barber* by considerations of legal certainty.[189] In the context of different pensionable ages, the Court had reasoned that the exceptions contained in Directive 79/7 and Directive 86/378[190] had led pension funds to believe that derogations from the equality principle were permitted in occupational pensions.[191] However, the temporal limitation in

---

[187] Although this was formally before the *Bundesverfassungsgericht* handed down its judgment in *Brunner* v. *The European Union Treaty*, [1994] 1 CMLR 57, on 12 October 1993, it must surely have been clear to the ECJ that the TEU was going to enter into force.

[188] Case C-109/91, cited *supra* at para. 20.

[189] Case C-262/88, *Barber* cited *supra* at para. 44.

[190] In fact, pensionable age and survivors pensions. A transitional regime was also envisaged for employee contributions. However, as will be discussed in the section on contributions below, in *Neath* and *Coloroll*, the Court held that employee contributions were pay and had had to be equal since 8 April 1976.

[191] This differs however slightly from what the Court actually said at the time in *Barber*. There it cited the exceptions in relation to pensionable age contained in the Directive and continued that "In the light of those provisions, the Member States and the parties concerned were reasonably entitled to consider that Article 119 did not apply to pensions paid under *contracted-out* schemes and that derogations from the principle of equality between men and women were still permitted in that sphere." (emphasis added). With respect, the exceptions to the Directives could by no stretch of the imagination be interpreted as excluding contracted-out schemes from the obligation to implement equality. However, this passage of the judgment prompt some to argue that the temporal limitation ought to be limited to contracted-out schemes; see Curtin 1990, op. cit. at 485.

Barber, the Protocol and the judgment in *Ten Oever*[192] all appeared to be worded generally, and accordingly not restricted, as logic might perhaps have demanded, to those subjects which were excluded from the Directive. Equally, the general terms employed in the temporal limitation suggest that it also extends to cover access to occupational schemes which the Court had held in *Bilka*, and *Barber* itself, to fall within Article 119. One of the questions raised by the temporal limitation was therefore whether in respecting the pension fund's legitimate expectations the Court had overruled *Bilka* and ignored the legitimate expectation of individuals based on that judgment.[193]

In *Vroege* and *Fisscher* the Court revealed that this interpretation of the temporal limitation was much too broad. It confirmed the logic which had moved it in *Barber*, holding that the temporal limitation applied only in respect of

> "those kinds of discrimination which employers and pension schemes could reasonably have considered to be permissible owing to *the transitional derogations for which Community law provided* and which were capable of being applied to occupational pensions." (emphasis added)[194]

The temporary derogations for which European law had made provision were in relation to pensionable age and survivor's benefits.[195] As the Court stressed, there was no justification for extending this to cover access to occupational schemes, which therefore continues to be governed by *Bilka*, which requires equality in access to and benefits from occupational schemes.

---

[192]   The latter confirmed in this respect by the judgments in Case C-110/91, *Moroni*, cited *supra*; Case C-152/91, *Neath*, cited *supra*.

[193]   See the comments of Advocate General Jacobs to this effect in his opinion in Case C-7/93, *ABP* cited *supra* at para. 51. See also E.A. Whiteford, "Collectief Geheugenverlies? Het EG-recht en de aanvullende pensioenen", 18 NJCM (1993), 998-1004.

[194]   Case C-57/93, *Vroege* cited *supra* at para. 27; Case C-128/93, *Fisscher*, cited *supra* at para. 24. See in general, Curtin (1990), op. cit. at 485; Whiteford 1995b, op. cit. at pp. 832-839; E.A. Whiteford, "Eindelijk Duidelijkheid? Het Hof van Justitie en aanvullende pensioenregelingen", 50 *Sociaal Mandblad Arbeid* (1995), 638-643.

[195]   Art. 9(a) and (b) of Directive 86/378. See in greater detail, Whiteford (1995) *supbra* at 832-839.

These considerations indicate that the temporal limitation applies as follows. Women and men have to be granted equal access to occupational schemes for post 8 April 1976 employment, and the resulting benefits must also be equal, unless the schemes had previously differentiated in respect of pensionable age and or survivors' benefits, in which case benefits need only be equal for employment subsequent to 17 May 1990.[196] In other words, where an employer requires that men have been employed for 2 years before they qualify for scheme membership, he may not set a different threshold for female members. In addition, where he offers men benefits of, say, 70% of their final salary on retirement, he may not offer women benefits of a mere 50%. The only differentiation which is permissible is where in the past schemes had differentiated in relation to pensionable age or survivor's pensions.[197]

Having established the scope of the temporal limitation which the Court imposed on the effects of Article 119 on occupational pension schemes, the final matter which has to be addressed is whether this conclusion has to be adjusted because of the Protocol. The Court observed that

"while extending it to all benefits payable under occupational social security schemes and incorporating it in the Treaty, Protocol No 2 essentially adopted the same interpretation of the Barber judgment as did the Ten Oever judgment".[198]

It is suggested that this indicates that the temporal limitation[199] and the Protocol are to be read as synonymous. The Protocol merely confirmed the future service

---

[196]   This is the interpretation supported by Advocate General Cosmas in Case C-435/93, *Dietz* v. *Stichting Thuiszorg Rotterdam*, opinion of 13 July 1995.

[197]   The logic of this interpretation is demonstrated by an example of what any other interpretation would mean. If equal access does not have to lead to equal benefits, it would mean that the employer would be free to offer men benefits of 70% of their final salary but restrict the benefits accrued for the same contributions by female employees to a mere, say, 50%. This hardly seems consistent with the principle of equal pay.

[198]   Case C-57/93, *Vroege* cited *supra* at para. 41.

[199]   As clarified in the case law.

interpretation and that it was available to all kinds of occupational pension schemes operating in Europe, not just the contracted-out schemes at issue in *Barber*.[200]

The alternative interpretation would be that the Protocol extends the temporal limitation of *Barber*[201] to all benefits provided for post-8 April 1976 service.[202] On this interpretation, the Protocol differs significantly from the case law,[203] making it difficult to state that the Protocol contains an interpretation of the temporal limitation which is "essentially the same" as that in the case law. Consequently, it is suggested that this interpretation ought to be rejected.[204]

To conclude, if this interpretation is accepted,[205] it means that the logic which moved the Court in *Barber* remains intact. Only for those matters for which Directive 86/378 provided a derogation is the obligation to pay equal benefits relaxed. Individuals relying upon the judgment in *Bilka* that pension benefits constitute pay and that they must obtain equal access to such schemes are respected. Any other interpretation leads to *Bilka* having been entirely overruled.[206] In addition, the Court's recognition that individuals have been

---

[200]   See also the opinion of the Advocate General in Case C-435/93, *Dietz*, cited *supra*.

[201]   Only those schemes which had differentiated in relation to pensionable age or survivors pensions are exempted from the obligation to provide for the accrual of equal benefits for service lying after 8 April 1976, and only to that extent.

[202]   M. Tether, "Sex Equality and Occupational Pension Schemes", 24 ILJ (1995), 194-203 at 196-198; J. Wouters, "Gelijke Behandeling van mannen en vrouwen inzake bedrijfspensioenen: de "post-*Barber*"-arresten van het Hof van Justitie", 20 NJCM Bulletin (1995), 274-302, at 280-287; Hoving, op. cit. at 27.

[203]   In practice, this interpretation would mean that an employer *could* offer male employees benefits of 70% of their final salary and female employees 50%.

[204]   See the opinion of the Advocate General in Case C-435/93, *Dietz*, cited *supra*.

[205]   Only schemes which had differentiated in relation to pensionable age and/or survivors' pensions enjoy an exemption from the obligation to provide equal benefits for service accruing after 8 April 1976.

[206]   Which was not the intention of the Court. It stated in *Vroege* that "Protocol No 2 does not affect the right to join an occupational pension scheme, which continues to be governed by the *Bilka* judgment." (para. 43). As has repeatedly been stated, *Bilka* recognises that access to and benefits from occupational pension schemes are pay.

entitled to obtain equal access since 8 April 1976 would have been rendered
meaningless since it would hold that although individuals would have to be granted
access on equal terms, and pay equal contributions, the employer could choose to
provide lower benefits in return for these contributions. Put in a different way, it
would in fact allow the employer to offer women and men access to different
things.

4.6.2   INTRODUCING EQUAL PENSIONABLE AGES

Although the statement that schemes are obliged to operate equal pensionable ages
in relation to periods of service after 17 May 1990 may appear to be quite
straightforward, in practice a number of problems arose which were laid before the
Court in the cases of *Smith*[207] and *Van den Akker*.[208] Both these pension
schemes chose to implement the *Barber* decision by raising the pensionable age
for women. The pension scheme in *Smith* operated different pensionable ages for
men and women until 30 June 1991. As a consequence of the *Barber* decision
equal pensionable ages were introduced as of 1 July 1991, whereby in fact,
women's pensionable age was raised from 60 to 65. In *Van den Akker*, pensionable
ages had been equalized (women's raised from 55 to 60) with effect from January
1985, although for one group of women the possibility of retirement aged 55 was
retained. However, in response to the judgment in *Barber*, this latter possibility
was abolished as of 1 June 1991. The alterations at issue thus altered retroactively
the pension rights of the women concerned.

A first subject of debate was whether schemes were entitled to raise
pensionable age at all, or whether EC law compelled them to lower male
pensionable age. In *Defrenne II* the Court had observed that

> "since Article 119 appears in the context of the harmonization of
> working conditions while the improvement is being maintained,
> the objection that the terms of that article may be observed in

---

[207]   Case C-408/92, *Smith*, cited *supra*.

[208]   Case C-28/93, *Van den Akker*, cited *supra*.

other ways than by raising the lowest salaries may be set aside."[209]

This was seen to support the view of those arguing for "levelling up" of the rights of the disadvantaged group to the levels enjoyed by the favoured group.[210] In the case of pensionable age, this means allowing men to retire at the same age as women without their pension being reduced.[211] Again, like the solutions proposed by the schemes in *Smith* and *Van den Akker*, the proposal was to treat all individuals retiring after a set date as if the terms of the scheme had always provided equal pensionable ages.

The Court's approach was, like that of its Advocate General, more nuanced. In *Smith* and *Van den Akker*, it clarified its previous case law in relation to levelling up. As has become clear in relation to the temporal limitation, the Court is sensitive to the fact that pensions are built up by individuals over time and that both pension funds and the individual members develop (legitimate) expectations in relation to the pension scheme. This explains why pension schemes themselves, when introducing new rules, do so only *vis-à-vis* future service periods and (partly) explains why the Court adopted the future service interpretation of the temporal limitation in *Barber*.[212]

In answering the question as to how pensionable ages are to be equalized, the Court was consistent with this approach and distinguished three different periods of service, requiring different legal treatment. First, the period after the scheme rules have been adjusted to comply with the directly effective norm of

---

[209] Case 43/75, *Defrenne II*, cited *supra* at para. 15.

[210] See the observations to this effect in Curtin 1990, op. cit. at 505-6. Note that requiring that employers level up can be seen to amount to a sanction, in that it is the employer who would bear the burden of funding the extension of the more favourable treatment to the group previously discriminated against.

[211] The Court's judgment in Case C-184/89, *Nimz*, cited *supra*, was also cited in support of levelling up. There the Court had held that the national court must set aside any discriminatory provision of national law and apply to members of the disadvantaged group the same arrangements as those enjoyed by the other employees, arrangements which, failing correct implementation of Article 119 in national law, remain the only valid point of reference.

[212] The future service approach is also recognised in Article 8(2) of Directive 86/378.

Article 119. In adjusting scheme rules **for the future**, schemes are free either to level up or level down, that is to raise or to lower pensionable age. As the Court emphasized, the Community law obligation imposed by Article 119 is merely one of equality, it does not impose any qualitative obligations on the schemes. Accordingly it would be entirely in conformity with the Treaty for a scheme to change its rules per 1 July 1991 to provide that all pension rights built up after that date are accrued on the basis of a pensionable age of 65.

The second period which was identified by the Court was that lying between 17 May 1990 and the date from which the scheme rules had been cured of their discriminatory provision. During this period, Article 119 enjoys direct effect but here requires that equality must be ensured by granting "to the persons in the disadvantaged class the same advantages as those enjoyed by the persons in the favoured class."[213] In casu, the Court interprets this as requiring that the pension rights accrued by men over this period must be calculated on the basis of the same retirement age as applies to women.

The third period identified by the Court was that lying prior to 17 May 1990 in which period it considers that Article 119 enjoys no direct effect in relation to pensionable age. Consequently, the Court held that employers were not required to ensure equal treatment as far as benefits related to those periods are concerned. The scheme remains unburdened by Community law obligations and remains free to retain the regime which was in place at that time, i.e. to continue to allow women to retain the rights to an unreduced pension at a different age from men.

In effect, what the Court has done is to allow the phasing in of equal pensionable ages. Totally equal pensions at the same pensionable age will only be ensured - at least in relation to schemes which pre-*Barber* operated different ages - some 40 years after *Barber*. On the other hand, pension rights for current employment are being built up now under equal conditions. In introducing equality of pensionable ages in such a manner, the Court demonstrates a sensitivity to both the expectations of the schemes but also those of the members. As the situations put in place by the schemes in *Smith* and *Van den Akker* demonstrate, introduction

---

[213]   See for example, Case C-184/89, *Nimz*, cited *supra* at para.s 18-20; Case C-408/92, *Smith*, cited *supra* at para. 17.

of equal pensionable ages overnight can cause considerable disappointment to individual employees who expected to be able to retire at a certain moment in time.

Nevertheless, the fact that Article 119 has no direct effect in relation to pensionable age for the period prior to 17 May 1990 leaves a certain degree of uncertainty as to the position of rights accrued prior to this date. For example, may the employer retroactively remove the advantages enjoyed by one group? The Court made it clear that Community law did not require that individuals lose the advantages which they had enjoyed in the past.[214] In other words, European law does not appear to require that these advantages be removed retroactively. However, the Court seems to suggest at paragraph 29,[215] that because Article 119 has no direct effect in that period, European law does not pose a barrier to levelling down.[216] This would allow funds to argue that there is no principle of European law which can be invoked to prevent the reduction with retroactive effects of pension rights which an individual had accrued as a result of service completed prior to 17 May 1990. While on all fours with the temporal limitation in *Barber*, this result would seem to be a little harsh upon the individual who is told that not only does European law not grant directly effective rights in relation to pensionable age prior to this date, but it also fails to prevent schemes from retroactively lowering the rights which have been accrued. Such a result would seem to ignore completely the legitimate expectations and accrued rights of individuals and would not seem to be compatible with a "Community based on the

---

[214] Para. 29 of Case C-408/92, *Smith*, cited *supra*. "Community law imposed no obligation which would justify the retroactive reduction of the advantages which women enjoyed."

[215] Where the Court observes that it is only in relation to periods of service between 17 May 1990 and the amendment of the scheme rules that "levelling down" is not possible.

[216] There is a general principle of EC law against retroactivity, (see for example, Case 108/81, *Amylum* v. *Council*, [1982] ECR 3107; see T.C. Hartley, *The Foundations of European Community Law*, 3rd ed., Oxford, 1994 at pp. 149-152; see in general T. Heukels, *Intertemporales Gemeinschaftsrecht*, Baden-Baden, 1990). However, it could be argued that the absence of direct effects of Article 119 in the period in question means that there is in fact no retroactive stripping of individual rights because Community law gave no enforceable rights. On the extent to which there are principles of European law which preclude particular forms of action, see C. Curti Gialdino, "Some Reflections on the *Acquis Communautaire*", 32 CML Rev. (1995), 1089-1121.

rule of law". Consequently, it is suggested that this interpretation should be rejected and the passage above read restrictively as meaning merely that advantages granted to one group in a period during which Article 119 lacked direct effect, may not be reduced.[217]

The UK[218]

After a number of years of discussion, the UK has finally adopted legislation equalising statutory pensionable ages.[219] However, until the adoption of the Pensions Act 1995, the UK scheme took advantage of the option contained in Article 7(1)(a) of Directive 79/7. As has already been highlighted above, both the Equal Pay Act 1970 and the Sex Discrimination Act 1975 exclude from their scope

> "terms related to death or retirement, or to any provision made
> in connection with death or retirement".[220]

This provision had been thought to justify the widespread practice of retiring women when they reached state pensionable age, which had the effect of retiring them five years earlier than men. This practice was finally outlawed as a consequence of the Court's decision in *Marshall*[221] which drew a distinction between pensionable and retirement age. Pensionable age may be different for

---

[217]   It seems to be clear that such retroactive reduction of accrued rights will generally not be countenanced by national law, since even raising pensionable ages for the future may raise difficulties. See for example the observations made by Nobles, loc. cit. at pp. 220-222; Lutjens 1989, loc. cit. at pp. 443-467.

[218]   For some of the issues, see Hannah, loc. cit. at pp. 122-137; Ellison, loc. cit. at pp. 61-79.

[219]   See the discussion in Chapter 2 and the literature cited therein.

[220]   EPA s. 6(1A)(b); SDA s. 6(4). The inclusion of the provision in the SDA was necessary to counter the argument that occupational pension schemes form a condition of employment. See D. Pannick, *Sex Discrimination Law*, Oxford, 1985. According to Ellison (loc. cit. at p. 32) two reasons prompted the decision to exclude occupational pension schemes from the scope of the EPA. First, it would require detailed definition of what exactly was meant by equal treatment in the field of pensions. Second, it was felt that Industrial Tribunals, the competent tribunal for equality cases at first instance, were an inappropriate forum in which to raise such questions.

[221]   Case 152/84, cited *supra*.

women and men pursuant to Directive 79/7 but retirement age much be equal for men and women because it falls within Directive 76/207. This judgment led to the adoption of the Sex Discrimination Act 1986 which made it unlawful for an employer to maintain different retirement ages for the sexes.[222]

Prior to the SDA 1986 it had been very common for occupational schemes to mirror the statutory scheme and offer women an unreduced retirement pension five years earlier than men.[223] In the post-*Marshall* period, this continued, the only difference being that women were no longer compelled to retire at the earlier date. According to the CBI, prior to the entry into force of the SDA 1986, only 19% of employers operated a system of equal retirement ages.[224] By 1988, 60% of employers operated schemes with equal retirement ages.[225] By the time of the 1991 NAPF survey, 75% of the schemes surveyed had equalised pensionable ages[226] a figure which had risen to at least 90% by 1993. This suggests that European law, particularly *Barber*, played a key role in persuading UK pension

---

[222]   Section 2 of the SDA 1986. On this subject, see Prechal and Burrows, loc. cit. at pp. 223-224; S. Atkins, L. Luckhaus and E. Szyszczak, "Pensions and the European Community Equality Legislation", in C. McCrudden (ed.) *Women, Employment and European Equality Law*, London, 1987 at pp. 123-142 at pp. 129-130.

[223]   In 1983, 85% of male members of occupational schemes in the private sector belonged to schemes with a normal retirement age of 65. 90% of women belonged to schemes with a normal retirement age of 60. Extract from "Flexible Retirement Policies and Equality in Pensions Provision - A CBI Strategy", cited in House of Lords Select Committee on the European Communities, Session 1988-1989, 10th Report, *Equal Treatment for Men and Women in Pensions and Other Benefits*, London, 1989 at p. 47.

[224]   Extract from "Meeting the Challenge in '88": The CBI survey of Company Pensions Policy - March 1988, cited in House of Lords Select Committee on the European Communities, Session 1988-1989, 10th Report, *Equal Treatment for Men and Women in Pensions and Other Benefits*, London, 1989 at p. 44. Of these 69% operated the age of 60 and 21% 65.

[225]   68% opting for the age of 65 as compared to 6% opting for 60. Ibidem.

[226]   64% of the schemes had a male NPA of 65 and 24% a male NPA of 60, whereas 42% of schemes had a female NPA of 65 and 49% one at 60. Figures cited in Fenton et al, loc. cit. at pp. 188-189.

schemes to introduce equal pensionable ages. Of these schemes, the 1993 data suggests that 63% introduced a common age of 65.[227]

It seems safe to conclude that the role played by EC law in persuading UK occupational pension schemes to introduce equal pensionable ages has been significant.[228] Nevertheless,

> "So long as the State continues to discriminate here [state pensionable age - EAW], it is difficult, or perhaps impossible, for schemes to be both fair, and in line with European law, in this area."[229]

This problem will be discussed in the section dealing with links between statutory and occupational schemes.

The Netherlands

As has already been explained, in the Netherlands, statutory retirement pensions are payable to both men and women from the age of 65. In 1989 a mere 2% of members belonged to schemes which operated different pensionable ages for women and men.[230] In 1985 65,000 Dutch employees belonged to schemes operating different pensionable ages. The remaining schemes were reported to have equalised in the recent past, generally allowing existing female members to choose

---

[227]   Interestingly, where pensionable age has been raised, 84% of schemes permit retirement at the previous normal retirement age, and 77% of schemes extend this facility to service completed after the date of change. Reported in EOR No. 56, July/August 1994 at p. 5; this is confirmed by S. Ward, *Managing the Pensions Revolution*, London 1995 at p. 85. See also the detailed information given in the 1991 Survey by the Government Actuary at pp. 47-50. This will be discussed in the final section dealing with pensionable age.

[228]   It is interesting to note that the majority of schemes have chosen to equalise at the higher age. This is itself out of step with an observable trend for activity rates in men between the ages of 60 and 64 to drop. For example, in 1971 the activity rate was 82.9% a figure which had fallen back to 54.6% in 1987. House of Lords, op. cit. at p. 21.

[229]   S. Ward, "Equal Treatment in Pensions", presentation made at the Industrial Law Society Seminar on May 19th, 1990 at p. 9; these comments are also echoed in P. Docking and S. Trier, *EC Pensions Law*, London, 1992 at p. 2-42 and by Ellison, loc. cit. at p. 61.

[230]   Pensioenkamer, *Pensioenkaart van Nederland*, The Hague, 1989 cited in de Veer et al, loc. cit. at p. 51.

to continue to have a lower pensionable age than men, or to equalise.[231] Although these figures would seem to suggest that few schemes will have been directly affected by the pensionable age part of the *Barber* judgment, the incidence of transitional regimes phasing in equality in pensionable age does raise issues of European law which will be considered briefly in the concluding section on pensionable age.

Germany

Like the scheme in the UK, the German statutory scheme continues to allow women to retire earlier than men.[232] However, in contrast to the situation in the UK, occupational schemes in Germany generally operate with equal pensionable ages for women and men.[233] Consequently, it is not to be suspected that the case law of the Court on this point has caused significant alteration in practice in this country. Nevertheless, paragraph 6 BetrAVG which provides that where an individual can qualify for his full state pension prior to the age of 65 he can also require that his occupational pension be paid out, allows the differentiation contained in the statutory scheme to be carried into occupational schemes. This will be considered in the section below on links between statutory and occupational schemes.

Conclusions relating to pensionable age

In terms of the schemes operating at the national level, it appears that in none of the three Member States examined has the Court's law caused a revolutionary alteration of course in relation to the setting of pensionable age. Rather, the case

---

[231]   Women choosing for the lower age generally accrued no entitlement to a survivor's pension and had to pay a higher premium. By contrast, if the higher pensionable age was chosen, survivor's benefits were included and premiums were lower. See Dierx 1991, op. cit.

[232]   See the discussion in Chapter 2.

[233]   See the comments of Rühmann, op. cit. at 110; Rühmann and Heissmann, op. cit. at 14.

law appears to have confirmed, perhaps accelerated, developments which had already been taking place at national level.

The Court's approach to the introduction of equality in pensionable age has already been described. Introducing changes to the rules of occupational pension schemes tends to be carried out only for future periods of service, as is recognised in the Court's temporal limitation. The introduction of changes is particularly tricky in relation to pensionable age. As was already discussed, for a scheme to announce that as of a given date, pensionable age is to be raised for everyone retiring after that date results in the existing pension rights of all members being altered retroactively. Additionally, for groups of employees close to retirement it can come as something of an unpleasant shock to learn that an extra number of years will have to be worked before that individual qualifies for an unreduced pension. To respect the plans and expectations of individual employees, many schemes operate a transitional regime for a number of years whereby individuals are permitted to choose between the options. In the Netherlands, the parliamentary debates concerning the implementation of Directive 86/378 reveal that the Dutch government considered such transitional regimes to be compatible with Community law.[234] Similarly, according to the 1993 NAPF survey, 84% of schemes which have introduced equality in relation to pensionable age continue to allow retirement at the previous normal retirement age of which 77% extend the facility to service completed after the date of change.[235]

It would seem to be clear that such transitional regimes conflict with Community law. The Court was confronted with transitional arrangements in *van den Akker* where women members of the scheme were allowed to choose which

---

[234]   The government planned to allow women who had reached the age of 50 on 31 July 1986 (later 31 July 1989 because of the length of time consumed by the legislative process) to choose whether to retain a retirement age of 60 or to work on until they reached the age of 65 and accrue extra pension rights. TK 1988-1989, 20 890, nrs. 1-3. It maintained this view despite of the comments of some (notably the NJCM, *Commentaar NJCM op de notitie over tenuitvoerlegging van de 4de EG-Richtlijn*, Leiden, 1987) that the approach was flawed as a matter of EC law. The debates were finally suspended to await the outcome of the "post-*Barber*" cases.

[235]   EOR No. 56, July/August 1994 at p. 5.

regime they would like to fall under.[236] In rejecting transitional regimes, the Court explained its reasoning in robust terms:

> "once discrimination has been found to exist, and an employer takes steps to achieve equality for the future by reducing the advantages of the favoured class, achievement of equality cannot be made progressive on a basis that still maintains discrimination, even if only temporarily."

> "... the step of raising the retirement age for women to that for men, which an employer decides to take in order to remove discrimination in relation to occupational pensions as regards benefits payable in respect of future periods of service, cannot be accompanied by measures, even if only transitional, designed to limit the adverse consequences which such a step may have for women."[237]

Thus the only transitional regime for introducing equality in pensionable ages in occupational schemes which is permissible is that which the Court envisaged itself.[238] This would seem to rule out the kinds of transitional arrangements envisaged by many UK schemes and the Dutch government.

Supporters of such measures might wish to argue that they represent a form of positive discrimination in favour of women. Indeed, within Germany[239] and the Netherlands[240] at least, there is a body of opinion which considers that different pensionable ages for women and men represents a form of positive discrimination in favour of women, an argument which seems bound to fail if raised before the Court as a consequence of the uncategorical nature of the Court's *Barber* decision on pensionable age. Furthermore, the Court has limited the application of measures of positive discrimination to

---

[236]   Case C-28/93, cited *supra*.

[237]   Case C-408/92, *Smith* cited *supra* at paras. 26 and 27.

[238]   Drawing lines in time, as described above.

[239]   The BVerfG has held different pensionable ages in the statutory scheme to amount to a form of positive discrimination. See decision of 28 January 1988, BB 1987, 619; Bloch, loc. cit. at p. 168; Rühmann, op. cit.

[240]   See the comments of the government of the time in TK 1986-1987, 19 936 nr. 3 at p. 13; de Veer et al, loc. cit. at p. 17.

"measures which, although discriminatory in appearance, are in fact intended to eliminate or reduce actual instances of inequality which may exist in the reality of social life."[241]

It is difficult to see how allowing a woman to retire earlier than a man reduces an existing inequality and therefore it seems unlikely that different pensionable ages would be found to form an acceptable form of positive discrimination under Community law.

However, on the entry into force of the Treaty on European Union an additional line of argument has been extended to proponents of positive discrimination in this field. Article 6(3) of the Agreement on Social Policy[242] provides that

"This Article shall not prevent any Member State from maintaining or adopting measures providing for specific advantages in order to make it easier for women to pursue a vocational activity or to prevent or compensate for disadvantages in their professional careers."

German commentators in particular[243] have seized on this provision as justifying differing pensionable ages per se. However, it is suggested that this argument is similarly misconceived. First, according to its express terms, the Protocol is to operate without prejudice to the provisions of the *acquis communautaire* upon which any measures adopted pursuant to the Agreement on Social Policy are to

---

[241]   Case 312/86, *Commission* v. *French Republic*, [1988] ECR 6315 at para. 15. It is worth noting that this statement was made in the context of Directive 76/207, not Art. 119. The Court has recently had the opportunity to interpret Article 2(4) again. See Case C-450/93, *Kalanke* v. *Freie Hansestadt Bremen*, [1995] ECR I-3051; S. Moore, "Nothing positive from the Court of Justice", 21 EL Rev. (1996), 156-161; D. Schiek, "Positive Action in Community Law", 25 ILJ (1996), 239-246; I. van der Steen, "Voorkeursbehandeling of gelijke kansen?", *Nederlands Tijdschrift voor Europees Recht* (1995), 273-277. See also the Recommendation on the promotion of positive action for women adopted by the Council on 13 December 1984, O.J. 1984 L 331/34. The Commission has also recently issued a communication on *Kalanke*, COM(96) 88; see *Agence Europe* of 28 March 1996, at 12-13.

[242]   See the discussion in Chapter 3.

[243]   See for example, Rühmann, op. cit.; Rühmann and Heissmann, op. cit. at 14; Ahrend and Beucher, op. cit.; U. Langohr-Plato, "Auswirkung das europarechtlichen Lohngleichheitsgrundsatzes auf das deutsche Betriebsrentenrecht", 6 EuZW (1995), 239-243; P. Clever, "Soziale Sicherheit im Rahmen der europäischen Integration - Perspectieven nach dem Maastrichter Gipfel", DAngVers (1992), 296-304.

build. The *acquis* clearly includes the Court's case law on pensionable age. Second, it is difficult to see how allowing a woman to retire earlier than a man could "make it easier" for her to pursue a vocational activity. Similarly, it would not seem to prevent her from suffering disadvantage in her professional life. Finally, although such a measure could be considered to compensate her for disadvantages in her professional life, granting all women the right to retire earlier than men would not seem an appropriate and necessary method of doing this, since it grants the compensation also to women who have not been doubly taxed. Consequently, Article 6(3) would not seem to be justify the conduct suggested.

However, the question which arises is whether the transitional regimes which seem to have been put in place in the UK and which obtained the support of the Dutch government would be permissible under Article 6(3).[244] Here again, however, the Court's view that

> "... the step of raising the retirement age for women to that for men, ... , cannot be accompanied by measures, even if only transitional, designed to limit the adverse consequences which such a step may have for women."

seems to preclude this. Consequently, the vast majority of pension schemes surveyed by the NAPF would seem, in trying to soften the consequences of the raising of pensionable ages for women and respect their legitimate expectations, to be acting contrary to Community law.[245] In this respect, it seems likely that the Court's judgments on pensionable age will have far-reaching consequences for the manner in which equality is introduced into occupational schemes.

---

[244] Of course, this argument will be of only theoretical importance in the UK context as a consequence of the fact that the provisions of the Agreement on Social Policy do not apply in the UK.

[245] Consequently, they would be vulnerable to challenge from aggrieved male scheme members who objected to women being granted advantages denied to them. Equally, in the context of granting previously excluded employees retroactive membership, the pension funds noted *supra* at footnote 98 would seem to be acting contrary to EC law.

4.7   Contributions

It has already been observed that occupational pensions are generally funded by contributions paid by employers and or employees. Where an employee is required to pay a contribution to a scheme, this can be viewed as amounting to a condition of obtaining the right to benefits. Deciding whether employer and/or employee contributions fall within the scope of Article 119 is considerably complicated by funding practice. The contributions which are levied are calculated as those which are considered sufficient to cover the expected liabilities of the scheme. In calculating at what level these liabilities should be assessed, actuaries take account of a number of factors, such as the expected return on scheme investments, developments in wage and price levels and the period for which it is expected the benefit will have to be paid out. In relation to the latter estimate, actuaries commonly base their calculations on mortality tables which distinguish between women and men because of the alleged greater average longevity of women.[246] This means that because the woman is assumed to live longer than a man, a greater sum will have to be accrued to pay her the same level of benefit.

The use of these different mortality tables can be seen to be the source of a number of forms of differentiation in occupational pension provision and, unsurprisingly, their use has long been the subject of controversy.[247] The use of tables which differentiate between women and men results in individual members being treated in a particular manner as a result of their membership of a group, the average characteristics of which need not necessarily be replicated in their individual cases. Such treatment is seen to be antithetical to the individual right to equal pay and consequently it has been argued that the use of these tables conflicts

---

[246]   See for example the discussion in Lutjens and van Poppel, loc. cit.

[247]   See the discussions in Curtin (1987), op. cit. at 225-229; T.K. Hervey, "Case C-152/91, *Neath* v. *Hugh Steeper Ltd.*", 31 CML Rev. (1994), 1387-1397; Laurent, op. cit. at 681-682, Lutjens and van Poppel, loc. cit at pp. 41-45. While Directive 79/7 was being drafted and the intention was still to include occupational schemes within its scope, the use of these tables was identified as one of the most pressing sources of discrimination in occupational schemes.

with Article 119.[248] In its original proposal for a Directive introducing equality into occupational schemes the Commission proposed that they be abolished.[249] However, this part of the proposal did not survive the legislative procedure with amendments being introduced by virtue of which the use of different actuarial tables was permissible.

The situation envisaged by the Directive can be summarized as follows:[250]

money purchase schemes

> may have different levels of **benefit** where this reflects actuarial differences
>
> **employee** contributions must be equal **after 30 July 1999**
>
> **employer** contributions may be different to reflect the use of different actuarial factors

final salary schemes

> **benefits** must be equal
>
> **employee** contributions must be equal **after 30 July 1999**
>
> **employer** contributions must be equal[251]

---

[248] See the authors cited in the previous footnote. Opponents of the use of differentiating tables took inspiration from developments in the US. In the *Manhart* decision (*City of Los Angeles, Department of Water and Power* v. *Manhart* (1978) 435 US 702), the Supreme Court held that it was a violation of Title VII of the Civil Rights Act of 1964 to require women to pay more than men for the same benefit. The Court was apparently prompted to adopt this position because such tables involve treating individuals on the basis of class characteristics while the legislation in question focused upon individuals; J. Mamorsky, "Equal Opportunity and Civil Rights: Employee Benefits Law: Employment Discrimination." in Mok (ed), loc. cit. at pp. 591-600; Additionally, in *Arizona* v. *Norris* (1983) 463 US 1073, the Supreme Court found that the use of sex-based actuarial tables in contribution defined schemes, resulting in lower periodic payments to women represented a prohibited form of discrimination on grounds of sex.

[249] COM (83) 217 final.

[250] See Articles 6(1)(d), (h), (i) and (j) and Article 9(c) of Directive 86/378.

[251] In relation to benefits from and employer's contributions to final salary schemes, the position set out can be deduced from the silence of the Directive on these points. Differentiation is only envisaged in relation to money-purchase schemes. Consequently, the permissible differentiation must be read as an exception to the general equality principle, and therefore limited to money purchase schemes. It is consistent jurisprudence that exceptions to Directives must be interpreted as restrictively as possible. Case 222/84, *Johnston* v. *Chief Constable of the RUC*, [1986] ECR 1651.

According to the Directive, these factors may also be reflected in the level of contributions which are reimbursed to an early leaver and in relation to deferred benefits.

In the discussion which follows, attention will first focus on the Court's conclusions on whether employer's and employee's contributions constitute pay within the context of Article 119. Subsequently, attention will turn to the use of different actuarial tables for women and men and whether this alters the general position which has already been described.

The subject of contributions to occupational schemes was first raised before the Court in *Worringham*.[252] It will be recalled that the scheme at issue there obliged men but not women younger than 25 to contribute to their employer's contracted-out occupational pension scheme. This contribution was reimbursed by the employer by means of an addition to the men in question's gross salary. In its judgment the Court held that

> "A contribution to a retirement benefits scheme which is paid by
> an employer in the name of employees by means of an addition
> to the gross salary and which therefore helps to determine the
> amount of that salary constitutes "pay" within the meaning of the
> second paragraph of Article 119"[253]

The formulation chosen by the Court creates the impression that its focus was upon the (consequences of the) difference in gross salaries paid to women and men rather than upon the classification as pay of contributions to occupational schemes.[254] An equally evasive approach appears to have been taken in the subsequent *Newstead* case.[255] There, although gross salaries were the same, net salaries differed as a result of the obligation, incumbent upon male employees

---

[252]   Case 69/80, cited *supra*.

[253]   Para. 1 of the *dispositief*.

[254]   This is confirmed by para. 17 of Case 192/85, *Newstead*, cited *supra*. This does however contrast with the Court's interpretation of *Worringham* in Case C-152/91, *Neath*, cited *supra* and Case C-200/91, *Coloroll*, cited *supra*. On which, see *infra*.

[255]   At para. 14 of *Newstead*, the Court observed that "a contribution paid by the employer to a pension scheme on behalf of the employee, ..., might be regarded as 'consideration ... which the worker receives, directly or indirectly' as referred to in Article 119."

only, to pay contributions towards a contracted-out widow's pension scheme. The Court found that this was entirely in conformity with Article 119 because the source of the

> "reduction in net pay ...[is] a contribution paid to a social security scheme[256] and in no way affects gross pay on the basis of which other salary related benefits ... are normally calculated."[257]

Taken together, *Worringham* and *Newstead* appeared to suggest that employee contributions fell outwith the scope of Article 119[258] but that at least where employer contributions affected the level of the gross salary received by the employee, these contributions did fall within Article 119.[259]

The Court's apparent position on employee contributions was clarified in its recent judgments in *Neath* and *Coloroll*. There it observed that

> "The contributions paid by the employees are an element of their pay since they are deducted directly from their salaries, which, by definition, constitute pay."[260]

---

[256] To the extent that *Newstead* was read as holding that contracted-out schemes do not fall within the scope of Article 119 it must be read as having been overruled by Case C-262/88, *Barber*, cited *supra*. Mr Newstead was a civil servant. Case C-7/93, *ABP*, cited *supra* clarified unambiguously that civil service pension schemes fall within the scope of Article 119.

[257] Case 192/85, cited *supra* at para. 18.

[258] This is the conclusion reached by A. Arnull, "Widows' Mite", EL Rev. (1988), 135-140 at p. 138; also Banks, loc. cit. at pp. 55-68.

[259] This is the conclusion reached by Curtin 1990, op. cit. at p. 481 and by the Advocate General in *Barber*, at para. 22.

[260] Case C-200/91, *Coloroll*, cited *supra*, at para. 80. A preferable ground for considering that employee contributions in fact constitute pay is that their level is negotiated between employer and employee representatives; see COM(95) 186 final. Alternatively, as has already been observed, an employee's contribution can be considered to constitute a condition of access to the occupational scheme.

Consequently, employee contributions must be equal for women and men, and this has been the case for all contributions levied since 8 April 1976.[261]

The Court's findings on employer contributions were limited to final salary schemes. It held that "inequality of employer's contributions paid under funded defined-benefit schemes, which is due to the use of actuarial factors differing according to sex, is not struck at by Article 119."[262] This is because "the use of actuarial factors differing according to sex in funded defined-benefit occupational pension schemes does not fall within the scope of Article 119 of the Treaty."[263] They are identified by the Court as funding arrangements falling outwith the scope of the equal pay principle. Consequently, where employer contributions to final salary schemes differ between women and men as a result of the use of actuarial tables differentiating on grounds of sex, this does not conflict with Article 119.[264]

The subject of actuarial factors and money purchase schemes was raised in *Coloroll* but the Court chose not to make a finding on this point. Certainly in relation to **employee** contributions, the logic which propelled the Court to decide that employee contributions to final salary schemes are pay would seem to require that the same conclusion be reached in relation to contributions to money purchase schemes. Turning to **employer** contributions and the eventual benefits provided

---

[261]   By basing its findings in *Coloroll* and *Neath* on employee contributions on its judgment in *Worringham*, the Court indicated that its case law on this point ought to have been clear (although in fact, as has already been observed, *Worringham* in fact suggested that the position was entirely different). Its finding on this point was based squarely on Article 119 and no reference was made to the temporal limitation of *Barber* as mitigating the consequences of this aspect of its ruling. Nor did the Court refer to the 13 year period which schemes are granted by Directive 86/378 to bring employee contributions in line with the requirements of equality after July 1986. Consequently, it would seem that the 13 year transitional period for employee contributions is not available to funds which, according to the Court, have always been obliged to levy equal contributions from women and men. See further, Whiteford 1995b, op. cit. at 829-830 and 835-836.

[262]   Case C-152/91, *Neath*, cited *supra* at para. 32.

[263]   Case C-152/91, at para. 34; confirmed by Case C-200/91, *Coloroll*, cited *supra* at para. 76.

[264]   See Whiteford 1995b, op. cit. at 830 for a discussion of the Directive on this point. In the proposal for a Directive amending Directive 86/378, the Commission proposes to alter the Directive to remove this anomaly. See COM(95) 186 final.

under such schemes, again the Court's view that "the employer commits himself ... to pay his employees defined benefits or to grant them specific advantages" is what falls within Article 119 suggests that the situation countenanced by the Directive is unlikely to be disturbed by the Court. This is because in a money purchase scheme, the employer generally undertakes to pay a certain fixed amount periodically rather than to ensure that the employee receive a particular level of benefit. It would therefore seem that the Court in *Coloroll* gave a number of indications that money purchase schemes can continue to utilize different actuarial tables for women and men in relation to **employer** contributions or the levels of benefit.[265]

The practice of reflecting average differences in longevity in occupational pensions is not limited to contributions. Where an individual changes employment he may transfer his accrued pension rights to the scheme being operated by his new employer. The difference in the anticipated longevity of men and women will be reflected in these sums. It will be assumed that a woman will receive a benefit for longer than a man and therefore a larger sum will be transferred as representing her accrued rights in accordance with the anticipated greater total which will be paid to her.[266]

Additionally, the same strand of reasoning which enabled the Court to exclude certain employer's contributions from the scope of Article 119 allowed it to place transfer values in a similar situation. It referred to its view that Article 119 does not cover "funding arrangements" and observed that the differences in the levels of transfer values paid were a consequence of these arrangements and consequently, are also not struck at by Article 119.

This is not to say that, in general, employer contributions and transfer values do not fall within the definition of pay. Rather, inequalities in the amounts

---

[265]   This subject will be returned to in the section on links between statutory and occupational schemes *infra*.

[266]   In money purchase schemes, life insurance companies will assume that a woman lives longer than a man. Consequently, she will receive a lower periodic payment for the same lump sum invested, or will require to pay more than a man to receive the same periodic benefit.

paid by employers to schemes,[267] or transferred to another scheme in respect of an early leaver, can be justified where they are the result of the use of actuarial tables which differentiate between women and men. This amounts to classifying the use of such different actuarial tables as a form of justifiable direct discrimination[268] - the only ground for the differentiation is the sex of the individual. If this is indeed the case, that differences caused by reliance on different tables amount to justifiable direct discrimination, this means that should actuarial science come up with a more accurate base than sex for making predictions about the expected liabilities facing a scheme, this form of justification ought to disappear and with it this controversial practice.

The conclusion of this section on contributions must be that since the Court has essentially left national practice in this area untouched, it is unlikely to have significant repercussions for the pensions received by women from occupational schemes.[269]

---

[267]   In money purchase schemes, it is submitted that the use of tables which differentiate between women and men can be used to justify different benefit levels, where the employer has chosen to pay equal contributions in respect of his male and female employees.

[268]   This seems to be the conclusion reached by Advocate General Van Gerven in his opinion in Cases C-109/91, C-110/91, C-152/91 and C-200/91, cited *supra*. For a discussion of the position as to the justifiability or otherwise of direct discrimination in EC law, see the observations of C. McCrudden, "Issues from the Discussion", in McCrudden (ed.) 1994 pp. 215-223 at pp. 215-217.

[269]   This section is not subdivided into specific sections on the individual Member States. Two considerations prompted this. First, it was extremely difficult to obtain any information whatsoever as to the practice in these Member States as to the levying of contributions. Second, since the Court of Justice has held that the use of actuarial tables which differentiate on grounds of sex does not conflict with Article 119 EC, existing national practice can continue unaltered.

4.8   Benefits

The benefits paid to members by occupational pension schemes constitute pay within the context of Article 119.[270] As such, where individuals are engaged in the same employment, they must receive the same pension benefit. As the Court stressed in *Barber*, "the principle of equal pay applies to each element of the remuneration granted to men or women."[271] Consequently, the periodic, not total lifetime, pension payments made to men and women must be equal.[272]

The various requirements of European law in relation to occupational pension schemes can be summarised with the aid of an example. An employer offers a final salary scheme providing members with benefits of 70% of their final salary. He is obliged to open this scheme to male and female members on the same conditions, which includes the requirement that in a contributory scheme, he levy equal contributions from them. Where his scheme uses actuarial tables which differentiate on grounds of sex to calculate its future liabilities, the employer is released from his obligation to pay equal contributions in respect of his male and female employees to enable him to make good any funding shortfall which would otherwise arise because of the use of such tables.

For money purchase schemes, the position is slightly more complex. There as with final salary schemes, the employer must open the scheme to male and female employees on the same conditions, including the condition that their contributions be equal. In money purchase schemes, it is submitted that equality requires either that the employer contributions be equal[273] or, he is released from the obligation to pay equal contributions in respect of his male and female

---

[270]   Case 170/84, *Bilka* cited *supra* at para. 22; confirmed in *inter alia*, Case C-262/88, *Barber*, cited *supra* at para. 30.

[271]   Case C-262/88, cited *supra* at para. 34.

[272]   This was clearly the consideration which prompted the statement of the Court in *Barber* cited above. See also Prechal 1992, op. cit. at 1152.

[273]   Which, where the insurance company uses separate actuarial tables, will result in female employees being offered a lower level of benefit.

employees where he intends to make the levels of benefit received by the sexes equal.

Most schemes in fact, provide a wide variety of different benefits, such as survivors' pensions and lump sums, and some allow individual members to accrue higher benefits by paying additional voluntary contributions to the scheme. The Court has been confronted by all these different types of benefits and has stated more or less clearly what Community law requires in this respect. These various subjects will be touched upon briefly below.

4.8.1   SURVIVORS' PENSIONS

An occupational survivors' pension is a benefit paid by a pension scheme to the survivor of a deceased employee.[274] The level of benefit received is generally linked to the pension and therefore salary previously received by the deceased. In undertaking to continue to provide financial support to the spouse of the deceased employee, the employer assumes that the spouse was financially dependent upon the deceased.[275] This assumption is also reflected in the fact that the survivor receives only a part of the benefit previously enjoyed by the deceased.[276] The lower level of payment can be seen to reflect the reduced expenses of the smaller

---

[274]   The recent Dutch survivor's benefits law, the *Algemene Nabestaandenwet* (ANW), grants rights also to unmarried cohabitees. These proposals caused a huge amount of controversy during the drafting of the statute. On the ANW, see J. Bol, "De zachte dood van het weduwenpensioen", 11 Nemesis (1995), 88-91; Raaphorst, loc. cit.; "Kabinet houdt vast aan wet op nabestaanden", *NRC Handelsblad*, 26 May 1995; also the special issue 7 *PS* (1996).

[275]   Only the presumption of dependence can adequately explain the development of the practice of continuing payment after the death of the employee whose labour resulted in the accrual of the pension rights in question.

[276]   This in turn suggests that the retirement pension is conceptualised as providing a family income. It is worth noting that in the past one of the reasons given by employers to justify paying women lower wages than men was the fact that a man's salary had to be used to support a family, unlike that received by the women. These provisions and assumptions ought to have been eradicated through legislation on equal pay. The payment of a survivor's pension can be seen to represent one last example of these older assumptions. Similarly, the Dutch practice of deducting the family AOW from occupational pension benefits can also be seen to reflect the same assumptions. This will be discussed in the section on links between statutory and occupational schemes.

household. In other words, the very concept of paying the surviving spouse of an ex-employee benefit after the death of the employee is premised on the financial dependence of couples, in reality the assumed economic dependence of women on men.[277] This assumption explains why over the years, legislative attention, when it deigned to consider women's pensions at all, focused on improving the prevalence and levels of widows' pensions rather than on stimulating pension provision for women in their own right.[278] In the UK, for example, the 1975 Social Security Pensions Act made provision of an adequate widow's pension (but not widower's pension) a condition for obtaining contracted-out status.[279] As Groves has observed, this helps to endorse and indeed reinforce the "traditional" division of labour into male, remunerated employment, and female domestic, unpaid employment.[280]

It is only recently that changes have begun to made in this area. In the discussion which follows, attention will first focus on European law. Subsequently, a brief description will be given of the requirements of national law in relation to occupational survivor's pensions. In the concluding section, an evaluation will be made of the role played by European law in introducing changes to national practices.

Although European law on survivors' pensions is now clear, this has not always been the case. As has already been discussed, secondary legislation was adopted by the Community legislator to introduce the principle of equality into *inter alia* statutory and occupational social security because of the perceived limitations of Article 119. Both Directive 79/7 and Directive 86/378 exclude

---

[277]   Groves, op. cit at p. 195; L. Fletcher, "Problems Specific to State Social Security, in Particular Regarding State Pension Age and Survivor's Benefits", in McCrudden (ed.), loc. cit. at pp. 79-87.

[278]   See Groves 1992, loc. cit. at p. 203; Westerveld, loc. cit. at pp. 308-322.

[279]   Prior to 1973 no tax relief was provided for contributions to a widower's pension scheme; J. Masson, "Women's Pensions", JSWL (1985), 319-340 at 325.

[280]   Groves 1992, loc. cit. at p. 203.

benefits paid to survivors from their scope.[281] The unequivocal nature of the Court's judgment that benefits paid out under statutory schemes of social security fall outwith the scope of Article 119[282] meant that the exclusion of survivor's benefits from Directive 79/7 has not been the subject of legal challenge. By contrast, the applicability of Article 119 to occupational pensions remained for many years the subject of heated debate, and consequently, in view of the fact that secondary European law can in no way limit the scope of primary European law,[283] the exclusion of survivors' pensions from the scope of Directive 86/378 was by no means the end of the debate.

As with so many other areas of pension law, the Court tried for many years to avoid giving an answer to this question. On the first occasion that the Court was asked whether men and women had to be given equal opportunities to accrue survivors pensions, the relevant legal provision was not Article 119 but the Community's own Staff Regulations. Although the Court found that male and female members of staff had to accrue equal survivor's pensions, it expressly based its finding on the broader equality principle binding the Community in its activities, rather than the narrower principle of equal pay.[284] In the next case in which the subject of survivors' pensions was raised, *Newstead*, the Court and the Advocate General appeared to be in agreement that survivors' pensions did not at that time have to be provided equally to women and men.[285]

Although both the Court and the Council appeared to be in agreement on this point, academic opinion continued to insist that Article 119 required that

---

[281] Art. 3(2) of Directive 79/7; Art. 9(b) of Directive 86/378. Equality was to be introduced by means of another Directive. See COM(87) 494 final.

[282] Case 80/70, *Defrenne I*, cited *supra*.

[283] See in this respect Case 96/80, *Jenkins*, cited *supra*; confirmed post-*Barber* in Case C-110/91, *Moroni*, cited *supra*.

[284] Joined Cases 75/82 and 117/82, *Razzouk and Beydoun* v. *Commission*, [1984] ECR 1509 at paras. 16 and 17. The Advocate General appeared to share this view; see the opinion of the Advocate General at p. 1540.

[285] Case 192/85, *Newstead*, cited *supra* at para. 28; opinion of the Advocate General at p. 4769.

equality be introduced to this type of benefit.[286] *Barber* implied that Article 9(a) of the Directive was invalid which raised the question whether Article 9(b) was equally unreliable.

In *Ten Oever*[287] the Court finally recognised that pensions paid to survivors of ex-employees constitute pay within the meaning of Article 119. In reaching this conclusion, it focused on the fact that the source of the right to the benefit was the same employment relationship as formed the source of the right to the occupational retirement pension which the survivor's pension would eventually replace.[288] Interestingly, the Court did not appear to be swayed by arguments that the survivor's pension formed an undertaking made by the employer to the employee that, on his death, he would care for his surviving spouse. Rather, it preferred to view the right to the survivor's pension as an independent right accruing to the spouse, even during the currency of the employment relationship.[289] In so doing, it broadened the personal scope of Article 119 beyond the direct parties to the employment relationship,[290] rejecting the

---

[286]   See for example, Curtin (1990), op. cit. at 491-492; M. Kraamwinkel, "Weduwnaarspensioenen en gelijke behandeling", *Tijdschrift voor Pensioenvraagstukken* (1990), 84-87 at 85.

[287]   Case 109/91, cited *supra*. Confirmed in Case C-200/91, *Coloroll*, cited *supra*.

[288]   This in turn is consistent with the Court's insistence that the nexus for the applicability of Article 119 to benefits is the employment relationship.

[289]   I shall return to this point in the final section dealing with survivor's pensions. It is however worth noting that if this is the Court's view, it does not correspond to the position at national law in many of the Member States as the Report of the EP Committee on Women's Rights on the splitting of pension rights on divorce or separation (A3-0418/93) reveals. However, in the Netherlands provision has just been made for splitting pension rights on divorce (see *Wet verevening pensioenrechten bij scheiding*, law of 28 April 1994, Stb. 342). In the UK context, the government was forced by a House of Lords revolt to introduce provisions to the Pensions Act 1995 (s. 166; s. 167 makes some alterations to the law of Scotland which, by virtue of the Family Law (Scotland) Act 1985 already contained provisions on the subject) to provide for pension splitting on divorce. These rules have yet to be fleshed out; see *Treatment of pension rights on divorce*, Cm 3345.

[290]   In Case C-200/91, *Coloroll*, cited *supra*, it ensured that the scope of Article 119 was symmetrical, broadening also the circle of persons upon whom Article 119 places obligations to include the trustees of a pension scheme.

argument that only benefits paid to the employee himself fall within the scope of Article 119.

However, as with *Barber*, the Court imposed a temporal limitation on the effects of its ruling. Recognising the legitimate expectations which had been created on the part of pension providers by the Directive, it held that the obligation to introduce equality in relation to survivors' pensions only applies in relation to benefits accruing in respect of periods of employment after 17 May 1990.

The UK

In principle, the UK statutory scheme pays only widow's pensions[291] although a man widowed after 6 April 1979 whose wife and he were both over pensionable age when she died and whose wife's contribution record was satisfactory can also be paid a Category B widower's pension.[292] As was mentioned above, it was originally a condition of receiving approval for contracting-out that the scheme provided a widow's pension, with no similar requirement being made in respect of widower's benefits. It was the 1986 Social Security Act which introduced change in this area, requiring that similar provision be made for widowers as is made for widows for tax years from 1988-1989.[293] The change of approach was prompted by recognition of the increased incidence of female employment, which made the assumptions of the previous legislation inappropriate.[294] However, the

---

[291]   A woman will be entitled to a widow's pension if she was over the age of 55 when she was widowed. Additionally, if a woman has dependent children on being widowed, she gains entitlement to widowed mother's allowance until the last of her children has reached the age of 16. If a woman is widowed between the ages of 45 and 55, she is entitled to a widow's pension, the amount of which is reduced by 7% for each year that the woman is younger than 55.

[292]   See SSCBA 1992, ss. 51 and 52. In fact, this will be paid out only rarely because the man will generally have qualified in his own right for a Category A pension which will be more valuable than his derived Category B entitlement.

[293]   See now ss. 12A,12B (inserted by s. 136 PA 1995) 17 of the 1993 PSA. Reg.s 26, 57-59 of the 1996 Contracting-Out Regulations.

[294]   The Green Paper which led to these reforms (Cmnd. 9518, para. 5.45 and 49) spoke of the changed social environment as justification.

UK government took the opportunity envisaged in Directive 86/378 to exclude survivor's benefits from its implementing legislation.[295] Nevertheless, by 1987, 67% of women in private sector schemes belonged to schemes which provided for widower's pensions, with a further 6% making such pensions available on proof of dependency.[296] The corresponding figures for widow's pensions are that 85% provided benefits as of right, with 2% granting benefits in circumstances of dependency,[297] suggesting that discrimination continues in a significant number of schemes.

It must therefore be concluded that national law formed the impetus behind the introduction of equality into survivor's pension in UK occupational schemes.[298]

The Netherlands

Prior to 1988, the Dutch statutory scheme discriminated between women and men in relation to survivor's pensions, with men having to satisfy much more stringent conditions to qualify for benefit than women.[299] However, as a consequence of judicial activity, the legislature was forced to treat women and men equally in this

---

[295]   Schedule 5 of the Social Security Act 1989 contained the relevant provisions. Its entry into force was delayed until the outstanding uncertainties caused by the Court's judgment in *Barber* had been clarified. Ultimately it was only ever partially brought into force. The maternity and family leave provisions were brought into force during 1991 (SI 1994/1661). It appears that Schedule 5 itself has not been repealed, with the exception of para.s 4 and 14 (see Schedule 7 PA 1995, parts I and III; see the discussion of the legislative amendments provided in McCrudden, 1995, op. cit. The equal treatment clause introduced by the PA 1995 will in future cover these matters.

[296]   Dependency will be discussed in the concluding section on survivor's pensions.

[297]   Government Actuary, *Occupational Pension Schemes 1987 Eighth Survey by the Government Actuary*, London, 1991 at p. 53.

[298]   The fact that UK law already required equality can be seen to explain why in *Ten Oever* and *Coloroll*, the UK government was prepared to argue that occupational survivor's pensions constituted pay within the meaning of Article 119.

[299]   For a description, see Westerveld, loc. cit. at pp. 453-456; Loenen, loc. cit. at pp. 248-251.

sphere for benefits paid after 23 December 1984.[300] In research dating from 1990-1991, the Dutch *Emancipatieraad* discovered that of the 70 occupational schemes examined, 63 offered married women membership,[301] of which 51 provided equal widower's and widow's pensions. In 7 of the schemes which allowed married women to be members, no widower' pension whatsoever was built up and in 5 schemes, the widower's pension was less attractive than the widow's. It is clear from the Dutch parliamentary debates surrounding the implementation of Directive 86/378 that the government initially hoped to utilise the possibility contained in the Directive to postpone the introduction of equality in relation to occupational survivors' pensions at least until 1 January 1993.[302] From this date, men and women would each accrue a survivor's pension at the same rate.[303] The judgment in *Ten Oever* removes this possibility. Consequently, in contrast to the situation pertaining in Germany and to a lesser extent the UK, the judgment of the Court in *Ten Oever*, will form the impetus for Dutch occupational schemes to introduce change.

---

[300]   In 1988 the *Centrale Raad van Beroep* decided that the Dutch statutory legislation relation to survivors' pensions was in conflict with Article 26 of the Convention on Civil and Political Rights. Furthermore, in the line of the European case law concerning Directive 79/7 it held that individuals could claim rights, irrespective of the individual's contributions history, as of 23 December 1984. See Rspr. SV 1989/67, CRvB 7-12-'88, AWW 1987/17 and AWW 1987/46. See Westerveld loc. cit. at pp. 453-456; Borgesius, op. cit.; Loenen, loc. cit. at pp.196-200; L. Andringa, Nemesis (1992), 1 and 2.

[301]   De Veer et al, loc. cit. at p. 67.

[302]   In fact, the major focus of concern during the parliamentary debates was not the potential of the Court of Justice to upset these national legislative plans. Instead, attention focused on the likelihood that the *Centrale Raad van Beroep* would decide that article 26 of the Convention on Civil and Political Rights would cover occupational survivor's pensions and require that women and men be treated equally in this area also. It was finally concluded that the danger of this occurring was slight since it was improbable that Article 26 enjoyed direct effects. Consequently, individuals would have been unable to rely on this provision before national courts. See TK 20 890 and 22 695.

[303]   This position was defended despite warnings that the Court of Justice could well decide that occupational survivors' pensions were pay within the meaning of Article 119 EC. NJCM *Commentaar NJCM op de notitie over tenuitvoerlegging van de 4de EG-Richtlijn*, Leiden, 1987.

Germany

The German statutory scheme was amended to lay down equality in relation to survivors' pensions as of 1 January 1986.[304] The practice of granting a survivor's pension only to women, that is to the survivors of men, found its echo in occupational pension schemes. However, the case law of the BAG has imposed more far-reaching obligations on the employer than the legislator. In a judgment handed down in 1989, the BAG held that because occupational pensions form part of the pay which the employer pays to his employees in return for their loyalty to the company, differentiation between men and women in relation to survivor's pensions conflicts with articles 3(2) and (3) of the Constitution, Article 119 EC and the general *arbeitsrechtlichen Gleichbehandlungsgrundsatz*.[305] Despite the latitude

---

[304]   *Gesetz über Hinterbliebebebrenten und Erziehungszeiten*, 11 July 1985, BGBl. 1450. This alteration was prompted by two judgments handed down by the BVerfG in which the statutory scheme which granted only widow's pensions, unless the woman was a breadwinner, was found to be compatible with the Constitution, a situation which the Court found would have changed by the end of 1984. The first judgment of these judgments was handed down in 1963 (BVerGE 17, 1, judgment of 24 July 1963; see Westerveld, loc. cit. at pp. 166-168; van Rooij et al, loc. cit. at p. 119) where the Court characterised the survivor's pension as serving to compensate the survivor for the loss of income caused by the death of the insured party. The statistics which were made available to the Court indicated to it that it could not be considered to be unreasonable to assume that on the death of a woman her surviving partner would not be deemed to suffer a loss of income. This conclusion was based on figures concerning the level of economic activity carried out by women. Apparently, only 7.5% of married women in Germany belonged to the labour market (see Westerveld, loc. cit. at p. 167). However, by 1975 (BVerfGE 39, 169; see Westerverld, loc. cit. at pp. 188-190; van Rooij et al, loc. cit. at pp. 119-120) women's economic activity had increased to such an extent that the Court held that the premise upon which the statutory scheme was based - women's economic dependence on men - while not yet false, would in time become so. Westerveld, loc. cit. at pp. 308-323 deals thoroughly with the reform process surrounding the amendment of the RVen relating to survivors benefits and places it in the context of the search in Germany for a solution to what was seen as the problem of the pension position of women.

[305]   Judgment of 5 September 1989, BB 1989, 2400; see R. Höfer, "Betriebliche Altersversorgung und deutsches Gleichberechtigungs- sowie europäisches Lohngleichheitsgebot", BB 1994, Beilage 15 at 9; P. Hanau and U. Preis, "Beschränkung der Rückwirkung neuer Rechtsprechung zur Gleichberechtigung im Recht der betrieblichen Altersversorgung", DB 1991, 1276-1284. This was preceded by a judgment of the LAG Hamm of 23 January 1983, where it was held that from 1985, and in the light of the altered economic activity levels of women, together with the new provisions of the statutory scheme, discrimination in occupational schemes was no longer permissible. NJW 1983,

granted to the legislator in relation to the statutory scheme, the Court held that the case law relating to equality of women and men in relation to pay was clear and that the employers had no grounds for considering that women could be treated less favourably than men in relation to such benefits.[306] Accordingly, no temporal limitation was imposed on the judgment and, subject to the relevant national prescriptive periods, equality can be claimed for periods of employment falling after 1972, the date at which the BAG recognised the remunerative qualities of occupational pensions.[307] In this regard, German law can be seen to require considerably more of schemes than European law.

Conclusions concerning survivor's pensions

On the basis of the brief discussions of the national situations it appears to be the case that the case law of the Court has formed a significant motor for change relation to occupational survivor's benefits in the Netherlands only. In the UK and particularly in Germany, it was national developments which prompted occupational schemes to stop discriminating in relation to survivors' pensions.

There are indications for both the UK and for Germany that some schemes are toying with the idea of making payment of occupational survivor's pensions dependent on the survivor's financial dependence on the deceased.[308] However, this would seem to be vulnerable to challenge since it seems to raise a

---

1510; see Bloch, loc. cit. at pp. 168-169.

[306]   Concerning the possibility of prescriptive periods and limitations on back-dating, see the comments of V. Matthiessen, N. Rössler and J. Rühmann, "Die nachholende Anpassung von Betriebsrenten - Zu den Entscheidungen des BAG vom 28.4.92", DB Beilage 5/93 at 7; H.-D. Steinmeyer, "Richtungsweisende Entscheidungen des BAG - u.a. Nachholung unterlassener Anpassungen, Anpassung im Konzern, Gehaltsumwandlung, Unverfallbarkeit bei zusätzlichen Zusagen, Begriff des Arbeitgebers im Insolvenzrecht", in in *Bewährungsprobe der Alterssicherungssysteme in Zeiten wirtschaftlicher Rezession*, Wiesbaden, 1993 at pp. 43-58.

[307]   See also Rühmann, op. cit. at 108.

[308]   For example, a small number of UK schemes already offer benefits only under such conditions. The German BAG (BB 1989 2400 at 2402) appeared to consider that this would be acceptable.

prima facie presumption of indirect discrimination to the disadvantage of women workers. Even given the increase in female participation in the workforce which prompted the BAG and the UK legislator to instigate reforms, it still seems more likely that an employed man will be the breadwinner[309] and therefore that more women than men will qualify for survivor's pensions made available under such circumstances.[310] Consequently, a breadwinner requirement seems likely to represent indirect discrimination against female employees. Community law is clear that where a suggestion of indirect discrimination has been raised, the respondent can rebut this presumption by demonstrating that the measure is objectively justified by factors which have nothing to do with sex discrimination.[311] Arguably, were an employer to be able to demonstrate that paying a pension to all survivors of deceased female employees would cause him severe financial difficulties, then such a provision could be found to amount to objectively justifiable indirect discrimination.[312] However, since European law only requires that survivor's pensions be provided in relation to periods of employment lying after 17 May 1990, this seems unlikely to succeed.[313]

---

[309] Lubnow, loc. cit. cites at pp. 278-279 figures which demonstrate that the pension rights of women are lower than those of men, which in turn reflects the lower wages of women, supporting this thesis. Holtmaat, loc. cit. at pp. 46-51 discussed the relative income positions of women and men.

[310] The case law relating to Directive 79/7 contains examples of breadwinner requirements being found to conflict with the equality principle (Case C-300/90, *Commission* v. *Belgium*, [1992] ECR I-305; Case C-226/91, *Molenbroek*, cited *supra*). Additionally, the Court has observed that the mere fact that some of the advantages granted by an employer to his employees may reflect considerations of social policy, does not preclude the applicability of Article 119 where the entitlement to the benefit arises by reason of the existence of the employment relationship (Case C-262/88, *Barber*, cited *supra* at para. 18).

[311] See Case 170/84, *Bilka*, supra; Case C-109/88, *Danfoss* cited *supra*; Case C-127/92, *Enderby*, cited *supra*. See also the draft Directive on the burden of proof in the area of equal pay and equal treatment for women and men O.J. 1988 C 176/5.

[312] The Court was not willing to reject such arguments out of hand in Case C-408/92, *Smith*, cited *supra* at para. 30.

[313] On the other hand, the judgment in Case C-200/91, *Coloroll*, cited *supra* at para.s 57-60 indicates that where benefits are paid at a particular level irrespective of the individual's insurance history, the benefits paid after 17 May 1990 must be equal. This will be of relevance to those schemes which pay a survivor's pension unrelated to the individual's

It has been suggested that paying a survivors' pension only to the female survivor of a male employee constitutes a form of positive discrimination[314] in favour of women.[315] The problem in this context, apart from the clarity of the case law rejecting such practices, is that as has repeatedly been stressed, European law requires equality only for women participating in the labour market. Were the Court to accept that paying a survivor's pension to the female survivor of a male employee did amount to positive discrimination, it would seem that this ought, logically, to be limited to those women who have already participated in the employment market. This would in fact exclude from payments precisely that group whose need for continued income on the death of a spouse was greatest.

In conclusion, although it would seem that for two of the three Member States which have been examined the case law of the Court has not been the cause of the changes which have been introduced into occupational schemes, European law may require that a potential development - a requirement of dependency - be halted.

4.8.2   ADDITIONAL VOLUNTARY CONTRIBUTIONS

Some schemes provide a facility whereby members can pay additional voluntary contributions (AVCs) which can be used to secure additional benefits such as an additional (survivors') pension or (increased) lump sum benefit. If differentiation is permitted in this area, it can result in the equality requirements being undermined. Directive 86/378 excluded from its scope the optional provisions of occupational schemes offered to participants individually to guarantee them, inter

---

contributions history.

[314]   See the discussion in the section on pensionable age, *supra*.

[315]   See Hanau and Preis, op. cit. at 1278. This seems to be derived from the judgment of the BVerfG in which it was held that different pensionable ages for women and men are a form of justifiable positive discrimination in favour of women because it compensates for the double role fulfilled by women during their active lives. Similarly, a widow's pension can be seen to compensate women for their inability to accrue independent pension rights because of their traditional, home based roles.

alia, additional benefits (Article 2(2)), although this exclusion was quickly challenged as contrary to Article 119.[316]

This issue was finally brought before the Court in *Coloroll*. Somewhat surprisingly, particularly in view of the Advocate General's conclusion that the answer to this question was "obvious"[317] and that such benefits did fall within Article 119, the Court decided that this was not the case. Focusing on those issues which the Advocate General had rejected as not altering the fundamental remunerative character of the resulting benefits, the Court considered that the fact that the benefits were maintained in a fund separate from the main pension fund and funded solely by employee contributions[318] excluded the applicability of Article 119.

With respect, this conclusion does appear to be open to criticism. As has already been discussed, the Court has held that access to an occupational pension scheme falls within the scope of Article 119. Logically, this requires that women and men be offered membership on the same terms.[319] In addition, it held that employee contributions to occupational pension schemes constitute pay. This logic would also seem to require that the same conclusion be reached in relation to benefits funded through AVCs.[320] However, the Court was not convinced. Thus, it will be perfectly compatible with Article 119 for an employer to offer a low occupational pension to all his employees and to offer substantial benefits through "voluntary" options funded by AVCs. In determining to which employees such benefits are to be made available, the employer can apparently differentiate

---

[316] Curtin 1987, op. cit. at 220-1; Curtin 1990, op. cit. at 498-9.

[317] Opinion of Advocate General Van Gerven in Cases C-109/91, C-110/91, C-152/91 and C-200/91, cited *supra* at para. 62.

[318] Which as the discussion in s. 4.7 reveals the Court considers to be part of the employee's remuneration.

[319] See the discussion, *supra*.

[320] The only ground which could perhaps justify the opposite conclusion is that access to a scheme is only pay because the resulting benefit is pay. However, this would seem to fly in the face of the future service logic expounded by the Court in relation to the temporal limitation, on which see the discussion in s. 4.6.1.

between male and female employees or full and part time employees if he so desires without risking being found to have acted in conflict with Article 119.

4.8.3   LUMP SUMS

A feature of some pension schemes is that on retirement the member can convert part of his accrued pension rights into a lump sum in return for receiving a reduced periodic pension.[321] The use of different actuarial tables[322] in respect of male and female members means that to obtain the same level of lump sum, a man will have to be satisfied with a lower periodic benefit than his female colleague.[323] The Court's finding in *Neath* and *Coloroll* that differences resulting from the use of different actuarial tables do not conflict with Article 119 would seem to mean that national practice in this area can continue unaltered.

4.9   Links with Statutory Schemes[324]

Despite the fact that they generally pre-date state involvement in old age income provision, occupational pension schemes traditionally link their conditions of entitlement to benefit and or benefit levels, to payments made from the state scheme. This explains why it has been common for schemes to provide that occupational benefits become payable at the same age as the state pension becomes payable. Similarly, occupational schemes often deduct statutory entitlement from the levels of benefit which they pay to beneficiaries, to mention only two of the

---

[321]   The Dutch *Commissie Witteveen*, convened to examine occupational pensions in the Netherlands, recommended allowing individuals to trade pension benefits for lump sums of a particular amount.

[322]   See the discussion, *supra*.

[323]   In a final salary scheme at least, and in a money purchase scheme to which the employer has made different contributions. In a money purchase scheme to which the employer has paid equal contributions, the position will be reversed.

[324]   The first part of this section borrows heavily from my contribution to T. Hervey and D. O'Keeffe (eds.), loc. cit.

most common of the ways in which occupational schemes build upon the pension provision made by the state.

Given the close links which exist between occupational and statutory schemes, any difference in the applicable legal regimes will cause considerable difficulty.[325] As a matter of EC law, statutory schemes are subject to the provisions of Directive 79/7 which has already been discussed in Chapter 3, whereas occupational schemes fall under Article 119. As a comparison between Chapter 3 and the present Chapter reveals, the obligations imposed on the state on the one hand and on the employer on the other differ significantly, posing schemes with a number of difficult dilemmas with which the Court has been confronted on a number of occasions. In the discussion of this topic which follows, first the problematic aspects of Directive 79/7 will be highlighted, together with the older body of case law. Finally, three relatively recent cases which may signal a refining of the Court's approach to this area will be discussed.

As has been described in Chapter 3, Directive 79/7 which aims progressively to implement the principle of equal treatment for men and women in matters of social security contains a number of exceptions, the most controversial of which has been Article 7(1)(a) which permits the Member States to postpone the implementation of equality in relation to

> "the determination of pensionable age for the purposes of granting old-age and retirement pensions and the possible consequences thereof for other benefits". [326]

Directive 86/378 originally contained a provision mirroring for occupational schemes, the temporary derogation contained in Article 7(1)(a) of Directive 79/7 for statutory schemes.[327] This suggested that the practice which occupational schemes had developed of linking entitlement and the amount of benefits they paid to those paid under the statutory scheme, would be compatible

---

[325] As Sue Ward observed ("Equal Treatment in Pensions", presentation made at the Industrial Law Society Seminar, 19 May 1990, at p. 9) "So long as the State continues to discriminate here [state pensionable age - EAW], it is both difficult, or perhaps impossible, for schemes to be both fair, and in line with European law, in this area."

[326] See the discussion, *supra*.

[327] Art. 9(a) of Directive 86/378.

with European law. However, in a series of judgments in relation to another Directive,[328] doubt was cast about the accuracy of this conclusion.

The Court was first asked to consider linkage between statutory pensionable age and other employment conditions in *Burton*.[329] Here the employer offered women voluntary redundancy from a lower age than men, the difference in ages reflecting the differences in statutory pensionable age. The Court held that the employer's practice was in conformity with EC law, suggesting that different age conditions linked to differences in the statutory scheme, were legitimate. However, by 1986 the Court's position on this matter appeared to have changed. In *Marshall*,[330] *Roberts*[331] and *Beets-Proper*[332] the Court concluded that employers could not set different age conditions for terminating employment even where they reflected different normal statutory pensionable age. In the context of Article 119, in *Barber*[333] and *Moroni*[334] the Court held that making occupational pensions payable at ages which differ as between women and men is contrary to EC law.

With the exception of *Burton*, all these cases suggest that no reliance could be had on differentiation in the statutory scheme for matters falling outwith the ambit of the national social security scheme. It also raised serious doubts as to the compatibility with European law of the widespread practice of linking occupational schemes to their statutory counterpart. However, three recent judgments, although at first glance contradictory, can be interpreted in a manner

---

[328]   Directive 76/207 on the implementation of the principle of equal treatment for men and women as regards access to employment, vocational training and promotion and working conditions, O.J. 1976, L 39/40.

[329]   Case 19/81, *Burton*, cited *supra*.

[330]   Case 152/84, *Marshall*, cited *supra*.

[331]   Case 151/84, *Roberts*, cited *supra*.

[332]   Case 262/84, *Beets-Proper*, cited *supra*.

[333]   Case C-262/88, *Barber*, cited *supra*.

[334]   Case C-110/91, *Moroni*, cited *supra*.

which suggests that established practice is compatible with European law, at least where it satisfies the requirements of the what might be termed overall objectives of European equality law. On this interpretation, these cases provide elucidation about both the extent to which links may be maintained for the purposes of setting conditions of entitlement to occupational benefits and also the extent to which schemes may take account of the benefits received from the statutory scheme in calculating the amount of occupational entitlement.

In *Commission* v. *Belgium*[335] the Commission had raised an Article 169 infringement action in respect of the provisions of a collective agreement which had been declared compulsory in Belgium. According to the collective agreement, all those made redundant over the age of 60 qualified for a supplementary payment financed by their last employer, where they also qualified for unemployment benefit. However, individuals ceased to qualify for unemployment benefit when they passed state pensionable age, which at that time was 60 for women and 65 for men. The effect of the provision was to exclude women from entitlement to the supplementary payment.

The Court appeared to have no difficulty in concluding that the supplementary payment in question constituted pay within the meaning of Article 119 and that to provide that only men between the ages of 60 and 65 who have been made redundant qualify for it while women in the same situation do not, violated Article 119. This suggests, in line with *Marshall, Roberts, Beets-Proper, Barber* and *Moroni* that links between entitlement to benefits under the statutory scheme and those under occupational schemes may not be maintained, where this imports into the occupational scheme differentiation in the statutory scheme.

In *Birds Eye Walls* v. *Roberts*[336] however, the Court reached an apparently different conclusion. Ms. Roberts had complained about the method of calculating bridging pensions[337] under the scheme operated by her employers

---

[335]   Case C-173/91, [1993] ECR I-673.

[336]   Case C-132/92, *Birds Eye Walls*, cited *supra*.

[337]   A bridging pension is a pension, usually but as the facts of *Birds Eye Walls* demonstrate not exclusively, paid to men between the ages of 60 and 65 to compensate them for the unavailability of their statutory pension. The scheme pays to the men a sum of money representing the statutory benefit payable to women from the age of 60 resulting in the total

whereby account was taken of the amount of pension payable under the statutory scheme. Where an employee had ceased paid employment due to ill health prior to the age of 60,[338] the scheme paid equal amounts to women and men. However, on reaching the age of 60, women saw their payments under the occupational scheme reduced by the amount of statutory pension to which they were deemed entitled,[339] a reduction which took place in relation to men only from the age of 65. According to Ms. Roberts, the reduction in the amount paid to her under her employer's scheme resulted in her receiving less pay than her male colleague.

The Court's apparently uncategorical rejection of links between statutory and occupational schemes in its previous case law seemed clearly to suggest that the scheme operated by *Birds Eye Walls* would be found to conflict with Article 119. However, the Court in fact held that the payment of the statutory pension to men and women at different ages constituted an

> "objective premise, which necessarily entails that the *amount* of the bridging pension is not the same for men and women and cannot be considered discriminatory." (emphasis added)[340]

---

amounts received by women and men being equal. This subject has not received much attention in the academic press. For an exception, (pre-*Barber*) see L. Luckhaus, "Bridging pensions a question of difference?", 19 ILJ (1990), 48-54.

[338]   It is submitted that there is nothing in the judgment to suggest that ill-health benefits form a special category separate from retirement pensions proper.

[339]   It will be recalled that in the past married women in the UK could choose to pay reduced NI contributions in return for obtaining only derived entitlement to social security benefits. The Category B pension to which such individuals gained entitlement on the basis of their husband's contributions was lower than the normal Category A pension. The scheme operated by *Birds Eye Walls* subtracted a standard sum representing statutory entitlement without enquiring into the actual entitlement of individual members.

[340]   Case C-132/92, cited *supra* at para. 20. Fitzpatrick (1994, op. cit. at 162) suggests that *Birds Eye Walls* may represent a first step by the Court to subsume Article 6(3) of the Agreement on Social Policy into Article 119. However, besides the arguments against this on the basis of the Court's interpretation of Article 119, on which, see ss. 4.6.2.4. and 4.8.1.4. above, the text of Article 6(3) itself would seem to preclude such an approach, at least on the facts of *Birds Eye Walls*. Article 6(3) is concerned with "measures providing for specific advantages in order to make it easier for women" etc. In other words, it seems clearly to be limited to measures which are aimed at women, which the bridging pension at issue in *Birds Eye Walls* was not.

In this case, in other words, links between the statutory scheme and the occupational scheme were found compatible with European law.

Although these various judgments would seem at first sight to be contradictory, it is suggested that they can in fact be reconciled. It has already been mentioned that after a false start in *Burton*, the Court had consistently held that differences in statutory pensionable age could not be replicated in matters falling outside the scope of the statutory social security system. This would suggest that *Commission* v. *Belgium* was consistent with this line of case law and that *Birds Eye Walls* represented a break with the past. However, if we turn again to the previous cases, they share one feature which is not to be found in *Birds Eye Walls*. In all the previous cases, the age condition which the occupational schemes proposed to import from the statutory scheme resulted in women and men being granted different *access* to benefits under the occupational scheme. In other words, it meant that women and men could claim their benefits at different ages. Seen from this perspective, *Birds Eye Walls* can be seen to raise a different issue. In *Birds Eye Walls* there was no differentiation in relation to the age at which individuals were granted access to the benefits under the scheme; instead the differentiation concerned the level of benefits. Women and men qualified for payment of the bridging pension at the same age but women saw the amount of their entitlement to the employer-funded part reduced five years earlier than men. If this analysis is correct, it suggests that although differentiating conditions of access may not be replicated in occupational schemes, occupational pension schemes may continue to take account of benefits received from statutory schemes in calculating the levels of benefits which they will pay.

Tentative support for this conclusion is to be found in the third of the recent cases on links between occupational and statutory schemes. If the interpretation suggested here is followed, it also indicates in which circumstances schemes will be allowed to link the amount of benefit which they offer to entitlement to a statutory pension.

It will be recalled that the *ABP* case concerned the system of taking account of the Dutch social security pension in the pensions paid to Dutch civil servants. The ABP promised its members pensions of 70% of final salary over a 40 year career, with the 70% being defined as including the benefit paid by the state. Prior to 1985, the Dutch statutory old age pension scheme, the AOW, paid single individuals benefits at 70% of the minimum wage. Married men received an AOW of 100% of the minimum wage, to reflect the extra expenses involved in providing for a household of two individuals. Married women accrued no independent entitlement to an AOW pension. In taking account of the AOW in calculating benefits payable by the ABP, 100% minimum wage was deducted from married male civil servants, whereas merely 70% AOW was subtracted from the ABP entitlement of married women. This resulted in married male civil servants receiving lower payments from the ABP than their married female colleagues.

At first glance, the analysis of *Birds Eye Walls* outlined above would suggest that the rules of the ABP should have been found to be compatible with European law because the link with the statutory scheme did not affect access to benefits but their amount. Instead, the Court found that the scheme operated by the ABP conflicted with Article 119.

It would be possible to take the view that the Court's case law was simply inconsistent on this point. Perhaps this is so. However, it is also possible to develop an argument according to which the judgment in the *ABP* case is not inconsistent, and instead contributes to an understanding of the requirements of equality in the field of pensions.

The key to reconciling these apparently diverse judgments is to be found in the opinion of the Advocate General in *Birds Eye Walls*.[341] He cited with apparent approval the observations of the Commission pointing out that the linkage which had previously fallen foul of the Court in *Marshall*, *Roberts*, *Beets-Proper* and indeed *Barber* perpetuated the differentiation in the statutory schemes which European law currently, but temporarily, tolerates. By contrast, in *Birds Eye Walls*, reducing the levels of bridging pensions paid to women after the age of 60 to take account of the amounts they received under the statutory scheme resulted in male and female ex-employees receiving the same total pension. In this sense, the linkage in *Birds Eye Walls* was considered not to perpetuate, but rather to reduce the differentiation currently countenanced by European law in relation to statutory pensionable age.

That this was not the situation in the ABP case is clarified by an example. 100% of the minimum wage is set at, say, *f*100; 70% of the minimum wage is

---

[341]   It is true that the Court does not mention this line of argument.

ƒ70. A married man and woman who are both promised a total pension of ƒ200 receive the following amounts from the ABP having taken account of the AOW. The man received ƒ100 and the woman receives ƒ130. However, unlike the rule in *Birds Eye Walls* this does not eradicate the discrimination in the statutory scheme. Rather, because the woman receives no AOW at all, it perpetuates the discrimination and the Court consequently rejects it. In this way, it is possible to reconcile the Court's apparently contradictory judgments, although it remains to be seen whether the Court will indeed follow this path.[342]

To recapitulate, these recent cases can be interpreted as suggesting that occupational schemes may not use age conditions operated in the statutory scheme to determine entitlement to payment of benefits under the occupational scheme, at least where the age conditions used in the statutory scheme differ between women and men. On the other hand, even where the statutory scheme pays pensions to women and men at different ages, occupational schemes can take account of payment of statutory benefits to their members in calculating the levels of benefits to which members gain entitlement where as a result of this calculation the benefits to which male and female members are entitled become more equal.[343]

Reaching the conclusion that the linkage with the statutory scheme in *Birds Eye Walls* resulted in a reduction in discrimination relied upon examination

---

[342]   It is true that in *Birds Eye Walls* the Court did not focus on the precise amount obtained by Ms. Roberts. However, that concerned a situation in which she had chosen to contribute lower amounts to the UK statutory scheme in return for which she accrued entitlement to a lower level of benefit. To have required that her employer compensate her for the results of her choice, can be seen to amount to unjust enrichment, *pace* the Advocate General. The difference between this and the *ABP* case, is that there the deduction made for female employees was for an amount to which they were not entitled under the law; choice had nothing to do with it, nor was there any question of unjust enrichment.

[343]   Still in the field of pensions, other evidence for such an approach can be gleaned. It will be recalled that the Court was willing to countenance employers paying different levels of contribution to final salary schemes in respect of his male and female employees, where the funding of the scheme required this as a consequence of the use of different actuarial tables for women and men. There, the objective served was to equalise benefits. It was suggested that the Court would also accept an employer contributing higher amounts in respect of female employees to money purchase schemes where this resulted in more equal benefits being paid. This possible equality of result orientation on the part of the Court can be seen as a new development. For a critique of the Court's previous position see Fenwick and Hervey, op. cit.

of the "total" pension income received by an individual from the statutory scheme and the occupational scheme. Great store was set by the Court in *Birds Eye Walls* on the fact that the result of the rules in question was equality of total pension income (thus defined). In taking the view that the scheme in *Birds Eye Walls* reduced discrimination, the Court appeared to acquiesce in account being taken of sources of income (the statutory pension) falling outwith the scope of Article 119.[344] The total income received from both sources may well have been equal as a result of the scheme operated by *Birds Eye Walls*, but the "pay" (the amounts paid by the occupational scheme) of male and female employees between the ages of 60 and 65 was different.[345] A discrimination in the statutory scheme which is generally seen to favour women was used in this case to justify a discrimination in the occupational scheme which favours men, because the outcome was seen to be neutral.[346] Two wrongs do apparently make a right.

Commission v. *Belgium*, *Birds Eye Walls* and the *ABP* suggest that links can indeed be maintained between statutory and occupational schemes. However, this is only permissible where it results in the total benefits received by male and female employees being equal. Links may not, however, be maintained when setting conditions of access to benefits under the scheme.

---

[344] See Case 80/70, *Defrenne I*, cited *supra*.

[345] The Advocate General appeared to recognise that this was a weak point in his reasoning. He attempted to bolster his reasoning by focusing on the fact that were no deduction to be made for the statutory pension payable to the woman, the employer would for that period be paying her twice: once in the form of her pension and a second time in the form of his contribution to the statutory scheme. The weakness of this argument is that, as the same Advocate General recognised in *Barber*, employer contributions to the statutory scheme do not constitute pay in the hands of the employee. Accordingly, his subsidiary argument is flawed by the same features as the principle argument.

[346] This approach suggests that the Court's observation in *Barber* that "the principle of equal pay applies to each of the elements of remuneration granted to men or women" (para. 34) no longer accurately states the law, at least where the occupational schemes links benefit levels to those provided under the statutory scheme.

4.9.1   THE UK

In the UK, most schemes make provision for retirement on immediate pension for members over a certain age (for example 50) or within a certain period of the member's normal retirement date.[347] In calculating the level of benefit paid to those taking early retirement, as with normal retirement, many schemes utilise a formula whereby account is taken of the state pension which it is expected that the individual will receive. In this way, the perfectly legitimate (in terms of European law) continuing differentiation between women and men in relation to statutory pensionable age carries through into occupational schemes. The Court's judgment in *Birds Eye Walls* will have come as a relief to parties in the field as considerable uncertainty had surrounded the topic for a number of years.[348]

Another feature of UK pension schemes which would seem to be allowed to continue as a result of the Court's approach in *Birds Eye Walls* relates to Guaranteed Minimum Pensions (GMPs).[349] It is currently a requirement of the contracting-out legislation[350] that salary related schemes provide benefits at least equal to those which would have been provided by SERPS. This guarantee is called the GMP and is built up for every year in which earnings factors are earned in an individual's working life. This forms a source of discrimination in that a

---

[347]   Government Actuary, at p. 59.

[348]   See for a pre-*Barber* discussion of the subject, Luckhaus 1990, op. cit. The UK government had taken the view that bridging pensions would have become unlawful as a result of Directive 86/378. HC Deb, 26 April 1989, Cols. 1048-1051, cited in House of Lords Select Committee on the European Communities, 10th Report, Session 1988-1989, *Equal Treatment for Men and Women in Pensions and Other Benefits*, London, 1989 at p. 16. Apparently the CBI was able subsequently to convince the government that its arguments were not as cut and dried as it had originally thought as a result of which the government undertook to try and secure other Member States' agreement to an appropriate amendment of the Directive in its "post-adoption phase" (whatever that might mean). HL Deb, Col 950, June 29, 1989, cited in Luckhaus 1990, op. cit. at 49. For a discussion of the various positions taken in the run up to the litigation, see S. Ward, "Equality of Treatment between Women and Men in Occupational Social Security", in McCrudden (ed.) 1994, pp. 99-113 at pp. 105-107.

[349]   See the discussion in Chapter 2.

[350]   Although, pursuant to s. 136 PA 1995 GMPs are abolished for service after April 1997. See the discussion of the contracting-out arrangements in Chapter 2 above.

man continues to 65.[351] Accordingly, she has a higher rate of accrual of GMP than a man of the same age and earning that same amount. Given the abstract nature of this legislation, an example may help.[352]

A man and a woman enter contracted-out employment on reaching the age of 25. Their careers follow uninterrupted parallel paths. On reaching the age of 60, the appropriate percentage by which the woman' earnings factors will be multiplied to calculate her GMP rights will be (20/35)%. The man on reaching pensionable age will find that his appropriate percentage is (20/40)%. Thus, that part of the pension which represents the GMP rights will differ.[353] However because the differentiation is in the level of benefits paid rather than in the conditions of access to them, it seems that this specifically British consequence for occupational schemes of differences in the statutory scheme will be left undisturbed by European law. Although GMPs will no longer have to be provided in relation to service after April 1997, those which have accrued to that date will have to be protected and consequently, the differentiation which the GMP currently brings will continue for up to 40 years into the future.

4.9.2   THE NETHERLANDS

In the Netherlands, occupational schemes are commonly linked to statutory schemes, not in relation to age conditions, but through the levels of benefit paid

---

[351]   See Schedule 3 para. 5(8) to the SSCBA 1992.

[352]   For ease of calculation it will be assumed that the working years all fall after 5 April 1978. According to s. 14(1)(5)(b) of the 1993 Act, the appropriate percentage by which earning factors for such years is to be multiplied is (20/N)% (where N represents the number of years in the earner's working life to pensionable age).

[353]   Admittedly, this problem is somewhat hypothetical since no separate payment is ever made reflecting GMPs. However, in terms of the obligation to index rights when a pension is deferred beyond normal pensionable age (that operating in relation to the statutory scheme) differentiation continues. See S. 15 of the 1993 PSA. If the pensionable age operated under the occupational scheme is lower than 65, male employees will not be entitled to payment of benefits reflecting GMPs.

out. The manner through which account is taken of the AOW has been the subject of controversy[354] and will be briefly discussed here.

The franchise is that part of an individual's salary over which no occupational pension rights are built up because it is assumed that this part of the income is replaced by the AOW. The problem is that the AOW pays benefits at two different levels: 70% of the minimum wage for single individuals, and 50% of the minimum wage to married individuals. Most pension schemes set the franchise at a standard rate without taking individual circumstances into account.[355] The figure chosen is generally twice the married individual's AOW entitlement. This results in single individuals and those who are married but both of whom work receiving a lower total pension income than a married person with a non-economically active spouse.[356] It has been suggested[357] that because it will predominantly be men who are married with a non-economically active spouse, the current practice in relation to the franchise is indirectly discriminatory against women.

It is submitted that this is not the case, or in any event that it does not conflict with European law. If the totalisation of family income is not carried out, all married individuals suffer equally from the practice, less so than single persons. To extrapolate from any of these statistics that one of the sexes suffers more than another seems simply to be too tenuous. Dutch tax law currently requires that total pension benefits do not exceed what is deemed socially acceptable, which in practice means 70% of an individual's final salary.[358] In a situation in which the AOW differentiates on the basis of an individual's "marital" status, something which can and does change over time, it can be argued that requiring actual AOW

---

[354]   De Veer et al, loc. cit. at pp. 15-16;

[355]   Lutjens and Wessels, loc. cit. at p. 15; Kraamwinkel, loc. cit. at pp. 28-31.

[356]   The married couple both of whom work are the worst off because their total AOW entitlement is deducted twice.

[357]   De Veer et al, loc. cit. at p. 11.

[358]   See the discussion in Chapter 2 and note that this may change shortly as a result of the recommendations of the *Commissie Witteveen*.

entitlement to be the basis for the franchise is unreasonable. The statutory scheme is not (sexually) discriminatory and so it seems difficult to conclude that the manner in which occupational schemes deal with the differentiation in the statutory scheme is discriminatory.[359]

4.9.3   GERMANY

The Court's case law on linkage would however seem to require that German practice alter. Paragraph 6 of the BetrAVG provides that where an individual can qualify for his full pension prior to the age of 65 he can also require that his occupational pension be paid out.[360] The terms of this provision are clearly sexually neutral but the possibilities of basing a claim on paragraph 6 are different for women and for men. The standard pensionable age for men is 65, unless the man in question has satisfied the 35 year waiting period to qualify for a pension payable to those with long insurance records aged 63. By contrast, women can require the payment of their statutory pension from the age of 60 where they satisfy the 15 year waiting period and have had at least 10 years compulsory insurance from the age of 40.[361] Despite the neutral terms of paragraph 6, it will be considerably easier for a woman to require that her occupational pension be paid from an age prior to 65 than it will be for a man.

Unlike the provisions on bridging pensions which were at issue in *Birds Eye Walls*, paragraph 6 does not concern the amount of benefit received by individual pensioners. Rather it concerns the benefit's very availability. As such it would not seem to fall within the Court's dicta in *Birds Eye Walls* but rather within that of *Barber*, *Moroni* and *Commission* v. *Belgium*. Consequently, this part

---

[359]   Note that the exception made for pensionable age in Directive 79/7 does not mean that the conduct is not discriminatory. It merely means that the discriminatory conduct does not violate European law (yet).

[360]   The second sentence of para. 6 concerns partial pensions. Where an individual is in receipt of a partial pension, he can request that his occupational pension also be paid out. However, in contrast to the situation for full pensions, he cannot require that this happen.

[361]   These conditions are laid down in para.s 33-40 and 50 of the *Sozialgesetzbuch* (SGB) VI. For detailed treatment, including the subject of when an individual is subject to compulsory insurance, see Gitter, loc. cit; Kittner and Krasney, loc. cit.

of the German legislation on occupational pensions, which perpetuates current discrimination in the statutory scheme, would seem to be in conflict with European law.

4.10   Directive 86/378: A Recapitulation

At the beginning of this Chapter, Directive 86/378 was introduced. It was adopted in July 1986 to implement the principle of equality in the field of occupational pension schemes. However, like Directive 79/7, discussed in the previous Chapter, it is subject to a number of exceptions. More specifically, Article 9 allows schemes to continue to defer the application of the equality principle in relation to pensionable ages and survivors' pensions. They are also entitled temporarily to continue to differentiate in relation to employee contributions to occupational schemes.[362]

However, as the discussion above demonstrates, Article 119 has been interpreted as requiring that employee contributions be equal, as should the ages from which pensions become payable. Similarly, survivors' pensions must be made available to women and men on the same conditions. In the judgments in which it made these findings, the Court was not asked to make a finding on the status of the Directive and it did not make any observations of its own motion. Earlier case law had however indicated that secondary legislation cannot limit the scope of norms of primary EC law.[363] Consequently, the requirements of Article 119 override those of the Directive, and the relevant provisions were simply of no effect. The continuing existence of a piece of secondary legislation which contained provisions inconsistent with Community law cried out for reform. Consequently, in the wake of the judgments of 28 September 1994, the

---

[362]   Until 30 July 1999; see Art. 9(c) of the Directive.

[363]   Order of the President in Case R 45/87, *Commission* v. *Ireland*, [1987] ECR 1369 at para. 19. See in the specific context of Article 119 and Directive 86/378, for example, Case 96/80, *Jenkins*, cited *supra* at para. 22; see Curtin (1987), op. cit. at 255; Curtin (1990), op. cit. at 480; Prechal (1990), op. cit. at 1301.

Commission presented a draft for a Directive to amend Directive 86/378.[364] In making the proposal, the Commission was motivated by considerations of legal certainty and clarity, and by the desire to avoid misunderstandings on the part of the national courts which have to apply Community law.[365] It seeks nothing more than to bring the Directive in line with the provisions of the case law.

Thus, it proposes that Article 2 be amended so that the exclusion of individual contracts and schemes with only one member now only applies to the self-employed. Also optional provisions of schemes offered to participants individually to guarantee them a choice of date upon which normal benefits will start, or a choice between several benefits will be of application to the self-employed only. To reflect the judgments in *Ten Oever* and *Coloroll*, Article 3 delimiting the Directive's personal scope is expanded to include those claiming derived entitlements on the basis of the worker's rights. The main substantive clarifications are to be found in Article 6 and concern the use of sex-specific actuarial tables. The provisions now state clearly that employers may contribute different amounts in respect of male and female employees in relation to both money purchase and salary related schemes, citing the Court's judgment in *Birds Eye Walls* as authority for the proposition that Article 119 permits different levels of contributions to be paid by employers where this will lead to equal benefits for individuals.[366]

The exceptions contained in Article 9[367] which have proved so problematic will continue to apply to the self-employed. Consequently, schemes offering benefits to the self-employed may continue to differentiate in relation to pensionable age, survivor's pensions and, temporarily, in relation to individual's

---

[364]   Proposal for a Directive amending Directive 86/378 on the implementation of the principle of equal treatment for men and women in occupational social security schemes, O.J. 1995 C 218/5; COM(95) 186 final. See I. van der Steen, "Gelijke behandeling van mannen en vrouwen in de aanvullende pensioenregelingen: een nieuw richtlijnvoorstel", *Nederlands Tijdschrift voor Europees Recht* (1995), 123-125.

[365]   COM(95) 186 final at p. 3.

[366]   See the discussion at s. 4.9.

[367]   Permitting the introduction of equality to be delayed in relation to pensionable age, survivor's pensions and employee contributions to occupational schemes.

contributions. The provisions of the Directive are to have retroactive effects for employees back to 17 May 1990,[368] but for the self-employed, it enters into force only as of 1 January 1993, and it does not affect rights accrued prior to the Directive's entry into force.

When it eventually enters into force, the amended Directive will not change the scope of the law which has been described in this Chapter. It will merely consolidate the Court's case law and remove inconsistencies from the secondary legislation. To what extent the changes which the equality principle has required be introduced into the rules of occupational schemes will enable women to accrue adequate levels of retirement income will be assessed in the final section of this Chapter.

4.11   Evaluation

In this Chapter we have ben concerned with the changes which have been required by the introduction of the equality principle into occupational pension schemes. Women are more likely than men to live to a ripe old age[369] but for a number of reasons, they are also more likely than men to be poor in old age.[370] As we saw in the previous Chapter, not only was the practice widespread for women to cease paid employment on marriage, to enable them to devote themselves to their home-based role, but this was also encouraged by the social security systems which created incentives for individuals to behave in precisely this way.

However, as the discussion in this Chapter reveals, those women who rejected the "traditional" paths and roles laid down for them were unable to accrue

---

[368]   In this respect, the Directive is ambiguously drafted as to which of the two interpretations discussed above in s. 4.5 it concerns. So whichever way the Court decides Case C-435/93, *Dietz*, cited *supra*, the text of the Directive should not require amendment.

[369]   See the mortality tables cited by Lutjens and van Poppel, loc. cit. at p. 47.

[370]   See for example, the discussion in Walker, loc. cit., esp. at pp. 177-182; Groves 1992, loc. cit.; J. Allmendinger, E. Brückner and H. Brückner, "Arbeitsleben und Lebensarbeitsentlohnung: Zur Entstehung von finanzieller Ungleichheit im Alter", in Gather et al (eds.), loc. cit. pp. 133-174 at p. 160; A. Kuhley-Oehlert, "Das Alter ist weiblich", in Gather et al (eds.), pp. 247-257 at p. 250.

a pension which would have freed them from financial dependence on a spouse. First many schemes simply excluded women from membership, while more enlightened employers excluded only married women. Second, where women were permitted to join a scheme, they may have been offered membership only from a later age than men. Another discriminatory practice was offering women different benefits from men. Equally, their pension accrual would suffer from the fact that their careers were often shorter than those of men, in part because of the practice of retiring women earlier than men. On the other hand, the fact that women generally outlive men brought with it that women's pensions were more expensive than those of men, and so sometimes to reflect their greater longevity, women would be paid lower levels of periodic benefits.

In virtually all these areas, schemes have been forced to change. With the exception of employer contributions where actuarial tables which differentiate on grounds of sex are used, the pension schemes to which men and women are offered access must be equal in all respects. This will undoubtedly improve significantly the levels of occupational pension which women will be able to accrue. But does it mean in fact that women will receive adequate pensions? Are the reforms such that women will now be able to accrue their own pension at such a rate as to enable them to be financially independent of a spouse? For a number of reasons, this will not commonly occur.

As was discussed in Chapter 2, occupational pension schemes gradually developed into a device by which an employer could bind his particularly valuable employees to his undertaking. As such, they came to be designed to reward most generously the individual working full-time for that employer for as many as 40 years. This is a pattern of employment followed, even today, by relatively few women. The primary reason for this is that the childbearing and often childrearing burden falls upon them which leads to lower pension rights in two main ways.

First, pension rights are only accrued during periods of paid employment. Although the states under consideration provide for pension rights to continue to accrue during periods of paid maternity leave, women who decide to take a longer period of childcare leave[371] will lose what protection this offers.[372] Unless their pension scheme allows voluntary contributions to be paid to continue pension accrual,[373] any such period will have negative consequences for women's pension accrual.

A second way in which childbirth negatively affects the levels of pensions accrued by women is that many women returning to work after the birth of a child do so on a part-time basis.[374] Although part-time workers must be offered access to a pension scheme on the same basis as full-timers,[375] unless the employer can

---

[371]   For example, in the Netherlands, 57% of women with children between the ages of 0 and 5 do not undertake any paid employment, a figure which drops marginally to 50% when the child is between the ages of 6 and 11.*Emancipatie in Cijfers 1994* at p. 30. Landenberger, loc. cit. at p. 85 indicates that the birth of a child reduces a woman's years of paid employment by 4.5 years.

[372]   Rolf, loc. cit. at pp. 177-185 produces tables which indicate how particular periods outside of paid employment, or in part-time employment caused by childcare affects pension accrual. Tölke, loc. cit. at pp. 37-41 discusses the effects of marriage and childbirth on paid employment, as does Prinz, loc. cit. at pp. 56-59. See also for the Netherlands Holtmaat, loc. cit. at p. 52. For the UK, Groves 1992, loc. cit. at p. 201; Field and Prior, loc. cit. at pp. 51-52.

[373]   The twin characteristics of myopia and free-riding partly explain why voluntary contributions are never as satisfactory as compulsory ones.

[374]   For example, in the Netherlands, 57% of women with a child between the ages of 0-5 undertake no paid employment; dropping to 50% where the child is between 6-11; 12% of women with children between the ages of 0-5 work between 1-11 hours per week; where the children are between 6-11, this figure is 14%. 9% of mothers with children in the youngest age group work between 12-19 hours, whereas when the child is slightly older this figure is 10%. Only 22% of mothers with children in the youngest age group work over 20 hours per week, a figure which rises to 25% for slightly older children. *Emancipatie in Cijfers 1994*, at p. 30. The 1991 research carried out for the *Emancipatieraad* (de Veer et al, loc. cit.) reveals that 73% of the schemes surveyed excluded part-time employees from membership. And a mere 9.1% of the members of occupational schemes in the Netherlands work part-time. Figures for Germany from 1988 indicate that 44.1% of West German women worked; the birth of a child reduced the numbers of women working full-time by 5% per child. Field and Prior, loc. cit. at pp. 51-52 provide a detailed overview of the effects of children on women's working patterns.

[375]   Where the part-timers are predominantly one sex and the full-timers the other.

point to an objective justification for their exclusion[376] the levels of pension which that individual will accrue will be proportionate to her reduced hours and wages. Consequently, even where a woman returns to work part-time after the birth of a child, her pension accrual will suffer. The judgments in *Nolte* and *Megner and* Scheffel[377] also provide an indication that despite the fact that the Court has held that the exclusion of part-time workers from pension scheme membership amounts to indirect discrimination which must be justified, it may not in fact increase the number of women who will obtain the right to belong to an occupational scheme. This is because the Court found compatible with EC law a threshold of 15 hours per week, combined with an earnings threshold. In the UK, some 1,940,000 individuals belong to schemes which require that members work between 9 and 26 hours per week to qualify for the scheme. The figures for the Netherlands discussed above suggest that the minimum hours thresholds there is between 12 and 20 hours per week with almost 50% of the schemes surveyed using such a threshold. This indicates the practical importance of a robust approach to what thresholds can be set for qualifying for scheme membership.

Another explanation for women's poor occupational pension provision is that the coverage of occupational schemes remains patchy. In the UK, only 48% of employees belong to schemes.[378] In Germany, private sector schemes cover 46.7% of employees[379] and it is only in the Netherlands that coverage is high, at 82%.[380] This of itself indicates that many individuals do not currently enjoy the benefit of occupational provision. However, those excluded from schemes are predominantly women: a recent survey indicates that only 43% of British female

---

[376]   See the discussion in Chapter 3 of the judgments of the Court in Case C-317/93, *Nolte*, cited *supra* and Case C-444/93, *Megner and Scheffel*, cited *supra*. See also Joined Cases C-50/96, C-234/96 and C-235/96, *Schröder, Vick and Conze* v. *Deutsche Bundespost Telekom* where the Court has been asked about the legality of a provision excluding individuals working fewer than 18 hours per week from an occupational pension scheme.

[377]   Discussed in Chapter 3.

[378]   Government Actuary, loc. cit. at p. 4.

[379]   *Supplementary Pensions*, loc. cit. at p. 60.

[380]   Harrison, loc. cit. at p. 11; Kraamwinkel, loc. cit. at p. 23.

employees belong to an occupational pension scheme.[381] 31.5% of scheme members in Germany were women, while in the Netherlands 60% of those without pension provision are women.[382] These statistics indicate that women are less likely than men to belong to a scheme, and it appears that they are more likely than men to work for an employer who does not operate an occupational scheme.[383] This is a consequence of the fact that it is currently entirely at the employer's discretion whether or not to offer employees membership of an occupational scheme.[384]

A final reason why the levels of pension to which a (married) woman accrues entitlement may not be adequate to free her from economic dependence upon her spouse is that despite the requirement that women and men receive equal pay for equal work, women's wages continue to lag behind those of men.[385] Lower wages are in turn reflected in lower pensions on retirement. It remains true that

---

[381]   Field and Prior, loc. cit. at pp. 71-72.

[382]   Kraamwinkel, loc. cit., at p. 36. Dutch pension scheme coverage is particularly high, at 82%. 11.4% of Dutch female employees are without occupational pension provision as compared to 7.6% of men.

[383]   For example, 30% of part-time employees and only 22% of full-time employees surveyed in the UK worked for an employer with no pension scheme; see Field and Prior, loc. cit. at p. 71. German research, which is echoed by UK and Dutch experience, reveals that the likelihood that a firm offers employees membership of an occupational pension scheme increases with the size of the firm. Consequently, it is relevant that 41% of German women, as compared to 20% of German men work for a firm with fewer than 5 employees. 27% of men and 14% of women work for firms with more than 500 employees; see Allmendinger et al, loc. cit. at p. 149. In the Netherlands, it appears that in firms with fewer than 10 employees, 43.8% of employees were without occupational provision; firms with between 10 and 49 employees, 20.7% had no pension scheme. Employers without pension schemes generally employ proportionately more women and part-time employees; see Kraamwinkel, loc. cit. at p. 37.

[384]   Unless the employer operates within a branch of industry in relation to which a Dutch scheme has been declared of compulsory application. See the discussion in Chapter 2.

[385]   For example, the ratio of female to male non-manual earnings ranges between 55% to 69% in 12 of the 15 Member States; see Social Europe, Supplement 4/94, *Wage Determination and Sex Segregation in Employment in the European Community*, at p. XXVI.

> "the main determinants of the poverty of older women and the
> inequalities between them and older men have already been
> established long before retirement age. As in other spheres of
> women's lives, the key to their poverty and deprivation in old
> age is the socially constructed relationship between gender and
> the labour market. The labour market is the primary source of
> the inequalities which are carried into retirement."[386]

As a consequence of the fact that their career patterns diverge from those which occupational pension schemes are designed most generously to reward, women will continue to accrue lower levels of retirement pensions than men. In this respect, despite the significant improvements in the levels of women's pensions which will ensue from the introduction of the equality principle into this area of the law, the alterations do not go far enough to ensure that women will be able to accrue adequate levels of occupational entitlement, enabling them to be financially independent on retirement.

---

[386]   Walker, loc. cit. at p. 190.

PART III

PENSIONS AND MOBILITY

STATUTORY PENSIONS AND MOBILITY

5.1   Introduction

In Chapter 1 the three main challenges which have been perceived to confront statutory pension schemes as they have been put in place in the countries of the EU in the post war period were described. It was observed that demographic predictions have persuaded some that the role played by Pay-As-You-Go statutory schemes will have to be reduced and pre-funded occupational schemes will have to be encouraged to take their place. However, two other challenges to the status quo were also described. The impact of the first - the increased number of women participating in paid employment - has been discussed in the preceding two Chapters. In the next two Chapters, attention will turn to the second major challenge facing pension provision - the internationalisation of the market, and, more specifically here, the fact that there are increasing numbers of employees who work in a number of different states.

In this part of the book, the structure of the preceding part will be adhered to. Consequently, in this Chapter, the focus of attention will be statutory pension provision. First, the features of statutory pension provision will be described which could potentially create problems for the international migrant worker. The measures which have been taken to ameliorate the social security difficulties faced by the international migrant find their origin in the EC legal order. In the next section, therefore, the EC legal background to the measures will be described. Thereafter the scope of the provisions will be described as will the main features of their operation. Next, the impact of the rules on the statutory pension schemes in the jurisdictions in question will be considered before finally, an evaluation will be made of the efficacy of the measures in eradicating the barriers to labour mobility caused by the rules of statutory pension schemes.

5.2   Problematic Features of Statutory Pension Schemes

As the discussion of statutory pension provision in Chapters 2 and 3 reveals, there are a number of profound differences between the pension schemes in place in these three Member States. Nevertheless, their systems also exhibit a number of similarities and it is in fact the shared features of the schemes which are of concern to the international migrant. These features are the use of the insurance principle combined with the territorially limited scope of pension schemes. Both will be discussed briefly below.

In all the countries of the EU, and consequently in the three jurisdictions considered here, pension benefits accrue on the basis of periods of insurance completed over a period of time. Irrespective of whether the basis of insurance is residence[1] or employment,[2] entitlement to benefit under the scheme, and often its level, depends upon having completed periods of insurance. Additionally, the legislation may require that the individual have completed a certain minimum period of insurance before he can accrue entitlement to any benefit at all.[3]

The second feature of pension schemes which when combined with the insurance principle makes accruing full pension entitlement problematic for migrants is the territorially limited scope of statutory pension schemes. This means that insurance must be completed within a specific scheme to count towards benefits entitlement: the UK scheme takes account only of periods of insurance in the UK scheme. Periods of insurance which are completed under another scheme are ignored. Consequently, a period of employment abroad may result in the international migrant accruing a lower pension entitlement than had he remained in his original state. Equally, territorial limitations on the scope of a national pension scheme may lead it to require that the pensioner be resident within the territory of the paying state to be entitled to payment of benefits. This makes it impossible for the migrant to return to his home state on retirement after a period

---

[1]   As with the UK and the Netherlands.

[2]   As in Germany.

[3]   For example, the 25% rule in the UK, described in Chapter 2, or the minimum of 5 years insurance found in German legislation.

of employment abroad, and the problems which these sorts of requirement pose for the migrant who has worked successively in a number of different jurisdictions are clear.

The combination of the insurance principle with the territorial limitations of pension schemes could result in the following situation arising. An individual has been employed in a series of different States without interruption between leaving full-time education and reaching pensionable age. He has paid contributions to the various social security schemes for his entire career. However, it is possible that according to the national legislation of the state in which he was employed he has not been insured by the national scheme for long enough to accrue entitlement to payment.[4] Even if this is not the case, the level of benefit to which he has accrued entitlement will reflect only the period of insurance carried out under that scheme. Consequently, it will be of vital importance to the migrant if he is to receive an adequate pension that the other states within which he has accrued entitlement do not require that he reside within their territory if he is to be paid his pension. As this demonstrates, by electing to work abroad, the international migrant risks being penalised in terms of his pension accrual. An even more acute example could result from the legislation of two of the Member States under consideration here. In the Netherlands, insurance depends upon residence. In Germany, insurance is linked to employment.[5] If, in the absence of overriding legislation, someone chooses to work in the Netherlands but to live in Germany, they will not be insured. Equally, someone living in the Netherlands but working in Germany would be insured in both states.

As this brief discussion reveals, the differences which exist between the social security schemes of the various Member States could have created significant barriers to employee mobility since, on moving abroad, an individual would risk losing entitlement to benefits which he was in the process of building up, or receiving a lower level of benefit to that to which he would otherwise have been entitled.

---

[4] For example, an individual must have been insured for 15-20 years in Italy to qualify for payment of a pension (Cornelissen, op. cit. at 451).

[5] There is provision for voluntary insurance, but we are concerned here with compulsory insurance.

5.3   EC Law - The Background

The difficulties which different social security rules could cause international migrant workers are a matter of concern to the EC because one of the foundations upon which its single market[6] is to be constructed is the free movement of persons.

The free movement of persons mentioned in Article 7A EC, can actually be subdivided into freedom of movement of workers, the freedom of movement of the self-employed and the freedom of movement of the non-economically active. Since the focus of the main body of this research is pre-funded employer-based pension schemes, it would seem appropriate to focus this discussion on the free movement of workers.[7] Equally, the fact that the free movement provisions have formed the impetus for the activities which have been undertaken in relation to social security, and are the reason for concern in relation to occupational schemes, it would seem appropriate to spend a little time outlining their precise scope.

---

[6]   An area without internal borders in which the freedom of movement of goods, persons, services and capital are to be guaranteed according to the provisions of the Treaty; see Art. 7A EC.

[7]   Similar principles inform the freedom of movement of the self-employed - whether concerning their freedom of establishment (Artt. 52 et seq. EC) or freedom to provide services (Artt. 59 et seq. EC). On the specific details of these freedoms see, for example, the discussion in S. Weatherill and P. Beaumont, *EC Law*, 2nd ed., London, 1995 at pp. 575-612. The rights of those who are no longer or have never been economically active are considerably less than those of the economically active; see in this respect, Directive 90/364 on the right of residence, O.J. 1990 L 180/26; Directive 90/365 on the right of residence for employees and self-employed persons who have ceased their occupational activity, O.J. 1990 L 180/28; Directive 93/96 on the right of residence for students, O.J. 1993 L 317/59, replacing Directive 90/366 on the rights of residence for students, O.J. 1990 L 180/30 annulled by the judgment of the ECJ in Case C-295/90, *Parliament* v. *Council*, [1992] ECR I-4193. On the effects upon this situation of the introduction of European citizenship (Artt. 8 - 8e EC) see, *inter alia*, C. Closa, "The Concept of Citizenship in the Treaty on European Union", 29 CML Rev. (1992), 1137-1170; C. Closa, "Citizenship of the Union and Nationality of Member States", in O'Keeffe and Twomey (eds.) loc. cit. at pp. 109-119; D. O'Keeffe, "Union Citizenship", in O'Keeffe and Twomey (eds.) loc. cit. at pp. 87-107; B. Wilkinson, "Towards European Citizenship? Nationality, Discrimination and Free Movement of Workers in the European Union", 1 European Public Law (1995), 417-437.

5.3.1   FREE MOVEMENT OF WORKERS[8]

The realisation of the free movement of workers was the focus of the Commission's social work programme during the 1960s and has long been the cornerstone of the social dimension of Community activity.[9] Drafted at a time of high Italian unemployment and German jobs surplus, it was considered that liberalising labour movement between the Member States would solve the social ill of unemployment. The barriers which states traditionally erected to exclude foreigners from their job markets included immigration controls, and restricting particular occupations to nationals. However, in the new Europe, apart from any more socially oriented goals, the efficient allocation of resources required a mobile labour market free of such artificial barriers.

The provisions on the free movement of workers are contained in Title III Chapter 1 of the Treaty. Article 48 provides that the free movement of workers was to be realised by the end of the transitional period, after which period the Court has held that Article 48 enjoys direct effect,[10] in both vertical and horizontal relationships.[11]

---

[8]   See the discussions in Bercusson, loc. cit. at pp. 383-412; E. Johnson and D. O'Keeffe, "From Discrimination to obstacles to free movement: Recent developments concerning the free movement of workers 1989-1994", 31 CML Rev. (1994), 1313-1346; Kapteyn VerLoren van Themaat, loc. cit. at pp. 405-421; C. Laske, "The Impact of the Single European Market on Social Protection for Migrant Workers", 30 CML Rev. (1993), 515-539; G.F. Mancini, "The Free Movement of Workers in the Case-Law of the European Court of Justice", in Curtin and O'Keeffe (eds.) loc. cit. at pp. 67-77; Nielsen and Szyszczak, loc. cit. at pp. 55-80; P. Watson, "Wandering Students: Their Rights under Community Law" (hereafter Watson 1992), in Curtin and O'Keeffe (eds.) loc. cit. at pp. 79-88

[9]   As is observed, for example, by Bercusson, loc. cit. at p. 383. For a discussion of the social dimension, see the literature cited in Chapter 3.

[10]   See inter alia, Case 167/73, Commission v. France, cited supra; Case 41/74, Van Duyn v. Home Office, [1974] ECR 1337; most recently, Case C-415/93, Union Royale Belge des Sociétés de Football Association v. Jean-Marc Bosman, [1995] ECR I-4921, noted by J.M. Fernández Martin in 21 EL Rev. (1996), 313-326; D. O'Keeffe and P. Osborne in 12 IJCLLIR (1996), 111-130; S. Weatherill in 33 CML Rev. (1996), forthcoming.

[11]   Inter alia, Case 36/74, Walrave and Koch v. AUCI, [1974] ECR 1405; Case 13/76, Dona v. Mantero, [1976] ECR 1333; Case C-415/93, Bosman, cited supra.

The central concept of Article 48 - that of the "worker" is not defined in the Treaty. However, focusing on the fact that this freedom constitutes one of the foundations of the Community,[12] the Court has taken a broad brush to defining the elements of this particular Treaty right. Early on the Court decided that "worker" must be a Community law concept[13] independent of the vagaries of national legislation. If national law was free to determine precisely who fell within the scope of Article 48, the scope of rights granted by European law could be changed unilaterally and differ between States, contrary to the overriding principle of the uniformity of the scope of EC law rights throughout the Community.

For the purposes of Article 48, an individual will be deemed to be a worker where he performs an "effective and genuine economic activity"[14] "for remuneration ... the nature of which [employment] is not determined by himself for and under the control of another, regardless of the legal nature of the employment relationship."[15] Consequently, those working part-time in an activity with some economic value,[16] even where they earn less than any legally

---

[12]   For example in Case 167/73, *Commission* v. *France*, cited *supra* at para 43.

[13]   Case 75/63, *Unger* v. *Bestuur der Bedrijfsvereniging voor Detailhandel en Ambachten te Utrecht*, [1964] ECR 177. This contrasts to the approach taken in many of the Directives adopted in the social field, where the delimitation of the workers falling within the Directives scope is expressly left to national law. See for example, Directive 91/533 on the employer's obligation to inform employees of the conditions applicable to the contract or employment relationship O.J. 1991, L 288/32.

[14]   Case 53/81, *Levin* v. *Staatssecretaris van Justitie*, [1982] ECR 1035 at para. 17.

[15]   Case 66/85, *Lawrie-Blum* v. *Land Baden-Württemberg*, [1986] ECR 2121 at para. 17. As has been discussed in Chapter 3, the Court has recently indicated that the same definition of "worker" applies in the sex discrimination sphere. See Case C-444/93, *Megner and Scheffel*, cited *supra*.

[16]   Compare in this respect the judgment handed down in Case 196/87, *Steymann* v. *Staatssecretaris van Justitie*, [1988] ECR 6159 with that in Case 344/87, *Bettray* v. *Staatssecretaris van Justitie*, [1989] ECR 1621. This can also cover trainees, see Case C-357/89, *Raulin* v. *Minister van Onderwijs en Wetenschappen*, [1992] ECR I-1027 and Case C-3/90, *Bernini* v. *Minister van Onderwijs en Wetenschappen*, [1992] ECR I-1071, both of which clarified Case 39/86, *Lair* v. *Universität Hannover*, 1988] ECR 3161 and Case 197/86, *Brown* v. *Secretary of State for Scotland*, [1988] ECR 3205. On the subject of the extent of the rights granted to students generally, see Watson 1992, loc. cit.; W. van Gerven, P. van den Bossche, "Freedom of Movement and Equal Treatment for Students in Europe:

prescribed social minimum,[17] fall within the scope of the definition developed by the Court. In essence,

> "any person who pursues an activity which is effective and genuine, to the exclusion of activities on such a small scale as to be regarded as purely marginal and ancillary is to be treated as a "worker" within the meaning of Article 48 of the Treaty."[18]

However, the rights to free movement are limited to nationals of one of the Member States,[19] which excludes a considerable number[20] of individuals from the Community regime.

In terms of the substantive rights granted to migrants, it is clear that the worker can move for the purposes of taking up a particular employment, but also that he can move to another Member States in search of employment.[21] To this end, the Court has held that a migrant can stay in another Member State for a reasonable period for the purposes of seeking employment and that even if national legislation provides that an alien can be deported if he has not found employment within a given period, this can not be invoked against a migrant who can

---

An Emerging Principle?", in H.G. Schermers et al (eds.), *Free Movement of Persons in Europe*, Dordrecht, 1993 at pp. 405-426.

[17] Case 139/85, *Kempf* v. *Staatssecretaris van Justitie*, [1986] ECR 1741.

[18] Case C-107/94, *Asscher* v. *Staatssecretaris van Financiën*, judgment of 27 June 1996, nyr, para. 25.

[19] See Art. 48(2) EC and for example Arts. 1 and 2 of Regulation 1612/68. See W. Alexander, "Free Movement of Non-EC Nationals; A Review of the case law of the Court of Justice", in H. G. Schermers et al (eds.), loc. cit. at pp. 485-496; T.K. Hervey, "Migrant Workers and their Families in the European Union: The Pervasive Market Ideology of Community Law", in Shaw and More (eds.) loc. cit. at pp. 91-110; T. Hoogenboom, "Free Movement and Integration of Non-EC Nationals and the Logic of the Internal Market", in H.G. Schermers et al, loc. cit. at pp. 497-511; P. Oliver, "Non-Community Nationals and the Treaty of Rome", 5 YEL (1985), 57-93; J.H.H. Weiler, "Thou Shalt Not Oppress a Stranger (Ex. 23:9): On the Judicial Protection of the Human Rights of Non-EC Nationals - A Critique", in H.G. Schermers et al, loc. cit. at pp. 248-271.

[20] Cornelissen, op. cit. at 444-445, fn 16, indicates that there are about 2 million EC migrant workers, but that the number of non-EC national migrant workers is much higher.

[21] Joined cases 115 and 116/81, *Adoui and Cornuaille* v. *Belgium*, [1982] ECR 1665; Case C-292/89, *R.* v. *Immigration Appeal Tribunal, ex parte Antonissen*, [1991] ECR I-745.

demonstrate that he is still in search of employment and has a genuine chance of securing said employment.[22]

Having obtained employment, or while in search of it, the migrant enjoys the right to reside in the host State,[23] and, having worked there, to remain on that territory after having ceased employment.[24] Additionally, irrespective of their nationality, the spouse[25] and dependents in the descending and ascending lines[26] can move to reside with the migrant.[27]

The essence of the rights to which the migrant worker is entitled is the right not to be discriminated against on grounds of nationality.[28] As such, the freedom laid down in Article 48 merely constitutes a specific elaboration of the general non-discrimination principle contained in Article 6 EC.

Nevertheless, the Treaty itself lays down some limitations on these rights. First, the Member States are entitled to limit the free movement of workers in the interests of public policy, public security or public health.[29] For such a limitation to be found to be legitimate, it must be based on the personal conduct of the

---

[22]   Case C-292/89, *Antonissen*, cited *supra* at para. 21.

[23]   Article 48(3)(b) and (c) EC, Regulation 1612/68 and Directive 68/360 O.J. Sp. Ed. 1968, L 257/13. See on the extent to which limitations can be imposed on this freedom, *inter alia*, Case 36/75, *Rutili* v. *Ministre de l'interieur*, [1975] ECR 1219.

[24]   Article 48(3)(d) EC.

[25]   See Case 59/85, *The Netherlands* v. *Reed*, [1986] ECR 1283.

[26]   Art. 10(1) of Regulation 1612/68.

[27]   For the limitations on the rights of non-EC national spouses, see Case 267/83, *Diatta* v. *Land Berlin*, [1985] ECR 567 and Case C-370/90, *R.* v. *Immigration Appeal Tribunal and Surinder Singh, ex parte Secretary of State for the Home Department*, [1992] ECR I-4265.

[28]   Art. 48(2) explains that freedom of movement entails "the abolition of any discrimination based on nationality between workers of the Member States as regards employment, remuneration and other conditions of work and employment."

[29]   Article 48(3) EC. See Directive 64/221 O.J. Sp. Ed. 1964, No. 850/64, p. 117.

individual[30] which remains a current threat[31] to one of the fundamental interests of society.[32] Additionally, employment in the public service is still excluded from the scope of the free movement provisions,[33] although the Court has limited this to occupations

> "which involve direct or indirect participation in the exercise of powers conferred by public law and duties designed to safeguard the general interests of the State or of other public authorities."[34]

Since the entry into force of the TEU, all nationals of the Member States of the EU are now designated European citizens. As a consequence, it can be questioned whether this is not an exclusion which should be reconsidered as incompatible with the current state of Community law.

The ECJ has described the right of free movement as a right of integration in the host state.[35] To facilitate the realisation of this objective, the Council has adopted Regulation 1612/68[36] which fleshes out the skeleton rights enumerated

---

[30] Article 3 of Directive 64/221. Case 67/74, *Bonsignore* v. *Oberstadtdirektor der Stadt Köln*, [1975] ECR 297.

[31] Case 131/79, *R.* v. *Secretary of State for Home Affairs, ex parte Santillo*, [1980] ECR 1585.

[32] Case 30/77, *R.* v. *Bouchereau*, [1977] ECR 1999.

[33] Article 48(4) EC. See D. O'Keeffe, "Judicial Interpretation of the Public Service Exception to the Free Movement of Workers", in Curtin and O'Keeffe (eds.), loc. cit. at pp. 89-106.

[34] Case 149/79, *Commission* v. *Belgium*, [1980] ECR 3881. See also Case 152/73, *Sotgiu* v. *Deutsche Bundespost*, [1974] ECR 153; Case 307/84, *Commission* v. *France*, [1986] ECR 1725; Case 33/88, *Allué and Coonan* v. *Universita degli Studi di Venezia*, [1989] ECR 1591; Case C-4/91, *Bleis* v. *Ministère de l'Education Nationale*, [1991] ECR I-5627; Case 225/85, *Commission* v. *Italy*, [1987] ECR 2625. See also the Commission's Action Plan, *Freedom of movement of workers and access to employment in the public service of the Member States*, O.J. 1988, C 72/2. See most recently, Case C-473/93, *Commission* v. *Luxembourg*, judgment of 2 July 1996; Case C-173/94, *Commission* v. *Belgium*, judgment of 2 July 1996; Case C-290/94, *Commission* v. *Greece*, judgment of 2 July 1996.

[35] Case C-308/93, *Bestuur van de Sociale Verzekeringsbank* v. *Cabanis-Issarte*, judgment of 30 April 1996, nyr, at para. 38.

[36] Regulation 1612/68 on freedom of movement for workers within the Community O.J. Sp. Ed. 1968, L 257/2, p. 475.

in the Treaty. Basically, it provides that it is unlawful to discriminate between nationals of different Member States in relation access to employment.[37] Further, the Regulation provides for equality in working conditions as between nationals and non-nationals.[38] The most far-reaching of these provisions is Article 7(2) which requires that the migrant worker receive the same "social and tax advantages" as are enjoyed by the nationals of the state in question.[39] These are all those facilities

> "which, whether or not linked to a contract of employment, are generally granted to national workers primarily because of their objective status as workers or by virtue of the mere fact of their residence on the national territory and whose extension to workers who are nationals of other Member States therefore seems likely to facilitate the mobility of such workers within the Community."[40]

Matters such as access to reduced rail travel,[41] interest-free loans on childbirth,[42] cohabitation rights with a non-spouse[43] and educational scholarships for study abroad[44] have all been held by the Court to fall within the scope of this provision which consequently provides migrant workers with an important means of ensuring that they are treated equally.

---

[37]   Artt. 1-6 of Regulation 1612/68. For discrimination of this sort, see for example, Case 167/73, *Commission* v. *France*, cited *supra*. According to Art. 3(1) requirements as to linguistic knowledge may be imposed. On which see Case C-379/87, *Groener* v. *Minister for Education and the City of Dublin Educational Committee*, [1989] ECR 3967.

[38]   Artt. 7-9 of Regulation 1612/68.

[39]   On this subject, see the discussion by D. O'Keeffe, "Equal Rights for Migrants: the Concept of Social Advantages in Article 7(2) of Regulation 1612/68", 5 YEL (1985), 93-123.

[40]   Case 249/83, *Hoeckx* v. *Openbaar Centrum voor Maatschappelijk Welzijn Kalmhout*, [1985] ECR 973 at para. 20.

[41]   Case 32/75, *Cristini* v. *SNCF*, [1975] ECR 1085.

[42]   Case 65/81, *Reina* v. *Landeskreditbank*, [1982] ECR 33.

[43]   Case 59/85, *The Netherlands* v. *Reed*, [1986] ECR 1283.

[44]   Case 235/87, *Matteucci* v. *Communauté Française de Belgique*, [1988] ECR 5589.

In recent years, the Court has been asked about the tax treatment to be afforded to individuals who have exercised one of their rights to free movement.[45] Are they to be treated like nationals of their own or their host state, or is an entirely separate regime to be created for them? Since migrants are likely to deviate from the employment and living patterns followed by nationals of their state of residence, a whole range of difficult questions arise for resolution, something not facilitated by the fact that direct tax remains within the exclusive competence of the Member States.

The situation of the individual who resides in the state in which he is employed is problem-free: he is entitled to the same treatment as nationals of the host state residing there. However, the situation of the migrant worker who resides in a state other than that in which he is employed is more complex. In principle, direct taxation remains a matter over which the Member States continue to enjoy exclusive competence, subject to the overriding requirement that this competence is not exercised contrary to Community law.[46] The Court has found that non-resident taxpayers may be taxed more heavily than residents[47] in relation to personal allowances and benefits, unless the individual receives virtually all of his income from the state of employment such as not to qualify for allowances in any other state from which he receives income.[48] This is because otherwise, the individual might be able to benefit twice from allowances granted in respect of a

---

[45]   See for example, Case C-204/90, *Bachmann* v. *Belgium*, [1992] ECR I-249; Case C-300/90, *Commission* v. *Belgium*, [1992] ECR I-305; Case C-279/93, *Finanzamt Köln* v. *Schumacker*, [1995] ECR I-225; Case C-80/94, *Wielockx*, cited *supra*; Case C-107/94, *Asscher*, cited *supra*. See the observations by P.J. Wattel, "The EC Court's attempts to reconcile the Treaty Freedoms with International Tax Law", 33 CML Rev. (1996), 223-254; F. Vanistendael, "The Consequences of *Schumacker* and *Wielockx*: Two Steps forward in the Tax Procession of Echternach", 33 CML Rev. (1996), 255-269.

[46]   See Case C- 279/93, *Schumacker*, cited *supra* at para.s 21 and 26; Case C-80/94, *Wielockx*, cited *supra* at para. 16; Case C-107/94, *Asscher*, cited *supra* at para. 36.

[47]   The Court accepts that in relation to direct taxation, the situations of residents and non-residents are not generally comparable; See Case C-279/93, *Schumacker*, cited *supra* at para. 31; Case C-80/94, *Wielockx*, cited *supra* at para. 18; Case C-107/94, *Asscher*, cited *supra* at para. 41.

[48]   See, for example, Case C-279/93, *Schumacker*, cited *supra*, introducing the concept of what Wattel terms the "virtual resident" (op. cit. at 226-228) into Community law.

single fact, for example, marriage. However, where double tax Treaties have been
concluded between the states and cover the situation at issue, it is likely that
differential treatment will be found to be indirectly discriminatory and without
objective justification.[49] Where such a Treaty has been concluded, the signatory
states have agreed that the equivalence in deductibility and tax which is generally
ensured in relation to every individual is to be replaced by a coherence between
the tax regimes operating at the level of the State. By concluding such treaties the
Member States in the eyes of the Court waive their right to insist on coherent tax
treatment of particular individuals.

As this brief discussion, reveals, the Treaty, Community legislator and the
Court have worked together to create a legal regime within which the migrant
worker is not discriminated against by virtue of his decision to migrate. Despite
the far-reaching rights granted to the migrant to equality in relation to social and
tax advantages, separate legislation[50] has been adopted to govern his social
security rights. This will be discussed in the next section.

5.4   Social Security[51]

5.4.1   INTRODUCTION

In section 5.2 above, a brief overview was given of the features of pension
schemes which will penalise the migrant worker. That social security schemes

---

[49]   See the discussion in Case C-107/94, *Asscher*, cited *supra* at para.s 42-62.

[50]   Which nevertheless may apply simultaneously with Reg. 1612/68. See for example, Case C-
111/91, *Commission* v. *Luxembourg*, [1993] ECR I-817, at para. 21; Case C-310/91, *Schmid*
v. *Belgian State*, [1993] ECR I-3011, at para. 17; Opinion of Advocate General Jacobs in
Joined Cases C-245/94 and C-312/94, *Hoever and Zachow* v. *Land Nordrhein-Westfalen* at
para.s 85-86.

[51]   See the introduction contained in Chapter 14 of Ogus, Barendt and Wilkeley, loc. cit.; I. van
der Steen, *Grensarbeid en Sociale Zekerheid*, Kluwer Reeks Sociale Verzekeringswetten,
part 2A, Deventer, Looseleaf provides an exhaustive treatment of the subject, as do H. von
der Groeben, J. Thiesing, C.-D. Ehlermann, *Kommentar zum EWG Vertrag*, Baden-Baden,
4th edn. 1991 at pp. 719-902; F. Pennings (ed.), *Introduction to European Social Security
Law*, Deventer, 1994.

could create practical problems for the realisation of the free movement of workers came as no surprise to the original Member States. Since the beginning of the century states have concluded an ever greater number of bilateral treaties and international conventions to regulate the situation of the international migrant.[52] Article 69(4) of the European Coal and Steel Community Treaty required that the Member States "settle amongst themselves any matters ... to ensure that social security arrangements do not inhibit labour mobility." Pursuant to this, the European Convention on Social Security was drafted and signed in December 1957. When the Treaty of Rome entered into force, this text was seized by the Member States as the method of fulfilling the Article 51 EC mandate.[53] However, before considering the precise scope of Article 51 and the rules which have been adopted to ameliorate the social security position of the migrant worker, the variety of options open to Member States to deal with this situation will be considered.

The Options

In solving the social security problems faced by the migrant worker, states have a choice between a number of options. The first option is one canvassed by Pieters.[54] He advocates creating a separate social security system (the 13th state[55]) specifically for migrant workers.[56] On leaving their home state the migrant would become subject to the social security regime organised and administered, probably, by the EC for the remainder of his working life.

---

[52]   See the discussion provided in P. Watson, *Social Security Law in the European Communities*, London, 1980 at pp. 8-11 and 16-29.

[53]   See *infra*.

[54]   See for example, D.C.H.M. Pieters, "Brengt '1992' coördinatie en harmonisatie van de sociale zekerheid?", in A.A. Franken, P.C. Gilhuis and J.A.F. Peters (eds.), *Themis en Europa. Een Opening van Nieuwe Grenzen?*, Zwolle, 1989 at pp. 165-187.

[55]   At the time the proposal was made, the EC had 12 members.

[56]   He also seems to be willing to allow individuals to opt out of their national scheme in favour of the new scheme. In the following discussion, the criticism will focus on this proposal from the perspective of the migrant.

Although this suggestion is very interesting and *communautaire*, it does suffer from a number of problems. First, it runs entirely counter to the basic principles of EC law on free movement which, as the discussion in the previous section reveals, seek "national" treatment of migrants. Singling them out for special treatment for their entire working life, even after a relatively short period abroad is far from this. Second, given the relatively small numbers of individuals involved,[57] it would also seem to be a somewhat disproportionate response to create a system taking them entirely outside any national scheme. Third, it has repeatedly been stated that the social security schemes, and the benefits to which they provide entitlement differ widely between Member States. Any so-called "13th state" would have to provide benefits at least equivalent to the most generous national system if no obstacles to free movement are to be created by social security. But if this course is in fact followed, incentives will be created for other workers from other states to migrate.[58] Finally, it would be an extremely complex task to devise a method of financing such a system.

Although solutions could undoubtedly be devised to deal with these technical difficulties, they can do nothing to address the fundamental criticism of the proposal - that it runs entirely counter to Community policy of providing migrant workers with "national" treatment. Since this policy is based on the non-discrimination principle contained in Article 48 and, more generally, Article 6 of the Treaty, it would be necessary to alter the Treaty and the entire *acquis communautaire* to bring about such a change.

A second option would be for states to decide entirely to harmonise conditions of entitlement and levels of benefits amongst all members of the Union. This would allow the migrant to remain a member of the same scheme irrespective of where he worked in the Union, although its administration might have been in the hands of a different organisation. Clearly this does not suffer from incompatibility with the objective of securing "national" treatment for migrants. However, the basic problem with harmonisation is that in the context of social

---

[57]   Cornelissen, op. cit. at 444-5, fn 16, indicates that there are about 2 million such migrants.

[58]   Pieters sees this as a good thing (op. cit. at p. 184). However, it is difficult to see why benefits shopping, generally portrayed as something to be avoided and discouraged, is suddenly desirable within this regime.

security benefits, it requires that a degree of consensus be reached between the participating members as to the specific function of the benefit in question. If, for example, the old age pension schemes of the UK, the Netherlands and Germany are compared, it emerges that although both the UK and the Netherlands pay flat rate benefits, the levels of benefit provided under each national scheme differ significantly. In Germany, benefits are considerably more generous and earnings-related. The UK is also characterised by the fact that the statutory scheme has a second limb, the earnings-related SERPS. Although it forms a welcome addition to the level of benefit provided under the basic scheme, because of the earnings ceiling in place, it provides only a relatively low replacement rate for many individuals.[59]

Harmonisation would require that agreement be reached amongst a politically and economically diverse group of states as to the precise role of social security provision. Irrespective of the details of the resulting regime, harmonisation would require wholesale adjustment of all participating national systems, raising difficult questions of transitional regimes, but more importantly, at least in political terms, bringing about a fundamental alteration in the national consensus[60] as to the role played by social security within a particular jurisdiction. To harmonise the social security pension schemes of the Member States of the European Union would bring about widespread and far-reaching alteration in the status quo merely to solve the problems faced by a relatively small group of migrant workers - in other words, harmonisation can be seen to be disproportionate.

Coordination of statutory pension schemes, on the other hand, allows the various national systems be left largely intact, but requires that a regime be created to allow the national systems to fit together to maintain the social security coverage of the migrant worker.[61] The advantage of this system is that it allows

---

[59]   But see the observations of P. Whiteford, "The use of replacement rates in international comparisons of benefit systems", 48 *International Social Security Review* 2/1995, 3-30 on the difficulties of comparing the benefits provided by different schemes.

[60]   Which must be assumed to exist, at least in broad lines, in all countries.

[61]   Note that even were the Member States to decide to harmonise social security, some form of coordination would be required for the purposes of calculating an individual's total entitlement and for dividing responsibility for paying benefits.

a migrant worker to be treated in the same way as nationals while employed in that state. Additionally, it does not require States to overhaul their existing regimes, and can consequently be regarded as a less intrusive, more proportionate response to the situation. It respects the autonomy and choice of the individual Member States as to the role to be played by social security within their particular jurisdiction. Finally, by subjecting a migrant to the social security regime of his host state, the equal treatment with nationals which coordination ensures can be seen to contribute to a migrant's integration into the society of his host state.[62]

There are broadly two alternative shapes which a coordinating regime can take.[63] The first is to provide that all periods of employment carried out in the Union be totalled and the Member State in which the migrant was last employed be deemed responsible for paying the entire resulting benefit. The problem with this approach, from the perspective of the Member States is that it would impose a great financial burden on the last Member State in which an individual worked. It could also encourage a form of benefits shopping, whereby workers would arrange their working lives so as to end up in a Member State paying relatively generous benefits. In the context of the three Member States in this research, this would encourage the migrant to work in Germany at the end of his career.

Seen more generally, such a system would amount to a form of lottery for the individual concerned. His benefit levels would not reflect his employment history, but rather where he happened to retire. This might work to his advantage, but where an individual moved, say, from an earnings related to a flat rate system, significant disadvantage and loss of rights could occur. Additionally, the parity of treatment with national employees would vanish to a certain degree, existing only in relation to employees in his final state.

The other alternative is to allow each individual state to retain responsibility for paying the levels of benefits corresponding to the employment

---

[62]   As the Court observed in Case C-308/93, *Cabanis-Issarte*, cited *supra* at para. 38, a migrant's integration in the host state is the objective pursued by the Community provisions on the free movement of workers.

[63]   See Pennings, loc. cit. at p. 147.

carried out in its territory.[64] The advantages of such an approach are that individuals receive the benefits to which they have accrued entitlement throughout their working lives and neither benefit unduly nor are they unduly penalised for their decision to migrate. Inevitably however, because premised on an individual retaining multiple entitlements, any such system would be horribly complex.

The drafters of the Treaty of Rome elected for this form of co-ordination. Article 51 provides that the Council is to adopt

> "such measures in the field of social security as are necessary to provide freedom of movement for workers; to this end, it shall make arrangements to secure for migrant workers and their dependants:[65]
> (a) aggregation, for the purpose of acquiring and retaining the right to benefit and of calculating the amounts of benefit, of all periods taken into account under the laws of the several countries;
> (b) payment of benefits to persons resident in the territories of Member States."

It is worth noting at this juncture that the formulation of the Council's mandate in Article 51 requires only co-ordination to the extent necessary to bring free movement of workers about.[66] Additionally, Article 51 identifies techniques through which coordination is to be accomplished, rather than the principles which it ought to respect, which forms a striking contrast with Article 48.[67] This gap has been plugged by the Court which considers that since the primary purpose of

---

[64]   Within this, a sub-division can be made into benefits on the basis of national law alone (autonomous pensions) or those resulting from the calculation laid down in the coordinating regime (the Regulation pension). This will be outlined in more detail below.

[65]   Note that in the other language versions of Article 51, the equivalent of "in particular" are added at this juncture. For example, *met name* (Dutch); *insbesondere* (German); *notamment* (French).

[66]   The scope of the Regulation was extended to cover the self-employed by Regulation 1390/81, O.J. 1981 L 143. Reg. 3795/81 (O.J. 1981 L 378) provided for a similar extension of Reg. 574/72.

[67]   As is noted by Cornelissen, op. cit. at 445.

Article 51 is to bring about the greatest possible freedom for migrant workers,[68] it seeks to create a system of rules which prevent the migrant worker from suffering any disadvantage from his decision to exercise his right of free movement.[69] This overriding objective forms the context within which the coordinating provisions must be interpreted.

5.4.2   THE MAIN FEATURES OF THE COMMUNITY SYSTEM OF CO-ORDINATION

The provisions by which the Community legislator gave form to the obligations contained in Article 51 was through the adoption of Regulations. The rules are currently to be found in Regulations 1408/71 and 574/72.[70] In the outline which follows, attention will first focus on the personal scope and then the material scope of the Regulation. Subsequently, the main principles of co-ordination - non discrimination on grounds of nationality, aggregation and apportionment, exportability, and insurance with a single state - will be discussed.

Personal Scope

The personal scope of Regulation 1408/71 is contained in Article 2(1) which provides that it

> "shall apply to employed or self-employed persons who are or
> have been subject to the legislation of one or more Member

---

[68]   See for example, Case 75/63, *Unger*, cited *supra* at p. 384.

[69]   See for example in the pensions sphere, Case 1/67, *Ciechelski* v. *Caisse Régionale de sécurité sociale de centre d'Orléans*, [1967] ECR 181; Case 2/67, *de Moor* v. *Caisse de Pension des Employés Privés*, [1967] ECR 197; Case 24/75, *Petroni* v. *Office National des Pensions pour Travailleurs Salaries*, [1975] ECR 1149; Case 62/76, *Strehl* v. *Nationaal Pensioenfonds voor Mijnwerkers*, [1977] ECR 211; Case 112/76, *Manzoni* v. *Fonds National de retraite des ouvriers mineurs*, [1977] ECR 1647.

[70]   Most recently consolidated in O.J. 1992 C 325.

States and who are nationals[71] of one of the Member States ...
as well as to the members of their families and their survivors."
In principle, therefore, those falling within its scope can be divided into two
distinct groups: workers and the self-employed on the one hand, and family
members and survivors on the other.[72]

As far as workers are concerned, as has already been observed, they - but
not their family members or survivors - must have the nationality of one of the
Member States, replicating in relation to social security the discrimination
characteristic of the more general free movement regime. For the purpose of
benefitting from the Regulation, it is not formally the quantity of work carried out
which is decisive, by contrast to the situation in relation to the free movement title,
but rather the fact of insurance or affiliation to one of the branches of social
security listed in Article 4 of the Regulation.[73] Part-time employment,[74] or
insurance for only one of the risks listed in Article 4 is sufficient in this regard.[75]
If someone is insured against one of the risks listed, they are covered by

---

[71]   It should be noted that the facts of any case are examined in the light of the legal regime
         in force at the time the facts occurred. See Case 10/78, *Belbouab* v. *Bundesknappschaft*,
         [1978] ECR 1915; Case C-105/89, *Buhari Haji* v. *Rijksinstituut voor de Sociale
         Verzekeringen der Zelfstandigen*, [1990] ECR I-4211. Thus, where someone had the
         nationality of one of the Member States at the time the rights were accrued, he falls within
         the scope of the Regulation despite subsequently losing this nationality. Art. 94 deals with
         periods of employment prior to the Regulation's entry into force.

[72]   See for example, the observations of Advocate General Tesauro to this effect at para.s 8 and
         9 of Case C-308/93, *Cabanis-Issarte*, cited *supra*.

[73]   It is only formally that the quantity of work is not relevant, because, as the discussion in
         Chapter 3 above reveals, the quantity of work carried out will be decisive as to whether
         someone is insured under a national scheme. This in turn, is decisive of whether someone
         falls within the scope of the Reg.

[74]   See for example, Case C-2/89, *Kits van Heijningen*, cited *supra*.

[75]   Case 388/87, *Warmerdam-Steggerda* v. *Bestuur van de Nieuwe Algemene Bedrijfsvereniging*,
         [1989] ECR 1203; Case C-71/93, *van Poucke* v. *Rijksinstituut voor de Sociale Verzekeringen
         der Zelfstandigen en Algemene Sociale Kas voor Zelfstandigen*, [1994] ECR I-1101

Regulation 1408/71, irrespective of whether or not they have exercised their right to free movement.[76]

The second group covered by the Regulation is family members and survivors of workers, irrespective of their nationality. Until recently, it appeared that it was necessary to distinguish between rights in personam and derived rights in the context of the Regulation. Family members were only entitled to rights in their capacity as family members of a worker. Thus, the spouse of a migrant worker was not entitled to unemployment benefit from the host state where the spouse had not exercised her right to free movement under the Treaty.[77] However, the Court has recently had occasion to reconsider this rule. In *Cabanis-Issarte*[78] the Court appears to have collapsed this distinction for all benefits but unemployment benefit, which suggests that the scope of the Regulation is wider than was previously thought.

In short, the personal scope of the Regulation extends to those covered by one of the listed branches of social security operated by the Member States. Somewhat strangely given that the coordinating regime is only required to the extent necessary to facilitate the free movement of workers, the factor which is determinative of an individual's falling within the coordinating regime is not that he is a worker within the meaning os Article 48 EC, but merely that he is covered by one of the branches of a national social security scheme.

---

[76] Case C-2/89, *Bestuur van de Sociale Verzekeringsbank* v. *Kits van Heijningen*, [1990] ECR I-1755. See also the observations of Cornelissen, op. cit. at 444. This contrasts with the position *vis-à-vis* Reg. 1612/68.

[77] Case 40/76, *Kermaschek* v. *Bundesanstalt für Arbeit*, [1976] ECR 1699, confirmed in Case 94/84, *ONEM* v. *Deak*, [1985] ECR 1873; Case 157/84, *Frascogna* v. *Caisse des Dépôts et Consignations*, [1985] ECR 1739; Case 147/87, *Zaoui* v. *Cramif*, [1987] ECR 5511; Case C-243/91, *Belgian State* v. *Taghavi*, [1992] ECR I-4401; Case C-310/91, *Schmid* v. *Belgian State*, [1993] ECR I-3011.

[78] Case C-308/93, cited *supra*. See the discussion in I. van der Steen, "Gelijke behandeling gezinsleden migrerende werknemers", *Nederlands Tijdschrift voor Europees Recht* (1996), 173-176.

Material Scope

According to Article 4, the Regulation applies to all national legislation concerning a number of benefits, including old age and survivor's benefits. The Member States are obliged to notify the Commission of which of their social security benefits they deem to be covered by the Regulation.[79] Although such a declaration is decisive for the purposes of a benefit's falling within the scope of the Regulation, the fact that a particular benefit is not to be found on the national list does not automatically exclude it from the scope of the Regulation.[80] Any other approach would allow the Member States unilaterally to determine the scope of the co-ordination regime. However, the Member States need not offer the benefits listed in Article 4; it is only if they have such benefits within their social security systems that the benefits fall within the co-ordination regime.[81]

As should already be clear, one of the objectives pursued by the Court in this area is that of the uniformity of the rights enjoyed by migrant workers, irrespective of the idiosyncrasies of the individual national schemes. Consequently, although social assistance schemes are excluded[82] from the scope of the Regulation, the Court has held that what constitutes social security is a matter of Community law, rather than dependent upon national classification. To fall within the scope of the Regulation, therefore, a benefit must be

> "granted without any individual and discretionary assessment of personal needs, to recipients on the basis of a legally defined position ... provided that it concerns one of the risks expressly listed in Article 4(1)."[83]

The Regulation has recently been extended to cover special non-contributory benefits other than those falling within Article 4(1), intended to provide

---

[79]   Article 5.

[80]   Case 35/77, *Beerens* v. *Rijksdienst voor Arbeidsvoorziening*, [1977] ECR 2249.

[81]   This in turn can be seen as a reflection of the EC's limited competence in the social sphere, as has already been touched upon in Chapter 3.

[82]   Art. 4(4) of Reg. 1408/71.

[83]   Case C-78/91, *Hughes* v. *Chief Adjudication Officer*, [1992] ECR I-4839, at para. 15.

"supplementary, substitute or ancillary" cover against the risks listed there.[84] However, Article 10a provides that these benefits may only be received in the state of residence and by virtue of that legislation, in so far as the benefits are mentioned in Annex IIa.[85] Additionally, where these benefits are supplementary to a particular benefit, it is permissible to take account of similar benefits paid from another source.

It can therefore be concluded that the coordination regime only covers some of the benefits provided by states to individuals within their territory. However, pension benefits, the focus of this research are clearly caught. In designing the system which allows the individual social security schemes of the Member States to fit together, a number of different issues had to be addressed. The solutions which were adopted will be described in the next sections.

Applicable Legislation

Despite these rules, it should always be borne in mind that the scope of national schemes, and the conditions which have to be satisfied to gain entitlement to a particular benefit, remain within the exclusive competence of the individual Member States,[86] subject to the requirements of the Regulation. Thus, European law does not require that the Dutch legislator scrap his requirement that all persons insured for the AOW be resident in the Netherlands, nor that of the German legislator that only those employed in Germany are compulsorily insured for the German old age pension scheme. Nevertheless, the Regulation does contain provisions which affect the freedom of the Member States to determine which

---

[84]   See Art. 4(2a). For a discussion of some of the difficulties of classification, see Ogus et al, loc. cit. at pp. 703-705. Note that Art. 4(2b) provides that the Reg. does not apply to provisions in the legislation of a Member State concerning special non-contributory benefits, referred to in Annex II, Section III, the validity of which is confined to part of its territory.

[85]   The ECJ has been asked whether the export prohibition in relation to these benefits is compatible with Article 51 EC; see Case C-20/96, *Kelvin Snares* v. *Adjudication Officer*, O.J. 1996 C 77.

[86]   Case 1/78, *Kenny* v. *Insurance Officer*, [1978] ECR 1489; Case 110/79, *Coonan* v. *Insurance Officer*, [1980] ECR 1445; Case C-297/92, *Baglieri*. v. *Instituto Nazionale delle Previdenza Sociale*, [1993] ECR I-5211; Cornelissen, op. cit. at 443-444.

individuals are covered by their particular social security regime. This is necessary to prevent a situation arising in which an individual is covered either by two schemes, or by none.[87] The Regulation accordingly provides that a migrant worker shall only be subject to the legislation of one Member State at any one time.[88] In general, this will be the State in which he is employed even if he lives elsewhere.[89] Consequently, an individual who lives in the Netherlands while working in Germany will be insured in Germany rather than the Netherlands.[90] This rule can be seen to be the logical consequence of the thrust of Community law in this field towards granting migrant workers "national" treatment. The obligation to be affiliated to only one social security scheme at any one time can be seen to be the first main principle of the co-ordination regime put in place by Community law.

Non-discrimination

The next major principle of the co-ordination regime is that an individual shall not suffer discrimination on grounds of his nationality.[91] This strikes not only at provisions which specify that only, say, French workers qualify for a particular benefit, but also at residence conditions in national legislation.[92] However, this

---

[87]   See the example given in section 5.2 above.

[88]   Regulation 1408/71 Art. 13(1).

[89]   Regulation 1408/71 Art. 13(2)(a). According to Art. 13(2)(b), a self-employed person is subject to the legislation of the state in which he carries out his activities. Mariners are subject to the social security legislation of the flag state (Art. 13(2)(c)); civil servants are subject to the legislation of the State to which the administration employing them is subject (Art. 13(2)(d)); members of the armed forces are subject to the legislation of that state (Art. 13(2)(e)).

[90]   For the exceptions in the case of posted workers, see artt.s 14 and 17.

[91]   Art. 3 1408/71.

[92]   See in this regard, Case 41/84, *Pinna* v. *Caisse d'allocation familiales de la Savoie*, [1986] ECR 1 (*Pinna I*), in which a provision to this effect in Reg. 1408/71 itself (Art. 73(2)) was annulled by the Court.

is not to say that residence requirements are automatically unlawful. Rather, they raise a prima facie presumption of (indirect) discrimination which the Member State must then seek to justify.

Exportability

The third main principle - exportability of benefits - will strike at any provisions of national law which make it a condition for receiving benefits that the individual in question reside in the paying state.[93] Thus, states may not require that an individual be resident within their territory to receive pension benefits from their scheme.

Aggregation and Apportionment

The final principle of co-ordination - aggregation and apportionment - has two elements. Aggregation is a technique for combining the various parts of the career of a migrant worker.[94] It leads to all the periods of insurance completed within the EU by an individual being totalled. This can be useful in relation to systems which operate a waiting period[95] prior to an individual being given a right to benefit.[96] Suppose for example, a migrant worker, having worked for, say 20 years in Italy and 10 years in the Netherlands, returns to the UK where he works for 8 years prior to retiring. The 25% rule[97] would appear to exclude him from

---

[93]   Art. 10 1408/71. Note that this is mainly applicable to long term benefits, such as old age pensions. See further, Ogus et al, loc. cit. at p. 713. For the extent to which unemployment benefit can be exported, a short term benefit, see Ogus et al, loc. cit. at pp. 715-717.

[94]   See the observation of the Court to this effect in Case C-165/91, *Van Munster* v. *Rijksdienst voor Pensioenen*, [1994] ECR I-4661 at para. 29.

[95]   As is discussed at greater length in Chapter 6 in the context of occupational pension schemes, a waiting period is a period of employment or insurance which must be completed before the individual begin to acquire an enforceable right to a benefit under the scheme.

[96]   Art. 45 of Reg. 1408/71.

[97]   See the discussion in Chapter 2.

entitlement to a UK pension. However, where his employment in the other Member States is taken into account, he will have sufficient insurance to qualify for a UK pension. In this way, aggregation can help a migrant worker to qualify for benefits to which he would otherwise not be entitled.

The second aspect of this final principle - apportionment - concerns the calculation and funding of the benefit. Under the present regime, for the purposes of apportionment rights to an "autonomous" pension and those to a "Regulation" pension must be distinguished. An autonomous pension is one granted solely by reference to the national legislation without there having been any need for aggregation.[98] A "Regulation" pension on the other hand, is a little more complex. First the theoretical amount of entitlement is calculated on the basis that all periods of insurance fulfilled in the Union were fulfilled under the legislation of that state. The actual amount of the Regulation benefit is equivalent to the sum produced by apportioning the amount on the basis of the actual period of insurance carried out in that jurisdiction. So for example, where someone has worked for, say, 10 years in Germany and 30 years in the UK, the highest theoretical amount (calculated in both Germany and the UK) is the benefit to which an individual would accrue entitlement on the basis of 40 years of insurance. The actual levels of benefit which the German and UK authorities are due to pay are, respectively, 10/40ths and 30/40ths of the relevant national amounts.[99] An individual is entitled to the higher of the autonomous or the Regulation pension.[100] As the Court has observed,

> "the aim of Articles 48 to 51 would not be attained if, as a consequence of the exercise of their right to freedom of movement, workers were to lose the advantages in the field of social security guaranteed to them by the laws of a single Member State."[101]

---

[98]   Art. 46(1)(a)(i).

[99]   See Art. 46(2).

[100]   Art. 46(3).

[101]   Case 284/84, *Spruyt* v. *Sociale Verzekeringsbank*, [1986] ECR 685, para. 19.

These rules can be seen to provide the migrant worker with a guarantee that he will not lose out as a consequence of his decision to migrate. Their importance is nowhere more clearly in evidence than in relation to the pension rights of the migrant worker. Aggregation and apportionment ensure that no rights are lost as a result of the individual's having worked abroad, and that his fragmented career does not prevent him from accruing rights to benefit.

Rules against Overlapping

However, equally, the Court and Community legislator have sought to ensure that individuals do not profit unduly from their decision to migrate by accruing multiple entitlements.

It is common for national legislation to make provision against the overlapping of benefits. Pursuant to such rules, the competent national institution will subtract from the benefits which it pays, any similar benefits received from another source, in casu, another Member State. If the Regulation did not make provision for this, national rules against overlapping of benefits could reduce an migrant's pension entitlement to nil. To this end it is necessary to distinguish first, between benefits of a similar kind and benefits of a different kind.

Benefits are of the same kind when they are calculated or provided on the basis of periods of insurance and or residence completed by one and the same person.[102] Benefits of a different kind are simply defined as those which are not of the same kind.[103] Thus, where someone is entitled to an invalidity pension in one state and to an old age pension in another, these will be benefits of the same kind. However, a survivors' pension and an old age pension are not two benefits of the same kind. This is because a survivor's pension is generally paid on the basis of the insurance of a deceased spouse and an old age pension is generally paid on the basis of the insurance record of the recipient.

The first requirement which must be satisfied before a state can reduce, suspend or withdraw benefits on the basis of overlapping benefits received from

---

[102]   Art. 46a(1).

[103]   Art. 46a(2).

another state, is that its legislation must make provision for this.[104] Second, account is to be taken of the gross amount of benefits,[105] but no account may be taken of entitlements accrued on a non-compulsory basis.[106] Finally, where only one of the Member States involved makes provision against overlapping, the deduction must remain within the bounds of that which is actually received by the migrant from other Member States.[107]

Article 46b deals with the overlapping of benefits of the same kind from two or more Member States. The first main rule here is that national rules on overlapping may not be applied to what is described above as a "regulation" pension, that is, one calculated on the basis of Article 46(2). Equally, national provisions on overlapping may be applied to an autonomous pension[108] only if the level of benefit provided is independent of the length of periods of insurance or residence completed. Similarly, they may be applied in respect of benefits the amount of which has been calculated on the basis of a credited period deemed completed after the materialisation of the risk. In this case, national provisions on overlapping may be applied where the benefits overlap with benefits of the same kind, or benefits the level of which is independent of periods of insurance or residence.

Article 46c is concerned with the subject of the overlapping of autonomous benefits with benefits of a different kind. If receipt of benefits of a different kind leads to reduction, suspension or withdrawal of two or more autonomous benefits, the amounts of the reductions are to be divided by the numbers of benefits to be reduced.[109] In the case of a "Regulation" benefit, the

---

[104] Art. 46a(3)(a).

[105] Art. 46a(3)(b).

[106] Art. 46a(3)(c).

[107] Art. 46a(3)(d).

[108] That calculated on the basis of national legislation alone, without reference to aggregation, see Art. 46(1)(a)(i).

[109] Unless the national legislation provides for reduction in proportion to the period of insurance in question; see Art. 46c(4).

amount of the deduction which the national authority is permitted to make in respect of other benefits is in proportion to the periods of insurance actually completed.

Finally, the situation of overlapping which leads to reduction of both autonomous and "Regulation" benefits is considered.[110] The amount by which autonomous benefits may be reduced by virtue of the application of national law is to be divided by the number of states making reductions, unless the national legislation in question provides that reduction is to be proportionate. The reduction which may be made in respect of a "Regulation" benefit is proportionate.

These complicated rules have been put in place to ensure that the migrant worker neither profits nor suffers from his decision to work in another Member State. The Regulation provides a complete system of rules for the calculation of the pensions entitlement of the migrant worker.[111] It enables the diverse national systems to fit together, while at the same time respecting the individual autonomy of the Member States to determine the precise content of their social security systems, and the conditions of acquiring entitlement to benefits. Nevertheless, as will be discussed in the final section, it has limited the prerogatives of the Member States in this field.

5.5   Exceptions and Exclusions

Although it may indeed be true to say that the system put in place by Regulations 1408/71 and 574/72 provides migrants with an efficient, if complicated, means of maintaining their pension rights on exercising their right to free movement, it should be pointed out that it has a number of limitations. First, because the Regulation merely seeks to co-ordinate the operation of national schemes for those already falling within the national systems, it depends on national legislation to determine which individuals are actually caught by the co-ordinating Regulation. A change in the design of national legislation may result in a whole category of

---

[110]   Art. 46c(3).

[111]   Case 302/84, *Ten Holder,* cited *supra* at para. 21.

individuals who previously fell within the scope of the Regulation, suddenly being excluded from its scope.[112]

A second limitation in the scope of the Regulatory scheme is that although one particular category of workers, civil servants, are expressly held to fall within the personal scope of the Regulation, special schemes operating in their favour do not fall within the scope of the co-ordination provisions. One of the concerns about this gap in the regulatory framework protecting migrant workers, is that the group of civil servants excluded from Regulation 1408/71 is not coterminous with those public employees excluded from the scope of Article 48.[113] As a consequence, some individuals who have the right freely to move throughout the Community do not enjoy the benefit of the co-ordination of their social security rights. The Commission has relatively recently introduced specific provisions to extend the scope of the co-ordination regime to include this group.[114] However, no agreement has yet been forthcoming from the Council.

The Court has recently taken the initiative to protect this groups of workers in the face of the inertia of the Council. In its judgment in *Vougioukas*,[115] the Court held that in the absence of co-ordinating measures, individuals may be able to require the direct application of Articles 48-51 EC. In the instant case, this required that the Greek social security scheme treat periods of service in a German hospital as equivalent to those in a Greek hospital. In this way, the Court was able to ensure that this individual not suffer disadvantage as a consequence of working abroad. It is not clear at this moment precisely how many situations can be dealt with by a "straight" application of Articles 48-51 in this way. However, it would seem that a robust approach to this issue by the Court, displaying scepticism in the face of arguments as to the "impossibility" of a

---

[112]   See the examples cited by Ogus et al, loc. cit. at p. 705.

[113]   See the discussion above.

[114]   O.J. 1992 C 46/1, COM(91) 528 final.

[115]   Case C-443/93, *Vougioukas*, cited *supra*; discussed by Cornelissen, op. cit. at 447-448; I. van der Steen, "Vrij verkeer en social zekerheid van ambtenaren", *Nederlands Tijdschrift voor Europees Recht* (1996), 53-57.

particular course of action by the Member States, may provide an effective spur to the Council finally to regulate this issue.

Another limitation on the scope of the co-ordinating regime is that migrants with the nationality of a third country do not benefit from its provisions.[116] In the EC context, the rights granted to third country nationals will only ever be as generous as the least generous Member State and it seems unlikely at present that this restriction will be lifted.

However, the most significant limitation in the scope of the Regulation from the perspective of this research is that it is limited to statutory social security schemes. Article 51 obliged the Council to adopt co-ordinating legislation at Community level in the field of *social security* to the extent necessary to provide for free movement of workers. In interpreting the term "social security" the Commission and Council[117] were conservative[118] as a result of which Regulation 1408/71 only covers "legislation" concerning a number of specified risks.[119] Legislation is in turn defined as

> "in respect of each Member State statutes, regulations and other
> provisions and all other implementing measures ... relating to the

---

[116]   See the discussion in B. Wilkinson, "Towards European Citizenship? Nationality, Discrimination and Free Movement of Workers in the European Union", 1 European Public Law (1995), 417-437.

[117]   But interestingly, not the European Parliament. In its proposal for the Regulation which became 1408/71, the Commission expressly excluded occupational schemes from its scope. The European Parliament suggested that the material scope of the proposed Regulation be extended to include such schemes. See *Resolutie houdende advies van het Europese Parlement inzake de voorstellen van de E.E.G. Commissie aan de Raad voor een verordening betreffende de toepassing van de stelsels van sociale zekerheid op werknemers in loondienst en op hun gezinsleden die zich binnen de Gemeenschap verplaatsen, een besluit tot toepassing van artikel 51 van het Verdrag op de Franse overzeese departementen* PB 1968, C 10/30.

[118]   As has already been discussed, a similar pattern was adopted in relation to the introduction of equality between women and men into social security schemes. First attention focused on the statutory schemes with action on occupational schemes being postponed until equality in statutory schemes had been achieved. However, the *traveaux préparatoires* for what became Directive 79/7 demonstrate an initially generally held view that the term "social security" used in Article 1(2) of Directive 76/207 covered both types of schemes.

[119]   Art. 4(1).

branches and schemes of social security covered by Article 4(1) and (2)."[120]

It is expressly provided that

"The term excludes provisions of existing or future industrial agreements, whether or not they have been the subject of a decision by the authorities rendering them compulsory or extending their scope."

However, where these sorts of provisions are used to put compulsory insurance into effect, or to set up a scheme administered by the same institution as administers the national schemes, the Member States can, by declaration, bring such schemes within the scope of the Regulation.[121] This express exclusion was designed to pre-empt arguments about the applicability of the Regulation to some types of occupational schemes.[122] It is true that without the reference to "industrial agreements" the reference to legislation could have been interpreted as embracing statutes such as the Social Security Pensions Act, the *Pensioen- en Spaarfondsenwet* or the *Gesetz zur verbesserung der Betriebliche Altersversorgung* and therefore as covering all employers who had chosen to provide their employees with pension cover in addition to that provided by the State. This argument could however have been countered by observing that the beneficiary's entitlement to benefits under occupational schemes does not flow from the statute which rather imposes a number of obligations on the employer.[123] Be that as it may, the express exclusion of provisions of "industrial agreements" makes it clear that benefits of a contractual nature are excluded from the scope of the Regulation.[124]

---

[120]   Art. 1(j).

[121]   This exclusion can be lifted by a declaration by the Member State in question in which it specifies the schemes of that kind to which the Regulation is to be deemed applicable (art. 1(j)). In the event of such a declaration being made, the publication provisions contained in Art. 97 must be followed.

[122]   Ogus et al, loc. cit. at p. 705.

[123]   This argument can be seen to be analogous to that adduced in Case 80/70, *Defrenne I*, cited *supra*. It also dovetails nicely with the Court's definition of social security for the purposes of distinguishing the latter from social assistance as outlined above.

[124]   Occupational pension schemes and mobility will be the subject of the next Chapter.

5.6   Conclusion

Despite these limitations, the coordinating regime put in place by virtue of Regulations 1408/71 and 574/72 does form an effective, if complicated method of linking the autonomous social security systems operating in the individual Member States. The rules which it contains allow the migrant workers covered to enjoy the benefits of uninterrupted insurance for the social security risks covered, including the focus of attention here, pensions. The REgulation identifies the system to which the individual is to be affiliated and precludes it from discriminating against him on grounds of his nationality or residence abroad. Additionally, the principle of aggregation and apportionment forms a safety net for the migrant, preventing him from suffering gaps in protection as a consequence of his geographically fragmented career. Equally, rules have been put in place to prevent migrants from benefiting from the fact that they have worked in a number of jurisdictions and accruing multiple entitlements far beyond the benefits accrued by non-migrants.

Although this system has been put in place, it merely coordinates the autonomous systems of the individual Member States, in relation to which they retain their full prerogatives. EC law merely precludes them from discriminating on grounds of nationality and obliges them to take account of events occurring abroad.

Although there are a number of areas and groups excluded from the coordinating regime, it must be concluded that for those falling within its scope, it provides an effective solution to the difficulties of pension accrual which an international migrant would otherwise face. Consequently, it can be concluded that by virtue of Regulations 1408/71 and 574/72, statutory pension schemes have been forced to adapt to the challenges posed by international migrant workers.

OCCUPATIONAL PENSIONS AND MOBILITY

In Chapter 2 where the development of occupational pension schemes in the UK, the Netherlands and Germany was discussed, it was observed that schemes were originally unilateral undertakings on the part of the employer to care for his long-serving but infirm employees. However, as the economy developed and grew, they began to be seen by employers as a means of rewarding particularly valuable employees and persuading them to remain in that employment. To the carrot was added a stick, in that those employees who chose to leave the employment - despite the benefits of the occupational scheme - were penalised in terms of their pension for doing so. Consequently, schemes have gradually come to be designed to reward the long-serving, highly skilled members of the workforce, with those leaving prior to reaching pensionable age generally being subject to severe penalisation in the form of more or less complete forfeiture of the pension rights which were accruing. In this way, the employer has been able to use his pension scheme to bind particular employees to his undertaking and erect barriers to their leaving him.

However, as has been stressed on a number of occasions in this research, the labour market is altering. Gone are the days when an individual could expect to work for a single employer for all of his or her active life. It is now increasingly the case that individuals expect to work for a number of different employers during their career.[1] Where the labour market itself is more flexible, the rigidities which

---

[1]   Reliable statistics are not easy to find on this matter. However, a recent survey carried out in the UK reveals that married men had 5.3 spells of economic activity, as compared to 5.6 for married women; see Field and Prior, loc. cit. at p. 52. As is discussed in Chapter 4 above, the significant difference between married men and married women is in relation to the years of full-time employment.) German research concerning the current generation of pensioners reveals that men changed their employment on average 3.5 times, compared to a figure of 2.5 for women. Note that this generation of women will have been likely to cease employment on marriage; see J. Allmendinger, E. Brückner and H. Brückner, "Arbeitsleben und Lebensarbeitsentlohnung: Zur Entstehung von finanzieller Ungleichheit im Alter", in Gather et al (eds.), loc. cit. pp. 133-174 at pp. 145-146.

occupational pension schemes introduce will affect its efficient functioning, besides reducing the pension entitlement of individuals and it can be expected that legislatures will act to counter this. Unsurprisingly, the legislatures and courts of the jurisdictions under examination have intervened to limit the degree to which employers are free to use their schemes to bind employees to their undertaking by penalising harshly employees who leave prior to reaching pensionable age.

The two challenges to existing forms of pension provision upon which this research is focusing are the increasing levels of economic activity undertaken by women and the internationalisation of the market. Both of these groups are likely to have been penalised by the rules of pension schemes designed to penalise early leavers. Women will often have lost out in the past because even where they were permitted to join a scheme,[2] and those women offered membership now will continue to lose out, because their patterns of employment are characterised by breaks from employment to care for family members.[3] Consequently, they will rarely have worked long-term for a single employer until reaching pensionable age and will consequently have been penalised by the scheme as a result.

The international migrant - in precisely the same manner as the job-changer within a single state[4] - will fail to follow the pattern of employment the scheme was designed to reward. Consequently, it appears that both women and the international migrant ought to benefit from the measures taken nationally to ameliorate the situation of the domestic migrant. These measures will be the subject of the present Chapter. In the discussion in this Chapter, the measures will

---

[2]   See the discussion in Chapter 4 of the access which women were granted to occupational schemes.

[3]   Landenberger, loc. cit. at p. 85 indicates that the birth of a child reduces a woman's years of employment by 4.5 years. Field and Prior, loc. cit. at pp. 51-52 indicate that the real significance is now in terms of years of full-time employment. German figures for 1988 indicated that 44.1% of West German women worked; of those with no children the figure was 27.3% working full-time; the % working full-time dropped by approximately 5% per child; see E. Kirner and E. Schulz, "Die Erwerbsbeteiligung im Lebensverlauf von Frauen in Abhängigkeit von der Kinderzahl - Unterschiede zwischen der Bundesrepublik Deutschland und der ehemaligen Deutschen Demokratischen Republik" in Gather et al (eds.), loc. cit., pp. 62-79 at p. 67.

[4]   For the reasons discussed in Chapter 1, the focus of attention here will be the international migrant.

be assessed for their adequacy in ensuring that international migrants do not suffer disproportionate penalisation in terms of occupational pension accrual because of their decision to deviate from the patterns of employment taken as typical for the purpose of scheme design. The extent to which they improve women's pension accrual will be discussed in the final Chapter.

In this discussion, the focus of attention will be upon the individual who has moved to another Member State for the purpose of taking up new employment. The situation of the posted worker or the individual employed in one Member State and residing in another will not be considered here. The former will not be considered because specific personal arrangements are typically made for individuals who are posted abroad, about which it is both difficult to obtain information, and from which it is also difficult to generalise. The latter group will not be considered separately because generally they are in precisely the same position as a local worker,[5] except for residing abroad. Consequently, the only difference in their situation is possibly tax-based. However, the judgments of the Court in *Schumacker*, *Wielockx*, and *Asscher*[6] ought to solve any specific difficulties which they face.

6.1   Waiting Periods and Vesting

It may be the case that the scheme rules provide that an individual is only entitled to begin to accrue pension rights after he has worked for the employer for a particular period of time. Such a period is called a waiting period, the period which the individual must wait prior to beginning to accrue pension rights. This differs from the vesting period which is the period of membership of the scheme which an individual must have completed before he obtains enforceable pension rights under the scheme rules. Both kinds of rule can have negative effects on the

---

[5]   Entire or virtually entire income from employment in the state of employment.

[6]   See the discussion in Chapter 5.

pension accrual of an individual who changes employment.[7] A scheme which has a long waiting period, leaves individuals who have not yet fulfilled it with no pension accrual at all.[8] Similarly, a long vesting period means that the employee who leaves the employment before it has expired will not obtain enforceable pension rights pursuant to that employment.[9] The operation of both types of provision is such as to increase the chances that an individual will not accrue pension rights for employment periods carried out in the undertaking to which the scheme is attached. A final, related, form of provision which may be found in scheme rules is offering scheme membership only to those over a particular age and the effect of such a provision on younger members of the workforce will be the same as vesting or waiting periods for the workforce in general.

As this brief discussion makes clear, vesting and waiting periods are rules which may potentially restrict the pensions accrual of those with interrupted employment patterns. In the following sections, the position in the UK, the Netherlands and Germany will be considered.

6.1.1   THE UK

Neither the Pension Schemes Act 1993 nor the Pensions Act 1995 contains provisions on waiting periods. According to the 1991 Survey by the Government

---

[7]   Both kinds of requirement, when viewed from the perspective of the pension provider, can be seen to be reasonable. When the pension is viewed as a reward for company loyalty, a waiting period can be seen to be entirely justifiable. Why should someone who has displayed no loyalty automatically obtain benefits. In relation to a vesting period, this releases pension funds from the obligation to maintain the rights of early leavers (see *infra*) where the resulting benefits would be very small indeed because of the limited career of the employee in question.

[8]   In theory were a scheme to have a long waiting period, it could still pay a high level of benefit if annual accrual under the scheme rules was at a high rate. In the UK and the Netherlands, however, the provisions of tax law generally limit the practical possibilities for accelerated accrual. See the discussion in Chapter 2, although it should be noted that the Netherlands plans to relax these requirements somewhat. Similarly, in the UK, it seems that the government is toying with the idea of removing the ceiling on the occupational pensions which can be accrued.

[9]   He may be entitled to a return of any contributions which he has paid. See *infra*.

Actuary,[10] of the 6,500,000 members of private sector schemes, 4,500,000 belonged to schemes which had no waiting period whatsoever.[11] Even for the 2 million individuals who do have to fulfil some kind of waiting period,[12] they will accrue benefits under SERPS for such waiting periods since they must participate in SERPS if they are not in contracted-out employment.[13] It therefore seems that waiting periods in the UK are unlikely to have negative effects on the pension accrual of a migrant worker.

Another form of waiting period which some schemes utilise is a minimum age for membership. However, again, it would seem that practice in the UK in the majority of schemes is not such as negatively to affect pension accrual[14] since only a small number of individuals belong to schemes which make membership available only to those over the age of 20.[15]

Turning to vesting, the PSA 1993 affords protection of the accrued rights of employees who have at least two years pensionable service under the scheme

---

[10]   Government Actuary, loc. cit. at p. 36.

[11]   It should be noted that the definition of waiting period contained in the 1991 survey appears to cover both waiting periods as defined here, and vesting periods.

[12]   According to the survey, 750,000 belong to schemes which require less than one year of service, 680,000 1 year or more, 190,000 in schemes where it varies per category of employee, 110,000 is it discretionary and 270,000 belonged to schemes closed to new members.

[13]   This will allow them to accrue pension rights in respect of these periods, even if they are lower than those to which they would have built up entitlement had they been entitled to join the occupational scheme immediately.

[14]   See Government Actuary, loc. cit. at table 5.7, p. 37.

[15]   It should be noted that the possibility of obtaining discretionary approval of a scheme from the Inland Revenue, offers the possibility of a scheme offering accelerated accrual. In such a situation, less than 40 years service will be required to obtain maximum benefit accrual, which means that the operation of a higher minimum age need not have negative consequences for the pension accrual of members of the scheme. See the discussion in Chapter 1 above.

rules,[16] although these rules may provide that the rights vest in the employee after a shorter period, or immediately.[17] The two year period was introduced in April 1988 by the Social Security Act 1986, replacing the five year period of pensionable service required under the previous legislation.[18] Without doubt, the shortening of the period of service required before rights vest in the employee represents an improvement in his situation and the barrier which vesting periods pose to the pension accrual of migrant workers can be seen to have been lowered by this move. The protection which an individual obtains once his rights have vested will be discussed in the sections on early leavers below.

6.1.2   THE NETHERLANDS

Like the UK, the Dutch legislation contains no provisions concerning waiting periods. It has however been common for Dutch schemes to allow individuals to join only after they have reached the age of 25,[19] although the civil servants' pension scheme, the ABP, abolished the provision to this effect in its rules as of 1 May 1994. To the extent that it can be argued that individuals below this age generally earn lower salaries from which it can be expected that the statutory scheme will provide an adequate level of income replacement, setting such (low) age thresholds would not seem to be likely to damage the pension accrual of the

---

[16]   Ss. 69-82 PSA 1993. The definition of 2 years pensionable service is contained in s. 71(7) PSA:"2 years (whether a single period of that duration or two or more periods, continuous or discontinuous, totalling 2 years) in which the member was at all times employed either- (a) in pensionable service under the scheme; or (b) in service in employment which was contracted-out by reference to the scheme." It will be discussed in more detail in the section on early leavers below.

[17]   Where an individual leaves prior to completing two years of pensionable service, an individual may receive a refund of contributions, less the amount required to fund the GMP. See

[18]   S. 10 SSA 1986.

[19]   Utilised in 95% of schemes surveyed in 1991, see de Veer et al, loc. cit. at p. 9. In the past, it was quite normal for women to be offered membership at a later age than men, see *De aanvullende regelingen* at p. 63.

migrant employee.[20] However, it can be argued that a lower earnings threshold is a more appropriate method of pursuing this objective than an age threshold because the means are better suited to the end.[21]

The PSW provides lays down no period of membership which an individual must have fulfilled to obtain protected rights under the legislation. However, as will be discussed in the section on transfers below, it can be deduced from other provisions that the pension rights of the employee who changes employment after at least one years pensionable service will receive particular protection[22] which can be interpreted as providing for rights to vest after this period.[23]

It can therefore be concluded that the situation in the Netherlands is very similar to that in the UK, and consequently, that no significant obstacles seem likely to be created to employee mobility.

6.1.3   GERMANY

The situation in Germany differs considerably from the situation in the other two Member States. Prior to the entry into force of the BetrAVG, it was extremely

---

[20]   It has been argued that age thresholds may amount to indirect discrimination against women. An age threshold means that the pensionable career is limited, and because many women over the age of 25 take time off work to have children, it is seen to damage their accrual more than that of men. See de Veer et al, loc. cit. at pp. 63-64; I. de Veer, "Van het pensioenfront niets nieuws" in Kraamwinkel et al (eds.), loc. cit. at pp. 21-33; J. Dierx, "Indirecte discriminatie: oplossing of obstakel?", in Kraamwinkel et al, loc. cit., at pp. 111-127 esp. at pp.120-121.

[21]   Indeed, as was discussed in Chapter 4 in the section dealing with links between statutory and occupational pension schemes, most Dutch schemes operate on the basis of the franchise. This is the part of an individual's salary which is deemed to be replaced by the payments he receives from the AOW. On the subject of the franchise, see Kraamwinkel loc. cit., at pp. 28-33; Lutjens 1989, loc. cit. at pp. 503-510.

[22]   In general, Dutch pensions may not be redeemed. However, where an individual has been a member for less than a year, the scheme may choose to pay a lump sum rather than preserve the rights. In addition, there are separate provisions for very small pensions of less than ƒ600 p.a. Art. 32(5) PSW.

[23]   Schemes are obliged to protect the short service benefits (SSBs) of early leavers who have at least one year of service. See the discussion *infra*.

common for pension schemes to require their members to remain active participants until reaching pensionable age to gain entitlement to a pension.[24] In this situation, the right to a pension could be said to vest on reaching pensionable age. The BAG made significant inroads into the employer's virtually unfettered discretion to determine conditions for qualifying for an occupational pension by holding that an employee could maintain certain rights on leaving employment having completed at least 20 years of service with that employer,[25] protection which was built upon by the legislator. Paragraphs 1-4 of the BetrAVG provide that the employee obtains vested rights (*unverfallbaren Anwartschaften*) after the pension promise is at least 10 years old, or where the individual has been affiliated to the company for 12 years and the promise is at least three years old.[26] Although this is undoubtedly a great advance on the previous situation, the full ten year period must be fulfilled if the right is to vest,[27] which compares unfavourably with the periods of two years and one year to be found in the UK and the Netherlands. Prior to the expiry of the ten year period, the parties are in principle free to alter the pension promise as they see fit, without however jeopardising the running of the 10 year period.[28] In practice, this is limited to situations of economic necessity for the undertaking which go so far as to put at issue the continued viability of the undertaking.[29]

The alternative (shorter) vesting period of three years comes into play most commonly in a situation where a new pension scheme is begun, although it

---

[24]   See the example to be found at BB 1982, 1176.

[25]   BB 1972, 1005. This is discussed in Chapter 2.

[26]   Additionally, the individual in both cases must already be over the age of 35 on terminating his affiliation.

[27]   Ahrend et al, loc. cit. at pp. 10-14.

[28]   Ahrend et al, loc. cit., at pp. 18-19. Additionally, para. 10(2) MuScfG provides that periods of pregnancy leave do not interrupt the running of the 10 year period. Periods spent on parental leave receive similar treatment pursuant to the BErzGG.

[29]   See BAG 18 May 1977, DB 1977, 1655; Ahrend et al, loc. cit. at pp. 13-14.

is also useful in transfer situations.[30] The precise scope of the obligations imposed on the employer by the vesting provisions depends upon the funding vehicle chosen, and upon whether the right is based on the 10 year or three year promise period.[31]

It appears that most German schemes take full advantage of the possibility of requiring that individuals belong to the scheme for ten years prior to obtaining vested rights.[32] It seems clear that the operation of such long periods is likely to lead to more individuals in Germany having years of employment in respect of which no occupational pension rights are built up than is the case for the UK and the Netherlands. As such, it seems that the ten year period will form a significant barrier to labour mobility both between firms within Germany, and more crucially in the context of this research, migration to and from Germany.

It is clear that this aspect of German pension provision is problematic for both groups of workers with which this research is concerned but it is perfectly logical if the mechanics of occupational provision there are considered. It will be recalled that the most common method of making occupational pension provision is through book reserves. They do not require that physical assets be accrued to cover pension undertakings made. The employer need in fact only actually fund the pension promises made to his employees with more than 10 years service. To reduce this period in the legislation would be to oblige employers to fund a greater number of benefits for an greater number of individuals than is currently the case. While occupational provision remains voluntary, it will be difficult to pursue such a course of action without running the substantial risk that employers simply stop offering a scheme.

Linked to this is the fact that the majority of Germany pension schemes are cast in legal forms which preclude employee contributions. This can be seen to lead to ignorance on the part of employees (and their trades union

---

[30]   Pursuant to para. 613a BGB the employer who takes over an undertaking is in general obliged to apply any scheme which he operated at his original undertaking to his new employees also.

[31]   This is discussed in greater detail in the sections on early leavers below.

[32]   Steinmeyer 1994, loc. cit. at p. 21.

representatives) as to the value of occupational pension rights. Additionally, the lack of employee contributions to the capital fund makes it easier for employers to deny that pensions are pay, and to argue against the employees having "rights" to benefits or to particular forms of treatment.[33] A non-compulsory benefit[34] to which the eventual beneficiary makes no contribution can be argued to be a subject over which he can make no demands. It seems likely that were employees to be required (or even merely allowed) to contribute, the legislation would be amended to offer them greater protection.[35]

Another explanation for this acceptance of a provision which can be seen to offer very few employees protection is the role played by occupational schemes in Germany when compared to the role they play in the other Member States. In Germany, they supplement for the already well paid what will be a (relatively) high state benefit. Such employees are not perceived to be in need of the same level of protection as the employees for whom an occupational pension represents a vital addition to their meagre statutory pension.

Another area in which the legal regime within which occupational pension provision is made in Germany differs from that in the other Member States under consideration is in its treatment of waiting periods.[36] In a 1982 judgment,[37] the BAG held that as a consequence of paragraph 1 BetrAVG the running of a waiting period is not terminated by the termination of the employment relationship where at that moment in time the employee has acquired a vested pension right. Despite having left the employment, the employee can complete the waiting period while employed outwith the undertaking of the employer who made the pension promise

---

[33]   For example, short vesting periods after which the employee will have enforceable rights, transfer values, indexation of SSBs.

[34]   It must be recalled that cracks have only recently begun to appear in the edifice of occupational pensions are a reward for company loyalty rather than as a quid pro quo for services rendered.

[35]   In this regard, it is instructive to compare the treatment of early leavers in the various different forms of pension fund. See the discussion below.

[36]   G. Schaub, *Arbeitsrechts-Handbuch*, 7th edition, München, 1992 at p. 540.

[37]   Judgment of 6 April 1982, BB 1982, 1176 at 1178.

in question. The effect of this judgment appears to be that any waiting periods which the employer may wish to set must run consecutively with the period laid down in the statute for obtaining a vested right. Consequently, it is not possible for the employer to undermine the provisions of the BetrAVG by offering a pension only to those who have worked for him for say, 20 years.[38] In terms of age limits, it must be pointed out that the BetrAVG only protects those who were at least 35 on leaving the employment. Consequently, an individual with 10 years pensionable service who is 32 on leaving this employment does not enjoy the protection of the statute. In addition, it is possible for an employer to set upper age limits before which periods of affiliation must have been completed.[39] All these features of the German legislation combine to create a situation in which employees of German undertakings are more likely than the employees of the British or Dutch competitors to have breaks in pension accrual caused by a decision to change or take a break from employment prior to the expiry of the vesting period.

6.1.4   COMPARISON AND COMMENT

Examining the legislative provisions and scheme practice relating to waiting periods and vesting in the three Member States the following observations can be made. The situations in the UK and the Netherlands are in practice virtually identical and seem likely to pose few significant barriers to employee mobility. By contrast, the extremely long vesting period which many German schemes operate will form a major obstacle to employee mobility to, from and within Germany, at least for those individuals who belong to the scheme.

Consequently, it can be concluded that employee mobility will be maximised if States require that rights vest in particular employees after a relatively short period of time. The short periods selected by the UK and Dutch legislatures certainly allows the individual's interest in obtaining rights as quickly

---

[38]   The specific German context in which employee contributions to schemes are relatively rare, and in which the degree of advance funding is much less than in the other Member States, must be borne in mind.

[39]   DB 1985, 286.

as possible to be balanced with the scheme's legitimate concern about the administrative costs of administering a large number of minuscule benefits.[40] In this context, the German requirement of 10 years' membership can be regarded as somewhat disproportionate.[41]

Allowing rights to vest after a short period of time improves the chances of the migrant worker being able to accrue an adequate occupational pension. Additionally, if the finding that occupational pensions form pay in the hands of the employee is taken seriously, this also supports arguments in favour of short(er) vesting periods. If the pension right is pay, what possible justification can there be for requiring that an individual have completed a significant period of employment before he can obtain vested pension rights?

It is also suggested that a different form of waiting period - the use of age thresholds to exclude individuals from scheme membership - ought also to be discouraged. The only aim which this kind of requirement can be said to serve is to prevent individuals accruing more pension rights than the legislation permits.[42] However, this objective can be served by requiring that accrual cease once the maximum number of contribution periods under the scheme have been fulfilled.[43] Given that the likelihood of reaching maximum accrual is slight, this can be seen to be a better method of preventing over-accrual than age thresholds which penalise all workers for a risk which is unlikely to arise in their individual case.

It can therefore be concluded that although the reforms introduced in the Member States under consideration will considerably have improved the position

---

[40]   Note that long vesting periods also allow employers to reduce the cost of overall benefits to the scheme. This is because pay outs to early leavers need not be financed. See the discussion *infra*.

[41]   Although they are explained by the development of occupational provision in that jurisdiction.

[42]   For example, where accrual is 1/60th per annum and the legislation provides that benefits may not exceed 2/3rds of final salary, 40 years accrual will result in maximum benefits. If pensionable age is 65, this would suggest an age threshold for membership of 25.

[43]   If the other suggestions made in this research are followed - particularly in relation to the availability of transfers - it will become considerably easier than is currently the case to ascertain when an individual has reached maximum accrual because all pension rights will be contained within a single pension fund.

of international migrants, reducing the vesting periods further (especially in Germany) would improve their situation.

6.2   Early Leavers - Short Service Benefits

It has repeatedly been stated that occupational pension schemes have been designed to benefit long-serving employees and that legislative interference has brought about an improvement of the situation of the early leaver. Before outlining the obligations which national law imposes on the employer *vis-à-vis* early leavers, it is worthwhile stating briefly what the general consequences of leaving prior to pensionable age are in final salary and money purchase schemes.

It is traditionally the case that earnings increase over an individual's lifetime, peaking in the years prior to retirement. In a final salary scheme, the contributions paid in the early years of membership will generally be set at a higher level than is required to fund the pension on the basis of the individual's current salary, because the actuary will anticipate salary increases which can be expected in the future. In other words, the younger members of the scheme pay more than they actually need to at that moment in time to fund the benefits to which they are currently entitled, because it is anticipated that they will earn more in the future.[44] Where an individual leaves prior to pensionable age, he will accordingly have paid too much for the benefit to which he is entitled because on leaving, his pension benefit under that scheme freezes and does not grow in line with any other salary increases which he may receive from subsequent employment. In addition, where vested rights remain within the scheme as a short service benefit (SSB), the value of the SSB to which the individual has built up entitlement, may decline relative to prices and wages if no provision for indexation is made. Finally, if no provision is made for increasing the pension resulting from

---

[44]   A final salary scheme generally treats the beneficiary as if he had earned his final salary (which may be defined as his average salary over the last, say, five years of his employment) for his entire pensionable service.

an SSB once it is in payment, the individual will find that the value of his benefit reduces in the course of his retirement.[45]

For a money purchase scheme, contributions are paid on the basis of salary levels. Unlike final salary scheme, pension accrual can be seen to be constant over the individual's contributing lifetime, without the intertemporal subsidisation which takes place in final salary schemes. However, because earnings generally rise with age, the individual who leaves prior to retirement will have accrued a relatively small sum to invest in an annuity on retirement. For him, it will be vital that earnings on pension fund investments be shared equally amongst both active and passive participants, so as to ensure that the sum which he has accrued for the purchase of pension benefits retains its relative value. Finally, for both types of scheme, a relatively large share of the contributions of the early leaver will go to defer the administrative costs of the pension scheme.

It can therefore be said that there are certain structural disadvantages which the early leaver with vested rights will face. In particular, he will suffer because his benefit levels will reflect current and not future salary levels. However, if provision is made for indexation of the deferred benefits which have accrued to early leavers, the disadvantages of leaving prior to pensionable age can be ameliorated somewhat. The various national measures which have been adopted to protect the early leaver with SSBs from the erosion of his accrued rights will now be considered.

6.2.1   THE UK

The Social Security Act 1973 introduced protection for the early leaver for the first time. Prior to that, an early leaver could merely require that any contributions which he might have made to the scheme be returned, and many schemes failed to pay interest on the money which they had held for the employee in the event that he changed employment.[46] An early leaver accordingly forfeited the

---

[45]   This is of course true in relation to all benefits. The point here is that benefits resulting from SSBs ought to be treated equally with those resulting from pensionable service which continues until pensionable age.

[46]   See the Goode Report at p. 294.

contributions paid by his employer and any interest which they might have earned if he changed employment. This can be seen to be a severe punishment for the individual and one which would increase in severity with an increase in seniority.[47]

Pursuant to the 1973 Act, schemes became obliged to offer those who left prior to retirement but after April 1975 a deferred pension, or SSB. Originally, schemes only had to provide SSBs to employees who were over the age of 25 when they left and who had at least five years pensionable service. However, as of 1 January 1986, the age requirement was removed[48] and from April 1988 SSBs became payable to those with at least two years pensionable service.[49] The current provisions are to be found in sections 69-82 of the PSA 1993.

The basic principle underlying the legislation is that benefits paid to the deferred pensioner must be calculated on the same basis as those paid to the continuing member,[50] although where a particular scheme rule is introduced after the member's service has terminated, it need not be applied to him.[51] A scheme is not however obliged to exercise discretionary powers in the same way in relation to SSBs and normal benefits.

In relation to pensions in payment, where the scheme rules make provision for periodic increases in pensions, they must also be applied to SSBs in payment.[52] However, where the increase is at a non-fixed rate, SSBs may be treated less favourably and increased by a fixed rate, provided it is at least 3%.[53]

---

[47] In this context, seniority means years of service.

[48] By s. 1 of the Social Security Act 1985.

[49] S. 10 of the Social Security Act 1986. Note that reg. 18 of the 1991 Regulations excepts SSBs of a trivial amount (currently £260). Such amounts may be commuted.

[50] See s. 71 PSA 1993.

[51] S. 72 PSA 1993.

[52] S. 76 PSA 1993.

[53] S. 76(4) PSA 1993.

Originally, the UK legislation made no provision for SSBs to be revalued between the termination of the employment relationship and the individual's retirement. An obligation to revalue SSBs was however introduced for those with service ending after 1 January 1986.[54] Pursuant to this provision, the SSB over the GMP[55] must be revalued when it becomes payable by the increase in prices over the period of preservation, subject to a ceiling of 5% per annum compound.[56] This will go some way towards protecting part of the value of rights in a final salary scheme, but it cannot compensate the individual for the fact that his rights are based on his salary on leaving the scheme rather than upon his actual final salary.

6.2.2   THE NETHERLANDS

Article 8 PSW concerns the treatment to be accorded to SSBs. Originally, an individual had to have belonged to the scheme for 5 years before he obtained the right to an SSB,[57] a period which was reduced to 1 year in 1972. Since 1987 all references to periods of employment have been removed from the legislation, meaning that in principle, an individual obtains the right to this protection the minute he begins to accrue pensionable service.

When membership of the scheme terminates, the fund calculates the level of the "proportionate pension" to which the individual is entitled. This is equivalent to the difference between the pension which the member would have received had he remained in employment until reaching pensionable age, and the pension which he would have received had he been a member from the date upon which his

---

[54]   By the Social Security Act 1985.

[55]   Note that separate provisions (s. 16 PSA 1993) govern the revaluation of GMP benefits. For discussion of this legislation, see Chapter 2.

[56]   For those who service terminated between 1 January 1986 and 1 January 1991, only service accruing between these dates had to be revalued. For those leaving after 1 January 1991, all service must be revalued. See also the anti-franking provision contained in s. 87 of the PSA 1993.

[57]   PSW 1952. See Lutjens 1989, loc. cit. at p. 559.

membership terminated until pensionable age. For the purposes of making this calculation, the provisions governing the scheme at the moment at which membership ceased will be used.[58]

The SSB (*premie vrije aanspraak*) which the ex-member receives must be at least equivalent to the premiums paid by and for him, and those which are still owed pursuant to article 2(6)[59] to the extent that any requirement as to the length of membership have been satisfied. Where the SSB is less than the proportionate pension, the number of calendar months between the date upon which membership ceased and the date upon which the pension becomes payable is calculated. The resulting number is then used to divide the difference between the proportionate pension and SSB to produce the amount by which the SSB must be increased per month between cessation of membership and pensionable age. If after membership has ended, the date on which the pension becomes payable is changed, a re-calculation takes place of the remaining difference between the SSB and the proportionate pension.[60]

Where supplements are granted to pensions in payment of members whose membership ceased on reaching pensionable age, the early leaver has the right to the same supplements calculated on the same basis.[61]

The statutes and rules of a fund may provide that where someone leaves the scheme early having been a member for less than one year (unless he has transferred pension rights from another fund), this individual may receive a lump sum payment at least equal to the amount of the premiums which he has paid.[62] This provision leaves a pension scheme free to "punish" the very early leaver by forcing him to forfeit the contributions paid to his pension by his employer.

---

[58]   Art. 8(2) PSW.

[59]   Art. 2(6) concerns the periodic payment of employer's contributions. It provides that where the pension scheme provides that the level of employer contribution will be set at the end of a given period, that period may not be longer than one year.

[60]   The difference between the two amounts can be eliminated more quickly.

[61]   Art. 8(7) and (8) PSW.

[62]   Art. 8(10) PSW.

The PSW contains no provisions requiring that SSBs be indexed between the termination of employment and retirement age which allows the value of the SSB to wither.[63]

6.2.3   GERMANY

The protection introduced for early leavers in Germany requires that a number of distinctions be drawn. First, a distinction must be drawn between an individual whose rights have vested and those whose rights have not. Where rights have vested, a distinction must be drawn between those enjoying rights as a consequence of the 10 year promise, or as a result of 12 years company affiliation and a promise which is at least 3 years old. Finally, it is necessary to consider which funding vehicle has been chosen for the pension promise.

As was mentioned in Chapter 2, employees do not usually contribute to *Direktzusagen* or *Unterstützungskassen*. Accordingly, where they leave their employment prior their rights vesting, they receive nothing. By contrast, where the employee has contributed to a *Pensionskasse* or *Direktversicherung*, the rights which his contributions have purchased are not forfeited.

Where the individual's rights have vested, they must be maintained. Pursuant to paragraph 2 BetrAVG, *Direktzusagen* and *Unterstützungskassen* are obliged to maintain the vested rights of the employee pro rata, unless the scheme rules are more favourable to the employee. The requirement that benefits be pro rata (*ratierliches Berechnungsverfahrens*) means that the employer is first obliged to calculate the level of benefit to which the employee would have been entitled had he remained in the same employment until reaching pensionable age. The benefit which the scheme is obliged to maintain for the employee bears the same proportion to this highest theoretical benefit as his actual employment does to the maximum theoretical period of employment,[64] with all calculations based on the salary levels current when the employment terminates.

---

[63]   Although art. 71 AOW contains an anti-franking provision. On anti-franking, see generally Lutjens 1989, loc. cit. at pp. 468-511.

[64]   For a detailed exposé of this process, see Ahrend et al, loc. cit. at pp. 32-34. This resembles the process in the Netherlands.

The pro rata method is also applicable to *Direktversicherung* and *Pensionskassen*, but here the employer is offered an alternative. In *Direktversicherung*, the employer can choose to confine the claims of the early leaver to those benefits due by the insurer pursuant to the insurance contract, instead of the pro rata method.[65] However, to protect the rights of the individual, this choice is only made available to the employer when a number of conditions are fulfilled:

> - within three months of the termination, the rights have vested and all loans or transfers have been removed;
> - from the very inception of the scheme, any surpluses formed have been directed, pursuant to the insurance contract, to improving the levels of benefit provided under the scheme;
> - the employee must have been offered the option of continuing his insurance voluntarily after ceasing to be in the employ of the employer.[66]

If these conditions are not satisfied, the employer may not choose and must make the pro rata calculation.

Pensionskasse can limit the benefits granted to early leavers to those provided on the basis of an approved company plan.[67] However, again it is a requirement that any surpluses found in the scheme be used, as a matter of the insurance contract, to improve the levels of benefit provided to the beneficiaries. Unlike the *Direktversicherung*, where the employee's benefits follow developments in his wage levels, it is permissible for the benefits provided to early leavers from *Pensionskasse* to be limited to those which have been financed in advance. Again, it must be possible for the employee to continue his membership after having left the original employment.

---

[65]   Para. 2(2) BetrAVG. See Ahrend et al, loc. cit. at pp. 34-38. This could prove attractive to the employer in a situation in which the contract provides for many of the administrative costs to be paid in the early years.

[66]   It should be noted that in this situation the employee will move outwith the group insurance within which he had been participating and the conditions of the scheme will become considerably less favourable as the pooling of risks disappears.

[67]   Para. 2(3) BetrAVG. See Ahrend et al, loc. cit. at pp. 38-40.

One consequence of the relatively short vesting periods in the UK and the Netherlands is that it encourages a situation in which one individual has a succession of small pensions from a variety of sources. The general requirement of a promise of 10 years duration to obtain a vested right in Germany prevents this situation arising. However, it will be recalled that there is an alternative manner of obtaining a vested right. This is where the individual has belonged to the undertaking for at least 12 years and a pension promise has been made for at least 3 years. Where the individual leaves after his 3 year promise has vested, the risk does exist of an individual having a succession of small benefits, although it is unlikely and will be unusual. To solve this problem, paragraph 3 BetrAVG provides for a limited exception to the general prohibition of redeeming accrued pension rights.[68] Where the employee has a vested pension right pursuant to paragraph 1 BetrAVG but the promise is less than 10 years old, he may, if he so wishes, obtain a one-off payment representing his accrued pension rights on leaving the employment.[69] Generally, the level of cash provided is calculated on the basis of the pro rata method described above.[70] In relation to the choice offered to both *Pensionskassen* and *Direktversicherung* lump sums are only possible where the choice has fallen upon the pro rata method.[71]

In short, the early leaver whose pension rights have vested either retains a preserved pension within the pension scheme of his old employer or, in limited circumstances, obtains a lump sum by means of which all his previous claims against his employer are resolved.[72] There is no provision in the legislation or in the case law which obliges the employer to index SSBs.[73]

---

[68]   See generally Ahrend et al, loc. cit. at pp. 41-47 and the section on transfers below.

[69]   Where an individual wishes to use the monies to buy into the statutory scheme, this is also possible pursuant to para. 3 BetrAVG.

[70]   Para. 3(2) BetrAVG.

[71]   For an explanation, see Ahrend et al, loc. cit. at p. 44.

[72]   The subject of the lump sum will also be touched upon in the section on transfers below.

[73]   Note the anti-franking provision contained in para. 5 BetrAVG. On this subject, see Ahrend et al, loc. cit. at pp. 50-57.

6.2.4   COMPARISON AND COMMENT

In all three jurisdictions, pension schemes are obliged to protect the short service benefits to which early leavers have accrued rights. Although this protection is undoubtedly an improvement on the position in the past where the early leaver lost all his accrued pension rights where he changed employment prior to pensionable age, it does not and cannot place the early leaver in the same position as his immobile colleague. The first problem is that only in the UK are schemes obliged to revalue SSBs in line with increases in prices (or 5%) which have occurred between the ending of pensionable service and the pension becoming payable. Such indexation is vital if the value of the pension provided pursuant to the SSB is not to be eroded. The absence of provision to this end in the Dutch and German legislation means that the level of pension paid by a scheme in either jurisdiction may have dropped considerably in the period between leaving the employment and entering retirement. Even in the UK, because price inflation (or a maximum of 5% compound p.a.) has been required rather than wage inflation, the individual with an SSB may find that the relative value of his pension has dropped. This of itself will mean that the right to an SSB will never be the optimal solution for the employee who leaves an occupational scheme early.

Another reason why SSBs will only ever be a second best option for the early leaver is that the pensionable salary upon which pension entitlement is calculated is that which the individual received when his pensionable service with the employer in question ceased. Because of the phenomenon of back-service,[74] even if the preserved rights are fully indexed with price inflation, they will still be less valuable than those to which the immobile employee is entitled because his future salary increases are not taken into account in calculating his pension rights. To require that the old employer take account of his ex-employees' future salary developments can be seen to be at least unacceptable to employers, and maybe even unreasonable.[75]

---

[74]   In final salary schemes, an individual is treated as if he has always earned the salary which he received on retirement.

[75]   See the discussion in the Goode Report, loc. cit. at pp. 296-297.

Consequently, SSBs will almost always be less advantageous to the individual than a transfer of his accrued rights to his new employer's scheme because of the fact that future developments in salary levels are not taken account of. The preferred option for the early leaver will often be to take a transfer of his accrued rights which he can then invest in the scheme operated by his new employer. Transfers will be discussed in the next section. However, in the event that transfer is not available or viable, SSB provision which provides for some degree of indexation of accrued rights between leaving the employment and reaching pensionable age will improve the level of benefit which the individual eventually receives. Additionally, schemes should be obliged to treat pensions paid on the basis of SSB and those on the basis of service active until pensionable age equally, if job-changes or career breaks are not to work even more strongly to the detriment of the early leaver than is already the case.

6.3   Early Leavers - Transfers

In the preceding section, the requirements of national legislation in relation to the treatment which must be accorded to SSBs was described. It was stated that where an individual has an SSB it will be of great importance to him that some provision be made for his rights to be revalued between the end of his employment relationship and his pensionable age. However, even with revaluation in line with national wage developments[76] the level of benefit paid to the employee will still, in a final salary scheme, fail to reflect subsequent developments in the individual's wage. In this situation in particular, it will be preferable for an individual to be able to transfer his accrued rights from the scheme of his old employer to that run by his new employer. This sum will be used to purchase extra years of service in the new employer's scheme and may mean that the rights accrued on the basis of the old employment keep in line with the salary developments which the individual

---

[76]   See the Goode report at pp. 296-297 for a discussion of what it is not generally considered fair on the employer to require that SSBs be revalued in line with the wage developments of the particular individual.

experiences in the future.[77] Similar advantages accrue to the individual who belongs to a money purchase scheme. The possibilities for transfers between pension schemes nationally and internationally will be discussed below.

6.3.1   THE UK

In the past, a UK employee was not entitled to transfer his accrued pension rights to the scheme being run by his new employer. However, the UK government decided that transfers would contribute to an increase in individual choice and control, and employee mobility, and introduced a right to take a transfer of accrued pension rights by virtue of the Social Security Act 1985.[78]

The current provisions on transfers within the UK are to be found in Part IV Chapter IV of the 1993 Act. An employee whose pensionable service has terminated can ask for his accrued rights to be transferred out of the old scheme.[79] An individual can make such a request at any time until he is within one year of the scheme's normal pensionable age.[80] When pensionable service terminates, an individual gains entitlement to the "cash equivalent" of the rights he has accrued to that date.[81] If someone wishes to request a transfer, he must do so

---

[77]   The utility of transfers depends upon the early leaver being given a fair sum in translation of his rights, and these being converted at a roughly similar rate by the receiving scheme.

[78]   1985 c. 53. See the Contracting-Out (Transfer) Regulations 1985, SI 1985 1323.

[79]   Note that orignally, only individuals whose pensionable service terminated after 1 January 1986 were entitled to request a transfer. However, by virtue of s. 152 PA 1995, this provision has been removed. Individuals who had belonged to salary related schemes, and whose pensionable service terminated prior to 1 January 1986 in relation to whom prescribed conditions are satisfied may not request a transfer. See s. 152 PA 1995. See The Occupational Pension Schemes (Transfer Values) Regulations 1996, SI 1996 1847, reg. 2.

[80]   S. 93(1)(a) of (b) PSA 1993.

[81]   See s. 94(1) PSA 1993. The method of calculating the value of the cash equivalent is contained in s. 97 PSA 1993. See the Occupational Pension Schemes (Transfer Value) Regulations 1985, SI 1985 1931. These will be repealed with the coming into force on 6 April 1997 of the Occupational Pension Schemes (Transfer Values) Regulations 1996, SI 1996 1847.

in writing[82] and the trustees of both the old and the new schemes must be empowered to carry out such an action by the trust deed, and be willing to do so.[83]

A scheme can, first, make a transfer to another contracted-out occupational pension scheme or to a personal pension scheme. In this situation, the transfer can include the GMP[84] or protected rights.[85] A third possibility is to use the capital to purchase an annuity contract which is provided by a policy of insurance satisfying a number of requirements.[86] If the option of transferring accrued rights to purchase credits in a self-employed scheme is utilised, rights representing GMP or protected rights may not be transferred.

Special considerations apply to transfers from contracted-out schemes to personal pension schemes. In order to protect established schemes from haemorrhages of funds, provision was made that where the employee remained in the same employment after ceasing to be a member of the scheme, he could only transfer that part of his pension rights accruing after April 5 1988.[87]

The money representing the accrued rights under the scheme is known as the cash equivalent. Section 97 of the Pension Schemes Act 1993 deals with the calculation of cash equivalents, provisions which are worked out further statutory

---

[82]   See s. 95(1) PSA 1993; reg.s 2, 4, 6, 8, 10 or 11 (depending upon the situation) of The Contracting-Out (Transfer and Transfer Payment) Regulations 1996, SI 1996 1462.

[83]   S. 95(2) PSA 1993.

[84]   The precise details are set out in the Occupational Pension Schemes (Transfer Values) Regulation 1985, SI 1985 1931. These are to be repealed by the Occupational Pension Schemes (Transfer Values) Regulations 1996, SI 1996 1847.

[85]   The relevant provisions are contained in the Personal Pension Schemes (Transfer Payments) Regulations 1988, SI 1988 1014.

[86]   Set out in the Occupational Pension Schemes (Discharge of Liability) Regulations 1985, SI 1985 No. 1929 and the Occupational Pension Schemes (Transfer Values) Regulations 1985, SI 1985 No. 1931. See also the Personal and Occupational Pension Schemes (Protected Rights) Regulations 1996, SI 1996 1537.

[87]   This is to be continued by reg. 3 of the Occupational Pension Schemes (Transfer Values) Regulations 1996, 1996 SI 1847.

instruments.[88] The calculation must be made in a manner approved by an actuary and the Institute of Actuaries and the Faculty of Actuaries, the most recent guidelines having been published in the form of Guidance Note 11.

In principle, it is possible for rights to be transferred abroad, although a number of conditions will have to be satisfied.[89] Thus, as in the case of a transfer wholly within the UK, the member must consent and both the transferor and transferee schemes must make provision for the execution and/or acceptance of such transfers. A further condition which must be satisfied is that the scheme in question, the employer and the employee must all be resident in the same state. In principle, the transfer may not be of an amount in excess of 1/10th of the earnings cap.[90] However, if it is proposed that a higher amount is to be transferred, and no reciprocal arrangements are in force, the PSO will require to see the scheme documentation, including details of the benefits to which membership will lead and any conditions of forfeiture or withholding, and the amount of the transfer which is envisaged. The PSO must also be informed of the individual's date of birth, retirement age and the date at which UK employment ceased. No part of the pension may have already have come into payment if a transfer is to be allowed. An additional condition which has to be satisfied is that the individual give an undertaking that he has left the UK permanently and neither intends to work in the UK again, nor to retire there. A final requirement is that the individual have already commenced employment abroad and begun to pay contributions.

The OPB (OPRA) on the other hand will have to be satisfied of a number of other factors if a transfer involving GMP rights is to be agreed. Thus, the new scheme must offer benefits at least equivalent to those which would be paid out by SERPs. Additionally, in the event that the benefits finally paid out are of a

---

[88] Currently, the Occupational Pension Schemes (Transfer Values) Regulations 1985.SI 1985, 1931; soon the Occupational Pension Schemes (Transfer Values) Regulations 1996, SI 1996 1847.

[89] See reg.s 6 and 11 of the Contracting-Out (Transfer and Transfer Payment) Regulations 1996, SI 1996 1462.

[90] S. 590B(10) ICTA 1988. This is currently set at £82,200 (see the Retirement Benefits Schemes (Indexation of Earnings Cap) Order 1995, SI 1995 3034). Therefore, the maximum amount for transfer will be £8,220.

lower level than those to which the individual would have been entitled under
SERPS, the individual must sign a waiver of all claims against the ex-employer or
the UK state.

The situation is less complex where the member seeks to transfer his
rights from a foreign to a UK scheme. Again, the individual must request and both
transferor and transferee must be able and willing to undertake the transfer. The
first additional requirement which will have to be met is that the IR must be
convinced that the transfer does not in fact concern an unapproved UK pension
scheme.[91] The IR also will have to be convinced of the fact that the member has
been in non-UK employment for at least two years and the transfer must be direct
and unconditional. The maximum lump sum benefit under the receiving scheme
must be less than or equal to 2.25 or 3 times the initial pension produced by the
transfer payment.[92]

6.3.2   THE NETHERLANDS

The basic principle embodied in the PSW is that pension rights can not be
redeemed under any circumstances.[93] Nevertheless, in the past a number of
exceptions to this rule were countenanced, principally[94] permitting schemes to
facilitate redemption for the purposes of transfers to schemes subject to Insurance
Chamber supervision[95] or which had been approved by the Minister.[96]
Additionally, where the individual was able to convince the fund's board that he

---

[91]   An unapproved UK scheme is one which has not satisfied the requirements of the IR
       contained in ICTA.

[92]   The figure depends upon the precise details of the benefits provided under the scheme.

[93]   Article 32(4) PSW.

[94]   Article 32a PSW.

[95]   Insurance companies licensed for life insurance.

[96]   Generally, schemes subject to public law, the most of important of which was the ABP.

was about to emigrate, the scheme was entitled to redeem his accrued rights.[97] Only where an individual was going to work for an EC institution was the pension fund actually obliged to cooperate in redeeming the pension rights for the purposes of transfer.[98]

The necessity of transfers between schemes within the Netherlands ought not to be so acute as in the UK because of the practice, described in Chapter 2, of schemes being set up which cover an entire branch of industry. Where an individual changes employment but remains within the same branch of industry, he will remain a member of the same pension scheme.[99] However, in addition, on 24 June 1986, a number of employers and pension funds signed a cooperation agreement with the objective of facilitating the transfer of acquired pension rights between different funds on the termination of employment.[100] This voluntary arrangement is known as the SDS (*Stichting Dienstverlening Samenwerkingsverband*). Employers and pension funds which are party to the agreement are obliged to cooperate in arranging transfers where an employee changes employment within the circuit. The accrued pension rights will be transferred to the new scheme. As a result of the transfer, the employee obtains rights in the new fund and the right to participate without a waiting period. A transfer will not take place where the employee objects within three months of joining his new employer. If employers and schemes wish to join the circuit they have to satisfy a number of criteria. The scheme must be salary related and contain provisions concerning regular increases for back service. Additionally, pensions in payment must be regularly increased to maintain purchasing power. Finally, the PSW must be applicable to the scheme in question. Arrangements have been made between the various circuits which are in existence to facilitate movement from

---

[97]   Article 32a(2) PSW.

[98]   Article 32a(3) PSW.

[99]   Unless exemption from the decision of general applicability has been granted to one of the schemes.

[100]   See Lutjens 1989, loc. cit. at pp. 645-648.

one circuit to another.[101] According to the Pension Chamber (*Pensioenkamer*, PK) more than 80% of current members of pension schemes can utilise the current network of circuits on transfer of employment.[102] Thus, the existing consensual arrangements can be seen to offer a reasonably high level of transferability between schemes within the Netherlands.

Nevertheless, however much this system of circuits may contribute to the avoidance of gaps in pension acquisition, it has a number of inherent limitations. First, and obviously, it only offers a solution if both schemes belong to a circuit. Furthermore, where an individual transfers from, say, a final salary to a money purchase scheme, or vice versa, diminution of rights may occur. Finally, it does not solve the problems of the migrant abroad.

Partly in response to such difficulties, the legislation relating to transfers has recently undergone a significant alteration. Since the entry into force of recent amendments to the PSW,[103] individuals can now **require** that their accrued rights be transferred to the scheme of their new employer.[104] A request can only be refused where the Insurance Chamber takes the view that the financial condition of the scheme precludes making a transfer.[105] A number of additional conditions must be satisfied before the obligation applies, all of which are designed to ensure that the rights in question are used by a reputable retirement institution to provide retirement benefits for the individual. Unless the value of the accrued rights would produce a pension of less than ƒ625 per annum,[106] the consent of the individual is required for the transfer. The purpose of the redemption must be to allow the

---

[101]   For details, see Lutjens 1989, loc. cit. at pp. 647-648. For recent developments, see *Pensioenbrief* no. 1 1994 nr. 1.

[102]   TK 1992-1993, 23 123, nr. 6 at p. 15.

[103]   Law of 30 June 1994. Stb. 1994, 496.

[104]   Article 32b PSW.

[105]   Art. 32b PSW.

[106]   Article 32(5) PSW. This is to be adjusted annually pursuant to article 32(6). Originally the amount was ƒ600, but this was increased pursuant to *Regeling van 24 november 1995 nr. 95/5155*, Stcrt. 1995, 234.

beneficiary to acquire pension rights with another retirement institution to which the capital is to be directly transferred. Furthermore, the institution must be subject to the supervision of the Insurance Chamber or have been nominated by Ministerial decision if the transfer is to take place. A general administrative measure (*algemene maatregel van bestuur*) has been adopted laying down the procedure to be followed and the means of calculating the value of the accrued rights and the value of the rights which they will purchase in the new scheme.[107] This is to help ensure that the individual is not penalised by a decision to move by unfavourable calculation values which decimate his pension rights.

Schemes are still obliged to cooperate in transfers where the individual is going to work for an EC institution.[108] However, Article 32a(2) PSW which permitted redemption of accrued rights where the individual was clearly planning to emigrate has recently been repealed.[109] In its place come two new provisions. The first provides that where the value of the accrued pension would not exceed ƒ1250 per annum,[110] the accrued rights can be redeemed.

The second of the new provisions represents a total reversal of previous policy in relation to emigration.[111] The main consideration which seems to have prompted the government to change the legal regime was fiscal. It had come to ministerial notice that (particularly highly paid) individuals were emigrating to

---

[107]   *Besluit reken- en procedureregels recht op waarde overdracht*, Stb. 1994, 647.

[108]   Art. 32b(4) PSW. The old article, Art. 32a(3) PSW, has been repealed.

[109]   Article L of the amending legislation of 30 June 1994.

[110]   Article 32(5) PSW. This amount is to be annually adjusted, article 32(6), and as with the amount for internal transfers, has recently been increased from the original ƒ1200.

[111]   The regime described above according to which it was possible for an individual to redeem his pension rights if he was emigrating was, according to the government, dictated by the emigration policy being pursued by the government at that time. It now takes the view that individuals are more likely than before to return to their original state at some stage in their (later) life, which mitigates against exporting all accrued Dutch pension rights. Furthermore, since the AOW cannot be redeemed, the government sees no reason for maintaining the existing emigration policy in relation to occupational schemes. See TK 1992-1993, 23 123, nr. 3.

Belgium or the Netherlands Antilles.[112] Having built up a large capital within a Dutch pension scheme, utilising the tax advantages available, these individuals then emigrated and took their untaxed accrued capital with them for the purposes of buying into a foreign pension scheme. In Belgium and the Netherlands Antilles it is possible to redeem pension rights without that sum being subject to tax, allowing the emigres to obtain a large tax-free lump sum on emigration. This proved a very attractive tax loophole for wealthy individuals and one which the government was determined to plug.

Consequently, the provision facilitating redemption on emigration has been repealed and in its place comes a provision giving the Insurance Chamber competence to grant exemption from the general prohibition of redemption.[113] The Insurance Chamber is given the discretion to derogate from article 32(a)(c)[114] where the purpose of the redemption is the acquisition of pension rights from an insurer established abroad. The government was aware of the fact that by abolishing the existing provision, possible obstacles to free movement of workers would be created, because migrants would not be able to take their occupational pension rights with them when they emigrated. It nevertheless considered that by including the possibility of exemption from the provisions for funds established abroad where the destination of the capital could be maintained, it had satisfied the requirements of the EC Treaty. The most obvious candidates for exemption are life insurance companies operating on the basis of the single licence. It is worth stressing that pursuant to article 2a of the *Regelen PSW*[115] regardless of the legal system of the insurer chosen, the provisions of the *Regelen PSW* remain applicable to such transactions. Thus, the general prohibition of redemption of pension rights continues to apply, in principle, even if the transfer

---

[112]   In the Netherlands, unlike the UK, there is no limit on the salary over which pension rights can be built up while maintaining the tax advantages. The position of the company director or major shareholder are subject to different rules.

[113]   Article 29 PSW.

[114]   Transfers are permitted where the institution to which the transfer is made is subject to the supervision of the Insurance chamber or has been nominated by the Minister.

[115]   As introduced by the amendment of 17 May 1993, Stcrt. 1993, 93.

has been effected.[116] However, it is as yet unclear whether pension funds established in other Member States will be deemed to satisfy the requirements of the Insurance Chamber.

Although where accrued pension rights are put at the disposal of the employee, they are currently subject to tax at 45%, this provision is relaxed where the capital is transferred to an approved pension scheme. By a resolution of 11 August 1982,[117] the Minister of Finance let it be known that if pension rights are redeemed and subsequently invested with an insurer or pension scheme established within the Netherlands, the sum is exempt from wage or income tax or social security premium levying. The permission can only be granted where the employee wishes to redeem his acquired pension rights because the new employer is willing to let him buy in with this sum. Thus, in the situation of the legal right to a transfer outlined above, the sum would not be subject to tax.

Another ground for exemption from tax on the transfer value is if the employee can continue his acquisition of rights with the other insurer or pension scheme under better conditions than prevailed with the current institution. In a situation where an individual employee has rights to a collection of small pensions and he wishes to collect them all under one institution, this will also fall within the exempted set of transactions. Nor, if by the time of reaching pensionable age the employee can buy a pension under better conditions with the new insurer or pension fund, will his transfer value be subject to taxation. Finally, where the individual (or his surviving spouse) with a preserved pension can buy a deferred pension with the other insurer or pension funds under more favourable conditions the transfer value will not be taxed. It is clear that in all these situations, it is envisaged that the objective of the individual providing for himself to ensure that he is not dependent on the state is being furthered.

---

[116]   In practice, it seems likely that this will be used to prohibit transfers where the legislation of the State to which the money is to be transferred allows rights to be redeemed.

[117]   Resolution of 11 August 1982, nr. 282-11 423, V-N 4 September 1982, p. 1759 as amended on 31 July 1984, nr. 284-10275, V-N 18 August 1984, p. 1608. Also reproduced in L.G.M. Stevens, (ed.), *Pensioen en andere toekomstvoorzieningen*, Deventer VII.F.7.1., as amended on 27 January 1989, nr. DB 88/1258, BNB 1989/69. For details, see P. Kavelaars, *Toewijzingsregels in het Europees sociaalverzekeringsrecht*, Deventer, 1992 at p. 50.

The inspector can set the following conditions to a grant of his permission:

> 1. The scheme must be a pension scheme within the meaning of art. 11(3)(a) of the Wet LB or a scheme treated the same on the basis of article (b).[118]
> 2. The capital must be transferred directly to the institution or employer, and must not be deducted from the income of the employee or his spouse.

The Minister of Finance has stated that transfers are, in his view, in principle, redemptions and liable to tax. Therefore, in the situation of a redemption by someone planning to emigrate, the sum would normally be subject to tax at 45%. This is a consequence of article 49(1)(b)(1) of the Wet IB which treats income received by a non-resident in relation to employment in the Netherlands as taxable income in the Netherlands. However, transfers to foreign pension schemes were generally favourably viewed. Thus, the Dutch authorities would not tax an amount transferred abroad where it was transferred to the scheme of a foreign employer, where the benefit itself would be subject to taxation and where no part of the amount transferred be payable free of tax.[119]

6.3.3   GERMANY

In stark contrast to the situation in the UK and the Netherlands, the German legislation contains no provisions relating to the transfer of accrued pension rights to another pension scheme. A number of factors can be adduced to explain this "gap". As has often be stressed in this exposition of the law, one of the factors informing the legislator in designing the regulatory framework for occupational pension provision was to avoid creating a situation in which employers simply refused to offer these benefits to employees or to terminate the schemes which were in operation.[120] Expressed simply, the legislator was wary of encroaching

---

[118]   See the discussion in Chapter 2.

[119]   Problems in this regard can be seen with the UK practice of granting lump sums tax free.

[120]   In this vein, see the comments of Berenz, op. cit. who examines recent developments in legislation and case law and concludes that the future is very sombre indeed.

excessively on the contractual freedom of the employer and telling the employer how to treat an ex-employee was presumably seen as just that.

In theory, it is possible to transfer German occupational pension rights between pension schemes. Because of the absence of legislative provision, the consent of both the ex- and the new employer will be required.[121] It appears that the situation is particularly complex for *Unterstützungskassen* and difficult in respect of *Pensionskassen*. However, for promises funded through *Direktversicherung* a number of agreements have been concluded which make transfer possible. In addition, it appears that there are plans to extend the scope of this facility to cover insurers established abroad. However, again there are currently no legislative provisions covering these practices.

A number of other features of the German situation also help to explain why no provisions relating to transfer of pension rights are to be found in the BetrAVG. First, and approaching this matter from the perspective of the employer, given that the majority opinion has traditionally tended to regard occupational pension benefits as a reward for company loyalty,[122] it is entirely logical for no provision to be made in respect of an individual who has demonstrated little or no company loyalty by his decision to change employment. On the other hand, when it is recognised that the pension represents deferred remuneration, this argument begins to lose much of its convincing force. However, the real key to this matter can be found in the methods of financing chosen for pension schemes in Germany. In *Direktzusagen*, and to a lesser extent *Unterstützungskassen*, the employer undertakes to make a pension payment without receiving any contribution from the employee. The monies "reserved" to cover the occupational benefits appear in the company balance sheet and are put at the disposal of the employer who can utilise these funds to further develop his undertaking. Stating the case simply, the vast majority of German schemes are not designed in a manner which will countenance transfers, since transfers are premised on clearly identifiable employee rights, something which is not the norm in relation to *Directzusagen* and

---

[121]   Given that the employer can often use pension monies for the development of his undertaking, it seems unlikely that an employer will ever consent to such a transfer.

[122]   See the discussion in Chapter 2.

Unterstützungskassen. Were employers using *Pensionskassen* or *Direktsicherungen*[123] to be obliged to transfer accrued rights, the legislator would create a great incentive for employers to fund their schemes by one of the other possibilities. Accordingly, transfers can be seen to be at odds with the system of occupational pension provision which has developed in Germany.

Even if the arguments outlined above are accepted, it could be submitted that in a situation where an individual has accrued vested rights, there are good grounds for granting this individual who has a clear right to some benefit, a transfer. On the other hand it can be argued,[124] that this individual does not actually need a transfer[125] since his rights are protected under the BetrAVG in any event.[126] However, the protection afforded to SSBs is never sufficient to prevent some deterioration in the value of rights taking place.[127]

For the individual with protected rights, the lack of transferability is unlikely to pose an insurmountable barrier to mobility. However, the root of rigidity seems likely to be the extremely long periods of affiliation required of an employee before he obtains enforceable pension rights.[128] This combined with the current methods of financing places a great degree of power in the hands of the employer for whom the legislation relating to occupational pension can be regarded as a means of binding employees to his undertaking with all risks involved falling squarely on the shoulders of the employee.

---

[123]   Which are funded in advance.

[124]   H.-D. Steinmeyer, "Harmonisierung des Betriebsrentenrechts in der Europäischen Gemeinschaft?", EuZW (1991), 43-49, at 48.

[125]   Or at least that his need is not the same as that of someone in the UK or the Netherlands.

[126]   Para.s 1, 2 and 16 BetrAVG.

[127]   On which, see the discussion in the previous section.

[128]   The long period of affiliation which is required if an individual is to obtain vested rights means that the problem of minuscule pension benefits from a number of sources which dogs the UK and Dutch systems and begs for a transfers based solution, does not arise to the same extent.

One area which can be seen to form an exception to this situation is where a lump sum payment is paid to an employee who has a vested pension right but one which has been accrued over a period shorter than 10 years. He has no absolute right to contribute this money to any scheme which his new employer may run, the possibilities being dependent on the wording of the scheme's statute and rules, and the utility of this approach would seem for obvious reasons to be limited to *Pensionskassen* and *Direktversicherung*. As far as the tax law position is concerned, the lump sum will be taxable as income in the hands of the employee at the moment that it is paid out, but the tax on the benefit will be reduced to take account of the tax already paid.

6.3.4 COMPARISON AND COMMENT

In the UK and the Netherlands an employee is entitled to require that his pension rights be transferred when he changes employment and although a variety of conditions must be complied with before a transfer can take place, these can all basically be seen to have been designed to protect the individual's accrued pension. However, the additional requirement made of the international migrant that the emigration be permanent seems likely in fact to prove a significant obstacle to the transfer of pension rights - at least where the migrant is a national of the state he is leaving - because it is often not easy to say whether a move will be permanent or not. In this regard, the Dutch requirement that a request for a transfer be submitted within 2 months of commencing pensionable employment in the new scheme, seems likely to work more restrictively than the more flexible British regime. Nevertheless, the transfer regimes put in place in these Member States will go a long way towards removing the rigidities which occupational pension schemes introduce into the operation of the labour market by penalising early leavers of schemes. Migrant workers and individuals taking career breaks[129] should find that

---

[129]   As well as those changing job within a single state.

the transfer schemes significantly improve the level of pension which they receive on retirement.[130]

Both Member States afford transfers favourable tax treatment which is very important if the full value of a transfer is to be enjoyed by the migrant. Were the transfer sum to be taxed, the migrant would possibly suffer the risk of double taxation[131] which would reduce significantly the utility and attractiveness of the transfer option to him.

The situation in Germany contrasts sharply with this. There, transfers are virtually impossible which, because of the inadequacy of the protection of SSBs when compared to transfers, means that the early leaver from a German scheme will suffer inevitable disadvantage when compared to early leavers in the UK or the Netherlands. As such, it can only be concluded that the position in Germany must represent a significant obstacle to labour mobility.

Both the UK and the Netherlands have adopted provision to allow individuals to request transfers of their rights. The Dutch rules require that a request be submitted within 2 months of joining a new scheme,[132] whereas the UK legislation requires that the request be submitted by the later of 6 months of leaving the employment, or the year prior to reaching normal pensionable age. Both formulations extend the possibility of requesting a transfer to a larger group of employees than would be the case were the legislation to require that the request be submitted within, say, 6 months of leaving the pensionable employment. This is because in the latter situation, the option of taking a transfer is effectively denied those whose decision to leave pensionable employment was not prompted by the offer of more favourable pensionable employment elsewhere, for example, those

---

[130]   Because it will virtually never be the case that an individual is able to purchase precisely the same level of rights in the new scheme which he had in the old, even a favourable transfer regime will still leave the employee in a worse position than if he had remained in the old scheme.

[131]   In general contributions or benefits are taxed. If contributions are taxed, taxing the transfer sum leads to double taxation. If benefits are taxed, having already taxed the transfer sum will result in double taxation.

[132]   In this respect, see the *Besluit reken- en procedureregels waarde-overdracht*, Decision of 15 August 1994, Stb. 647 article 3 of which refers to a request being made within 2 months of joining a new scheme.

who cease employment to care for dependents or become unemployed. Additionally, as has already been discussed, the more restrictive formulation chosen by the Dutch legislator makes transfers for international migrants potentially more difficult than the UK formulation.

Another feature of the transfer rules found in both the UK and the Netherlands is provision concerning how transfer values are to be calculated. This ensures that the sum released to the individual to invest in the other fund is a reasonably fair reflection of the value of the rights which have been accrued to date and should enable the employee to purchase rights in the new scheme which bear a reasonably close relation to those which he has redeemed. Without such provision, it would be possible for either scheme to give the individual a "bad rate of return" in converting his accrued rights, something which could severely damage the individual's final pension benefit.

If the effectiveness of transfers in terms of pension accrual is to be maximised, it is important that the sums transferred not be subject to tax. The tax treatment of pensions is the subject of a separate section, but it is generally the case that either contributions or benefits are taxed. If that pattern were to be followed by the a legislator, taxing a transfer sum would be likely to lead to the individual being subject to double taxation,[133] and form a barrier to mobility. Equally, it would have a detrimental influence on the level of benefit to which the individual would eventually accrue entitlement.

The advantages of an effective transfer system are many. First, from the perspective of the employee, it results in there being a single pension accruing at a single source which makes it considerably easier for the individual to assess his likely future level of pension income.[134] Additionally, it reduces replicated administration in that only one benefit will be being administered by a single fund, rather than a whole host of small benefits being administered by an equivalent

---

[133]   Taxed on transfer value and subsequently on the benefit.

[134]   It will also, as has already been observed, significantly facilitate assessment of when maximum accrual has been reached.

number of funds.[135] If the time limit suggestions are followed, this leaves the transfer option open to the maximum number of people, which where government policy is to maximise retirement income from this source, must be seen as a positive development.

6.4   Taxation[136]

In Chapter 2, the way in which the legislator has used tax law to encourage individuals and their employers to make occupational pension provision was described. The legislation makes a number of rewards available to (members of) pension schemes which comply with certain legislative conditions.[137] In designing such measures, the legislator can be seen to be informed by a couple of different considerations. First, he may wish to encourage individual employers to make occupational provision to relieve pressure on state resources in supplying the elderly with retirement income.[138] Second, in particular where employees themselves are contributing to their occupational pension scheme, the legislator may wish to provide the employee with security[139] and to this end require that the pension fund take a particular form if maximum revenue approval is to be obtained.[140] Additionally, the exchequer may seek to prevent pensions being used as a method of avoiding paying tax. This can arise as a consequence of the tax

---

[135]   A single fund administering a single benefit, removes some of employers' objections to short vesting periods (because of the administrative expense of administering small benefits), as has already been mentioned.

[136]   See in general Philip Davis, loc. cit. at pp. 77-90.

[137]   For example, exempt approval in the UK.

[138]   Although this only works most obviously in situations in which state old age retirement income is means-tested, it is also relevant where the state provides other means-tested post-retirement income, particularly in situations where the level of income provided by the state scheme is relatively low.

[139]   This is clearly linked to the first objective mentioned.

[140]   Of course the Maxwell débacle in the UK illustrates the sometime futility of this aim.

deductibility of pension contributions which, in a jurisdiction in which different tax rates are levied, offers individuals the opportunity to make a lifetime tax saving. The legislature will wish to ensure that the individual who has benefitted from tax deductions does not avoid paying tax on the benefits by transferring the sum abroad. Additionally, the exchequer may wish to limit the size of funds which are allowed to accrue to a certain percentage above scheme liabilities, to prevent a different form of tax avoidance from being practised.

Basically, pensions can be taxed at three points: at the moment when funds are contributed, when investment income is earned, and when benefits are paid out.[141] In the discussion which follows, no mention will be made of taxation of investment income, since that seems primarily to be a concern of the *fund*. This research is concerned only with the recipients of occupational pension benefits, rather than with the scheme itself and so it seems appropriate to concentrate upon the taxation of benefits rather than on measures directed at the financial institution. Where the legislator has decided to use tax law to encourage occupational pensions, he basically has a choice between taxing the contributions or the benefit. The particular advantage to the individual of contributions being tax-deductible, but benefits taxed is that it offers the individual a chance to make a lifetime tax saving.[142] This is because in systems with different bands of tax applicable to different levels of income, the contribution will be subtracted from the employee's income before any tax is paid - in other words at a (relatively) high marginal rate, whereas the benefit may well be taxed at a lower rate.

Another argument for this approach, is that by allowing contributions to occupational pension schemes to be tax-deductible, the exchequer foregoes income to which it would otherwise be entitled now and gains instead the opportunity to levy tax in the future.[143] The demographic predictions discussed in Chapter 1

---

[141]   Philip Davis, loc. cit. at p. 77.

[142]   Philip Davis (loc. cit. at p. 77) cites figures which suggest that an individual can reduce his lifetime tax liability by between 20 and 40%.

[143]   Provisional figures indicate that the cost of tax relief for occupational pension schemes in the UK amounted to £7,700 million for the year 1992-1993 (figures quoted in Daykin, loc. cit. at p. 46). This figure does of course include the income received from taxing benefits in payment. Philip Davis, loc. cit. at p. 81 suggests that gross costs of tax relief in 1989-

suggest that the retired population in the future will be large relative to the working population. Taxing pensions then offers the exchequer the opportunity to obtain income at a time when receipts from the smaller working population could be expected to decline, unless tax rates were increased.[144] In a situation like this in which the working population is expected to contract *vis-à-vis* the retired population, postponing the moment at which tax is levied, generates a source of income for the future.

When the exchequer has delayed the collection of tax from an individual until the benefit is actually paid, it will be anxious to ensure that this tax is in fact paid. Where an individual remains resident in the State in which the pension rights were accrued, no particular problem seems to arise. Mechanisms can be put in place to ensure that the payments are taxed before they reach the beneficiary. However, where an individual is resident abroad while the benefits are being paid, a number of problems can and do arise. Further complications arise when the individual moves to another State prior to retirement and wishes to transfer his pension rights to his pension fund in his new state of employment. These two separate problems will be discussed in the sections below. However, prior to that, a brief outline will be provided of the general provisions on taxation of pensions in place in the UK, the Netherlands and Germany.

6.4.1   TAXATION OF PENSIONS

The general position in the UK is that contributions to approved pension schemes are tax deductible for both the employer and the employee, with benefits treated as taxable income in the hands of the employee.[145] In principle, therefore,

---

1990 were £12 billion.

[144]   See the discussion in Kuné 1996, op. cit.; Miles, op. cit.

[145]   See the discussion in Chapter 1. The basic provisions are to be found in ss. 595 and 596 ICTA. Where the employee's income is not chargeable to Schedule E, or concerns foreign emoluments (defined in s. 192 ICTA as "the emoluments of a person not domiciled in the United Kingdom from an office or employment under or with any person, body of persons or partnership resident outside, and not resident in, the United Kingdom, but shall be taken not to include the emoluments of a person resident in the United Kingdom from an office or employment under or with a person, body of persons or partnership resident in the

benefits originating from a UK scheme are liable to UK tax, irrespective of the residence of the pensioner.[146] Thus, for example, where an individual who has worked all his life in the UK retires to the Netherlands, in the absence of alternative provision, the UK tax authorities will tax the individual's benefits. However, as will emerge below, it is also customary for the Dutch authorities to tax pension benefits on payment, and so the individual could have to pay tax twice on the same benefit: once to the paying state and once to the state of residence.

In practice however, the situation is governed by Double Taxation Treaties[147] which generally allow occupational pensions to be taxed in the state of residence.[148] In the context of this research, this is the case between the UK and the Netherlands[149] and between the UK and Germany.[150] So, in the example cited above, the UK would waive its right to tax in favour of the Netherlands, as it would if the state of residence was Germany.

In the Netherlands, contributions paid to a pension scheme are generally tax-deductible for both the employer and the employee. As in the UK, the Dutch tax authorities tax the pension when it is paid. As has just been observed, the Double Tax Treaty between the UK and the Netherlands provides that pensions paid are taxable in the state of residence. Article 12 of the Netherlands-Germany

---

Republic of Ireland." S. 192(2) ICTA provides that foreign emoluments are exempted from Case 1 of Schedule E.

[146]   S. 597(1) ICTA 1988.

[147]   It should be stressed that all that Double Tax Treaties do is allocate competence to tax as between the signatory states. They do not provide the authority for the levying of taxation. This must be found in the national legislation. An example may clarify this point. A Treaty allocates competence to tax pension benefits to country X rather than country Y. The legislation of country X provides that the contributions to a pension scheme are taxable but that benefits escape tax, while country Y taxes contributions but not benefits. Although the Treaty allocates competence to country X, the benefit will not in fact be taxed, because there is no national legislation providing for this.

[148]   Reardon, loc. cit. at p. 208.

[149]   Art. 18 of the UK - Dutch Double Tax Treaty.

[150]   Art. X of the UK - German Double Tax Treaty.

Double Tax Treaty also provides that pensions are to be taxed in the state of residence.

In Germany an entirely different approach was taken. Employer contributions to *Pensionskassen* and *Direktversicherung* are treated as current income in the hands of the employee and taxed accordingly. The resulting benefit is subject to a lower than normal rate of tax. Contributions to *Unterstützungskassen* are deductible only in certain narrowly defined circumstances, but again benefits will only be taxed lightly. By contrast, the entries representing *Direktzusagen* can be set off completely against the company's liability to corporation tax, and the PSVaG premiums are tax-deductible. The benefits paid by such funds are taxable as income in the hands of the recipients. As was mentioned in Chapter 2, these provisions partly explain the popularity of *Direktzusagen* in Germany.

The Double Tax Treaties which are in force between the UK and Germany and the Netherlands and Germany provide for benefits to be taxed in the state of residence. This does not entirely solve the risk of double taxation for recipients of benefits from a German scheme, because should they belong to a scheme in relation to which contributions are taxed, allowing the state of residence to tax the benefits, may nevertheless result in the individual being taxed twice. This is a consequence of the different approaches to the taxation of pensions taken by the German exchequer on the one hand, and those of the UK and the Netherlands on the other.

Consequently, it can be concluded that individuals moving from the UK or the Netherlands to any of the other jurisdictions covered by this research ought not to face Double Taxation. However, the different approach taken by the German legislator means that individuals moving to another Member State may find that they are obliged to pay tax twice despite the existence of Double Tax Treaties.

Even where Double Tax Treaties eradicate the risk of paying tax twice, they are unable to offer any consolation to the individual who finds that the allocation of competence to tax results in his state of residence levying a higher rate of tax than the paying state would have done. However, since setting rates of direct tax remains a matter within the exclusive jurisdiction of the individual state, no alteration can be expected in this area in the foreseeable future.

6.4.2   TAXATION OF TRANSFERS

The provisions contained in Double Taxation Treaties on the taxing of pensions generally follow the pattern laid out in the OECD Model Treaty.[151] However, no agreement was reached on the subject of the taxation of transfer sums. In relation to transfers between the UK and the Netherlands, article 18(2) of the UK-Netherlands Double Taxation Treaty provides that "where remuneration is not of a periodic nature, and is paid in respect of employment in the other State, it may be taxed in the other state". In other words, if the UK pays a transfer sum to a pension scheme established in the Netherlands, the UK may choose to tax the transfer sum. By contrast, the provision in the Double Tax Treaty between Germany and the Netherlands requires that the transfer sum be treated like the benefit itself - and the state of residence is accordingly given the competence to tax this sum.[152] The UK-German Treaty similarly provides that it would be taxable in the state of residence. This suggests at first glance that there ought to be no problems caused for the international migrant worker seeking to transfer his or her pension rights to a pension scheme in another Member State.

However, as was already described in the sections on transfers in general, transfers from German schemes, although a theoretical possibility, are virtually impossible in practice. Consequently, these provisions will largely be concerned with transfers to German schemes. The fact that the majority of German schemes are cast in a form which prohibits employee contributions suggests that in practice very few migrant workers will in fact transfer accrued pension rights to a German scheme.[153]

It would therefore seem to be the case, that the tax treatment of pensions in the UK and the Netherlands need not pose insurmountable barriers to the

---

[151]   See art. 18 of the OECD Model Treaty.

[152]   Art. 12 of the Double Taxation Treaty between Germany and the Netherlands provides that where an individual resident in one of the states receives a retirement pension or other payments or benefits in respect of past services, it may be taxed in the state of residence.

[153]   It may well be the case that the degree of security of employee rights in *Direktzusagen* will be found unacceptable by the Dutch and UK authorities, and therefore, that transfers would not be permitted.

movement of labour between these two states, although the requirement that emigration be permanent may. This contrasts sharply with the position in respect of Germany. The framework within which occupational provision is made there seem likely to make transfers to and from Germany virtually impossible, creating a significant barrier to intra-Community migration. Double Tax Treaties are able to offer little consolation in this respect.

6.5 Evaluation

In this Chapter I have described the features of occupational pension schemes which seem likely to disadvantage individuals changing employment. Attention focused first on waiting and vesting periods, then moved on to consider the treatment of short service benefits (SSBs) left within the scheme of the old employer. In the next section the possibility of transferring accrued rights was addressed before, in the final section, the tax treatment of pensions and transfers was discussed.

In relation to waiting and vesting periods, it was concluded that the situation in Germany gave rise to significant barriers to employee mobility. The extremely long period of scheme membership which an individual was required to have before he could obtain a vested right to a pension was identified as posing a potentially serious barrier to employee mobility. The shorter periods operated in the UK and the Netherlands appeared to find a balance more favourable to the employee between an employee's interest in accruing pensions and the employer's interest in not having to administer a large number of small pensions.

In relation to the treatment of SSBs, for money purchase schemes at least, the protection granted to rights left in the old employer's scheme seems likely to prove adequate to protect the individual against substantial disadvantage on migration. Although the provisions in place improve significantly the position of the early leaver from a final salary scheme, they cannot compensate him for the fact that his frozen pension benefits are based on his salary on leaving that employment and do not grow in line with his future salary developments. Additionally, the absence of an obligation to index SSBs in the Netherlands and

Germany between leaving and retirement allows rights to be permitted to evaporate.

For a member of a final salary scheme, the most attractive option on changing employment[154] is to transfer his accrued rights to the scheme run by his new employer. In relation to transfers within the UK and the Netherlands, the framework appears to have been put in place to facilitate this. As a result, the individual will be able to buy in extra years of pensionable service with his new employer. Although in theory it is possible to transfer rights abroad from UK and Dutch schemes, in practice the requirement that an undertaking be given that the migration is permanent reduces significantly the likelihood that an individual will redeem his rights in this way.

The contrast with the situation in Germany could hardly be more stark. There transfers are in principle possible but in practice impossible and the regulatory framework of occupational schemes in Germany may cause the UK and Dutch authorities to refuse permission to individuals seeking a transfer to a scheme established there, because the guarantees provided that benefits will in fact be paid may be considered inadequate.

The difficulty of obtaining rights in German schemes and transferring accrued rights from or to German schemes represents the most significant obstacle to free movement of workers in this field. Equally, the practical obstacles placed in the path of the international migrant seeking to transfer accrued pension rights make this largely a theoretical possibility, even for migrants to and from the UK and the Netherlands. Even where a transfer is possible, it will result in some reduction in the value of the individual's accrued rights. Retaining rights in the ex-employer's scheme allows the value of the migrant's accrued rights to reduce even further. These difficulties are only compounded by the fact that the Dutch and British legislators took a different approach to taxing pensions than the German legislator.

This allows the conclusion to be drawn that occupational pension schemes in the jurisdictions studied have not yet adequately adapted to the situation of the international migrant worker and that as a result the international migrant with accrued occupational pension rights risks suffering a considerable reduction in the

---

[154] Assuming that the schemes have similar benefit terms.

value of the pension which he eventually receives, as a consequence of his decision to migrate.

6.6   Conclusion

In this Chapter the various devices which have traditionally been used by employers in the UK, the Netherlands and Germany to bind employees to their undertaking through their occupational pension schemes have been examined, alongside the measures which have been introduced by those national legislatures to counter some of the effects of these practices on the operation of the labour market. As the discussion makes clear, occupational pensions have the potential to introduce significant obstacles to labour mobility within the European labour market. It also seems clear that because of their potential to create barriers to employee mobility, if the other Member States choose to increase the role played by occupational pension schemes in the overall levels of pension provision provided in their territories, this could make considerably more difficult the exercise of one of the fundamental freedoms of the single market, the free movement of workers.

As might be expected, the potential of occupational pension schemes to create barriers to the free movement of workers is not something of which the Community legislator has remained ignorant. However, there is no equivalent of Regulation 1408/71 for occupational provision, despite the fact that Article 51 EC[155] is not limited to **statutory** social security schemes and that the Commission has carried out numerous studies on the topic. During the 1960s in the period after the predecessor of Regulation 1408/71 - Regulation 3 - was put in place, the Commission carried out a study of occupational pension provision in certain sectors of the then six Member States.[156] It concluded in general that the rigidities which occupational provision introduced into labour markets created the

---

[155]   See the discussion in Chapter 5.

[156]   Commission of the European Communities, *De aanvullende regelingen van de sociale zekerheid in de landen van de EEG* (hereafter *De aanvullende regelingen*), serie sociale politiek number 15, 1966, Luxemburg.

same obstacles to labour mobility within states as it did between them. It was only *vis-à-vis* waiting periods that the Commission foresaw particular problems for migrant workers. No action was however undertaken in response to this report, nor was anything done in respect of the recommendations of the Economic and Social Committee[157] and the European Parliament[158] that a coordinating regime be designed for occupational pension rights.

The next occasion on which the subject of the barriers to mobility created by occupational pension schemes was on the Community agenda was pursuant to the 1974 Social Action Programme.[159] The Council asked that the Commission report to it on the subject of the coordination of supplementary schemes for employees migrating within the Community. Pursuant to this the Commission proposed that a tripartite work group be convened to produce a report about the possibilities of bringing such coordination about.[160] However, again no proposals were forthcoming.

The subject was then basically ignored at Community level until the late 1980s. In 1989, eleven of the then twelve Member States adopted the Community Charter of the Fundamental Rights of Workers.[161] The Commission's Action Programme[162] designed to implement this initiative, contains some 47 proposals for measures to realise these rights. One of the areas highlighted by the Commission in the communication which accompanied this Action Programme was the obstacles to employee mobility caused by the lack of coordination of

---

[157]   PB 1967 1009/67.

[158]   PB 1968 C 10/30.

[159]   See the brief discussion in Chapter 3.

[160]   See Bull EC Supp. 2/74 at p. 28.

[161]   On which subject, see B. Bercusson, "The European Community's Charter of Fundamental Social Rights of Workers", 53 MLR (1990), 624-642; P. Watson, "The Community Social Charter", 28 CML Rev. (1991), 37-68; B. Hepple, "The Implementation of the Community Charter of Fundamental Social Rights", 53 MLR (1990), 643-654; Wedderburn, "The Social Charter in Britain - Labour Law and Labour Courts?", 54 MLR (1991), 1-47.

[162]   COM (89) 568 final.

occupational provision.[163] It commissioned a number of studies and reports on the subject of occupational pension provision in the EU,[164] but legislative proposals have been slow.[165]

The most recent statement on this issue is to be found in the Commission's Medium-Term Social Action programme. This stated that it was going to propose a draft Directive on the transferability of occupational pension rights to deal with the problems faced by migrant workers. However, even without it being published, the proposal generated such fierce opposition that the Commission felt obliged to retreat.[166] At the same time, a high-level working group chaired by Madame Veil has been convened to consider whether such a piece of legislation is even necessary.[167]

---

[163]   At p. 25 it observed that "The absence of coordination may cause workers to lose rights and may form an obstacle to the development of the occupational mobility of workers between the different Member States; this is especially true in the case of middle and upper managerial workers whose total social protection is more dependent on supplementary schemes. The diversity and multiplicity of supplementary schemes - also on the national level - makes the transferability of rights a very complicated matter. This is why, after studying the problem, the Commission intends - as a first stage - to stimulate debate by means of a communication and, on this basis, may propose appropriate measures. Furthermore, on a more general level, supplementary protection is taking on greater importance in relation to statutory schemes in several Member States."

[164]   Working Paper (*Completing the Internal Market for Private Retirement Provision*, XV(90)224); Communication on *Supplementary Social Security Schemes: The Role of Occupational Pension Schemes in the Social Protection of Workers and their Implications for Freedom of Movement*, SEC (91) 1332 final; Working Paper on Cross-Border Membership of Occupational Schemes (XV/2040-1/92); *Supplementary Pensions*, loc. cit.

[165]   See however, the draft Directive concerning the freedom of management and investment of funds held by institutions for retirement provision (O.J. 1991 C 312. COM (91) 301). For detailed discussion of some of the issues, see G.S. Zavvos, "Pension fund liberalization and the future of retirement financing in Europe", 31 CML Rev. (1994), 609-630; Philip Davis loc. cit. at pp. 127-229). However, this has now been withdrawn by the Commission after opposition in the Council proved insurmountable.

[166]   "Commission reconsiders Directive on occupational pension rights", EIRR 266, (1996) 3; *Agence Europe*, 9 February 1996 at 10. "Brussels fails on pensions portability" *Financial Times*, 8 February 1996, p. 2 citing German opposition in particular as the reason for failure.

[167]   See *Agence Europe* 25 January 1996 at 12; *Agence Europe*, 9 February 1996 at 10; *Agence Europe*, 10 February 1996 at 10.

It therefore appears that the likelihood of Community legislation being adopted to deal with the obstacles created for employee mobility by the operation of occupational pension schemes is as remote as ever.

We have however already seen in Chapters 4 and 5 that on occasion the Court has acted to resolve an issue in relation to which the Council has been unable to reach agreement. As the preceding discussion makes clear, it seems far from clear that the Council will be able (or willing) to agree to any legislative initiatives in this field. It would therefore seem appropriate before drawing any final conclusions in this Chapter to consider whether there are any clues in the case law of the Court that litigation might be a more fruitful strategy to pursue.

In discussing this issue, it would seem appropriate first to consider whether the operation of occupational pension schemes does in fact erect a barrier to the exercise of the right to free movement which is contrary to the Treaty. Thereafter, assuming that this question is answered in the affirmative, we will move on to consider whether the case law provides any potential solutions.

The main features of the legal regime governing the free movement of workers have already been outlined in Chapter 5. In essence, a migrant worker enjoys the right not to be discriminated against on ground of his nationality. In the situation at issue we must first consider whether the obstacles which the operation of occupational pension schemes erect to the exercise of the right of free movement, are contrary to Article 48 EC.

As the discussion in this Chapter reveals, the international migrant suffers disadvantage in terms of his occupational pension accrual by virtue of the fact, first, that there is no aggregation of periods of insurance completed with other employers for the purposes of completing a vesting or waiting period with a new employer. Second, an international migrant with an SSB in the scheme operated by his previous employer will be disadvantaged as compared to someone who remains faithful to that employer. Third, the international mgirant may not be permitted to transfer his accrued rights abroad, and if he is permitted to do so, there is a possibility that he will be taxed on the sum transferred. Finally, that which can be purchased by transferring rights is not usually exactly the same as the rights to which the individual would have been entitled in the scheme which he was leaving.

In the first two situations described - lack of aggregation and the SSB - the international migrant is treated in exactly the same manner as an individual changing employment within a single Member State. In relation to transfers, it is only where an individual is required to pay tax on the sum which he seeks to transfer abroad that his situation differs from the individual changing job within the state. In the discussion a distinction will accordingly be drawn between the first three situations, and the final situation, that where the individual is taxed on the value of the sum he seeks to transfer abroad.

It has been stated that the essence of the rights granted to migrant workers by Article 48 EC is the right not to suffer discrimination on grounds of nationality. It is clear that the treatment afforded to the international migrant is precisely the same as that afforded to a job-changer within the state. However, it appears from recent case law that the scope of Article 48 extends even to such situations.

In *Bosman*,[168] the Court was asked about the compatibility with EC law of the transfer system operating in European professional football.[169] In so far as is relevant for these purposes, the rules restricted the free movement of professional footballers seeking to change club within a state as much as footballers seeking to work abroad. The Court took the view that the rules

> "directly affect players' access to the employment market in
> other Member States and are thus capable of impeding freedom
> of movement for workers"[170]

and this conclusion was not affected by the fact that similar restrictions faced individuals seeking to change club within a single state. This suggests that the Court has altered the focus of its case law from eradicating discrimination to eradicating obstacles to market access.[171] If that is indeed the case, all rules which make it more difficult for an individual to exercise his right of free movement fall within the scope of the Treaty norm. Consequently, the rules on

---

[168]   Case C-415/93, cited *supra*.

[169]   For detailed discussion, see the opinion of Advocate General Lenz.

[170]   Case C-415/93, *Bosman*, cited *supra* at para. 103.

[171]   See the observations of S. Weatherill, "After *Keck*: Some thoughts on clarifying the clarification", 33 CML Rev. (1996), forthcoming.

vesting, treatment of SSBs and transfers would seem *prima facie* to form an obstacle to the exercise by individuals of their right to free movement.

The question which now arises is whether objective justification can be found for the rules. If they pursue a legitimate aim, are compatible with the Treaty (in the sense of not discriminating on grounds of nationality) and are appropriate and necessary to the achievement of the objective which they are designed to serve, they may not be incompatible with the Treaty.

Examining first, vesting and waiting periods, in the UK and the Netherlands, employers face obligations to preserve the value of accrued rights of those who have belonged to the scheme for at least one or two years. By contrast, the German employer may face this obligation only after the employee has been with him for 10 years. If vesting and waiting periods are regarded as a method of protecting the employer from the expense of having to administer a large number of small benefits, it can be argued that the 10 year requirement in Germany is not an appropriate and necessary measure to take to pursue this goal, particularly in the light of practice in the other two Member States. On the other hand, German employers will argue that occupational pensions play a different social role in Germany to that which they play in the UK and the Netherlands, in part as a consequence of the differences between the statutory schemes in place in these three jurisdictions. In the specifically German context, occupational pension benefits are not so much pay in the hands of the employee, but a *qui pro quo* for *Betriebstreue*, company loyalty.[172] In that situation, particularly since the majority of German schemes are non-contributory, it is not inconceivable that the Court would find the longer period required in Germany appropriate and necessary to the objective pursued.

The disadvantage suffered in relation to SSBs and transfers,[173] is a consequence of the way in which occupational pension schemes have been

---

[172] See the discussion in Chapter 2 and the literature cited. Note that an analogy with seniority perks would not seem to be appropriate here. An individual is offered the perk after the requisite period. In German occupational pension schemes, all employees in the class covered are offered membership of the occupational scheme. It is only once the 10 year period has elapsed that they can enforce any rights.

[173] Ignoring for now the taxation of transfers.

designed. The benefits received reflect the salary on the basis of which the rights are accrued. When accrual stops, the salary is frozen[174] and the loss which the international migrant suffers can be seen to be a necessary consequence of the scheme being salary-related. As a result, it can be concluded that this aspect of the disadvantaging of international migrants does not breach Article 48.

The taxation of transfer values on leaving a Member State to work elsewhere in the EU would seem on its face to constitute a breach of the free movement provisions. In this respect, the Court's decision in *Wielockx*[175] would seem effectively to prevent the Member States from arguing that the coherence of their fiscal systems depends upon taxing the sum of money when it leaves their jurisdiction, unless the Double Tax Treaty in question makes specific provision for taxation to take place at this point.[176]

It can consequently be concluded that all the features of occupational pension provision which were identified in this Chapter as posing possible barriers to employee mobility can be justified and consequently do not breach Article 48. As such, it seems unlikely that Article 48 could be used to plug these gaps in the protection of the international migrant.

However, another avenue is also open to the Court. It will be recalled that Article 51 obliges the Council to adopt the measures in the field of social security which are necessary to realise the free movement of workers. Nothing in the text of Article 51 indicates that the obligation is limited to statutory social security schemes, and excludes occupational social security. Indeed, the express exclusion from Regulation 1408/71 of occupational social security can indeed be seen to support this interpretation.[177]

It will be recalled that Regulation 1408/71 also excludes from its scope the social security schemes which apply to civil servants. This exclusion was the

---

174   Albeit that there is an obligation to index SSBs between the end of pensionable employment and pensionable age in the UK.

175   Case C-80/94, cited *supra* and discussed in Chapter 5 above.

176   See the UK-Netherlands Double Tax Treaty discussed above.

177   See the discussion in Chapter 5.

subject of a recent reference. A Greek doctor sought to have periods of employment in a German state hospital aggregated with period of employment in similar hospitals in Greece for the puposes of obtaining the right to pay contributions in repect of all these years. Payment of these contributions would entitle him to an old age pension under the scheme rules. His request was refused by the authorities in Greece on the basis that the special schemes for civil servants were excluded from the scope of Regulation 1408/71 and they were accordingly under no obligation to aggregate with period in Greece, periods of employment completed abroad.

However, the Court found differently. It recognised that the obligation imposed on the Council by Article 51 was one of result, and that the Council enjoyed some discretion as to how it brought this objective about. It upheld the validity of the exclusion of civil service schemes from Regulation 1408/71, recognising that at the time when the Regulation was drafted to attempt coordination of that type of scheme also would have been a huge undertaking, in addition to that already being attempted. However, the Court continued, this could not justify the Council's inaction in the intervening period. Although the Court recognised the Council's margin of discretion, it applied itself to the applicant's situation. In this case, all that he was requesting was for account to be taken of periods spent abroad (i.e. aggregation). This does not require legislation. Aggregation is one of the techniques mentioned in Article 51, and consequently, Mr Vougioukas' problem could be solved by a simple application of Article 51 to his case.

Is it conceivable that the Court would come to a similar conclusion in relation to occupational pension schemes? Of the obstacles to employee mobility which have been identified here, this technique would seem most appropriate in relation to vesting or waiting periods. A direct application of Article 51 could be used to oblige employers to take account of periods of employment carried out abroad.

But would the Court follow such a path? It is worth noting that the facts of *Vougioukas* were quite specific: the applicant sought aggregation to qualify him for the facility of paying contributions to gain entitlement under a particular social security scheme. It did not appears to entail any (substantial) financial consequences for the Member State concerned. By contrast, aggregation of periods of employment abroad would require employers to fund individuals' pension benefits at an earlier date than would otherwise be the case, particularly in Germany. This would represent a potentially significant financial burden for the employers concerned, particularly where the schemes in question were non-contributory (i.e. where the entire financial burden would fall upon the employer). While it might be considered acceptable to impose (more or less) far-reaching financial obligations on states in this way,[178] it is suggested that it is considerably more difficult to do so in relation to employers, particularly where, as here, they are under no obligation to offer their employees access to membership of an occupational scheme, Ultimately - and essentially unlike the state in relation to its statutory scheme - the employer can simply wind the scheme up if they consider that the obligations imposed by the legislator are too onerous. For this reason, therefore, it seems unlikely that the obstacles to employee mobility created by vesting and waiting periods - especially in Germany - would be eradicated by direct application of Article 51 EC. Positive legislation would instead be required.

The other obstacles which were identified - SSBs and transfers - could not be eradicated by a "mere" direct application of the principles of Articles 48-51 EC. Rather, some form of positive legislation would seem to be required because of the complexity of the subject-matter, which takes us back to the Council which appears politically unable to act in this field.

Consequently, it must be concluded that neither the Council nor the Court seems likely to act in the near future to eradicate the obstacles to labour mobility which are formed by the rules of occupational pension schemes. Therefore, it would seem that occupational pension schemes have not yet adequately adapted to the challenges posed by the international migrant worker.

---

[178]   The social security scheme is an aspect of the state's social policy. It cannot simply be abolished on a political whim. Additionally, because of their method of financiang, the financial burden falls on all contributors to the state scheme, and is consequently minute, and an expression of the social solidarity which the scheme ultimately embodies.

PART IV

CONCLUSIONS

SUMMARY AND CONCLUSIONS

7.1   Introduction

In Chapter 1 this research project was delimited and the questions which it was designed to answer were formulated. It was stated that a number of developments which had taken place over the last decades and which are predicted for the decades to come are posing fundamental challenges to the way in which pensions are provided in the countries of the EU.

First, the increased numbers of (married) women engaging in paid employment for significant periods of their lives and their rejection of the subordinate role to which they were traditionally consigned by social security posed a challenge to pension schemes which, as the discussion, particularly in Chapters 3 and 4 reveals, typically treated them as financially dependent upon their spouse. These developments, coupled with the rising divorce rate[1] which in fact deprived many women of this form of financial support, required that pension schemes adapt to provide adequate pensions to women, as well as to their more usual focus of attention, men.

Second, it was stated that the market had internationalised, deliberately so in Europe where an increasing number of states had joined the European Communities (now European Union) one of the objectives of which was to create a single market within which the factors of production - including crucially in this context workers - are able to move freely. This development required pension schemes to adapt to the fact that an individual might not work within a single state for his entire working life, and indeed, might even retire abroad. As the discussion, particularly in Chapter 5, reveals, the pension schemes created in the period after

---

[1]   For example, Backes, loc. cit. at p. 268 indicates that around 25% of marriages concluded in 1970 are expected to end in divorce.

the second world war were territorially limited. They were concerned only with those within the jurisdiction of the state which had created them, and were not designed to deal with the situation of someone who worked in a number of different states. So the second challenge to which pension schemes were required to respond, was the increased internationalisation of the market. A system had to be designed which allowed the international migrant to accrue adequate pension entitlement.

Finally, the demographic predictions as to the future age composition of the population were discussed. Statistics indicate that not only are people living longer[2] but that in the future a larger number of people will be in retirement at a given time.[3] However, at the same time as the retired population increases, statistics indicate that the size of the working population will decrease as a consequence of the drop in the fertility rate in the countries of the EU.[4] This has consequences for pensions because not only will an increased number of individuals claim benefits, but unless other factors change,[5] they will do so for a longer period of time. This means that the future pension bill will be greater than it currently is, which of itself can be seen to be a matter of concern. However, what has transformed this issue into a fundamental challenge to pensions in the EU, is that the relative shrinking in the size of the working population means that a smaller group of individuals will be asked to pay for these benefits.

The reasons why the smaller group will be asked to pay for the benefits of the larger group of individuals is because of the method of financing which the Member States of the EU chose for their pension systems. The "Pay-As-You-Go" method was advantageous when the schemes were introduced because it enabled

---

[2]   Life expectancy has increased from an EU average of 67 in 1950 to 74.4 in 1980, Besseling and Zeeuw, loc. cit. at p. 25.

[3]   The dependency ratio is set to drop from 21.2 in 1990 to 42.8 in 2040, Besseling and Zeeuw, loc. cit. at p. 20.

[4]   It has fallen from 2.6 children per female to 1.5, CEPS Working Party Report No 9, *Financing Retirement in Europe*, loc. cit. at p. 11.

[5]   I.e. increasing pensionable age. As the discussion in Chapter 1 indicates, this is not an easy change to accomplish.

schemes to be introduced quickly and to benefit the immediate pensioners. Equally, the funding vehicle chosen was able to reflect increases in the prosperity of society while the booming birthrate allowed all of this to be achieved at a relatively low cost. However, as was discussed in Chapter 1, given the drop in the birth rate, the only method of continuing the current system is either to increase the levels of contributions paid by the employees and/or the state, or to cut benefit levels. For the reasons discussed there, neither approach has been found particularly attractive. At the same time, the constraints imposed by EMU, together in some jurisdictions with ideological considerations, have persuaded some Member States to consider fundamentally reforming their pension systems. This challenge is the final one facing the pension schemes put in place by the Member States in the period following the second world war.

As is discussed in greater detail in Chapter 1, a variety of different solutions have been proposed to deal with this challenge. A feature which many such proposals share is that the role played by pre-funded employer based, "occupational" pension schemes is to be increased and indeed, surveying the countries of the EU, it is clear that many states are currently seeking ways of doing just this. However, whatever solution is found to deal with the perceived deficiencies of the current pension system, it will be necessary for that system also to be able to address the needs of women and international migrants. The first question which this research seeks to answer is accordingly, to what extent occupational pension schemes are currently able to address the needs of women and to ensure that they accrue adequate levels of retirement income. Second, it seeks an answer to the question whether occupational pension schemes will enable the international migrant worker to accrue an adequate pension. These questions were considered in detail in Chapters 4 and 6. In Chapters 3 and 5, the same questions were addressed, but in the context of the statutory schemes which some propose occupational schemes should (partly) replace.

In the next two sections of this Chapter, the findings of Chapters 4 and 6 will be summarised along with the conclusions drawn in Chapters 3 and 5. These summaries should allow some conclusions to be drawn in the final section of this Chapter as to whether the two groups with which this research is concerned would be better served by statutory or by occupational provision.

7.2   Pensions and Women

7.2.1   STATUTORY SCHEMES

In Chapter 3 the treatment which statutory pension schemes afford to women was
outlined. First, however, a brief summary was given of the main ways in which
pension schemes have tended to discriminate against women, largely as a
consequence of the fact that they assume that a married woman would and indeed
should be financially dependent upon her spouse. It was stated that the main
impetus for change has been the EC's social security Directive. Before providing
a description of its main provisions, the EC's competence in the social sphere was
discussed.

In discussing the Directive, it became abundantly clear that the
Community legislator - and in turn the ECJ when interpreting its provisions - had
been reasonably conservative in its approach. The Directive in fact has relatively
modest aims - to eradicate some direct discrimination against married women from
statutory social security schemes. Nevertheless, differentiation may continue in
relation to the provision of survivor's pensions and pensionable age. Additionally,
it continues to be permissible to grant advantages to those who have spent time out
of the labour market for the purposes of bringing up children. Additionally, derived
entitlements for wives continue to be legal, as does increasing long term old age
benefits to take account of a dependent wife. Finally, the rights of individuals who,
prior to the Directive's entry into force elected not to contribute to the social
security scheme because they would be able to benefit from derived entitlements,
are to be respected by the Directive. So although the Directive states that its aim
is to ensure the "progressive implementation, in the field of social security" of the
principle of equal treatment, in essence the exclusions which it contains allow the
Member States to leave in place the vast majority of structures and provisions
through which women have been encouraged to become financially dependent upon
their spouses.

Other features of the Directive limit its potential for ensuring the
eradication of discriminatory social security provisions. Thus, indirect
discrimination may continue if the Member States can demonstrate to the
satisfaction of the relevant judicial body that the measure is appropriate and

necessary to the pursuit of a legitimate aim of social policy. So for example, the ECJ has recently determined that German legislation which excludes from compulsory pension insurance those working fewer than 15 hours per week and earning less than a certain amount, is not incompatible with the Directive, despite the fact that the overwhelming majority of those excluded from insurance by this rule are women.

Nevertheless, as emerged from the discussion of statutory provision in that Chapter, the Directive played an important role in persuading the Dutch government to alter their old age pension legislation to grant married women a previously absent independent right to an old age pension. The Dutch and German judiciaries have insisted that their legislatures alter their statutes on survivor's pensions to eradicate their discriminatory features. Additionally, the UK and German governments have recently announced plans for equalising pensionable ages over the next few decades. As a consequence, the most obvious forms of discrimination in statutory pension schemes, but those which the Directive did not affect, have been, or are in the process of being eradicated.

This of itself ought to ensure that the women retiring in the future will receive better levels of pensions in their own right. The provisions which have been introduced to enable women to continue to accrue pension rights while on maternity leave, and while caring for young children ought to play an important role in this respect.

However, an important limitation in the scope of the Directive is its exclusive concern with those who participate in paid employment. Women who have ceased paid employment to care for dependents lose the protection of the Directive until they again seek to undertake paid work. More importantly, in the *Nolte* and *Megner and Scheffel* judgments discussed in Chapter 3, the Court took the view that relatively high hours thesholds - coupled with low earnings - could be set for membership of statutory pension schemes. As a result, many women working part-time can lawfully be excluded from the opportunity of accruing pension entitlement. The Directive offers such women no aid in obtaining access to scheme membership, focusing only upon those who have already managed to clear that particular hurdle. Statutory schemes now offer that group of women the possibility of accruing an adequate level of pension, but because of such thresholds continue to be unavailable to significant numbers of women[6] who seem likely to be poor and/or financially dependent on retirement.

It can therefore be concluded that as a result of recent reforms, women who have access to the statutory schemes operating in these jurisdictions ought to be able to accrue adequate levels of pensions.

7.2.2   OCCUPATIONAL SCHEMES

In Chapter 4 the issue of occupational pension schemes and women was addressed. As that discussion reveals, occupational pension schemes have already been required to introduce wholesale changes into their rules and operation to deal with the increased economic activity of women and the change in perception as to women's role which has accompanied this. In this context, EC law has played a very significant role. The ECJ has held that occupational pensions amount to pay in the hands of employees and consequently that they are caught by Article 119 EC which requires equality of pay between women and men.[7] This of itself has not always been the case in the Member States and in particular in relation to some of the details of schemes, its consequences have been far-reaching. For example, the equality principle contained in Article 119 has been found by the Court to require that the conditions upon which individuals are granted access to scheme membership have to be equal as between the sexes,[8] something which the discussion demonstrates was by no means common practice in any of the jurisdictions examined.

However, it is not only the access granted to occupational pension schemes which has to be equal as between comparable male and female workers. Another condition which is commonly set before an individual can obtain entitlement to a benefit under a scheme, is the payment of a contribution. The

---

[6]   For example, in the UK in 1990 some 2.25 million women were estimated to have been excluded from the compulsory contributory social security scheme because their earnings fell below the LEL. See McCrudden and Black, loc. cit. at p. 172.

[7]   Inter alia, Case C-262/88, *Barber* cited *supra*.

[8]   Inter alia Case 170/84, *Bilka* cited *supra*.

Court has recently stated very clearly that employee contributions to occupational pension schemes constitute pay within the meaning of Article 119.[9] The general rule in relation to employer contributions appears to be that they also fall within the concept of pay,[10] but that where they reflect the use of actuarial tables which differentiate between women and men, they need not be equal.[11] Finally, the benefits paid out by occupational schemes have to be equal as between women and men, payable from the same age[12] and if pensions are automatically paid to the female survivors of male employees, similar provision must be made in relation to the male survivors of female employees.[13]

The discussion in Chapter 4 appeared to suggest that equality law will have significantly improved pension provision for women. However, this conclusion becomes considerably less positive if the German situation is examined. It is unlikely that German women will accrue similar levels of occupational pension provision to those accrued by their Dutch and British counterparts, leaving aside for a moment the different roles currently played by occupational provision in Germany on the one hand and the UK and the Netherlands on the other.[14] The root of the explanation of why it is unlikely that German women will recoup the same degree of benefit from the various requirements of equality law is to be found in German occupational pension law. As was discussed in Chapter 2, most German pension schemes allow rights to vest in employees only after the employee has belonged to the scheme for ten years and is at least 35 years old on leaving the scheme. Although as a consequence of equality law, German employers are obliged to offer women and men access to the same scheme under the same terms and

---

[9]   Case C-200/91, *Coloroll*, cited *supra* at para. 80.

[10]   See Case 192/85, *Newstead*, cited *supra* at para. 14.

[11]   Case C-152/91, *Neath*, cited *supra* at para. 32; Case C-200/91, *Coloroll*, cited *supra*, at para. 81.

[12]   For example, Case C-262/88, *Barber*, cited *supra* at para. 32.

[13]   Case C-109/91, *Ten Oever*, cited *supra* at para. 14.

[14]   See the discussions in Chapters 1 and 2.

conditions, the ten year period, combined with the typically interrupted employment careers of women, suggests that German women are unlikely to accrue substantial levels of pension benefits. This suggests that, in this respect at least, the German model would require some further adjustment before women will be able to accrue significant levels of pension benefit.

As this brief summary indicates, EC equality law has required that schemes change their practice in a large number of ways. Many discriminatory practices which will have prevented women from accruing adequate levels of pensions in the past will have been eradicated, and consequently, this case law ought significantly to contribute to an improvement in the occupational pension provision made to women. However, at the end of Chapter 4 an assessment was made of the extent to which these measures seemed likely to be adequate to ensure that the levels of pension accrued by women match those accrued by men. It was stated that occupational pension schemes have traditionally been designed to reward long periods of full-time employment - often relatively highly paid - with a single employer between finishing full-time education and reaching pensionable age. On the other hand, the employment carried out by women is often low-paid, part-time and peppered with periods of economic inactivity, generally as a consequence of caring for dependents.

In this respect, women's employment patterns can be seen to resemble in one respect those of migrant workers in that they are interrupted rather than continuous. In Chapter 6 the various devices which the legislatures in the UK, the Netherlands and Germany have taken to ensure that interruption of employment does not lead to the undue penalisation of the accrued pension rights of the early leaver were examined and assessed. Since women's employment shares certain characteristics with this employment, it would seem appropriate, before drawing any conclusions as to the extent to which occupational pension schemes are able to provide women with adequate levels of pensions, to consider whether these reforms will improve the pension position of women.

The first feature of occupational pension scheme rules which was examined was the use of waiting or vesting periods, something which may also be effected by setting age thresholds for membership. Women are more likely than men to work on fixed-term contracts,[15] and it can therefore be expected that requiring a particular minimum period of employment to be completed (or age reached) before rights can be accrued (or before accrual can begin) will prevent many women on such contracts from accruing occupational pension rights.

For this reason, it can be argued that the use of such conditions amounts to a form of indirect discrimination against women.[16] The question which then has to be answered is whether the use of such periods can be regarded as objectively justified by reasons which have nothing to do with sex discrimination.[17] The justification most commonly adduced for providing that a particular period of membership must be completed before rights vest is to prevent the scheme from having to administer a large number of very small pensions.[18] While some force can probably be given to this line of argument, it can only justify relatively short vesting periods. It would certainly not seem to be of avail to German employers seeking to justify a 10 year vesting period. Additionally, where legislation provides for individuals to be able to transfer their rights to other pension schemes, the spectre of having to administer a large number of small benefits can be seen to recede, which in turn raises doubts as to this justification.

A waiting period, on the other hand, can be justified by reference to the fact that the pension is a form of reward for loyalty to the company. As such, it is possible to argue that an employer is perfectly within his rights only to offer this higher form of pay to employees who have demonstrated a particular level of loyalty to his undertaking and consequently, it can be said that where the pension is a higher form of pay offered to employees after they have been with the undertaking for a certain number of years, this can be justified.

Finally, in relation to age thresholds, the objective served by such

---

[15] See for example, the statistics cited in LRD Booklet, *Temporary Workers*, July 1995 at pp. 4-5; also the observations of McCrudden and Black, loc. cit. at p. 171.

[16] See the discussion in Chapter 4.

[17] See for example, Case 170/84, *Bilka*, cited *supra*.

[18] As the discussion in Chapter 6 reveals, providing for long vesting periods enables the employer to reduce the overall cost of providing a pension because he is able to avoid providing a pension for workers who are with him for a short period of time.

requirements would seem to be related to excluding employees whose wages fall below a particular level from the benefits of membership, because their needs are deemed to be satisfied by payments from the statutory scheme. In this case, it can be argued that the measure is not appropriate and necessary to the achievement of the objective, and consequently a breach of the proportionality principle.[19] Consequently, if a scheme wishes to exclude those for whom the statutory scheme would provide an adequate level of income replacement from membership of the occupational scheme, a more appropriate method of doing this would seem to be to set a lower earnings threshold for scheme membership.

In conclusion, it can be argued that because women are more likely than men to be employed on short-term contracts, vesting periods and age thresholds can be expected to work to their disadvantage and contribute to the poor levels of occupational pension benefits to which they accrue entitlement. The analysis also suggests that these provisions cannot be justified by factors which exclude discrimination grounds of sex. By contrast, it does seem possible to find an objective justification for the use of waiting periods.

This particular practice seems likely to preclude many women from obtaining vested right to occupational scheme benefits. However, once they have such rights, the reforms discussed in the previous Chapter ought to ensure that they are not unduly penalised by any decision to change or temporarily cease employment. The obligation to maintain SSBs will ensure that they do not forfeit their accrued rights on leaving the employment relationship in question. Similarly, the provisions on transfers in place in the UK and the Netherlands will allow women who have decided to take a career break to transfer the rights which have been maintained in the old scheme to the scheme run by the new employer. However, as with the situation in relation to equality, the extremely long vesting periods which German employers are permitted to operate will preclude many women from being able to reap the benefits of these reforms.

It can consequently be said that, in part as a result of the requirements of EC law, occupational pension schemes have already been required to introduce far-

---

[19]   See the discussion in G. de Búrca, "The Principle of Proportionality and its Application in EC Law", 13 YEL (1993), 105-150; T.C. Hartley, *The Foundations of European Community Law*, 3rd ed., Oxford, 1994 at pp. 155-156.

reaching alterations to adjust their rules to remove provisions designed to operate to the disadvantage of women. Equally, the reforms introduced to prevent occupational schemes from hindering employee mobility ought also to result in women being able to accrue higher levels of pension benefits. This is not however to say that schemes have as yet adapted adequately to women's participation in paid employment, in the sense of being able to provide women with adequate levels of income on retirement.

It has frequently been stressed that schemes are generally designed to reward highly-skilled/highly paid individuals. Statistics continue stubbornly to demonstrate that the majority of women workers are crowded into low-paid, low-skilled employment.[20] Consequently, one reason why women do so poorly in terms of accruing occupational pensions is that they do not belong to the category of employees that the schemes reward.[21]

A second characteristic of the employment which occupational schemes are generally designed to reward is that it is long, full-time and uninterrupted. Again, statistics demonstrate that women's employment patterns are anything but that, peppered all too often with periods out of paid employment to care for children and other dependents.[22] They change and interrupt their employment and

---

[20] See for example the discussion in I. Bruegel, "Women's Employment, Legislation and the Labour Market", in Lewis (ed.), loc. cit. at pp. 130-169; C. Buswell, "Training Girls to be Low-Paid Women", in Glendinning and Millar (eds.), loc. cit. at pp. 79-94; S. Lonsdale, "Patterns of Paid Work", in Glendinning and Millar (eds.), loc. cit. at pp. 95-109. For the European context, see the discussion in *Social Europe*, Supp. 4/94 at pp. 154-192.

[21] German research, which is echoed by UK and Dutch experience, reveals that the likelihood that a firm offers employees membership of an occupational pension scheme increases with the size of the firm. Consequently, it is relevant that 41% of German women, as compared to 20% of German men work for a firm with fewer than 5 employees. 27% of men and 14% of women work for firms with more than 500 employees; see Allmendinger et al, loc. cit. at p. 149. In the Netherlands, it appears that in firms with fewer than 10 employees, 43.8% of employees were without occupational provision; firms with between 10 and 49 employees, 20.7% had no pension scheme. Employers without pension schemes generally employ proportionately more women and part-time employees; see Kraamwinkel, loc. cit. at p. 37.

[22] For example, Joshi in Glendinning and Millar, loc. cit. at p. 115 has calculated the impact on average lifetime workforce membership of different numbers of children. One child was calculated to reduce full-time employment by 7.16 years, and an extra 2.83 years of part-time employment would be undertaken. For a woman with three children, this figures rise

are consequently penalised by the occupational scheme for their failure to adhere to the pattern of employment taken as typical for the purposes of scheme design. As such, an increase in the role played by occupational pension schemes in overall retirement income provision will leave women with inadequate levels of pension if schemes do not adapt to their different employment patterns. If women are to be enabled to accrue adequate levels of pension, schemes have to devise a method of recognising (crediting) that women typically spend some time out of employment or in part-time employment as a consequence of childbearing/childrearing activities. It is only when this mechanism is in place that women will in fact enjoy the same opportunity as men to accrue adequate levels of pension benefits. However, at present, this remains an area in which there is considerable scope for improvement. It can therefore be concluded that the changes which occupational pension schemes have been required to introduce do not go far enough to ensure that women will be able to accrue adequate levels of retirement income and that occupational pension schemes have not yet adequately adapted their rules to enable women to accrue adequate pension benefits.

7.3   Pensions and International Migrants

7.3.1   STATUTORY PENSIONS AND MIGRANTS

In Chapter 5, the focus was upon the statutory schemes which were put in place by the Member States of the EU in the period following the second world war. They typically provide benefits to those resident or working within their territory and who satisfy for the relevant period a whole variety of conditions. Thus for example, the UK requires an individual to have contributed to the scheme for at least 25% of his or her working life. In Germany, an individual has to have been insured for at least 5 years to gain entitlement to benefit. However, as the schemes

---

to 10.44 fewer years of full-time employment and an extra 3.10 years of part-time employment. According to her research, the mother of an infant is very unlikely to have paid work, while the mother of a child of school age has a 43% chance of being in some form of employment, usually part-time. Similar conclusions are reached in relation to Germany by Rolf, loc. cit. at pp. 177-185.

were originally designed, their rules operated in such a way as to preclude individuals who moved to work or possibly even live in another jurisdiction from accruing rights, or maintaining rights which had already been accrued.

In the period subsequent to the second world war, the market has internationalised, particularly in Europe, where an increasing number of states have collaborated in creating first the common, then the internal market and now the European Union. One of the basic pillars upon which this endeavour has been based has been the free movement of workers. However, as was discussed in Chapter 5, without some method of ensuring that individuals are protected against the loss of social security rights when they move to seek or take up employment abroad, a significant obstacle would have been placed in the path of individuals who wished to make use of this right.

The EC has acted to ensure that this situation does not come about, and has put in place a complex but effective system which co-ordinates the autonomous social security schemes of the individual Member States. As a result, Member States are obliged to take account of periods of insurance completed in other Member States where this is necessary for an individual to qualify for a benefit within a particular jurisdiction.[23] Thus, he is assured that he will not "lose" periods of insurance which he has completed, simply as a consequence of changing the state in which he is employed. However, to prevent the migrant from benefiting unduly from his decision to exercise his right to free movement, provisions are also in place according to which the individual's entitlement can be apportioned between the various Member States in question.

In this way, the autonomous social security schemes of the Member States are left virtually intact while at the same time, a safety net is created for the social security rights of the migrant worker. Directly discriminatory provisions of social

---

[23]   Cornelissen, op. cit. at 451 gives the example of an individual who works for 14 years in Italy and for 4 years in Germany. He does not fulfil the conditions of insurance in Italy, which requires 15 to 20 years of insurance to qualify for the payment of a pension, nor those of the German scheme which requires 5 years of insurance. However, the Regulation requires that these periods be aggregated, so that for the purposes of qualifying for an Italian pension (but not in relation to its amount, where this is relevant) he is treated as having worked for 18 years in Italy, which may then enable him to qualify for benefit. Similarly, for the purposes of qualifying for the payment of a benefit under the German legislation, he is treated as if he has been insured under that scheme for 18 years.

security schemes - such as nationality requirements - are eradicated as a consequence of the Regulation. Indirectly discriminatory provisions - such as residence requirements - are in principle outlawed, but may be justified in particular cases.

7.3.2   OCCUPATIONAL PENSIONS AND MIGRANTS

In Chapter 6 the focus shifted to occupational pension schemes. By contrast to the statutory pension schemes, which are concerned only with insurance completed within the territory of the state in question, occupational pension schemes are concerned only with insurance completed with the employer or group of employers operating the scheme in question. In this respect, the focus of occupational pension schemes is on a considerably narrower group of individuals than that of the statutory scheme. Consequently, in addition potentially to creating obstacles to intra-Community employee mobility, occupational schemes could create significant rigidities in the operation of the national labour markets.

In Chapter 6 the methods traditionally utilised by occupational pension schemes to bind employees to the undertaking sponsoring or connected with the scheme were discussed. It was observed that the Member States studied had all recognised the potential of occupational schemes to obstruct the operation of their national labour markets, and had acted to counteract this. In this Chapter, these measures were analyzed from the perspective of the international migrant worker.

It has already been observed that occupational schemes have traditionally rewarded employees with long-service records, using a variety of methods discussed in Chapter 6 to penalise the early leaver. In this respect, because an occupational scheme is designed to reward employment with a specific employer, the penalisation is not specific to the international migrant, but affects equally the job-changer within the state and someone taking a career break, who will usually be a woman.

As the discussion in Chapter 6 reveals, it was previously relatively common for scheme rules to provide that an employee only obtain enforceable rights to pension benefits if he remained in the employment in question until reaching pensionable age. The freedom of employers to set the vesting and waiting periods they wish has been significantly curtailed by the national legislator, although less so in Germany than in the other jurisdictions examined. As was discussed more extensively in that Chapter, setting maximum periods of membership which an employer may require prior to granting an individual an enforceable pension right, can be seen to protect the scheme from having to administer a large number of minuscule benefits. Nevertheless, in an environment in which job-changes are increasingly common, long vesting periods - while perhaps understandable in individual cases viewed in isolation - can result in individuals accruing very low levels of occupational pension rights. This led to the conclusion being drawn that it would be a favourable development were legislatures to require that rights vest after a shorter period, perhaps a year. It was observed that the long vesting periods which characterise German pension schemes seem likely to operate to the detriment of migrant workers and pose a considerable problem in this area. It is difficult for individuals to qualify for accrued rights - and the considerable protection which they enjoy - and as such, the long vesting periods operated by German schemes seem likely to penalise both women and migrant workers.

The extent to which vesting periods penalise relatively frequent job-changers can be minimised if individuals are granted a right to transfer accrued pension rights from the scheme run by their old employer to that run by their new employer.[24] Assuming - as was discussed in Chapter 6 - that the individual can require a reasonable degree of parity between that which he has redeemed and that which he is purchasing, this allows the job-changer to buy in a number of years of service in the new scheme roughly equivalent to the rights he had in the old scheme. In such a situation the vesting period does not form an obstacle to the early leaver's accrual of rights because he has a fictitious period of membership longer than the vesting period. Consequently, in a situation in which individuals have a right to require the transfer of their accrued pension rights, vesting periods do not pose as great a threat to pension accrual as would otherwise be the case.

In the jurisdictions examined, the position *vis-à-vis* the possibility of transferring pension rights diverged from this situation in a number of respects. In Germany, for example, although transfers are possible in principle, they are impossible in practice. In the Netherlands someone must make a request within 2

---

[24]   It also offers schemes the advantage that they are relieved of SSBs.

months of commencing pension employment in another scheme whereas in the UK, an individual can request a transfer at any time until he is within one year of normal pensionable age. As discussed in Chapter 6, the provisions of the UK legislation seem more conducive to international employee mobility than those in the Netherlands.

As was also discussed in Chapter 6, the national rules on transfers have been a relatively recent response to the rigidities caused by occupational pension schemes in the labour market. Prior to that individuals who ceased to be employed in the undertaking to which the scheme related had to leave their rights in the scheme.[25] These would then be translated into a pension when the relevant age was reached. However, particularly where there is a long intervening period, or where inflation is high, the value of the benefit produced can be eroded.[26]

To ameliorate the penalty which early leavers with accrued rights face, it is necessary that some kind of mechanism be introduced to maintain the level of benefit to which he has accrued entitlement, during the period between the cessation of employment and reaching pensionable age. All three jurisdictions have legislated to require that schemes do so. For the value of the rights to be maintained in relation to general wage developments,[27] it is necessary that the rights be revalued (periodically) in line with wage developments. However, in none of the jurisdictions examined is this the case, since revaluation is merely in line with developments in prices. This results usually in a lower rate of increase being given on benefits than if revaluation was in line with wages, which of itself makes the position of the early leaver with an SSB less favourable than that of the continuing member.

Consequently, it was concluded that although the measures taken in the jurisdictions examined have significantly improved the protection afforded to the holders of SSBs, they do not entirely remove the negative consequences of leaving

---

[25]   If they enjoyed any rights at all, see the discussions concerning vesting. Alternatively, they might be entitled to a return of their (but not their employer's) contributions. This appears to have been the case in Case 192/85, *Newstead*, cited *supra*.

[26]   See the discussion on this in Chapter 6.

[27]   Although not individual wage developments.

the scheme early. For this reason, it was concluded that a transfer would usually be the preferred option, at least if the transfer took the form discussed in Chapter 6 and above. However, it is worth noting that even if individuals are granted the right to require a transfer within a particular period of commencing new pensionable employment, this does not obviate the necessity of providing for a high level of protection of the level of SSBs while they remain with the old employer. For this reason, also, even where an effective system of transfers is put in place, it remains of considerable importance that SSBs are not allowed to evaporate through the effects of price or wage inflation, because this in turn could rob even the best structured and regulated transfer scheme of its effectiveness for transferees, because what they were transferring had become worthless.

The Chapter 2 discussion of the regulatory frameworks which have been put in place round occupational pension schemes in the three Member States at issue gave considerable prominence to the role played by tax law. The examination revealed that the national legislatures had to a greater or lesser extent used tax law to encourage individuals and employers to make pension provision to supplement that provided by the state. Tax law can be and is also used to cajole individuals into following particular courses of conduct deemed desirable by the legislator. Thus in the UK and the Netherlands for example, having allowed contributions to be deductible from tax for individuals and employers, the legislator tries to ensure that the contributions are in fact used for this purpose by attaching a sanction to a premature redemption of accrued rights - taxing the sum redeemed. This helps the legislator to ensure that the money is used for pension benefits, which was the reason why contributions were made deductible in the first place.

In principle, a transfer of pension rights amounts to a redemption of the accrued rights, albeit to reinvest them in another scheme but a transfer all the same. Were transfer values to be subject to tax, the role which transfers can play in allowing the job-changer to maximise the benefits he accrues would be reduced.[28] Consequently, the legislatures examined allow transfers which satisfy a number of criteria[29] to be free of tax.

---

[28]   As the discussion in Chapter 6 reveals, this can also raise questions of double taxation.

[29]   See the discussion in Chapter 6.

A particular problem might be faced by the international migrant in this regard when he seeks to export his accrued right abroad since the legislature of the state is faced with the loss of the possibility of taxing the benefit in the future. If it seeks to tax the sum as it leaves its jurisdiction, this reduces the efficacy of transfers for the individual, and may indeed confront him with a Double Taxation problem.[30] As the discussion in the preceding Chapter reveals, Double Tax Treaties concluded between the states in question largely remove many of the difficulties which the migrant between the UK and the Netherlands might face in this regard. However, the difficulties involved in transferring rights to and from German schemes seem likely to form a major problem in this area, despite the superficially clear solution offered by the Double Taxation Treaties. Consequently it was concluded that transfers to and from Germany remained an area in which obstacles to employee mobility remained.[31]

In the conclusion of Chapter 6 it was accordingly observed that the legislatures of the Member States examined have all intervened to prevent employers using occupational pension schemes to constrain the operation of the labour market by penalising migrant workers heavily. Despite this, particularly in relation to migrants to and from Germany, considerable obstacles to adequate pension accrual remain. Even if the broad pattern adopted by the UK and the Netherlands is followed, the international migrant will face some degree of penalisation in terms of the value of accrued rights by virtue of the fact that he has decided to migrate. Consequently, it can be concluded that additional measures would have to be taken to prevent the international migrant from suffering a reduction in the value of his accrued rights on changing employment.

---

[30]   Where both the sum transferred will be taxed and the resulting benefit. See the discussion in Chapter 6.

[31]   Additionally, the different approaches to the taxation of pensions taken by the UK and the Netherlands on the one hand, and Germany on the other, means that benefits paid to residents of other Member States may also be the subject of Double Tax. See the discussion in Chapter 6 *supra*.

7.4   Which is Better?

In delimiting this research project, three challenges to the pension status quo were
identified: first, the increased levels of economic activity undertaken by women.
Second, the internationalisation of the market. Finally, the demographic predictions
as to the future balance in the population between active and non-active members.
This third challenge was described as having been interpreted by some as meaning
that fundamental reform in the method of providing pensions was required. The
reform which seems to enjoy the support of the greatest number of people is to
increase the role played by employer-based, pre-funded occupational pension
schemes. Given that the other two challenges to the status quo will have to be
addressed by whatever system is chosen as the alternative to the current statutory
schemes, in Chapter 1 it was explained that in this research the primary focus
would be upon the extent to which the replacement system would be able to
provide adequate pensions to the two types of workers whose employment patterns
were requiring that the systems erected in the post-war period be adapted. Having
carried out this research, while also outlining the ways in which statutory schemes
had been required to adapt to these developments, we are now in a position to
draw some conclusions as to whether the two groups with which we are concerned
here are more likely to accrue adequate pensions under a statutory or an
occupational scheme.

7.4.1   WOMEN

Statistics demonstrate that not only are women more likely than men to live to an
advanced old age but they are also more likely to be poor in their old age. A
significant cause of female poverty in old age is the fact that pension schemes -
both statutory and occupational - have traditionally been designed to reward men.
As the discussions in Chapters 3 and 4 demonstrate, the methods used displayed
varying degrees of subtlety. However, significant reforms have been introduced
into both regimes which, as has been discussed, ought significantly to improve the
levels of pensions accrued by women in the future.

        Is a scenario in which the role played by occupational pension schemes
increases a positive scenario when viewed from the perspective of women's

pensions, or would they be better served were States to remain faithful to the existing arrangements?

The discussions in Chapters 3 and 4 revealed that, besides more blatant forms of discrimination, the reason why women generally failed to accrue adequate levels of pensions was because of their typically interrupted career patterns. The main cause of these interruptions was childbearing and childrearing. In this respect, women would seem to be better able to accrue adequate pensions under a statutory scheme. In all three jurisdictions under consideration, some form of credit is granted to individuals who are not participating in paid employment because they are caring for a dependent child,[32] which enables such individuals to continue to accrue statutory entitlement while out of the labour market for this reason. By contrast, as the discussion in Chapter 4 reveals, occupational schemes may well be obliged to enable women on paid maternity leave to continue to accrue pension rights on the basis of their salary during this period[33] but this does not extend to cover periods in which they are not in receipt of pay. This means that women taking career breaks to care for children are more likely to suffer in terms of occupational pension accrual than in terms of statutory accrual.

This is in essence a consequence of the funding vehicles chosen for each type of pension. It will be recalled that statutory schemes are funded on a Pay-As-You-Go basis, whereas in pre-funded schemes, each individual member builds up his or her own individual fund which will be used to finance his or her pension. Statutory schemes are characterised by a degree[34] of solidarity.[35] The benefits which an individual receives are not directly related to the contributions which he or she has paid in and some redistribution takes place between the lifetime rich and the lifetime poor, perhaps even between those who spend their entire life in paid employment and those who spend periods out of paid employment. By contrast,

---

[32]   See the discussion in Chapter 3 above.

[33]   Which may be lower than that to which they are usually entitled. Consequently, the pension
        rights which they accrue during this period will be lower than would otherwise be the case.

[34]   Which varies between states, and indeed within states over time.

[35]   See the discussion in L. van Vorselen, *Solidariteit en pensioen. Denkbeelden over een
        solidair ouderdomspensioen*, Deventer, 1993.

the solidarity exhibited by occupational pension schemes is considerably less, and amounts simply to a degree of subsidisation between good and bad risks, which also takes place in the statutory scheme. Occupational schemes are not incapable of being designed to reflect solidarity; it is simply not current practice.

The constraints of the funding vehicles of the respective types of pension also explain why interruptions in careers can be accommodated within statutory schemes in a manner more favourable to the individual than is possible in occupational schemes. In a statutory scheme, individuals accrue credits over time, which are then revalued on retirement in the light of a particular standard laid down in the legislation.[36] Although the level of benefit received is often related to the individual's contributions history,[37] the relationship is with the years during which contributions have been paid, rather than their precise amount. This is very different from the manner in which pre-funded schemes operate. In a pre-funded final salary scheme, while the member is active, the value of his pension is continually revalued in line with developments in his wages. This ceases when membership is no longer active. In a money purchase scheme, the value of accruing rights follows individual wage developments in a fairly similar manner. Where an individual returns to the same scheme after a break, scheme rules may allow the employment to be treated as uninterrupted,[38] but where someone changes employment, this is not generally possible. Because women's career patterns are more fragmented than those of men, it can consequently be considered that statutory schemes offer them a better chance of accruing an adequate level of pension than occupational schemes.

A final reason for this is that the coverage of occupational schemes remains patchy. In the UK, only 48% of employees belong to schemes.[39] In

---

[36] See the discussion in Chapter 2. In the UK and the Netherlands, the revaluation is in line with what is deemed the minimum wage, or social minimum. In Germany, wages for the context.

[37] Although for example, survivor's pensions may be paid at a flat rate, irrespective of the duration of the insurance.

[38] And indeed, in relation to periods spent caring for children may be obliged to do so.

[39] Government Actuary, loc. cit. at p. 4.

Germany, private sector schemes cover 46.7% of employees[40] and it is only in the Netherlands that coverage is high, at 82%.[41] This of itself indicates that many individuals do not currently enjoy the benefit of occupational provision. However, those excluded from schemes are predominantly women: a recent survey indicates that only 43% of British female employees belong to an occupational pension scheme.[42] 31.5% of scheme members in Germany were women, while in the Netherlands 60% of those without pension provision are women.[43] These statistics indicate that women are less likely than men to belong to a scheme, and it appears that they are more likely than men to work for an employer who does not operate an occupational scheme.[44] This is a consequence of the fact that it is currently entirely at the employer's discretion whether or not to offer employees membership of an occupational scheme.[45] The only method of ensuring that there are not pockets of non-provision is to make occupational pension schemes compulsory. It can consequently be concluded that even given the significant alterations which schemes have been forced to introduce, without making schemes compulsory it

---

[40]   *Supplementary Pensions*, loc. cit. at p. 60.

[41]   Harrison, loc. cit. at p. 11; Kraamwinkel, loc. cit. at p. 23.

[42]   Field and Prior, loc. cit. at pp. 71-72.

[43]   Kraamwinkel, loc. cit., at p. 36. Dutch pension scheme coverage is particularly high, at 82%. 11.4% of Dutch female employees are without occupational pension provision as compared to 7.6% of men.

[44]   For example, 30% of part-time employees and only 22% of full-time employees surveyed in the UK worked for an employer with no pension scheme; see Field and Prior, loc. cit. at p. 71. German research, which is echoed by UK and Dutch experience, reveals that the likelihood that a firm offers employees membership of an occupational pension scheme increases with the size of the firm. Consequently, it is relevant that 41% of German women, as compared to 20% of German men work for a firm with fewer than 5 employees. 27% of men and 14% of women work for firms with more than 500 employees; see Allmendinger et al, loc. cit. at p. 149. In the Netherlands, it appears that in firms with fewer than 10 employees, 43.8% of employees were without occupational provision; firms with between 10 and 49 employees, 20.7% had no pension scheme. Employers without pension schemes generally employ proportionately more women and part-time employees; see Kraamwinkel, loc. cit. at p. 37.

[45]   Unless the employer operates within a branch of industry in relation to which a Dutch scheme has been declared of compulsory application. See the discussion in Chapter 2.

seems unlikely that the measures will be adequate to ensure that in an environment in which state provision is being cut back, women and relatively low-paid and low-skilled employees - whether male or female - will be able to accrue adequate levels of benefits.

As a consequence, it can be concluded that in respect of the first group with which this research is concerned, on the basis of the manner in which occupational and statutory schemes currently operate, women will be better able to accrue an adequate level of pension within a statutory than within an occupational scheme.

7.4.2   MIGRANTS

A similar conclusion can be reached in relation to the second group of workers with which this research has been concerned - migrant workers. Through Regulation 1408/71, a system has been put in place whereby periods of insurance completed by an individual - whether on the basis of residence or employment - are never lost as a consequence merely of deciding to exercise the right of free movement. By contrast, the individual with occupational pension rights who seeks to exercise his right to free movement risks suffering a significant loss of rights which he is in the process of accruing, or seeing the value of accrued rights reduce as a consequence of moving to work abroad. However, a system like that of Regulation 1408/71 would be unworkable in relation to occupational pension schemes for a number of reasons.

First, occupational schemes are typically pre-funded, in which situation every individual member builds up his or her own individual fund,[46] for the purposes of financing his or her retirement income. There is a very close correlation in occupational schemes between the value of contributions paid in, and the value of the benefits ultimately received. It has already been mentioned that the financing methods of statutory schemes allow them to revalue accrued rights in

---

[46]   Notionally at least.

line with the scheme norm on an individual's retirement.[47] Norms in occupational schemes are much more closely linked to the actual developments in an individual's wage level. In final salary schemes, accrued rights are "revalued" in the light of the individual's final salary averaged over the relevant reference period.[48] The burden of ensuring that the funds in the scheme are adequate to cover the benefits due generally falls upon the employer. To require that an ex-employer revalue an individual's SSBs in line with his actual wage developments would be to impose a far-reaching obligation indeed.

Second, aggregation of periods of insurance elsewhere - in the absence of transfers[49] - would also appear to be a far-reaching obligation to impose on an employer. For example, this would amount to telling a German employer that he had to grant an employee enforceable pension rights after, say 2 years employment, because the individual in question had already been employed for 8 years elsewhere. As the discussion in Chapter 6 reveals, this would increase significantly the cost to the employer of operating the fund.

The reason why these obligations appear so far-reaching in the context of occupational pension schemes is that in none of the jurisdictions under consideration are occupational schemes compulsory. Imposing these requirements on employers - who will generally bear ultimate financial responsibility for the financing of the scheme - can be seen to be such that employers would be likely to simply cease to operate the scheme.

Consequently, it can be concluded that in the present situation, migrant workers are likely to face penalties in terms of their occupational pension accrual as a consequence of deciding to exercise their right to free movement. Creating a system which would remove these disadvantages would represent a possibly

---

[47]   In the UK system, in line with the "social minimum"; in the Netherlands with developments in the minimum wage; in Germany in line with an individual's qualifying earnings.

[48]   For example, an individual's average salary over the last three years of pensionable employment.

[49]   With transfers, an individual is able to buy in a number of years of service with the new employer. As such, he is able to buy off as such the waiting or vesting period. If this were not the case, no-one would take a transfer, since they would be vulnerable to the loss of the entire accrued pension entitlement should their new employment relationship cease before the end of the new employer's waiting or vesting period.

impossible intellectual challenge, at least where occupational provision is not made compulsory. By contrast, the co-ordinating regime which has been put in place for statutory schemes basically removes this risk for the migrant. In short, as with women, occupational schemes are less able than statutory schemes to provide the migrant worker with an "adequate" levels of retirement pension.

7.5   Conclusion

It can therefore be concluded that in relation to both groups of workers with which this research has been concerned, increasing the role played by pre-funded employer based occupational schemes will put in place a scheme less able to provide adequate levels of pensions than the scheme which it was designed at least partly to replace, at least if the patterns followed by these Member States are adhered to.

A common feature of both the preceding sections of this conclusion was the observation that particular advantages would attach to making occupational provision compulsory. In relation to women's pensions, it was observed that making schemes compulsory would eradicate the pockets of non-provision which currently disproportionately affect women. In relation to migrant workers, it was observed that aggregation and apportionment would be too far-reaching obligations to impose upon employers in the absence of schemes being made compulsory. Other considerations also plead in favour of making occupational pension provision compulsory. In Chapter 1 it was observed that some states are considering increasing the role played by pre-funded occupational pension schemes in their overall systems of pension provision in the hope that this will enable them to cut their spending on pensions in the future. For a number of reasons which will be outlined in the next paragraphs, it is suggested that if this objective is to be met, schemes will have to be made compulsory.

The first reason for this is the fact that individuals are typically myopic,[50] unable or unwilling to make the long-term savings commitments

---

[50]   See Philip Davis, loc. cit. at p. 11; Kraamwinkel, loc. cit. at pp. 89-90; SEC(91) 1332 final at pp. 6-7.

required to take the "prudent" and informed decisions required to fund adequate benefits in the future. This in part can be explained by the general lack of information available on occupational pensions, investments, rates of return and the operation of the markets upon which these instruments operate, which coupled with its technical and specialised nature make it impenetrable for all but a select few. This in turn suggests that intensive information campaigns should be undertaken to inform individuals of the need to make pension provision, together with information about the operation of pension funds and their markets. This would have to be made available to individuals in an accessible form if it was to be effective.

However, another phenomenon also suggests that, if statutory pensions are to become less important, membership of occupational schemes should be made compulsory. This is "free-riding", where individuals choose not to make the necessary provision in the assumption that the state will "bail them out" and provide them with funds to keep them from poverty on retirement. If significant numbers of individuals decided to follow such a course, the objective of reducing the numbers of individuals reliant on the state for their retirement income would not be realised.

Consequently, it can be concluded that if occupational schemes were to be made compulsory, the objectives pursued by the Member States would be more likely to be achieved. Additionally, it would be easier to put a legal framework in place whereby the two groups of employees upon which this research has focused - women and international migrants - could accrue adequate levels of pension benefits.

If this is in fact to be ensured, it will be necessary that the schemes which are put in place are able to take account of the fact that many women will have children and that this will affect their paid employment in a particular way. If this is not to have negative consequences for pension accrual, it will be necessary that the scheme be able to provide the woman with rights which reflect her normal earnings. This will entail breaking the link between contributions paid and benefits received which has traditionally been such a characteristic feature of occupational provision. It will also require that occupational schemes display a considerably greater degree of solidarity than is currently the case, in that it will be necessary for those not taking career breaks to have and care for children to subsidise those who do.

Second, it will require that the schemes do not operate such high wage or thresholds for entitlement to membership as to exclude large numbers of individuals. Connected to this is the fact that if the objectives of reducing state spending are to be met, the schemes will have to pay a certain minimum level of benefit, irrespective of the contributions history of the individual. If this does not occur, the individual whose pension falls below that level will have to turn to the state for a top up in his resources, which will not result in a lessening of the financial burdens on the state.

Turning to the international migrant, making schemes compulsory would enable legislators to oblige schemes to aggregate and apportion the accrued rights of individuals within schemes. If schemes were compulsory, it would also be possible to prohibit setting the kinds of extremely long vesting periods which are characteristic of the German situation and which operate to the disadvantage of both women and international migrants.

The scenario described as being more likely to produce the results sought can be seen to be far from the current situation and, perhaps, to represent an unjustifiably far-reaching incursion by the regulator into what is currently a matter for the social partners. However, without such measures, there is no guarantee that the objectives will be met.[51] Other advantages would also seem to ensue from a greater degree of state involvement in occupational provision than is currently the norm. For example, instead of pension schemes being employer or industry-based, it would be possible to have a state occupational scheme, to which all individuals and employers would contribute. Apart from the benefits which this would bring in terms of facilitating penalty-free internal employee mobility, it would offer a saving in terms of the administrative costs of operating a scheme.[52]

---

[51] Whether pre-funded schemes will be able to realise the objectives which it is said that they can achieve is a matter open to some doubt; see Beattie and McGillivray, op. cit.; Castle and Townsend, loc. cit; Voisin, op. cit.; Thompson, op. cit.

[52] It is apparently the case that in relation to individual personal pensions, up to 25% of the contributions paid go to defray administrative expenses; see "Security in Retirement Now", *UPS Intelligence*, 13 July 1996 at 4.

In this respect, the conclusion of this research is - like some of the more economics oriented comparisons of occupational and statutory provision[53] - that to shift the emphasis of pension provision from Pay-As-You-Go to pre-funded occupational schemes - even if the patterns followed by the UK and the Netherlands are followed - seems likely at the moment to put in place a system less able to provide adequate pensions to women and migrant workers than the scheme which it is designed to replace.

> "[A]t the end of the day, the question how far resources should be extended to the welfare state is a political one, just as much as is the question of how these resources are to be distributed."[54]

In the light of this fact, it is submitted that before proposals are accepted to reduce the role played by the state in retirement income provision and replace it with more individually oriented employer based provision, society has a duty to ensure that this will not result in significant numbers of individuals for whom the market is unable adequately to provide being trapped in poverty during their retirement. In heeding the cry to shoulder individual responsibility for our old age income provision, we should not ignore the situation of those who are unable to do so. Before we abandon the structures created in the post war period, we should be sure that any replacements are an improvement. At this time, this can not unequivocally be said of occupational schemes.

---

[53] See for example, Beattie and McGillivray, op. cit.; Castle and Townsend, loc. cit; Voisin, op. cit.; Thompson, op. cit.

[54] Ploug and Kvist, loc. cit. at pp. 38-39. This is echoed by Castle and Townsend, loc. cit. at p. 19.

A.

Achenbach, K. and E. Haneberg, "Rentenversicherung: Ermutigende Zukunftsperspektiven", *Bundesarbeitsblatt* 11/1995 at pp. 5-11.

Adema, M. and Dierx, J.R., "Pensioenbreuken van vrouwen", NJB (1992), 998-104.

Adinolfi, A., "The Implementation of Social Policy Directives through Collective Agreements", 28 CML Rev. (1988), 291-316.

Adinolfi, A., "Note on *Nimz*", 29 CML Rev. (1992), 637-645

Ahrend, P., Förster, W., Rühmann, J., *Gesetz zur Verbesserung der betrieblichen Altersversorgung mit zivilrechtlichen, arbeidsrechtlichen, steuerrechtlichen Voorschriften und Erläuterungen* 4th ed., München, 1991.

Ahrend, P., Beucher, D., "Die Gleichberechtigung der Geschlechter in der betrieblichen Altersversorgung seit dem Barber-Urteil des EuGH", BetrAVG 1993, 253-258.

Alcock, P., "The advantages and disadvantages of the contribution base in targeting benefits: A social analysis of the insurance scheme in the United Kingdom", 49 *International Social Security Review* 1/1996, 31-49.

Alexander, W., "Free Movement of Non-EC Nationals; A Review of the case law of the Court of Justice", in H. G. Schermers et al (eds.), *Free Movement of Persons in Europe*, Dordrecht, 1993 at pp. 485-496.

Alkema, E.A. and Jaspers, A.Ph.C.M. (eds.), *Lof der verscheidenheid. Rechtsgeleerden over vrouw en recht*, Zwolle, 1993.

Allmendinger, J., E. Brückner and H. Brückner, "Arbeitsleben und Lebensarbeitsentlohnung: Zur Entstehung von finanzieller Ungleichheit im Alter", in C. Gather et al (eds.), *Frauenalterssicherung. Lebensläufe von Frauen und ihre Benachteiligung im Alter*, Berlin 1991 at pp. 133-174.

Andringa, L., Nemesis (1992), 1 and 2.

Arnull, A., "Article 119 and Equal Pay for Work of Equal Value", EL Rev. (1986), 200-208.

Arnull, A., "Some More Equal than Others?", EL Rev. (1986), 229-232.

Arnull, A., "Sex Discrimination in Occupational Pension Schemes", 11 EL Rev. (1986), 363-366.

Arnull, A., "Widows' Mite", EL Rev. (1988), 135-140.

Arnull, A., *The General Prinicples of EEC Law and the Individual*, London, 1990.

Asscher-Vonk, I.P. and Wentholt, K., *Wet Gelijke Behandeling van Mannen en Vrouwen*, Deventer, 1994.

Asscher-Vonk, I.P., *European Community Equality Law: The Netherlands*, Deventer, 1994

Association Europe & Enterprises, *Fonds de Pension en Europe: Expreiences et Devenir*, Les Dorriers de l'AEE No. 5, Paris, 1994.

Atkins, S. and Luckhaus, L., "The Social Security Directive and UK Law" in McCrudden, C. (ed.), *Women, Employment and European Equality Law*, London, 1987 at pp. 103-122.

Atkins, S., L. Luckhaus and E. Szyszczak, "Pensions and the European Community Equality Legislation", in McCrudden, C. (ed.) *Women, Employment and European Equality Law*, London, 1987 at pp. 123-142.

Atkinson, A.B., "The Development of State Pensions in the United Kingdom", in Schmähl, W. (ed.), *The Future of Basic and Supplementary Pension Schemes in the European Community - 1992 and Beyond*, Baden-Baden, 1991 at pp. 117-134.

B.

Backes, G.M., "Was bedeuten sich verändernde Lebens- und Arbeitsbedingungen von Frauen für ihre künftige Situation im Alter?" in C. Gather et al (eds.), *Frauenalterssicherung. Lebensläufe von Frauen und ihre Benachteiligung im Alter*, Berlin 1991 at pp. 266-276.

Baldwin, S. and Falkingham, J. (eds.), *Social Security and Social Change. New Challenges to the Beveridge Model*, London, 1994.

Banks, K., "L'article 118A. Element dynamique de la politique sociale communautaire", CDE (1993), 537-554.

Banks, K., "Whither the Social Security Directives? Developments in Community Law Relating to Sex Equality", in C. McCrudden (ed.), *Equality of Treatment between Women and Men in Social Security*, London, 1994 at pp. 55-68.

Barnard, C., "A Social Policy for Europe: Politicians 1: 0 Lawyers", IJCLLIR (1992), 15-31.

Barnard, C., *EC Employment Law*, Chichester, 1995.

Barnard, C., "Workers' Rights of Participation", in in Neuwahl, N.A. and Rosas, A. (eds), *The European Union and Human Rights*, Deventer 1995 at pp. 185-206.

Barnard, C., "The economic objectives of Article 119", in T.K. Hervey and D. O'Keeffe (eds.), *Sex Equality Law in the European Union*, Chicester, 1996 at pp. 321-334.

Bates, J.D.N., "Gender, Social Security and Pensions: The Myth of the 'Everyday Housewife'?", in S. McLean and N. Burrows (eds.) *The Legal Relevance of Gender*, London, 1988, at pp. 119-145.

Beattie, R. and McGillivray, W., "A risky strategy: Reflections on the World bank Report *Averting the old age crisis*", 48 *International Social Security Review* 3/4/1995, 5-22.

Bercusson, B., "The European Community's Charter of Fundamental Social Rights of Workers", 53 MLR (1990), 624-642.

Bercusson, B., "Fundamental Social and Economic Rights in the European Community", in A. Cassese, A. Clapham and J. Weiler (eds.), *Human Rights and the European Community*, Baden-Baden, 1991 at pp. 195-289.

Bercusson, "Maastricht: A Fundamental Change in European Labour Law", 23 IRJ (1993), 177-190.

Bercusson, B., "The dynamic of European Labour Law after Maastricht", 23 ILJ (1994), 1-31.

Bercusson, B. and van Dijk, J.J., "The Implementation of the Protocol and Agreement on Social Policy of the Treaty on European Union", 11 IJCLLIR (1995), 3-30.

Bercusson, B., "The Collective Labour Law of the European Union", 1 ELJ (1995), 157-179.

Bercusson, B., *European Labour Law*, London, 1996.

Berenz, C., "Hat die betriebliche Altersversorgung zukünftig noch eine Chance?", 11 NZA (1994), 385-390, 433-438.

Berg, G.J. van den, *Ouderdom en overlijden*, Deventer, 1985.

Berghman, J.A.M., "Europese integratie en sociale zekerheid. Ontwikkelingen en perspectieven", in Engbersen, G., Hemerijck, A.C. and Bakker, W.E. (eds.), *Zorgen in het Europese Huis. Verkenningen over de grenzen van nationale verzorgingsstaten*, Amsterdam, 1994 at pp. 215-235.

Besseling, P.J., and Zeeuw, R.F., *The financing of pensions in Europe: Challenges and Opportunities*, CEPS Research Report No. 14, November 1993, Brussels.

Betten, L, "EG-Handvest van Sociale Grondrechten: Een hol vat?", *SMA*, 119-128.

Binon, J.-M., *Les Directives Européennes en matière d'assurance sociale complémentaire (Assurances, banques, institutions de retraite)*, Louvain-la-Neuve, 1994.

Birk, R., "The Influence of the German Pension Reform Act 1992 on Occupational Pension Schemes", in Schmähl, W. (ed.), *The Future of Basic and Supplementary Pension Schemes in the European Community - 1992 and Beyond*, Baden-Baden, 1991 at pp. 111-116.

Bloch, E., *Gleichbehandlung von Männern und Frauen im Verhältnis des Europäischen Gemeinschaftsrechts zum Deutschen Arbeitsrecht*, Diss., Göttingen, 1988.

Blom, J.A.H., *De Effectiviteit van de Wet Gelijke Behandeling M/V*, The Hague, 1994.

Blomeyer, C., *Das Verbot der mittelbaren Diskriminierung gemäß Art. 119 EGV. Seine Funktion im deutschen Arbeitsrecht*, Baden-Baden, 1994.

Blüm, N., "Vertrauen in die Rentenversicherung", *Bundesarbeitsblatt* 3/1996 at 5-10.

Bode, K.-J., Grabner, E.R., "Teuerungsanpassung der Betriebsrenten in 1993", DB 1993, 274-277.

Boelens, L. and Veldman, A., *Gelijkwaardige arbeid, gelijk gewaardeerd*, Utrecht, 1993.

Bol, J., "De zachte dood van het weduwenpensioen", 11 Nemesis (1995), 88-91.

Borchardt, K.-D., "Die EuGH-Rechtsprechung zur Gleichbehandlungsfrage im Hinblick auf Versicherungslösungen in der betrieblichen Altersversorgung", BetrAVG (1994), 137-140.

Borgesius, J. "Weduwenpensioen voor weduwnaars", TvP (1989), 6-10.

Born, C., "Zur Bedeutung der beruflichen Erstausbildung bei der Verbindung von Familien- und Erwerbsarbeit in weiblichen Lebensläufen", in C. Gather et al (eds.), *Frauenalterssicherung. Lebensläufe von Frauen und ihre Benachteiligung im Alter*, Berlin 1991 at pp. 19-31.

Boshuizen, G.R., "De gewezen deelnemer aan de pensioenregeling", TvP (1995), 91-94.

Bourn, C. and Neal, A.C., "European winds of change", NLJ (1992), 1131-1132.

Bradley, K. St. C., "Note on Case 12/81 and Case 19/81", 19 CML Rev. (1982), 625-634.

Brenninkmeijer, A.F.M., "Vrouwenstudies kwam te laat voor de sociale zekerheid", in Alkema, E.A. and Jaspers, A.Ph.C.M. (eds.), *Lof der verscheidenheid. Rechtsgeleerden over vrouw en recht*, Zwolle, 1993 at pp. 17-28.

Bruegel, I., "Women's Employment, Legislation and the Labour Market", in J. Lewis (ed.) *Women's Welfare Women's Rights*, London, 1983, at pp. 130-169.

Breuker, H.P., "Gelijke behandeling van mannen en vrouwen in pensioenregelingen: een 'mer à boire'", TvP (1995), 110-113.

Brouwer, J. Th. L., and Kappelle, H.M., "De maatschappelijke opvattingen omtrent pensioen bieden meer ruimte dan Financiën denkt", WFR 1994, 6116, 1243-1245.

Brouwer, O.W., "Bedrijfspensioenen: gelijke monniken, gelijke kappen", Staatscourant 3, 5 januari 1994, 5.

Bruyn-Hundt, M., "Gelijke behandeling in pensioenen", 3 TvA (1987), 12-23.

Búrca, G. de "The Principle of Proportionality and its Application in EC Law", 13 YEL (1993), 105-150.

Burri, S., "Tussen wens en werkelijkheid. Naar een volwaardig recht op deeltijdarbeid", 11 *Nemesis* (1995), 63-73.

Burri, S., "Gelijke Behandeling en Arbeidsduur", 12 *Nemesis* (1996), 18-26.

Buswell, C., "Training Girls to be Low-Paid Women", in C. Glendinning and J. Millar (eds.), *Women and Poverty in Britain: the 1990s*, London, 1992 at pp. 79-94.

Buul, W.J.J. van, *Waardering van Pensioenen*, 4th ed., Arnhem, 1992.

C.

Canata, R., "Judicial protection against Member States: A new *jus commune* takes shape", 32 CML Rev. (1995), 703-726.

Cass, D.Z., "The word that saves Maastricht? The principle of subsidiariyu and the division of powers within the European Community", 29 CML Rev. (1992), 1107-1136.

Castle, B., and P. Townsend, *We CAN Afford the Welfare State*, London, 1996

CEPS, Working Party Report No. 9, November 1993, *Financing Retirement in Europe*, Brussels.

CERR, *Les retraites en Europe*, Paris, 1990.

Clever, P., "Soziale Sicherheit im Rahmen der europäischen Integration - Perspectieven nach dem Maastrichter Gipfel", DAngVers (1992), 296-304.

Closa, C., "The Concept of Citizenship in the Treaty on European Union", 29 CML Rev. (1992), 1137-1170.

Closa, C., "Citizenship of the Union and Nationality of member States", in D. O'Keeffe and P.M. Twomey (eds.), *Legal Issues of the Maastricht Treaty*, London 1994, at pp. 109-119.

Collins, D., *The European Communities: The Social Policy of the First Phase*, Volume 2: *The European Economic Community 1958-1972*, London, 1975.

Commission of the European Communities, *De aanvullende regelingen van de sociale zekerheid in de landen van de EEG*, serie sociale politiek number 15, 1966, Luxemburg.

Conci, P., "Pensions Reform in Italy", 7 *International Insurance Law Review* (1996), 229-231.

Conrad, C., "Les Fonds de Pension Allemands", in Association Europe & Enterprises, *Fonds de Pension en Europe: Expreiences et Devenir*, Les Dorriers de l'AEE No. 5, Paris, 1994 at pp. 39-42.

Cornelissen, R.C., *De Europese Verordeningen inzake sociale zekerheid*, Antwerp, 1984.

Cornelissen, R., "The Principle of Territoriality and the Community Regulations on Social Security (Regulations 1408/71 and 574/72), 33 CML Rev. (1996), 439-471.

Cousins, M., "Equal treatment and social security", 19 EL Rev. (1994), 123-145.

Crijns, L.H.J., "Het Sociale Beleid van de Europese Gemeenschap", in F.A.J. van den Bosch and A.M. Dancot-Devriendt (eds.), *Sociaal en zeker*, Deventer, 1986, pp. 149-175.

Crisham, C.A., "Note on Case 43/75", CML Rev. (1977), 108-118.

Crisham, C.A., "The Equal Pay Principle: Some recent Decisions of the European Court of Justice", 18 CML Rev. (1981), 601-612.

Curti Gialdino, C., "Some Reflections on the *Acquis Communautaire*", 32 CML Rev. (1995), 1089-1121.

Curtin, D., "Occupational pension schemes and article 119: Beyond the fringe?", 24 CML Rev. (1987), 215-257.

Curtin, D., "Delimiting the Direct Effect of Directives in the Common Law Context", 15 EL Rev. (1990), 195-223.

Curtin, D., "Directives: The effectiveness of judicial protection of individual rights", 27 CML Rev. (1990), 709-739.

Curtin, D., "Scalping the Community legislator: Occupational pensions and "Barber"", 27 CML Rev. (1990), 475-506.

Curtin, D., "The constitutional structure of the union: A Europe of bits and pieces", 30 CML Rev. (1993), 17-69.

Curtin, D., "Simple Justice", 9 Nemesis (1993), 190-198.

Curtin, D., "Note on Case C-271/91, *Marshall* v. *Southampton and South West Hampshire Area Health*

Authority", 31 CML Rev. (1994), 631-652.

D.

Dallett, E., "Sex discrimination in pensions and nonretroactivity of relief", British Business Law (1992), 91-98.

Däubler, W., "Trends in German Labour Law", in Wedderburn et al, *Labour Law in the Post-Industrial Era. Essays in Honour of Higo Sinzheimer*, Aldershot, 1994 at pp. 105-131.

Davidson, F., "Occupational Pensions and Equal Treatment", (1990) JSWL 310-331.

Davies, B. and Ward, S., *Women and Personal Pensions*, London, 1992.

Davies, B., *Better Pensions for All*, IPPR, London, 1993.

Davies, B., *The New Contracting-Out Requirements*, London, 1996.

Davies, P., "The Emergence of European Labour Law", in W. McCarthy (ed.), *Legal Intervention in Industrial Relations: Gains and Losses*, Oxford, 1992, at pp. 313-359.

Davies, P., "Market Integration and Social Policy in the Court of Justice", 24 ILJ (1995), 49-77.

Davis, E. Philip. *Pension Funds. Retirement-Income Security and Capital Markets. An International Perspective*, Oxford, 1995.

Daykin, C.D., *Pension Provision in Britain*, London, 1994.

Daykin, C.D., "Financial management and control of supplementary pension schemes", 48 *International Social Security Review* 3/4/1995, 75-89.

Deakin, S., Wilkinson, F., "Rights vs Efficiency? The Economic Case for Transnational Labour Standards", 23 ILJ (1994), 289-310.

Deakin, S. and Barnard, C., "Social Policy in Search of a Role: Integration, Cohesion and Citizenship", in A. Caiger and D.A.M.-A. Floudas (eds.) *1996 Onwards: Lowering the Barriers Further*, Chichester, 1996 at pp. 177-195.

Denys, C., *Impliciete Bevoegdheden in de Europese Economische Gemeenschap. Een onderzoek naar de betekenis van 'implied powers'*, Antwerpen, 1990.

De Wildt, J., "Gelijke behandeling in aanvullende pensioenreegelingen", TvP (1988), 73-77.

Dickens, L., *Whose Flexibility? Discrimination and Equality Issues in Atypical Work*, Institute of Employment Rights, London, 1992.

Dierx, J. and Kraamwinkel, M., "Pensioenplicht", 1989 Nemesis 127

Dierx, J.R., "Barberisme", Nemesis nr. 4 (1991), 1-4.

Dierx, J.R., "De macht der gewoonte", Nemesis nr. 1 (1992), 1-2.

Dierx, J.R., "Indirecte discriinatie: oplossing of obstakel?", in Kraamwinkel, M.M.H., Schippers, J.J., Siegers, J.J., *De toekomst van de aanvullende pensioenen*, Zwolle, 1992 at pp. 111-127.

Dietvorst, G.J.B., *De drie pijlers van toekomstvoorzieningen en belastingen*, Deventer, 1994.

Driessen, C.C.H.J., "Op weg naar een wettelijke aanvullende pensioenrecht voor werknemers", in Kraamwinkel, M.M.H., Schippers, J.J., Siegers, J.J., *De toekomst van de aanvullende pensioenen*, Zwolle, 1992 at pp. 35-42.

Docking, P. and Trier, S., *EC Pensions Law*, London, 1992.

Docksey, C., "The Principle of Equality between Women and Men as a Fundamental Right under Community Law", 20 ILJ (1991), 258-280.

Due, O., "Artikel 5 van het EEG-Verdrag - Een Bepaling met een Federaal Karakter?", 40 SEW (1992), 355-366.

E.

Edward, D.A.O. and Lane, R.C., *European Community Law. An Introduction*, Edinburgh, 1995.

Eekeren, P.J. van, "De totstandkoming van aanvullende pensioenregelingen: verplichtingen van rechtswege", 1989 SR 165.

Ellis, E., and Morrell, P., "Sex Discrimination in Pension Schemes: Has Community Law changed the Rules?", 11 ILJ (1982), 16-28.

Ellis, E., *European Community Sex Equality Law*, Oxford, 1991.

Ellis, E., "Recent case law of the Court of Justice on the equal treatment of women and men", 31 CML Rev. (1994), 43-75.

Ellison,R., *Pensions: Europe and Equality*, Longman Pensions Report, London, 1994.

Emiliou, N., "Subsidiarity: An Effective Barrier against the Enterprises of Ambition?", 17 EL Rev. (1992), 383-407.

Emiliou, N., "Subsidiarity: Panacea or Fig Leaf?", in D. O'Keeffe and P.M. Twomey (eds.), *Legal Issues of the Maastricht Treaty*, London 1994, pp. 65-83.

Engbersen, G., Hemerijck, A.C. and Bakker, W.E. (eds.), *Zorgen in het Europese Huis. Verkenningen over de grenzen van nationale verzorgingsstaten*, Amsterdam, 1994.

ETUI, *The European Dimensions of Collective Bargaining after Maastricht*, Brussels, 1992.

ETUI, *The Social Architecture of Europe put to the Test: Trade Union Ideas for a European Model of Development*, Brussels, 1993.

ETUI, *The European Industry Committees and Social Dialogue: Experience at sectoral level and in multinational companies*, Brussels, 1993.

ETUI, *Bargaining in Recession: Trends in Collective Bargaining in Western Europe 1993-1994*, Brussels, 1994.

Everling, U., "Von der Freizügigkeit der Arbeitnehmer zum Europäischen Bürgerrecht?", EuR (1990), 81-103.

F.

Fenton, J., Ham, R. and Sabel, J., *Tolley's pensions handbook*, Croydon, 1993.

Fenwick, H. and Hervey, T.K., "Sex Equality in the Single Market: New Directions for the European Court of Justice", 32 CML Rev. (1995), 443-470.

Fitzpatrick, B., "Community social law after Maastricht", 21 ILJ (1992), 199-213.

Fitzpatrick, B., "Equality in Occupational Pension Schemes: Still Waiting for *Coloroll*", 23 ILJ (1994), 155-163 and 252.

Fletcher, L., "Problems Sepcific to State Social Security, in Particular State Pension Age and Survivors Rights", in C. McCrudden (ed.), *Equality of Treatment between Women and Men in Social Security*, London, 1994 at pp. 79-88.

Förster, W. and Rössler, N. (eds.), *Betriebliche Altersversorgung in der Diskussion zwischen Praxis und Wissenschaft. Festschrift für Peter Ahrend*, Köln, 1992.

Förster, W., Recktenwald, S. and Trevisany, M., "Das Rentenreformgesetz 1992 und seine Auswirkung auf betriebliche Versorgungssysteme", BB (1990) Beilage 29

Foster, N., "Equal Treatment and Retirement Ages", EL Rev. (1986), 222-229.

Foster, N., *German Law and Legal System*, London 1993.

Fredman, S., "European Community Sex Discrimination Law: A critique", 21 ILJ (1992), 119-134.

Fredman, S., "Poverty and Equality: Pensions and the ECJ", 25 ILJ (1996), 91-109.

Freestone, D., "Equal Pay in the European Court", 45 MLR (1982), 81-87.

G.

Gather, C., Gerhard, U., Prinz, K. and Veil, M., (eds.), *Frauenalterssicherung. Lebensläufe von Frauen und ihre Benachteiligung im Alter*, Berlin 1991.

Gerven, W. van, "Contributions de l'arret Defrenne au developpement du droit communautaire", 13 CDE (1977), 131-143.

Gerven, W. van, Bossche, P. van den, "Freedom of Movement and Equal Treatment for Students in Europe: An Emerging Principle?", in H.G. Schermers et al (eds.), *Free Movement of Persons in Europe*, Dordrecht, 1993 at pp. 405-426.

Gerven, W. van, "Bridging the gap between Community and national laws: Towards a principle of homogenity in the field of legal remedies?", 32 CML Rev. (1995), 679-702.

Ginn, J. and Arber, S., "Heading for Hardship: How the British pension system has failed women", in Baldwin, S. and Falkingham, J. (eds.), *Social Security and Social Change. New Challenges to the Beveridge Model*, London, 1994 at pp. 216-234.

Gitter, W., *Sozialrecht. Ein Studienbuch*, München, 1992.

Glendinning, C. and Millar, J. (eds.), *Women and Poverty in Britain: the 1990s*, London, 1992.

Gold, M. (ed.), *The social dimension. Employment policy in the European Community*, London, 1993.

Goldschmidt, J.E., and Holtmaat, R., *Vrouw en Recht*, Den Haag, 1993.

Government Actuary, *Occupational Pension Schemes 1987 Eighth Survey by the Government Actuary*, London, 1991.

Government Actuary, *Occupational Pension Schemes 1991 Ninth Survey by the Government Actuary*, London, 1994.

Green, M., "Social Security in Europe: The Only Certainty is Change", 25 *Benefits and Compensation International* no. 10 (1996), 2-7.

Griebeling, G., "Gleichbehandlung in der betrieblichen Altersversorgung", RdA (1992), 373-378.

Groves, D., "Members and Survivors: Women and Retirement-Pensions Legislation", in J. Lewis (ed.) *Women's Welfare Women's Rights*, London, 1983, at pp. 38-63.

Groves, D., "Occupational Pension Provision and Women's Poverty in Old Age", in Glendinning, C. and Millar, J. (eds.), *Women and Poverty in Britain: the 1990s*, London, 1992 at pp. 193-206.

Gulmann, C., "The Single European Act - some remarks from a Danish perspective", 24 CML Rev. (1987), 31-40.

H.

Hanau, P., Preis, U., "Beschränkung der Rückwirkung neuer Rechtsprechung zur Gleichberechtigung im Recht der betrieblichen Altersversorgung", DB 1991, 1276-1284.

Hannah, L., *Inventing Retirement. The Development of Occupational Pensions in Britain*, Cambridge, 1986.

Harrison, D., *Pension Provision in the EC. Opportunities for the private sector in the Single Market*, London, 1992.

Hartley, T.C., *The Foundations of European Community Law*, 3rd ed., Oxford, 1994.

Heijden, P. van der, "Post-Industrial Labour Law and Industrial Relations in the Netherlands", in

Wedderburn et al, *Labour Law in the Post-Industrial Era. Essays in Honour of Higo Sinzheimer*, Aldershot, 1994 at pp. 133-147.

Heither, F.H., "Aktuelle Rechtsprechung zu Fragen der betrieblichen Altersversorgung bei individualrechtlicher Ausgestaltung", DB (1991), 165-172.

Heither, F., "Bestandsschutz und Billigkeitskontrolle in der betrieblichen Altersversorgung", RdA (1993), 72-79.

Hepple, B. and Byre, A., "EEC Labour Law in the United Kingdom - A New Approach", 18 ILJ (1989), 129-143.

Hepple, B., "The Implementation of the Community Charter of Fundamental Social Rights", 53 MLR (1990), 643-654.

Hepple, B. and Szyszczak, E., *Discrimination: The Limits of Law*, London 1992.

Hervey, T.K., "Justification for indirect sex discrimination in employment", 40 ICLQ (1991), 807-.

Hervey, T.K., *Justifications for sex discrimination in employment*, London, 1993.

Hervey, T.K., "Legal Issues concerning the *Barber* Protocol", in O'Keeffe, D. and Twomey, P.M. (eds.), *Legal Issues of the Maastricht Treaty*, London, 1994 at pp. 329-337.

Hervey, T.K., "Case C-152/91, *Neath* v. *Hugh Steeper Ltd.*", 31 CML Rev. (1994), 1387-1397.

Hervey, T.K., "A Gendered Perspective on the Right to Family Life in European Community Law", in Neuwahl, N.A. and Rosas, A. (eds), *The European Union and Human Rights*, Deventer 1995 at pp. 221-234.

Hervey, T.K., "Migrant Workers and their Families in the European Union: The Pervasive Market Ideology of Community Law", in J. Shaw and G. More (eds.), *New Legal Dynamics of European Union*, Oxford, 1995 at pp. 91-110.

Heukels, T., *Intertemporales Gemeinschaftsrecht*, Baden-Baden, 1990.

Hill, M., *The Welfare State in Britain*, Aldershot, 1993.

Höfer, R., "Betriebliche Altersversorgung und deutsches Gleichberechtigungs- sowie europäisches Lohngleichheitsgebot", BB 1994, Beilage 15.

Holtmaat, R. and Loenen, T., *Inleiding vrouw en recht*, Alphen aan den Rijn, 1989.

Holtmaat, R., *Met zorg een recht? Een analyse van het politiek-juridisch vertoog over bijstandsrecht*, Zwolle, 1992.

Holtmaat, R., "Overtime Payments for Part-Time Workers" 24 ILJ (1995), 387-394.

Holtmaat, R., "Deeltijdwerk, Gelijkheid en Gender", 12 *Nemesis* (1996), 4-17.

Hon, L.P. de, "Verplichte bedrijfspensioenfondsen verenigbaar met Europees mededingingsrecht?", TvP 1992, 73-74.

Honeyball, S. and Shaw, J., "Sex, law and the retiring man", 16 EL Rev. (1991), 47-58.

Hoskyns, C. and Luckhaus, L., "The European Community Directive on Equal Treatment in Social Security", 17 *Policy and Politics* (1989), 321-335.

Hoskyns, C., *Integrating Gender. Women, Law and Politics in the European Union*, London, 1996.

Hoving, E., "Gelijke behandeling mannen en vrouwen in pensioenregelingen. Commentaar op Hof van Justitie EG 17 mei 1990 (Zaak *Barber*), TpV (1990), 50-55.

Hoving, E., "Gelijke behandeling en de gevolgen voor de pensioenaanspraken", TvP (1995), 26-29.

Hudson, D., "Some reflections on the implications of the *Barber* decision", 17 EL Rev. (1992), 163-171.

Hudson, R.B., "The evolution of the welfare state: Shifting rights and responsibilities for the old", 48 *International Social Security Review* 1/1995, 3-17.

Hulst, J. van der, "Beloning van deeltijdwerknemers volgens het Hof van Justitie", Sociaal Recht 1993 292-295.

Hutsebaut, M., "State of Implementation of the European Social Charter and the European Social Action Programme", in ETUI *The Social Architecture of Europe put to the Test: Trade Union Ideas for a European Model of Development*, Brussels, 1993, at

Hutton, S. and Whiteford, P., "Gender and Retirement Incomes: A comparative analysis", in Baldwin, S. and Falkingham, J. (eds.), *Social Security and Social Change. New Challenges to the Beveridge Model*, London, 1994 at pp. 199-215.

Hutton, S., Kennedy, S. and Whiteford, P., *Equalisation of State Pension Ages: The Gender Impact*, EOC Research Discussion Series No. 10, Manchester, 1995.

J.

Jacobs, A.T.J.M., *Het recht op collectief onderhandelen in rechtsvergelijkend en Europees perspectief*, Alphen aan den Rijn/Brussels, 1986.

Jansen, B., "Das Arbeits- und Sozialrecht im Zweck- und Kompetenzgefüge der Europäischen Gemeinschaften, EuR (1990), 5-33.

Johnson, P., *The Pensions Dilemma*, IPPR, London, 1994.

Johnson, P. and Falkingham, J., "Is there a future for the Beveridge pension scheme?", in Baldwin, S. and Falkingham, J. (eds.), *Social Security and Social Change. New Challenges to the Beveridge Model*, London, 1994 at pp. 255-270.

Johnson E. and O'Keeffe, D. "From Discrimination to obstacles to free movement: Recent developments concerning the free movement of workers 1989-1994", 31 CML Rev. (1994), 1313-1346.

Joshi, H., and Davies, H., "The Paid and Unpaid Roles of Women: How should social security adapt?", in Baldwin, S. and Falkingham, J. (eds.), *Social Security and Social Change. New Challenges to the Beveridge Model*, London, 1994 at pp. 235-254.

Junge, R. and Mulder, A.J., *Een nieuw pensioenperspectief. Overwegingen voor een ander beleid*, Deventer, 1995.

K.

Kam, A., "The Pension Schemes Act 1993", 55 BPL (1994), 12-13.

Kapteyn, P.J.G., "Denemarken en het Verdrag van Maastricht", 67 NJB (1992), 781-785.

Kapteyn, VerLoren van Themaat, *Inleiding tot het recht van de Europese Gemeenschappen - Na Maastricht*, Deventer, 5th ed. 1995.

Kavelaars, P., *Toewijzingsregels in het Europees sociaalverzekeringsrecht*, Deventer, 1992.

Keeken, G.J. van, "Wettelijke regeling waarde-overdrachten van pensioenaanspraken" PS (1993), 1832-1843.

Kenner, J., "EC Labour Law: The Softly, Softly Approach", 11 IJCLLIR (1995), 307-326.

Kilpatrick, C., "Deciding when Jobs of Equal Value can be Paid Unequally: An Examination of s1(3) of the Equal Pay Act 1970", 23 ILJ (1994), 311-325.

Kittner, M., Krasney, O.E., *Sozialgesetzbuch. Textausgabe mit Einleitungen*, 2nd ed., Bonn, 1991.

Kirner, E. and E. Schulz, "Die Erwerbsbeteiligung im Lebensverlauf von Frauen in Abhängigkeit von der Kinderzahl - Unterschiede zwischen der Bundesrepublik Deutschland und der ehemaligen Deutschen Demokratischen Republik" in C. Gather et al (eds.), *Frauenalterssicherung. Lebensläufe von Frauen und ihre Benachteiligung im Alter*, Berlin 1991 at pp. 62-79.

Klabbers, J., "Informal instruments before the European Court of Justice", 31 CML Rev. (1994), 997-1023.

Kok, L. and Schoneveld, E., "Arbeidsvoorwaarden voor deeltijdwerkers in cao's", 3 TvA (1987), 58-68.

Kolb, R., "Aspekte der Vereinheitlichung der Sozialversicherungssysteme in Ost- und Westdeutschland, in Förster, W. and Rössler, N. (eds.), *Betriebliche Altersversorgung in der Diskussion zwischen Praxis und Wissenschaft. Festschrift für Peter Ahrend*, Köln, 1992, at pp. 35-57.

Kraamwinkel, M., "Weduwnaarspensioenen en gelijke behandeling", *Tijdschrift voor Pensioenvraagstukken* (1990), 84-87.

Kraamwinkel, M.M.H., Schippers, J.J., Siegers, J.J., *De toekomst van de aanvullende pensioenen*, Zwolle, 1992.

Kraamwinkel, M.M.H., *Pensioen, emancipatie en gelijke behandeling*, Deventer, 1995.

Kraamwinkel, M., "Inhaalpensioen voor gediscrimineerde vrouwen", 50 *Sociaal Mandblad Arbeid*, (1995), 644-650.

Krämer, L., "The Single European Act and Environmental Protection: Reflections on Several New Provisions in Community Law", 24 CML Rev. (1987), 659-688.

Kravaritou, Y., "Women and the Law: In Search of an Ever-Evasive Equality", in S. Martin (ed.), *The Construction of Europe. Essays in Honour of Emile Noël*, Dordrecht, 1994 at pp. 227-238.

Kuhley-Oehlert, A., "Das Alter ist weiblich", in C. Gather et al (eds.), *Frauenalterssicherung. Lebensläufe von Frauen und ihre Benachteiligung im Alter*, Berlin 1991 at pp. 247-257.

Kuné, J.B., "Een ouder wordende wereldbevolking in een studie van de Wereld Bank. Pensioenvoorzieningen in mondiaal perspectief; met bijzonder aandacht voor de Nederlandse situatie", TvP (1995), 95-98 and 114-116.

Kuné, J.B., "Bevolkingsveroudering en de financiering van de AOW-voorziening. Is het creëren van een schommelfonds zinvol?", TPV (1996), 31-34.

Kyriazis, G., *Die Sozialpolitik der Europäischen Wirtschaftsgemeinschaft in bezug auf die Gleichberechtigung männlicher und weiblicher Erwerbstätiger*, Berlin, 1990.

L.

Landenberger, M., "Familiepolitische Maßnahmen und ihre Wirkungen auf Arbeitsmarktchancen und soziale Sicherung von Frauen", in C. Gather et al (eds.), *Frauenalterssicherung. Lebensläufe von Frauen und ihre Benachteiligung im Alter*, Berlin 1991 at pp. 83-105.

Lane, R.C., "New Community Competences under the Maastricht Treaty", 30 CML Rev. (1993), 939-979.

Lange, P., "Maastricht and the Social Protocol: Why did they do it?", 21 *Politics and Society* (1993, 5-36.

Lange, P., "The Politics of the Social Dimension", in A.M. Sbragia (ed.), *Euro-Politics. Institutions and Policymaking in the "New" European Community*, Washington, 1992, at pp. 225-256.

Langenfeld, C., *Die Gleichbehandlung von Mann und Frau im Europäischen Gemeinschaftsrecht*, Baden-Baden, 1990.

Langohr-Plato, U., "Gleichbehandlungsgrundsatz und betriebliche Altersversorgung", MDR (1992), 838-841.

Langohr-Plato, U., "Auswirkung das europarechtlichen Lohngleichheitsgrundsatzes auf das deutsche Betriebsrentenrecht", 6 EuZW (1995), 239-243.

Lanquetin, M. and Masse-Dessen, H., "Maastricht: consolidation ou remise en cause des principes en matière d'égalité professionnelle", Droit Social (1992), 386-390.

Laske, C., "The Impact of the Single European Market on Social Protection for Migrant Workers", 30 CML Rev. (1993), 515-539.

Laurent, A., "The elimination of sex discrimination in occupational social security schemes in the EEC", 125 *International Labour Review* (1986), 675-683.

Laurent, A., "De sociale zekerheid in de binnenmarkt van 1992", 52 Maandschrift Economie (1988), 363-371.

Leenders, M.A.J., "Gemeenschapsrecht en sexe-discriminatie", in burkens, M.C., and Kummeling, H.R.B.M., (ed.), *EG en Grondrechten. Gevolgen van de Europese integratie voor de nationale grondrechtenbescherming*, Zwolle, 1993 at pp. 97-139.

Le Grand, J., Robinson, R., *Privatisation and the Welfare State*, London, 1984.

Lenaerts, K., and van Ypersele, P., "Le principe de subsidiarité et son contexte: étude de l'article 3b du Traité CE", CDE (19950, 3-85.

Lewis, J., "Dealing with Dependency: State Practices and Social Realities, 1870-1945", in J. Lewis (ed.) *Women's Welfare Women's Rights*, London, 1983, at pp. 17-37.

Loenen, T., *Verschil in Gelijkheid. De conceptualisering van het juridische gelijkheidsbeginsel met betrekking tot vrouwen en mannen in Nederland en de Verenigde Staten*, Zwolle, 1992.

Lonsdale, S., "Patterns of Paid Work", in C. Glendinning and J. Millar (eds.), *Women and Poverty in Britain: the 1990s*, London, 1992 at pp. 95-109.

Lubnow, M., "Die Rechtsprechung zur Gleichbehandlung von Teilzeitbeschäftigten in der betrieblichen Altersversorgung - Folgen und Fragen", in Förster, W. and Rössler, N. (eds.), *Betriebliche Altersversorgung in der Diskussion zwischen Praxis und Wissenschaft. Festschrift für Peter Ahrend*, Köln, 1992, at pp. 273-294.

Luckhaus, L., "Bridging pensions a question of difference?", 19 ILJ (1990), 48-54.

Luckhaus, L., "Changing Rules, Enduring Structures", 55 MLR (1990), 655-668.

Luckhaus, L., "Intentions and the Avoidance of Community Law", 21 ILJ (1992), 315-322.

Luckhaus, L., "Individualisation of Social Security Benefits", in C. McCrudden (ed.), *Equality of Treatment between Women and Men in Social Security*, London, 1994 at pp. 147-162.

Lutjens, E., *Pensioenvoorzieningen voor werknemers. Juridische beschouwingen over ouderdomspensioenen*, Zwolle, 1989.

Lutjens, E., "Pensioenvoorzieningen voor gehuwde en ongehuwde partners", in Zwemmer, J.W., and Lutjens, E., *Partners in werk en rust*, Lelystad, 1991 at pp.79-137.

Lutjens, E. and Wessels, B., *Aanvullend Pensioen. Civiel- en sociaalverzekeringsrechtelijke hoofdzaken van aanvullende pensioenen in het bedrijfsleven*, Deventer, 1991.

Lutjens, E., "Cross-border membership of occupational pension schemes for migrant workers", EC Tax Review (1993), 164-169.

Lutjens, E., and van Poppel, F.W.A., *Levensverwachting en pensioen. Geslacht afhankelijke of sekse-neutrale actuariële factoren?*, Deventer, 1995.

Lyon-Caen, G., "The Evolution of Labour Law", in Wedderburn et al, *Labour Law in the Post-Industrial Era. Essays in Honour of Higo Sinzheimer*, Aldershot, 1994 at pp. 93-104.

M.

Mackenzie-Stuart, "Subsidiarity - A Busted Flush?", in D. Curtin and D. O'Keeffe (eds.), *Constitutional Adjudication in European Community and National Law*, Dublin, 1992, at pp. 19-24.

Majone, G. (ed.), *Deregulation or Re-Regulation? Regulatory Reform in Europe and the United States*, London, 1990.

Majone, G., "The development of Social Regulation in the European Community: Policy Externalities, Transaction Costs, Motivational Factors", 50 *Aussenwirtschaft* (1995), 79-110.

Mamorsky, "Equal Opportunity and Civil Rights: Employee Benefits Law: Employment Discrimination." in L. Mok (ed), *International Handbook on Pensions Law and similar employee benefits*, London 1989 at pp. 591-600.

Mancini, G.F., "The Free Movement of Workers in the Case-Law of the European Court of Justice", in D. Curtin and D. O'Keeffe (eds.), *Constitutional Adjudication in European Community and National Law*, Dublin, 1992 at pp. 67-77.

Martin, D., "Reflexions sur le champ d'application materiel de l'article 48 du traité CE (à la lumière de la jurisprudence récente de la Cour de justice", CDE (1993), 555-596.

Masson, J., "Women's Pensions", JSWL (1985), 319-340.

Masson, J., "Pensions, Dependency and Divorce", JSWL (1986), 343-361.

Matthiessen, V., Rössler, N., Rühmann, J., "Die nachholende Anpassung von Betriebsrenten - Zu den Entscheidungen des BAG vom 28.4.92", DB Beilage 5/93.

Maydell, B.B. von, "Betriebliche Altersversorgung und gesetzliche Rentenversicherung in der Zukunft", in Förster, W. and Rössler, N. (eds.), *Betriebliche Altersversorgung in der Diskussion zwischen Praxis und Wissenschaft. Festschrift für Peter Ahrend*, Köln, 1992 at pp. 79-88.

McCallum, I.M. and I. Snaith, "EEC Law and United Kingdom Occupational Pensions Schemes", 2 EL Rev. (1977), 266-273.

McCrudden, C. (ed.), *Women, Employment and European Equality Law*, London, 1987.

McCrudden, C. (ed.), *Equality of Treatment between Women and Men in Social Security*, London, 1994.

McCrudden, C. and J. Black, "Achieving Equality between Men and Women in Social Security: Some issues of costs and problems of implementation", in C. McCrudden (ed.), *Equality of Treatment between Women and Men in Social Security*, London, 1994, pp. 169-194

McCrudden, C., "Equal Treatment and Occupational Pensions: Implementing European Community Law in the United Kingdom following the Post-*Barber* judgments of the European Court of Justice", 46 NILQ (1995), 376-404.

McCrudden, C., "Third Time Lucky? The Pensions Act 1995 and Equal Treatment in Occupational Pensions", 25 ILJ (1996), 28-42.

McGlynn, C., "Equality, Maternity and Questions of Pay", 21 EL Rev. (1996), 327-332.

Meinhardt, H., "Betriebliche Altersversorgung - ein wesentliches Element der Personalpolitik - Ein Beitrag zur künftigen Entwicklung von Stellung und Aufgabe der Altersversorgung in Unternahmen, in Förster, W. and Rössler, N. (eds.), *Betriebliche Altersversorgung in der Diskussion zwischen Praxis und Wissenschaft. Festschrift für Peter Ahrend*, Köln, 1992, 310-318.

Meyer, P., *Auswirkungen des EG-Dirkriminerungsverbots von Mann und Frau auf das private und betriebliche Krankheits- und Altersvorzorge in Europa*, Karlsruhe, 1994.

Millett, T., "European Community Law: Sex Equality and Retirement Age", 36 ICLQ (1987), 616-633.

Ministry of Social Affairs, *Social Security in the Netherlands*, Deventer, 1990.

Mitchell, D.J.B., and Rojot, J., "Employee Benefits in the Single Market" in Ulman, L., Eichengreen, B. and Dickens, W.T. (eds.), *Labor and an Integrated Europe*, The Brookings Institution, Washington, 1993 at pp. 128-166.

Mittmann, A., "Das Zweite Gleichberechtigungsgesetz - eine Übersicht", NJW (1994), 3048-3054.

Moore, S., ""Justice Doesn't Mean a Free Lunch": The Application of the Principle of Equal Pay to Occupational Pension Schemes", 20 EL Rev. (1995), 159-177.

Moore, S., "Nothing positive from the Court of Justice", 21 EL Rev. (1996), 156-161.

Moore, S., "Enforcement of private law claims of sex discrimination in the field of employment", in T.K. Hervey and D. O'Keeffe (eds.), *Sex Equality Law in the European Union*, Chichester, 1996, at pp. 139-159.

Mortelmans, K.J.M., "Zaak C-262/88, Douglas Harvey Barber vs. Guardian Royal Exchange Assurance Group", 39 SEW (1991), 143-153.

Mortelmans, K., "De interne markt en het facettenbeleid na het Keck-arrest: nationaal beleid, vrij verkeer of harmonisatie", 42 S.E.W. (1994), 236-250

Mückenberger, U. and Deakin, S., "From deregulation to a European floor of rights: Labour law, flexibilisation and the European single market", 3 ZIAS (1989), 153-207.

N.

Nelissen, J.H.M. and Verbon, H.A.A., "Ouderen voor jongeren", ESB 1993, 817-821.

Nielsen, R. and Szyszczak, E., *The Social Dimension of the European Community*, Copenhagen, 1993.

Niemeyer, W., "Die gesetzliche Rentenversicherung drei Jahre nach der Wiedervereinigung und Perspektiven für ihre Weiterentwicklung", in *Bewährungsprobe der Alterssicherungssysteme in Zeiten wirtschaftlicher Rezession*, Wiesbaden, 1993 at pp. 11-22.

Nieuwenburg, C.K.F., "Pensioenen, arbeidskosten en het aanbod van risicodragend vermogen", SMA (1987), 39-58.

Nobles, R., "Pensions: The New Framework?", 49 MLR (1986), 42-67.

Nobles, R., *Pensions, Employment, and the Law*, Oxford, 1993.

Nobles, R., "Occupational Pensions", 23 ILJ (1994), 69-72.

Nobles, R., "Pensions Act 1995", 59 MLR (1996), 241-260.

Notz, G., "Frauen nun doch an den Herd? Erziehungsgeld, Erziehungsurlaub und die Auswirkung auf die Lebens- und Arbeitssituation von Müttern", in C. Gather et al (eds.), *Frauenalterssicherung. Lebensläufe von Frauen und ihre Benachteiligung im Alter*, Berlin 1991 at pp. 106-119.

O.

Ogus, A.I., and Barendt, E.M., *The Law of Social Security*, 3rd edition, London, 1988.

Ogus, Barendt and Wikeley, *The Law of Social Security*, 4th edition, London, 1995.

Ojeda-Avilés, A., "European Collective Bargaining: A Triumph of the Will?", IJCLLIR (1993), 279-296.

O'Keeffe, D., "Equal Rights for Migrants: the Concept of Social Advantages in in Article 7(2) of Regulation 1612/68", 5 YEL (1985), 93-123.

O'Keeffe, D., "Judicial Interpretation of the Public Service Exception to the Free Movement of Workers", in Curtin, D. and O'Keeffe, D., *Constitutional Adjudication in European Community and National Law. Essays for the Hon. Mr. Justice T.F. O'Higgins*, Dublin, 1992 at pp. 89-106.

O'Keeffe, D., "Union Citizenship", in D. O'Keeffe and P.M. Twomey (eds.), *Legal Issues of the Maastricht Treaty*, London 1994, at pp. 87-107.

O'Keeffe, "Third Generation Remedies and Sex Equality Law" in T.K. Hervey and D. O'Keeffe (eds.), *Sex Equality Law in the European Union*, Chichester, 1996, at pp. 161-172.

Oliver, P., "Non-Community Nationals and the Treaty of Rome", 5 YEL (1985), 57-93.

Olsen, F., "Legal Responses to Gender Discrimination in Europe and the USA", Collected Courses of the Academy of European Law, Volume II, Book 2, (1993), 199-268.

P.

Pannick, D., *Sex Discrimination Law*, Oxford, 1985.

Paulsdorff, J., "Der Begriff der betrieblichen Altersversorgung als Gegenstand der Insollvenzsicherung" in Förster, W. and Rössler, N. (eds.), *Betriebliche Altersversorgung in der Diskussion zwischen Praxis und Wissenschaft. Festschrift für Peter Ahrend*, Köln, 1992 pp. 195-207.

Pauly, H.-J., "Decisions by the Federal Labour Court and the Court of Justice of the European Communities on the Subject of Indirect Discrimination" in Mok, L. (ed.), *International Handbook on Pensions Law and Similar Employee Benefits*, London/Dordrecht/Boston, 1989, at pp. 601-610.

Peijpe, T. van, "EU and Adjustments in Dutch and Nordic Labour Law", 11 IJCLLIR (1995), 42-69.

Pennings, F. (ed.), *Introduction to European Social Security Law*, Deventer, 1994.

Pension Law Reform. The Report of the Pension Law Review Committee, Chairman Professor Roy Goode, Cm 2342-1, London, 1993.

Pieters, D.C.H.M., "Brengt '1992' coördinatie en harmonisatie van de sociale zekerheid?", in A.A. Franken, P.C. Gilhuis and J.A.F. Peters (eds.), *Themis en Europa. Een Opening van Nieuwe Grenzen?*, Zwolle, 1989 at pp. 165-187.

Pieters, D., *Introduction into the Social Security Law of the Member States of the European Community*, 2nd ed., Antwerpen-Apeldoorn, 1993.

Piso, I., "Het Ten Oever-arrest van het Hof van Justitie", Sociaal Recht 1993 288-292.

Ploug, N., "The welfare state in liquidation?", 48 *International Social Security Review* 2/1995, 61-71.

Ploug, N. and Kvist, J., *Social Security in Europe. Development or Dismantlement?*, Deventer, 1996.

Prakke, L and Kortmann, C.A.J.M. (eds.), *Het Staatsrecht van de landen der Europese Gemeenschappen*, Deventer, 1993.

Prechal, S., "De hordenloop in de sociale zekerheid: gelijke behandeling in de aanvullende stelsels", Nemesis (1984), 329-331.

Prechal, S. and Burrows, N., *Gender Discriination Law of the European Community*, Aldershot, 1990.

Prechal, S., "Ondeugdelijke communautaire wetgeving: de pensioenrichtlijn", NJB (1990), 1299-1303.

Prechal, S. "Zaak 109/88, *Handels- of Kantorfunktionaerernes Forbund i Danmark* v. *Dansk Arbejdsgiverforening*; Zaak C-33/89, *Kowalska* v. *Freie und Hansestadt Hamburg*; Zaak C-184/89, *Nimz* v. *Freie und Hansestadt Hamburg*", 40 SEW (1992), 183-196.

Prechal, S., "Bommen ruimen in Maastricht. Wijziging van Artikel 119 EEG", 67 NJB (1992), 349-354.

Prechal, S., "Combatting indirect discrimination in Community law context", (1993) LIEI 81-97.

Prechal, S., "Zaak C-9/91, The Queen v. Secretary of State for Social Security, ex parte the Equal Opportunities Commission", 42 SEW (1994), 191-196.

Prinz, K., "Die Bedeutung der Kindererziehung für die Erwerbsverläufe und die Alterssicherung von Frauen in der Bundesrepublik Deutschland und der ehemaligen Deutschen Demokratischen Republik" in C. Gather et al (eds.), *Frauenalterssicherung. Lebensläufe von Frauen und ihre Benachteiligung im Alter*, Berlin 1991 at pp. 46-61.

R.

Raaphorst, G.B., *De Algemene nabestaandenwet*, Zwolle, 1993.

Rating, S., *Mittelbare Diskriminierung der Frau im Erwerbsleben nach europäischem Gemeinschaftsrecht. Richterrecht des EuGH und die Voraussetzungen seiner Rezeption am Beispiel Spaniens und der Bundesrepublik*, Baden-Baden, 1994.

Reardon, A., *Allied Dunbar Pensions Guide*, 4th ed., London, 1992.

Reynaud, E., "Financing retirement pensions: Pay-as-you-go and funded systems in the European Union", 48 *International Social Security Review* 3/4/1995, 41-57.

Rhodes, M., "The Future of the Social Dimension: Labour Market Regulation in Post-1992 Europe", 30 JCMS (1992), 23-51.

Rhodes, M., "The Social Dimension after Maastricht: Setting a new Agenda for the Labour Market", IJCLLIR (1993), 297-325.

Riemens, R.C., "Wetsvoorstel wijziging Pensioen- en Spaarfondsenwet", TvP 1993 50-52.

Rische, H., "Finanzierungsperspektiven der gesetzlichen Rentenversicherung im geeinten Deutschland, in Förster, W. and Rössler, N. (eds.), *Betriebliche Altersversorgung in der Diskussion zwischen Praxis und Wissenschaft. Festschrift für Peter Ahrend*, Köln, 1992, at pp. 58-68.

Robinson, W., "Case C-91/92, *Paola Faccini Dori* v. *Recreb Srl*", 32 CML Rev. (1995), 629-639.

Roerbroek, J.M., "Europese sociale politiek en Europese verzorgingsstaten", in Engbersen, G., Hemerijck, A.C. and Bakker, W.E. (eds.), *Zorgen in het Europese Huis. Verkenningen over de grenzen van nationale verzorgingsstaten*, Amsterdam, 1994 at pp. 236-263.

Rolf, G., "Ideologiekritik am Rentenrecht und ein Reformvorschlag zur eigenständigen Alterssicherung von Frauen" in C. Gather et al (eds.), *Frauenalterssicherung. Lebensläufe von Frauen und ihre Benachteiligung im Alter*, Berlin 1991 at pp. 175-190.

Rood, M., "Labour Law in the 21st Century", in Wedderburn et al, *Labour Law in the Post-Industrial Era. Essays in Honour of Higo Sinzheimer*, Aldershot, 1994 at pp. 83-91.

Rooij, J.W.P.M. van, Schell, J.L.M., Vansteenkiste, S.M.E., Verwijmeren, C.J.M.M., *Rechterlijke toetsing aan het gelijkheidsbeginsel in het sociale-zekerheidsrecht in rechtsvergelijkend perspectief*, Den Haag, 1994.

Rühmann, J., "Auswirkung der neueren EuGH-Rechtsprechung auf die Gestaltung betrieblicher Versorgungsregelungen", BetrAVG (1994), 107-114.

Rühmann, J., Heissmann, E., "Sex Discrimination - The German View", *International Pension Lawyer* 1994, no. 16, 14.

Ruland, F., "Der Europäische Binnenmarkt und die sozialen Alterssicherungssysteme", 24 EuR (1989), 303-337.

S.

Saelaert, C., Taghon, A.G.G.D., Zeijen, J.P.M., "Gelijke behandeling van mannen en vrouwen in de sociale zekerheid", in Pieters, D. (ed.), *Europees sociale zekerheidsrecht. Commentaar.* Antwerp, Apeldoorn, 1988.

Salafia, A., "Italy. The draft legislation for reform of Italy's statutory and complementary pension schemes", 48 *International Social Security Review* 3/4/1995, 143-150.

Schaub, G., *Arbeitsrechts-Handbuch*, 7th edition, München, 1992.

Schermer, A., "Ontwerp vierde richtlijn", SMA (1985), 520-533.

Schiek, D., "Positive Action in Community Law", 25 ILJ (1996), 239-246.

Schmähl, W. (ed.), *The Future of Basic and Supplementary Pension Schemes in the European Community - 1992 and Beyond*, Baden-Baden, 1991.

Schmähl, W., "Unbau der sozialen Sicherung im Alter? - Zur Diskussion über die weitere Entwicklung der Alterssicherung in Deutschland", Staatswissenschaften und Staatspraxis (1995), 331-365.

Schösser, F., "Muß die gesetzliche Rentenversicherung umgebaut werden?", 4 Neue Zeitschrift für Sozialrecht (1995), 193-197.

Schuler, R., "Zwischenstaatliche und gemeinschaftsrechtliche Sozialrechtsintegration im Vergleich", 20 EuR (1985) 113-137.

Schulte, B., "Europäisches und nationales Sozialrecht", EuR (1990), 35-79.

Schuster, G. "Rechtsfragen der Maastrichter Vereinbarungen zur Sozialpolitik", 1992 EuZW, 178-187.

Schwartz, I.E., "EG-Kompetenzen für den Binnenmarkt: Exklusiv oder konkurriend/subsidär?", in O. Due, M. Lutter, J. Schwarze (eds.), *Festschrift für Ulrich Everling*, Baden-Baden, 1995 at pp. 1331-1354.

Sciarra, S., "Social Values and the Multiple Sources of European Social Law", 1 *European Law Journal* (1995), 60-83.

Séché, J.-C., "L'europe sociale après Maastricht", CDE (1993), 509-536.

Sevenster, H.G., *Milieubeleid en Gemeenschapsrecht. Het interne juridische kader en de praktijk*, Deventer, 1992.

Shanks, M., *European Social Policy Today and Tomorrow*, Oxford, 1977.

Shanks, M., "The Social Policy of the European Communities", 14 CML Rev. (1977), 375-383.

Shaw, J., "Recent Developments in the Field of Labour Market Equality: Sex Discrimination Law in the Federal Republic of Germany", Comparative Labor Law Journal (1991), 18-44.

Shaw, J., "Twin-Track Social Europe - the Inside Track", in O'Keeffe, D. and Twomey, P.M. (eds.), *Legal Issues of the Maastricht Treaty*, London, 1994 at pp. 295-311.

Shrubsall, V., "Article 119, Pensions and Part-Time Workers", 16 ILJ (1987), 52-54.

Sjerps, C.M., "Van Doornroosje en haar hardnekkige prins, oftwel: hoe het EG-Hof de pensioenwereld probeert te wekken", Sociaal Recht (1990), 212-217.

Snaith, I., "Two more Equal Pay cases from the United Kingdom", 6 EL Rev. (1981), 193-198.

Snyder, F., "The Effectiveness of European Community Law: Institutions, Processes, Tools and Techniques", 56 MLR (1993), 19-54.

Snyder, F., "Subsidiarity: An Aspect of European Community Law and its Relevance to Lesbians and Gay Men", in K. Waaldijk and A. Clapham (eds.), *Homosexuality - A European Community Issue - Essays on Lesbian and Gay Rights in European Law and Policy*, Dordrecht, 1993, 223-246.

Snyder, F., "Soft Law and Institutional Practice in the European Community", in S. Martin (ed.), *The Construction of Europe. Essays in Honour of Emile Noël*, Dordrecht, 1994 at pp. 197-225.

Sohrab, J.A., *Sexing the Benefit: Women, Social Security and Financial Independence in EC Equality Law*, dissertation, Florence, 1994.

Sohrab, J.A., "Women and Social Security: the Limits of EEC Equality Law", *Journal of Social Welfare and Family Law*, (1994), 5-17.

Steiner, J., "Subsidiarity under the Maastricht Treaty", in D. O'Keeffe and P.M. Twomey (eds.), *Legal Issues of the Maastricht Treaty*, London 1994, pp. 49-64.

Steiner, J., "The Principle of Equal Treatment for Men and Women in Social Security", in T.K. Hervey and D. O'Keeffe (eds.), *Sex Equality Law in the European Union*, Chichester, 1996, at pp. 111-136.

Steinmeyer, H.-D., *Betriebliche Altersversorgung und Arbeitsverhältnis - Das betriebliche Ruhegeld als*

Leistung im arbeitsvertraglichen Austauschverhältnis, München, 1991.

Steinmeyer, H.-D., "Harmonisierung des Betriebsrentenrechts in der Europäischen Gemeinschaft?", EuZW (1991), 43-49.

Steinmeyer, H.-D., "Die Gehaltsumwandlungsversicherung als betriebliche Altersversorgung", BB (1992), 1553-1559.

Steinmeyer, H.-D., "Richtungsweisende Entscheidungen des BAG - u.a. Nachholung unterlassener Anpassungen, Anpassung im Konzern, Gehaltsumwandlung, Unverfallbarkeit bei zusätzlichen Zusagen, Begriff des Arbeitgebers im Insolvenzrecht", in in *Bewährungsprobe der Alterssicherungssysteme in Zeiten wirtschaftlicher Rezession*, Wiesbaden, 1993 at pp. 43-58.

Steinmeyer, H.-D., "Nationaler Bericht Deutschland", in *Zusatzversorgungssysteme in der Bundesrepublik Deutschland, Frankreich und Großbritannien - Entwicklung, Tendenzen und offene Fragen*, Köln, 1994.

Stevens, L.G.M., *Pensioen in de winstsfeer*, 3rd ed., Deventer, 1993.

Stevens, L.G.M., *Pensioen in de loonsfeer*, 3rd ed., Deventer, 1993.

Stevens, L.G.M. (ed.), *Pensioen en andere toekomstvoorzieningen*, Deventer, looseleaf.

Steyger, E., "Hof van Justitie EG, 17 mei 1990", Actualiteiten nr. 116, Nemesis (1990), 210-215.

Steyger, E., "Het vervolg van de Ruzius-zaak of: hoe ver ligt Groningen van Luxemburg?", NJB (1990), 1405-1407.

Stocker, O., "Le second arret Defrenne. L'égalité des rémunerations des travailleurs masculins et des travailleurs feminins.", 13 CDE (1977), 180-226.

Stolz-Willig, B., ""Geregelte" Vereinbarkeit von Beruf und Familie - das Ende der Benachteiligung von Frauen im Erwerbsleben?", in C. Gather et al (eds.), *Frauenalterssicherung. Lebensläufe von Frauen und ihre Benachteiligung im Alter*, Berlin 1991 at pp. 120-129.

Streeck, W., "Neo-Voluntarism: A New European Social Policy Regime?", 1 ELJ (1995), 31-59.

Supplementary Pensions in the European Union: Developments, Trends and Outstanding Issues, Report by the European Commission's Network of Experts on Supplementary Pensions, Brussels, 1994.

Szyszczak, E., "L'espace sociale Européenne: Reality, dreams, or nightmares?", 33 German Yearbook of International Law (1990), 284-307.

Szyszczak, E., "Social Policy: a Happy Ending or a Reworking of the Fairy Tale?", in O'Keeffe, D. and Twomey, P.M. (eds.), *Legal Issues of the Maastricht Treaty*, London, 1994 at pp. 313-327.

Szyszczak, E., "Future Directions in European Union Social Law", 24 ILJ (1995), 19-32.

Szyszczak, E., "Social Rights as General Principles of Community Law", in Neuwahl, N.A. and Rosas, A. (eds), *The European Union and Human Rights*, Deventer 1995 at pp. 207-220.

T.

Taverne, D., *The Pension Time Bomb in Europe*, Federal Trust Report, London, 1995.

Taschner, H. C., "Free Movement of Students, Retired Persons and Other European Citizens - A difficult legislative process", in H.G. Schermers et al (eds.), *Free Movement of Persons in Europe*, Dordrecht, 1993 at pp. 427-436.

Tegtmeier, W., "Supplementary Pension Schemes within the Overall System of Provision for Old-Age in the Federal Republic of Germany", in W. Schmähl (ed.), *The Future of Basic and Supplementary Pension Schemes in the European Community - 1992 and Beyond*, Baden-Baden, 1991 pp. 99-110.

Tegtmeier, W., "Zum Einfluss gesellschaftlicher und rechtlicher Rahmenbedingungen auf die betriebliche Altersversorgung", in Förster, W. and Rössler, N. (eds.), *Betriebliche Altersversorgung in der Diskussion zwischen Praxis und Wissenschaft. Festschrift für Peter Ahrend*, Köln, 1992 at pp. 89-100.

Temple Lang, J., "Community Constitutional Law: Article 5 EEC Treaty", 27 CML Rev. (1990), 645-681

Tether, M., "Sex Equality and Occupational Pension Schemes", 24 ILJ (1995), 194-203.

Thomas, M. and Dowrick, B., *Blackstone's Guide to the Pensions Act 1995*, London, 1995.

Thompson, L.H., "The advantages and disadvantages of different social welfare strategies", 48 *International Social Security Review* 3/4/1995, 59-73.

Tölke, A., "Heirat und Geburt als Einschnitte in der weiblichen Erwerbsbiographie", in C. Gather et al (eds.), *Frauenalterssicherung. Lebensläufe von Frauen und ihre Benachteiligung im Alter*, Berlin 1991 at pp. 32-45.

Toth, A.G., "The principle of subsidiarity in the Maastricht Treaty", 29 CML Rev. (1992), 1079-1105.

Toth, A.G., "A Legal Analysis of Subsidiarity", in D. O'Keeffe and P.M. Twomey (eds.), *Legal Issues of the Maastricht Treaty*, London 1994, pp. 37-48.

Trommel, W., *Eigentijds met pensioen. Een beschouwing over flexibele pensioenering en arbeidsdeelname in Nederland, aan de hand van Amerikaanse, Zweedse en Japanse voorbeelden*, Den Haag, 1993.

U.

Ulman, L., Eichengreen, B. and Dickens, W.T. (eds.), *Labor and an Integrated Europe*, The Brookings Institution, Washington, 1993.

V.

Van der Steen, I., *Grensarbeid en Sociale Zekerheid*, Kluwer Reeks Sociale Verzekeringswetten, part 2A, Deventer, Looseleaf.

Van der Steen, I., "Gelijke behandeling van mannen en vrouwen in de aanvullende pensioenregelingen: een nieuw richtlijnvoorstel", *Nederlands Tijdschrift voor Europees Recht* (1995), 123-125.

Van der Steen, I., "Voorkeursbehandeling of gelijke kansen?", *Nederlands Tijdschrift voor Europees Recht* (1995), 273-277.

Van der Steen, I., "Vrij verkeer en social zekerheid van ambtenaren", *Nederlands Tijdschrift voor Europees Recht* (1996), 53-57.

Van der Steen, I., "Gelijke behandeling gezinsleden migrerende werknemers", *Nederlands Tijdschrift voor Europees Recht* (1996), 173-176.

Vanistendael, F., "The Limits to the New Community Tax Order", 31 CML Rev. (1994), 293-314.

Vanistendael, F., "The Consequences of *Schumacker* and *Wielockx*: Two Steps forward in the Tax Procession of Echternach", 33 CML Rev. (1996), 255-269.

Van Veen, "Verjaring van pensioenopbouw", NJB 1995, 213-4

Vaubel, R., "Social Regulation and Market Integration: A Critique and Public-Choice Analysis of the Social Chapter", 50 *Aussenwirtschaft* (1995), 111-132.

Veer, I. de, Bruyn, R.A., Linden, M. van der, *Gelijke behandeling naar geslacht in aanvullende pensioenregelingen. Juridisch, beleidsmatig en empirisch bekeken*, Den Haag, 1991.

Veil, M., ""Es wächst zusammen, was nicht zusammen gehört" - Die Frau im Rentenrecht der ehemaligen Deutschen Demokratischen Republik und der Bundesrepublik Deutschland" in C. Gather et al (eds.), *Frauenalterssicherung. Lebensläufe von Frauen und ihre Benachteiligung im Alter*, Berlin 1991 at pp. 191-204.

Veldman, A., "De bescheiden functie van het juridisch gelijkheidsbeginsel", 12 *Nemesis* (1996), 31-38.

Verburg, L.G. and Banz, J.C., "Maastricht voorbij: gelijke behandeling man/vrouw in pensioenregelingen", SMA (1992), 429-436.

Vogel-Polsky, E., "L'Acte unique ouvre-t-il l'espace social européen?", Droit Social (1989), 177-189.

Vogel-Polsky, E., "Welk Juridisch Instrumentarium is Nodig voor een Sociaal Europa?", SMA (1990), 60-70.

Vogel-Polsky, E., L'europe sociale 1993: Illusion, alibi ou réalité?, Brussels, 1991.

Voirin, M., "Private and public pension schemes: Elements of a comparative approach", 48 International Social Security Review 3/4/1995, 91-141.

Vonk, G.J., De coördinatie van bestaansminimumuitkeringen in de Europese Gemeenschap, Deventer, 1991.

Voorden, W. van, "Flexibilisering van de arbeidsmarkt als spanningsbron voor de sociale zekerheid", SMA (1987), 726-736.

Vorselen, L. van, Solidariteit en pensioen. Denkbeelden over een solidair ouderdomspensioen, Deventer, 1993.

Verbon, H., "De financiering van de oudedagsvoorziening", 18 Tijdschrift voor Politieke Ekonomie (1995), 32-51.

W.

Walker, A., "The poor relation: poverty among older women", in Glendinning, C. and Millar, J. (eds.), Women and Poverty in Britain: the 1990s, London, 1992 at pp. 176-192.

Waltermann, R., "Wieder Altersgrenze 65?", NZA (1994), 822-830.

Wanders, W., "Freizügigkeit statt Sozialunion - Zur Kompetenz der Sozialrrechtsintegration in der Gemeinschaft", 20 EuR (1985) 138-157.

Ward, S., "Equality of Treatment between Women and Men in Occupational Social Security", in C. McCrudden (ed.), Equality of Treatment between Women and Men in Social Security, London, 1994 at pp. 99-113.

Ward, S., Managing the Pensions Revolution, London 1995.

Warner, H., "EC Social Policy in Practice: Community action on behalf of women and its impact in the Member States", 23 JCMS (1984), 141-167.

Wartenberg, L.-G. von, "Zur Bedeutung der betrieblichen Altersversorgung für die Finanzierung deutscher Unternehmen, in Förster, W. and Rössler, N. (eds.), Betriebliche Altersversorgung in der Diskussion zwischen Praxis und Wissenschaft. Festschrift für Peter Ahrend, Köln, 1992, at pp. 141-159.

Wattel, P.J., "The EC Court's attempts to reconcile the Treaty Freedoms with International Tax Law", 33 CML Rev. (1996), 223-254.

Watson, P., Social Security Law in the European Communities, London, 1980.

Watson, P., "The Community Social Charter", 28 CML Rev. (1991), 37-68.

Watson, P. "Wandering Students: Their Rights under Community Law", in D. Curtin and D. O'Keeffe (eds.), Constitutional Adjudication in European Community and National Law, Dublin, 1992 at pp. 79-88.

Watson, P., "Social Policy after Maastricht", 30 CML Rev. (1993), 481-513.

Watson, P., "Equality of Treatment: A Variable concept?", 24 ILJ (1995), 33-48.

Weatherill, S. and Beaumont, P., EC Law, 2nd ed., London, 1995.

Weatherill, S., Law and Integration in the European Union, Oxford, 1995.

Weatherill, S., "Subsidiarity and Responsibility", University of Nottingham Research Papers in Law, No.

6, 1993.

Weatherill, S., "Beyond Preemption? Shared Competence and Constitutional Change in the European Community", in D. O'Keeffe and P.M. Twomey (eds.), *Legal Issues of the Maastricht Treaty*, London 1994, pp. 13-33.

Webb, J., "Limiting reliance on discriminatory pensionable ages: The possible consequences for other benefits", 55 MLR (1992), 393-400.

Wedderburn, , "The Social Charter in Britain - Labour Law and Labour Courts?", 54 MLR (1991), 1-47.

Wedderburn, "European Community Law and Workers' Rights. Fact or Fake in 1992?", 13 *Dublin University Law Journal* (1991), 1-35.

Wedderburn et al, *Labour Law in the Post-Industrial Era. Essays in Honour of Higo Sinzheimer*, Aldershot, 1994.

Wedderburn, W., "Labour Law and the Individual in Post-Industrial Societies", in Wedderburn et al, *Labour Law in the Post-Industrial Era. Essays in Honour of Higo Sinzheimer*, Aldershot, 1994 at pp. 13-82.

Weiler, J.H.H., "The Community System: The Dual Character of Supranationalism", 1 YEL (1981), 267-306.

Weiler, J.H.H., "The Transformation of Europe", 100 Yale LJ (1991), 2403-2483.

Weiss, M., "The significance of Maastricht for European Community Social Policy", 1992, IJCLLIR 3-14.

Wellens, K.C. and G.M. Borchardt, "Soft Law in European Community Law", 14 EL Rev. (1989), 267-321.

Westerveld, M., *Keuzes van gisteren...een blauwdruk voor morgen? Honderd jaar sociale-verzekeringspensioenen in de Bondsrepubliek Duitsland, Groot-Brittannië en Nederland*, 1994, Den Haag.

Westerveld, M., "Yesterday's Choices ... Tomorrow's Blueprint? - One hundred years of Social Security Pensions in the Federal Republic of Germany, the United Kingdom and the Netherlands", in 10 IJCLLIR (1994), 16-35.

Westerveld, M., "Pensioenen in de 21e eeuw: gouden bergen, diepe dalen", NJB nr. 28 (1996), 1103-1109.

Whiteford, E.A., "De sociale dimensie van de EG na Maastricht: oude wijn in nieuwe zakken", 18 NJCM (1993), 110-132.

Whiteford, E.A., "Social Policy after Maastricht", 18 EL Rev. (1993), 202-222.

Whiteford, E.A., "Collectief Geheugenverlies? Het EG-recht en de aanvullende pensioenen", 18 NJCM (1993), 998-1004.

Whiteford, E.A., "Lost in the Mists of Time: The ECJ and Occupational Pensions", 32 CML Rev. (1995), 801-840.

Whiteford, E.A., "Eindelijk Duidelijkheid? Het Hof van Justitie en aanvullende pensioenregelingen", 50 *Sociaal Mandblad Arbeid* (1995), 638-643.

Whiteford, E.A., "W(h)ither Social Policy?", in More and Shaw (eds.), *New Legal Dynamics of European Union*, Oxford, 1995 at pp. 111-128.

Whiteford, E.A., "Occupational Pensions and European Law: Clarity at Last?", in T.K. Hervey and D. O'Keeffe (eds.), *Sex Equality Law in the European Union*, Chichester, 1996, at pp. 21-34.

Whiteford, P., "The use of replacement rates in international comparisons of benefit systems", 48 *International Social Security Review* 2/1995, 3-30.

Wienk, M., "Wettelijk recht op waarde-overdracht: mag het een onsje meer zijn?", Sociaal Recht 1993 193-199.

Wildt, J.H.J. de, "Gelijke behandeling in aanvullende pensioneregelingen", TpV (1988), 73-77.

Wilkinson, B., "Towards European Citizenship? Nationality, Discrimination and Free Movement of Workers in the European Union", 1 European Public Law (1995), 417-437.

Wincott, D., "Is the Treaty of Maastricht an adequate "Constitution" for the European Union?", 72 *Public Administration* (1994), 573-590.

Winter, J.A. "Direct Applicability and Direct Effect: Two Distinct and Different Concepts in Community Law", 9 CML Rev. (1972), 425-438.

Wissmann, M., "Die ordnungspolitischen Herausforderungen der 90er Jahre", in Förster, W. and Rössler, N. (eds.), *Betriebliche Altersversorgung in der Diskussion zwischen Praxis und Wissenschaft. Festschrift für Peter Ahrend*, Köln, 1992, at pp. 69-77.

Woolcock, S., Hodges, M., Schreiber, K., *Britain, Germany and 1992. The Limits of Deregulation*, London, 1991.

World Bank, *Averting the Old Age Crisis. Policies to Protect the Old **and** Protect Growth*, Oxford, 1994.

Wouters, J., "Gelijke Behandeling van Mannen en Vrouwen inzake Bedrijfspensioenen: De "Post-*Barber*"-Arresten van het Hof van Justitie", 20 NJCM-Bulletin (1995), 274-302.

Würtenberger, T., "Equality", in Karpen, U. (ed.), *The Constitution of the Federal Republic of Germany. Essays on the Basic Rights and Principles of the Basic Law with a Translation of the Basic Law*, Baden-Baden, 1988, at pp. 67-90.

Wyatt, D. and Dashwood, A., *European Community Law*, 3rd ed. 1993, London

Z.

Zachert, U., "Trade Unions in Europe - Dusk or a new Dawn?", IJCLLIR (1993), 15-

Zavvos, G.S., "Pension fund liberalization and the future of retirement financing in Europe", 31 CML Rev. (1994), 609-630.

Case 75/63, *Unger* v. *Bestuur der Bedrijfsvereniging voor Detailhandel en Ambachten te Utrecht*, [1964] ECR 177   226, 238

Case 1/67, *Ciechelski* v. *Caisse Régionale de sécurité sociale de centre d'Orléans*, [1967] ECR 181   238

Case 2/67, *de Moor* v. *Caisse de Pension des Employés Privés*, [1967] ECR 197   238

Case 80/70, *Defrenne* v. *Belgian State*, [1971] ECR 445 (*Defrenne I*)   93, 122, 123, 126, 134, 186, 204, 251

Case 152/73, *Sotgiu* v. *Deutsche Bundespost*, [1974] ECR 153   229

Case 167/73, *Commission* v. *France*, [1974] ECR 359   91, 225, 226, 230

Case 36/74, *Walrave and Koch* v. *AUCI*, [1974] ECR 1405   225

Case 41/74, *Van Duyn* v. *Home Office*, [1974] ECR 1337   225

Case 67/74, *Bonsignore* v. *Oberstadtdirektor der Stadt Köln*, [1975] ECR 297   229

Case 24/75, *Petroni* v. *Office National des Pensions pour Travailleurs Salaries*, [1975] ECR 1149   238

Case 32/75, *Cristini* v. *SNCF*, [1975] ECR 108   230

Case 36/75, *Rutili* v. *Ministre de l'interieur*, [1975] ECR 1219   228

Case 43/75, *Defrenne* v. *Sabena*, [1976] ECR 455 (*Defrenne II*)   91, 92, 118, 120, 121, 122, 134, 150, 165

Case 13/76, *Dona* v. *Mantero*, [1976] ECR 1333   225

Case 40/76, *Kermaschek* v. *Bundesanstalt für Arbeit*, [1976] ECR 1699   240

Case 45/76, *Comet BV* v. *Produktschap voor Siergewassen* [1976] ECR 2043   137, 138

Case 62/76, *Strehl* v. *Nationaal Pensioenfonds voor Mijnwerkers*, [1977] ECR 211   238

Case 112/76, *Manzoni* v. *Fonds National de retraite des ouvriers mineurs*, [1977] ECR 1647   238

Case 30/77, *R.* v. *Bouchereau*, [1977] ECR 1999   229

Case 35/77, *Beerens* v. *Rijksdienst voor Arbeidsvoorziening*, [1977] ECR 2249   241

Case 149/77, *Defrenne* v. *SABENA*, [1978] ECR 1365, (*Defrenne III*)   92, 118, 119, 127, 129, 153

Case 1/78, *Kenny* v. *Insurance Officer*, [1978] ECR 1489   242

Case 10/78, *Belbouab* v. *Bundesknappschaft*, [1978] ECR 1915   239

Case 177/78, *Pigs and Bacon Commission* v. *McCarren and Company Ltd.*, [1979] ECR 2161   137

Case 110/79, *Coonan* v. *Insurance Officer*, [1980] ECR 1445   242

Case 131/79, *R.* v. *Secretary of State for Home Affairs, ex parte Santillo*, [1980] ECR 1585   229

Case 149/79, *Commission* v. *Belgium*, [1980] ECR 3881   229

Case 69/80, *Worringham and Humphreys* v. *Lloyds Bank Ltd.*, [1981] ECR 767   114, 123, 124, 178

Case 96/80, *Jenkins* v. *Kingsgate (Clothing Productions) Ltd.*, [1981] ECR 9194, 118, 122, 186, 209

Case 12/81, *Garland* v. *British Rail Engineering Ltd.*, [1982] ECR 359   119, 120

Case 15/81, *Gaston Schul* v. *Inspecteur der Invoerrechten en Accijnzen*, [1982] ECR 1409   88

Case 19/81, *Burton* v. *British Railways Board*, [1982] ECR 554   153, 198

Case 53/81, *Levin* v. *Staatssecretaris van Justitie*, [1982] ECR 1035   96, 226

Case 65/81, *Reina* v. *Landeskreditbank*, [1982] ECR 33   230

Case 108/81, *Amylum* v. *Council*, [1982] ECR 3107   167

Joined Cases 115 and 116/81, *Adoui and Cornuaille* v. *Belgium*, [1982] ECR 1665   227

Joined Cases 75/82 and 117/82, *Razzouk and Beydoun* v. *Commission*, [1984] ECR 1509   186

Cases 14/83, *von Colson and Kamann* v. *Land Nordrhein-Westfalen*, [1984] ECR 1891   132

Case 79/83, *Harz* v. *Deutsche Tradax GmbH*, [1984] ECR 1921   132

Case 184/83, *Hofmann* v. *Barmer Ersatzkasse*, [1984] ECR 3047   120

Case 249/83, *Hoeckx* v. *Openbaar Centrum voor Maatschappelijk Welzijn Kalmhout*, [1985] ECR

973   230

Case 267/83, *Diatta* v. *Land Berlin*, [1985] ECR 567   228

Case 293/83, *Gravier* v. *City of Liège*, [1985] ECR 593   140

Case 41/84, *Pinna* v. *Caisse d'allocation familiales de la Savoie*, [1986] ECR 1   243

Case 94/84, *ONEM* v. *Deak*, [1985] ECR 1873   240

Case 151/84, *Roberts* v. *Tate and Lyle Industries Ltd.*, [1986] ECR 703   105, 154, 198

Case 152/84, *Marshall* v. *Southampton and South West Area Health Authority*, [1986] ECR 723

105, 154, 168, 198

Case 157/84, *Frascogna* v. *Caisse des Dépôts et Consignations*, [1985] ECR 1739   240

Case 170/84, *Bilka Kaufhaus* v. *Weber von Hartz*, [1986] ECR 1607

100, 119, 122, 133, 134, 183, 193, 316, 319

Case 222/84, *Johnston* v. *Chief Constable of the RUC*, [1986] ECR 1651   177

Case 262/84, *Beets-Proper* v. *van Landschot Bankiers NV*, [1986] ECR 773   105, 154, 198

Case 284/84, *Spruyt* v. *Sociale Verzekeringsbank*, [1986] ECR 685   245

Case 302/84, *Ten Holder* v. *Bestuur van de Nieuwe Algemene Bedrijfsvereniging*, [1986] ECR 1821

248

Case 59/85, *The Netherlands* v. *Reed*, [1986] ECR 1283   228, 230

Case 66/85, *Lawrie-Blum* v. *Land Baden-Württemberg*, [1986] ECR 2121   96, 226

Case 71/85, *State of the Netherlands* v. *FNV*, [1986] ECR 3855   99

Case 139/85, *Kempf* v. *Staatssecretaris van Justitie*, [1986] ECR 1741   227

Case 150/85, *Drake* v. *Chief Adjudication Officer*, [1986] ECR 1995   97

Case 192/85, *Newstead* v. *Department of Transport*, [1987] ECR 4753

       115, 125, 126, 178, 179, 186, 317, 326

Case 225/85, *Commission* v. *Italy*, [1987] ECR 2625   229

Case 309/85, *Barra* v. *Belgian State and City of Liège* [1988] ECR 355   140

Case 384/85, *Borrie-Clarke* v. *Chief Adjudication Officer*, [1987] ECR 2865   100

Case 39/86, *Lair* v. *Universität Hannover*, 1988] ECR 3161   226

Case 126/86, *Giminez Zaera* v. *Instituto Nacional de la Seguridad Social y Tesorería General de la Seguridad Social*, [1987] ECR 3697   91

Case 197/86, *Brown* v. *Secretary of State for Scotland*, [1988] ECR 3205   226

Case 312/86, *Commission* v. *French Republic (Re the protection of women)*, [1988] ECR 6315   174

Case R 45/87, *Commission* v. *Ireland*, [1987] ECR 1369   209

Case 80/87, *Dik* v. *College van Burgemeester en Wethouders der Gemeente Arnhem en Winterswijk*, [1988] ECR 1601   100

Case 147/87, *Zaoui* v. *Cramif*, [1987] ECR 5511   240

Case 196/87, *Steymann* v. *Staatssecretaris van Justitie*, [1988] ECR 6159   226

Case 235/87, *Matteucci* v. *Communauté Française de Belgique*, [1988] ECR 5589   230

Case C-379/87, *Groener* v. *Minister for Education and the City of Dublin Educational Committee*, [1989] ECR 3967   230

Case 344/87, *Bettray* v. *Staatssecretaris van Justitie*, [1989] ECR 1621   226

Case 388/87, *Warmerdam-Steggerda* v. *Bestuur van de Nieuwe Algemene Bedrijfsvereniging*, [1989] ECR 1203   239

Case 33/88, *Allué and Coonan* v. *Università degli Studi di Venezia*, [1989] ECR 1591   229

Joined Cases 48/88, 106/88 and 107/88, *Achterberg-te-Riele and others* v. *Sociale Verzekeringsbank*, [1989] ECR 1963   96

Case C-102/88, *Ruzius-Wilbrink* v. *Bestuur van de Bedrijfsvereniging voor Overheidsdiensten*, [1989] ECR I-4311   101

Case 109/88, *Handels-og-Kontorfunktionaerernes Forbund i Danmark* v. *Dansk Arbejdsgiverforening (ex parte Danfoss)*, [1989] ECR 3199   121, 193

Case 171/88, *Rinner-Kühn* v. *FWW Spezial Gebäudereiningung GmbH & Co Kg*, [1989] ECR 2743   101, 119

Case C-262/88, *Barber* v. *Guardian Royal Exchange*, [1990] ECR I-1889

                     105, 119, 121, 127, 152, 155, 157, 160, 179, 183, 193, 198, 316, 317

Case C-2/89, *Bestuur van de Sociale Verzekeringsbank* v. *Kits van Heijningen*, [1990] ECR I-1755

                                                                                    239, 240

Case C-33/89, *Kowalska* v. *Freie und Hansestadt Hamburg*, [1990] ECR I-2591   121

Case C-105/89, *Buhari Haji* v. *INASTI*, [1990] ECR I-4211   239

Case C-113/89, *Rush Portuguesa* v. *Office National d'Immigration*, [1990] ECR I-1417   91

Case C-184/89, *Nimz* v. *Freie und Hansestadt Hamburg*, [1991] ECR I-297   121, 165, 166

Case C-188/89, *Foster* v. *British Gas* [1990] ECR I-3313   120

Case C-292/89, *R.* v. *Immigration Appeal Tribunal, ex parte Antonissen*, [1991] ECR I-745 227, 228

Case C-357/89, *Raulin* v. *Minister van Onderwijs en Wetenschappen*, [1992] ECR I-1027   226

Case C-377/89, *Cotter and others* v. *Minister for Social Welfare and others*, [1991] ECR I-1155

                                                                                            100

Case C-3/90, *Bernini* v. *Minister van Onderwijs en Wetenschappen*, [1992] ECR I-1071   226

Case C-31/90, *Johnson* v. *Chief Adjudication Officer*, [1993] ECR I-3723   96, 98

Joined Cases C-87-89/90, *Verholen and others* v. *Sociale Verzekeringsbank*, [1991] ECR I-3757

                                                                                    12, 96, 100

Case C-204/90, *Bachmann* v. *Belgium*, [1992] ECR I-249   231

Case C-208/90, *Emmott* v. *Minister for Social Welfare and Attorney General*, [1991] ECR I-4269

                                                                                            137

Case C-243/90, *R.* v. *Secretary of State for Social Security, ex parte Smithson*, [1992] ECR I-467

                                                                                         97, 98

Case C-295/90, *Parliament* v. *Council*, [1992] ECR I-4193   224

Case C-300/90, *Commission* v. *Belgium*, [1992] ECR I-305   193, 231

Case C-370/90, *R.* v. *Immigration Appeal Tribunal and Surinder Singh, ex parte Secretary of State for the Home Department*, [1992] ECR I-4265   228

Case C-4/91, *Bleis* v. *Ministère de l'Education Nationale*, [1991] ECR I-5627   229

Case C-9/91, *R.* v. *Secretary of State for Social Security, ex parte the EOC*, [1992] ECR I-4297

                                                                                        32, 105

Cases C-63/91 and C-64/91, *Jackson and Cresswell* v. *Chief Adjudication Officer*, [1992] ECR I-4737

                                                                                             98

Joined Cases C-72/91 and C-73/91, *Sloman Neptun Schiffahrts AG* v. *Seebetriebsrat Bodo Ziesemer der Sloman Neptun Schiffahrts AG*, [1993] ECR I-887   91

Case C-78/91, *Hughes* v. *Chief Adjudication Officer*, [1992] ECR I-4839   241

Case C-109/91, *Ten Oever* v. *Stichting Bedrijfspensioenfonds voor het Glazenwassers- en Schoonmaakbedrijf*, [1993] ECR I-4879   120, 127, 160, 187, 317

Case C-110/91, *Moroni* v. *Collo GmbH*, [1993] ECR I-6591   152, 155, 161, 186, 198

Case C-111/91, *Commission* v. *Luxembourg*, [1993] ECR I-817   232

Case C-152/91, *Neath* v. *Hugh Steeper Ltd.*, [1993] ECR I-6935   124, 161, 178, 180, 317

Case C-165/91, *Van Munster* v. *Rijksdienst voor Pensioenen*, [1994] ECR I-4661   244

Case C-173/91, *Commission* v. *Belgium*, [1993] ECR I-673   199

Case C-189/91, *Kirshammer-Hack* v. *Sidal*, [1993] ECR I-6185   103

Case C-200/91, *Coloroll Pension Trustees Ltd.* v. *Russell et al*, [1994] ECR I-4389   121, 124, 129, 178, 179, 180, 187, 193, 317

Case C-226/91, *Molenbroek* v. *Sociale Verzekeringsbank*, [1992] ECR I-5943   102, 193

Case C-243/91, *Belgian State* v. *Taghavi*, [1992] ECR I-4401   240

Case C-310/91, *Schmid* v. *Belgian State*, [1993] ECR I-3011   232, 240

Case C-328/91, *Secretary of State for Social Security* v. *Thomas and others*, [1993] ECR I-1247   105

Case C-337/91, *Gemert-Derks* v. *Bestuur van de Nieuwe Industriële Bedrijfsvereniging*, [1993] ECR I-5435   104

Case C-338/91, *Steenhorst-Neerings* v. *Bestuur van de Bedrijfsvereniging voor Detailhandel, Ambachten en Huisvrouwen*, [1993] ECR I-5475   100, 139

Case C-91/92, *Paola Faccini Dori* v. *Recreb Srl*, [1994] ECR I-3325   120

Case C-127/92, *Enderby* v. *Frenchay Health Authority and Secretary of State for Health*, [1993] ECR I-5535   118, 121, 193

Case C-132/92, *Birds Eye Walls* v. *Roberts*, [1993] ECR I-5579   137, 199, 200

Case C-154/92, *Van Cant* v. *Rijksdienst voor Pensioenen*, [1993] ECR I-3811   60, 105

Case C-297/92, *Baglieri* v. *Instituto Nazionale delle Previdenza Sociale*, [1993] ECR I-5211   242

Case C-343/92, *Roks and others* v. *Bestuur van de Bedrijfsvereniging voor Gezondheid, Geestelijke en Maatschappelijke Belangen and others*, [1994] ECR I-571   103, 108

Joined Cases C-399/92, C-409/92, C-425/92, C-34/93, C-50/93 and C-78/93, *Helmig* v. *Stadt Lengerig*, [1994] ECR I-5727   100, 111

Case C-408/92, *Smith and others* v. *Avdel Systems Ltd*, [1994] ECR I-4435   121, 152, 164, 167, 173, 193

Case C-410/92, *Johnson* v. *Chief Adjudication Officer*, [1994] ECR I-5483   100

Case C-420/92, *Bramhill* v. *Chief Adjudication Officer*, [1994] ECR I-3191   106

Case C-7/93, *ABP* v. *Beune*, [1994] ECR I-4471   21, 128, 129, 161, 179

Case C-28/93, *Van den Akker and others* v. *Stichting Shell Pensioenfonds*, [1994] ECR I-4527

121, 152, 164, 173

Case C-57/93, *Vroege* v. *NCIV Instituut voor Volkshuisvesting BV and Stichting Pensioenfonds NCIV*, [1994] ECR I-4541   134, 150, 155, 159, 161,162

Case C-71/93, *van Poucke* v. *Rijksinstituut voor de Sociale Verzekeringen der Zelfstandigen en Algemene Sociale Kas voor Zelfstandigen*, [1994] ECR I-1101   239

Case C-128/93, *Fisscher* v. *Voorhuis Hengelo BV and Stichting Bedrijfspensioenfonds voor de Detailhandel*, [1994] ECR I-4583   121, 134, 135, 136, 138, 141, 150, 155, 161

Case C-279/93, *Finanzamt Köln* v. *Schumacker*, [1995] ECR I-225   121, 231

Case C-308/93, *Bestuur van de Sociale Verzekeringsbank* v. *Cabanis-Issarte*, judgment of 30 April 1996, nyr   229, 236, 239, 240

Case C-317/93, *Nolte* v. *Landesversicherungsantalt Hannover*, [1995] ECR I-4625   96, 143, 214

Case C-342/93, *Gillespie and Others* v. *Northern Health and Social Services Board and others*, judgment of 13 February 1996, nyr   118, 119, 121

Case C-415/93, *Union Royale Belge des Sociétés de Football Association* v. *Jean-Marc Bosman*, [1995] ECR I-4921   225, 302

Joined Cases C-430 and 431/93 *Van Schijndel and Van Veen* v. *Stichting Pensioenfonds voor Fysiotherappeuten*, [1995] ECR I-4705   53

Case C-435/93, *Dietz* v. *Stichting Thuiszorg Rotterdam*   162, 163, 211

Case C-443/93, *Vougioukas* v. *Idryma Koinonikon Asfalisscon (IKA)*, [1995] ECR I-4033   21, 249

Case C-444/93, *Megner and Scheffel* v. *Innungskrankenkasse Vorderpfalz*, [1995] ECR I-4741

96, 144,214, 226

Case C-450/93, *Kalanke* v. *Freie Hansestadt Bremen*, [1995] ECR I-3051   174

Case C-473/93, *Commission* v. *Luxembourg*, judgment of 2 July 1996   229

Case C-80/94, *Wielockx* v. *Inspecteur der Directe Belastingen*, [1995] ECR I-2493   102, 231, 304

Case C-92/94, *Secretary of State for Social Security and the Chief Adjudication Officer* v. *Graham, Connell and Nicholas*, [1995] ECR I-2521   106

Case C-107/94, *Asscher* v. *Staatssecretaris van Financiën*, judgment of 27 June 1996   227, 231, 232

Case C-173/94, *Commission* v. *Belgium*, judgment of 2 July 1996   229

Case C-228/94, *Atkins* v. *Wrekin District Council and Department of Transport*, judgment of 11 July 1996   97, 98, 99

Joined Cases C-245/94 and C-312/94, *Hoever and Zachow* v. *Land Nordrhein-Westfalen*, opinion of Advocate General Jacobs 2 May 1996   232

Case C-290/94, *Commission* v. *Greece*, judgment of 2 July 1996   229

Case C-20/96, *Kelvin Snares* v. *Adjudication Officer*, O.J. 1996 C 77   242

Case C-50/96, *Schröder* v. *Deutsche Bundespost Telekom*, O.J. 1996 C 133   150, 214

INDEX

A.

ABP 21, 129, 130, 162, 180, 202-205, 258, 278

access 36, 93, 94, 103, 114, 117, 120, 131, 132, 134-136, 138-143, 145, 148, 151, 152, 154, 156, 157, 162-165, 180, 196, 199, 202, 203, 205, 207, 213, 214, 229, 230, 254, 302, 306, 315-317

accrued rights 23, 38, 42, 143, 150, 168, 169, 182, 257, 266, 273-276, 279-281, 286, 289, 296, 297, 301, 303, 320, 325-328, 333, 334, 337

acquis communautaire 160, 168, 175, 234

actuarial factors 118, 153, 178, 179, 181-184, 197, 204, 211, 213, 317

aggregation 6, 237, 238, 244-247, 252, 301, 302, 305, 334, 335

ANW 84, 185

AOW 8, 11, 48-50, 55, 83, 107, 129, 185, 202-204, 208, 242, 259, 270, 281,

apportionment 238, 244-246, 252, 335

Article 51 6, 233, 237, 238, 242, 250, 298, 304-306

Article 48 225-229, 234, 237, 240, 249, 301, 302, 304

Article 119 21, 91-93, 116, 118-131, 135, 136, 139, 141, 149, 151, 153, 154, 156, 157, 158-163, 165-169, 177-184, 186-188, 190-192, 194, 196-201, 203, 205, 210, 211, 316, 317

AVC 195, 196

AWW 108, 190, 191

B.

back-service 273

bedrijfspensioenfonds 51, 121, 122

BetrAVG 64, 65, 67, 69-71, 85, 172, 209, 259, 260, 262, 263, 270-272, 285, 286

Betriebstreue 63, 150, 303

Beveridge 12, 49, 82, 83

BGB 133, 151, 261

breadwinner 100, 110, 192, 194

bridging pensions 201, 200, 201, 203, 206, 209

Bundes Gesetz Buch 133

Burgerlijk Wetboek 132

C.

cash equivalent 275, 276

changed role of women 5

childbearing 213, 322, 330

civil servant 126, 180

co-ordination 90, 237, 238, 241, 243, 244, 249

common market 6, 88

company pension fund 51

compulsory application 216, 332

contract-out 32, 34-37, 39, 45

contributions 3, 12-15, 17, 18, 31, 32, 36, 38, 40-43, 45, 47, 48, 56, 60, 61, 67, 71-74, 76, 82, 83, 85, 105, 108, 110, 111, 114, 116-118, 123-126, 137, 138, 141-143, 158, 161, 163, 165, 176-186, 190, 194-197, 201, 205, 210-214, 223, 256, 258, 261-263, 265-267, 269, 270, 277, 288, 289, 291, 292, 293-295, 305, 313, 317, 326, 327, 330, 331, 333, 336-338

contributory principle 82

D.

demographic developments 11, 60

dependency 83, 107, 115, 190, 195, 312

derived rights 38, 83, 201, 240

direct discrimination 100, 111, 122, 123, 147, 148, 183, 314

direct effect 99, 121, 123, 135, 136, 158, 161, 167-169, 225

Directive 76/207 94, 120, 121, 124, 127, 131, 132, 154, 156, 170, 175, 199, 250

Directive 79/7 81, 95, 97,. 99, 104, 109,

116-118, 124, 154, 155, 161, 169, 170, 177, 186, 187, 190, 194, 198, 209, 210, 250
Directive 75/117 93, 119, 132
Directive 86/378 95, 109, 116-118, 157, 161, 162, 164, 166, 173, 178, 181, 186, 187, 189, 191, 195, 198, 206, 210, 211
Direktversicherung 67, 270-272, 285, 287, 294
Direktzusage 66, 68, 71
discretionary approval 46, 47, 257
discrimination on grounds of sex 5, 99, 101, 117, 122, 178

E.
early leaver 57, 66, 179, 183, 265, 266, 269, 271-275, 288, 296, 318, 324-326
Einkommensteuergesetz 71
employee mobility 7, 29, 64, 69, 223, 259, 263, 275, 296, 298, 299, 301, 304-306, 321, 324, 326, 328, 337
employee contributions 43, 47, 118, 125, 137, 161, 177, 178, 180, 181, 196, 210, 211, 261-263, 295, 317
employer contributions 43, 71, 178, 180-182, 184, 205, 213, 294, 317
EMU 10, 11, 313
exempt approved 47, 48
exportability 6, 238, 244

F.
family members 239, 240, 254
fertility rate 8, 312
financial equilibrium 102, 105
franchise 208, 209, 259
free movement of workers 6, 22, 96, 224, 225, 228, 229, 233, 236, 237, 240, 250, 282, 297, 298, 301, 304, 323
full-time 86, 101, 125, 126, 134, 135, 149, 213, 214, 216, 223, 253, 254, 318, 321, 322, 332
FVP 147, 148

G.
GG 133, 134, 149, 151
Goode report 33, 35, 36, 41, 266, 273, 274
Graduated Pension Scheme 32-34

H.
harmonisation 6, 89, 234, 235
health benefits 22, 201

I.
indirect discrimination 99, 100, 111, 122, 123, 133, 134, 147, 148, 150, 193, 194, 215, 259, 314, 319
individualisation 109
industrial pension fund 51
Inland Revenue 45, 46, 48, 257
Insolvenzsicherung 67
insurance principle 222, 223
international migrant 19, 221-224, 233, 252, 254, 287, 295, 297, 301, 302, 304, 306, 312, 313, 324, 328, 337
internationalisation 7, 29, 81, 221, 254, 312, 329

J.
justification 10, 85, 101, 109, 144, 162, 183, 189, 215, 232, 264, 303, 319, 320

L.
legal certainty 139, 157, 158, 161, 211
legitimate expectation 162
levelling up 166
links with statutory schemes 114, 197
lump sums 46, 74, 114, 185, 197, 272, 284

M.
mandatory approval 46
married women 4, 38, 83, 84, 86, 106-108, 115, 147, 191, 192, 201, 203, 213, 253, 314, 315
Maxwell 35, 77, 290

MFR 41, 42

migrant worker 6, 221, 228, 230-233, 235, 236, 238, 240, 243-246, 248, 257, 264, 295, 297, 301, 306, 313, 323, 324, 335

mittelbare Versorgungszusage 66

money purchase 37, 43, 45, 57, 130, 178, 181-184, 197, 204, 211, 265, 266, 275, 280, 296, 331

mortality tables 116, 177, 212

N.

national time limits 141

nationality 224, 228, 238-240, 243, 250, 252, 301-303, 324

O.

occupational pension schemes 18, 20, 22, 24, 25, 27-29, 30, 33-36, 39, 44, 45, 47, 48, 55, 57, 63, 64, 76, 77, 94, 114-116, 118, 125-132, 134, 136, 138, 142, 143, 144, 146, 149-151, 154, 159, 160, 163, 164, 169, 171, 173, 181, 184, 190, 192, 196, 197, 202, 210, 212, 213, 217, 244, 251, 253, 254, 259, 265, 275-277, 287, 291, 296, 297-301, 303, 305, 306, 313, 316-318, 320, 322, 324, 326-329, 331-335

ondernemingspensioenfonds 51

P.

part-time 84, 86, 100-102, 110, 111, 125, 126, 134, 135, 144-146, 148-151, 214-216, 226, 239, 315, 318, 321, 322, 332

pay 3, 11-13, 16, 17, 21, 26, 30, 32, 38, 63, 65, 70, 72-75, 81, 84, 89, 91-94, 101, 105, 110, 114, 118-121, 123-126, 131, 132, 134-143, 146, 151, 157, 160, 161, 163, 164, 165, 169, 172, 177-185, 187, 188, 190-197, 200, 201, 202, 205, 216, 221, 235, 245, 256, 259, 262, 264-266, 277, 293, 294, 302, 303, 305, 312, 316, 317, 319, 330, 337, 338

Pay-As-You-Go 11-13, 16, 17, 21, 30, 81, 221, 312, 330, 338

pensionable age 8, 14, 16, 22, 24, 38, 41, 47, 49, 59, 61, 63, 65, 75, 85, 86, 98, 103-108, 114, 118, 122, 144, 147, 152-155, 157, 161-169, 171, 172, 173, 174, 176, 189, 195, 198-200, 202, 203, 206, 207, 209, 211, 223, 253, 254, 260, 264-266, 268-270, 273-275, 283, 288, 304, 312, 314, 318, 324, 326

Pensionskasse 67, 68, 73, 74, 270, 271

positive discrimination 174, 175, 195

pre-funded 12, 16-19, 24, 28, 29, 30, 55, 67, 81, 114, 221, 224, 313, 329-331, 333, 335, 337, 338

pregnancy 260

price inflation 137, 273

proportionality 320

protected rights 43-45, 259, 276, 286

Protocol and Agreement on Social Policy 87

PSVaG 67, 69, 72, 294

PSW 51, 52, 54, 55, 57, 145, 147, 259, 268-270, 278-282

public servant 21

R.

redress 136-142, 145-148, 151, 152

redundancy payments 120

reference scheme 40, 41

Regulation 1408/71 96, 238, 240, 243, 249, 250, 298, 304, 305, 333

Regulation 1612/68 227-230

regulatory regimes 28, 30

retirement age 155, 167, 169-171, 173, 174, 176, 217, 270, 277

rules against overlapping 246

S.

salary-related scheme 37

schedule of contributions 42

SDS 279

self-employed 95, 117, 211, 212, 224, 237-239, 243, 276

SERPS 25, 27, 34-39, 44, 45, 110, 127, 206, 235, 257, 277, 278

sick pay 101, 120

social charges 88-90
social policy 18, 87, 88, 90, 91, 94, 101, 109, 118, 121, 175, 176, 194, 201, 306, 314
social assistance 97-99, 107, 241, 251
social solidarity 12, 306
social and tax advantages 230, 232
social dimension 87, 88, 225
Social Action Programme 93, 94, 299, 300
SSBs 57, 259, 262, 266-268, 270, 272-274, 286, 288, 296, 303, 304, 306, 320, 325, 327, 334
statutory schemes 11, 15, 16, 19, 21, 22, 26-28, 31, 48, 58, 81, 82, 94, 97, 99, 104, 114, 115, 126, 129, 130, 145, 186, 197, 198, 202, 203, 207, 221, 250, 300, 303, 313-316, 322, 329-331, 333, 335
survivor's benefits 24, 144, 147, 162, 172, 185-187, 189, 190-194, 193, 211, 241, 314, 315, 331

T.

tax 15, 18, 37, 38, 41, 45, 47-49, 56, 57, 66, 70-74, 76, 77, 186, 189, 208, 230-232, 255, 256, 282-284, 287-296, 302, 304, 327, 328
temporal limitation 65, 136, 157, 159-164, 166, 168, 173, 181, 188, 193, 196
territorially limited 5, 222, 312
TEU 87, 88, 160, 161, 229
transfers 43, 259, 264, 271, 272, 274-286, 288, 289, 294-297, 302, 303, 306, 320, 325-328, 334
travel concessions 120

U.

uniformity 9, 128, 152, 226, 241
unjust enrichment 138, 204

V.

Van Rhijn 49, 83
Verzorgungszusage 66
vested rights 260, 261, 265, 266, 270, 286

W.

wage inflation 14, 273, 327
waiting periods 60, 111, 255-258, 262, 263, 299, 303, 305, 306, 320, 324
Wet LB 56-58, 284
Wet Gelijk Loon 132
Wet Bpf 53-55
Wet Gelijke Behandeling 132
widow 38, 41, 44, 46, 47, 83-85, 104, 127, 180, 186, 189-192, 195
widower 38, 44, 104, 186, 189-191
women 4, 5, 7, 14, 19, 20, 22, 27-29, 30, 32, 34, 38, 53, 59-61, 81-87, 91-100, 102-112, 114-123, 125, 126, 131-133, 135, 136, 138, 141, 142, 145-156, 161, 163, 165-179, 181-188, 190-196, 198, 199, 200-206, 208-217, 221, 250, 253-255, 258, 259, 311, 313-322, 325, 329-333, 335-338